Discourses of Global Politics

Critical Perspectives on World Politics

◇

R. B. J. Walker, Series Editor

Discourses of Global Politics

A Critical (Re)Introduction to International Relations

Jim George

Lynne Rienner Publishers • Boulder, Colorado

Published in the United States of America in 1994 by
Lynne Rienner Publishers, Inc.
1800 30th Street, Boulder, Colorado 80301

Library of Congress Cataloging-in-Publication Data
George, Jim, 1946–
Discourses of global politics : a critical (re)introduction to international relations / Jim George.
Includes bibliographical references and index.
ISBN 1-55587-444-4 (alk. paper)
ISBN 1-55587-446-0 (pbk., alk. paper)
1. International relations. I. Title.
JX1391.G467 1994
327—dc20 93-32719
CIP

Printed and bound in the United States of America

The paper used in this publication meets the requirements of the American National Standard for Permanence of Paper for Printed Library Materials Z39.48-1984.

Published and distributed outside North and South America, the Philippines, Australia, New Zealand, and Japan by:

The Macmillan Press Ltd.
Houndmills, Basingstoke, Hampshire RG21 2XS, England

British Library Cataloguing in Publication Data
ISBN 0-333-61868-8
ISBN 0-333-61685-5 (pbk)

For my daughter,
Sara

Contents

Preface

This book stands at that intersection of social theory and International Relations which in recent years has seen a range of critical scholars call to account the given, axiomatic, and taken-for-granted realities of orthodox theory and practice in the search for more incisive and less dangerous perspectives on contemporary social life. In this context it takes issue with an intellectual and policy agenda that, in the last quarter of the twentieth century, still resonates with cultural, political, and gendered privilege and narrowly conceived images of global reality. Its critical status, consequently, is related to a discursive regime of exclusion, silence, and intolerance that, as "International Relations," reduces a complex and turbulent world to a patterned and rigidly ordered framework of understanding, derived from a particular representation of post-Renaissance European historical experience, articulated in orthodox Anglo-American philosophical terms. In the 1990s, however, as ethnic hatreds, religious passions, and the ongoing struggles of race, culture, and gender illustrate the inadequacies of universalist schemas and grand theories of order and control, the traditional doctrines and protocols of International Relations are coming under widespread critical challenge.

This book takes up this challenge in acknowledging that, for all its dangers and uncertainties, the space beyond the Cold War provides us with the opportunity to confront the narrowness and closure of traditional perspectives and redirect our energies to more tolerant, inclusive, and sophisticated thought and behavior. In this regard, however, it has no quick-fix, alternative grand theories of global politics to offer. The issues at stake are too serious for such simplistic posturing. Rather, in critically (re)introducing International Relations in the 1990s, it offers a comprehensive reassessment of a range of ideas, issues, events, and perspectives that have rarely been addressed in the International Relations literature in the way they are addressed here. It seeks, in this way, to provide a contemporary audience with the opportunity to think beyond orthodox dogma and engage creatively with a diverse body of critical work, marginalized or excluded in the mainstream agenda.

In doing so, this book relocates International Relations as a discursive microcosm of a much larger cultural and philosophical enterprise that, in the post-Enlightenment era, has successfully transformed a particular meaning of *reality* into reality per se. This singular, homogeneous, and narrowly focused image of human society has *become* International Relations, in the post–World War II period, establishing the boundaries of legitimate and relevant theory and research and underpinning the "art of the possible" in policy terms.

Chapters 2 to 5 in particular speak to this issue, illustrating how, via an unproblematic appropriation of a particular way of understanding the modern world and its peoples, International Relations resonates with the problems, tensions, paradoxes, and potentials intrinsic to a dominant modernist agenda. These problems include a dichotomized frame of reference at all analytical levels (e.g., subject/object, fact/value, is/ought, self/other, domestic/international, Realist/idealist); an objectivist, linear sense of (Western) history; essentialist reading/writing practices; universalist strategies of categorization, definition, and exclusion; and a dangerously restrictive understanding of knowledge and reality that, in effectively detaching the observer/analyst from the vicissitudes of the world "out there," abrogates social and individual responsibility to one (perceived) irreducible foundational source or another (e.g., structural anarchy, human nature, historical recurrence and repetition).

This perspective is challenged here in a manner that does not simply dismiss the modernist traditions that have made contemporary International Relations what it is but also emphasizes how the critical potentials within these traditions (e.g., via Descartes, Hume, Kant, Marx, Weber, and Popper) have been largely ignored or marginalized in the search for a simple, self-affirming narrative of global life, represented as Realism (or neo-Realism) since World War II. I argue, nevertheless, that to begin to move beyond the narrow and dangerous confines of Realism as International Relations, it is necessary to expose it as a particular (interpretive) process of understanding the world and indicate how this process might be confronted and repudiated and its "reality" challenged, in theory and practice.

Chapters 6 to 8 are concerned primarily with this theme. As indicated already, they offer no easy answers, for there are none to offer. Their aim, rather, is to facilitate a broader, more inclusive understanding of global human relations by illustrating how it is possible to think and act beyond the seemingly irreducible principles of the International Relations orthodoxy. I seek, in this way, to provide for students of International Relations alternative points of entry into contemporary debates concerning a complex and dangerous global environment in the 1990s. In particular I explore the analytical possibilities inherent in perspectives such as critical theory and the discourse approach of postmodernist scholarship.

As an exercise in facilitation I have sought to make the book as accessible as possible, occasionally, perhaps, at the expense of nuance. Consequently, this (re)introduction to International Relations attempts to communicate sophisticated and often very complex themes in a manner that does them some interpretive justice, while accounting for the interested reader who might otherwise be inhibited or intimidated by the "foreignness" of some of the literary fare on offer. Accordingly, the discussion to follow is, for all its "foreign" influence, couched in a conventional language, and, wherever possible, the references used are from traditional sources.

The point is that it is not necessary to invoke a Foucault, a Derrida, or a Habermas to comprehend that which has been left unsaid, unthought, and unwritten in International Relations. On the critical margins of modern Western thought there have always been those working to open "thinking space," and even in the scholarship that has been integral to the framing of modern ways of thinking there were opportunities for critical reflection that have been effectively ignored, by Anglo-American social theory in general and by International Relations in particular. For all this, a discursive perspective on International Relations has never been more necessary than it is at present, because it explains how and why this continues to be the case and because it illustrates the power and (largely unrecognized) dangers of the unsaid, the unreflected, and the unwritten in a world that everyday and in so many ways defies simplistic, grand-theorized invocations of its "reality."

In this broad context this book represents a contribution to an ongoing conversation among a diverse range of scholars who, both directly and indirectly, have been sources of stimulation and insight for me over the past decade or so. In the indirect category I include, among others, Robert Cox, John Vasquez, Jane Flax, Roger Tooze, William Connolly, Susan Hekman, R. N. Berki, Mark Poster, Hayward Alker, Ralph Pettman, and Ian Clark. More directly, there is a group of people in North America in particular who via their fine minds and generous natures have given much to this project and its author. Michael Shapiro's kindness and encouragement is greatly appreciated in this regard, as is that of Rob Walker and Richard Ashley, who gave me the opportunity and confidence to push beyond traditional boundaries of understanding. I am indebted also to Michael Dillon, Bradley Klein, James Der Derian, Richard Leaver, Jim Richardson, and John Girling for their support at different stages of this enterprise. David Campbell has been integral to this work since its earliest articulations in various Antipodean hostelries, and he remains a friend and colleague integral to its critical purpose. So does Michael McKinley, whose everyday friendship, generosity, and moral example are sources of continuing stimulation and wonder. Finally, Susan Engel deserves special thanks for her friendship and commitment to me and to this project.

Jim George

1

(Re)Introducing the Theory as Practice of International Relations

Reality, it seems, is not what it used to be in International Relations.[1] The Cold War is over, and patterns of thought and behavior identified as corresponding with an enduring, universal "essence" of global existence are coming under increasing scrutiny as old ideological commitments and alliances are reformulated, territorial boundaries are hastily redrawn, and new symbols of identity are constructed or resurrected. The catalysts for much of the questioning and reassessment, of course, are the remarkable events in the Soviet Union following the Gorbachev era and the policies of perestroika and glasnost, which, in one form or another and with varying results, sparked off political tinderboxes from Beijing to Berlin.

In the West, the resultant sequence of events has been cause, generally, for widespread rejoicing at the new opportunities for personal and political liberty within the societies of, in particular, Eastern Europe. There has been smugness also. For those who represent capitalism and utilitarian social relations as the natural order in the modern world, it was the socialist system and not its market-based counterpart that was always destined to "wither away." However, notwithstanding these instances of well-rehearsed polemic and the triumphalism integral to claims for "new world" orders, there is also a widespread sense of crisis associated with the post–Cold War era.

At one level this is not at all surprising. As the tragedies in the former Yugoslavia have attested, the opportunities for future liberty in Eastern Europe are laced with the great dangers that have attended previous resurrections of national identity in that complex region. Similarly, the social revolution unleashed by Gorbachev in the Soviet Union, having devoured its architect, now has the potential for something other than a democratic outcome. And while celebration might be the appropriate response at scenes of erstwhile central balance foes actually transforming their swords into plowshares, there is well-founded apprehension about the increasingly lethal arsenals of the Third World, where, for all the change and talk of historical watersheds, there has been little, if any, change in the lives of those identified decades ago as the "wretched of the earth." Grinding poverty remains the most prominent characteristic of much Third World existence, where spiraling infant mortality rates, chronic unemployment, and inadequate shelter and health care are the stuff of everyday life. Meanwhile, former "comfort women," brutalized by the Japanese military in World War II, relive their agony and humiliation for the world's media in order that the violence perpetrated upon them be no longer rationalized as merely the "spoils of war." At the Group of Seven (G7) meeting in Tokyo, concern is expressed about Russia's use of the Sea of Okhotsk as a dumping ground for used nuclear reactors. The prime minister of Tuvalu seeks help in the quest to prevent his island nation from being submerged in the event of global warming. Salman Rushdie appeals against the death sentence imposed upon him by an Iranian mullah for denigrating Islam. Greek troops, following a recent Italian example, herd desperate Albanians back across their territorial frontier. And then there is the pall of smoke, the size of India, that hangs over the Amazon jungle.

These issues, integral to global politics in the 1990s, are integral also to this book, which seeks to speak to them, as its title suggests, in a critical manner. More explicitly, these issues of life and death, celebration, crisis, struggle, terror, and opportunity are to be addressed in this work in terms critical of an orthodox International Relations perspective on them, which, it will argue, is an increasingly inadequate reference point for understanding a complex and changing global environment. This book is critical, in particular, of that sociointellectual process that has transformed a particular discursive image of global life into a "reality" of International Relations, complete with ritualized manifesto for thought and action. It is at one level, therefore, an engagement with the "theoretical" processes by which we have traditionally understood and given meaning to reality in International Relations and the ways in which we continue to reproduce that meaning in the face of the great dangers and opportunities of the post–Cold War period. Simultaneously, it is always an engagement with the "practical" implications of this process of meaning-making—with this theory *as* practice.

The implications of this process were starkly illustrated in the Gulf War of 1990–1991, which, as the first major conflict of the post–Cold War period, provided a profound challenge to the policy and intellectual sectors of the International Relations community, faced with the kind of low-contingency threat to established order that is the most likely politicostrategic scenario in that space beyond the "balance of terror." In these terms, I suggest, the orthodox response to the Gulf War was a disaster, a devastating and tragic indictment of a moribund but lethal theory *as* practice, designed for violent response and big-power coercion and not at all for the kind of sensitive, preventative global strategies that will be required in the post–Cold War era.

In this first "new world" scenario, therefore, the U.S.-led alliance invoked traditional old-world images (e.g., of Hitlerism and appeasement) and acted in accordance with old-world strategic rituals in accomplishing what Cold War alliances had been unable to accomplish for forty years—that is, to actually punish the designated "Other" without fear of major retaliation. Consequently, at a moment when innovative and imaginative responses to small-time thuggery were the order of this particular day, a less endearing spectacle was evident—via the crudest juxtaposition of Machiavellian "theoretical" logic and the violent "practice" of contemporary technorationalist savagery. The whole event was then legitimated in terms of a rather desperate concoction of medieval and modernist rhetorics, which, for example, saw Kuwaiti "democracy" and "self-determination" articulated in terms of neo-Augustinian notions of "Just War."

This of course is not the only way to interpret the events in the Gulf. Nor indeed is it the way in which the policy sectors of the major Western powers and the mainstream intellectual sector within the International Relations community have generally recorded the experiences of Operation Desert Storm. On the contrary, the dominant policy and intellectual sectors have represented the Gulf War in exemplary traditional terms—as a response to a threatening reality "out there" that offered no alternative to violent strategic action. Thus, the general wisdom from within the problem-solving inner sanctums of the Pentagon and the disciplinary citadels of International Relations scholarship have maintained that the only "realistic" response to the squalid adventurism of Saddam Hussein in 1990 was the resort to the "massive retaliation" doctrine of the early Cold War years or, in broader terms, to the first (Machiavellian) principle of power politics strategic lore—that is, that vírtu in International Relations dictates that aggression must be met with greater aggression if meaningful order is to be maintained.[2]

This brings me directly to the critical focus of this book and a rejection of this kind of analytical approach, which, I will argue, continues to reduce highly complex historicopolitical phenomena to narrowly focused ahistorical rituals of thought and action, dominant in the era of imperialist power politics and four decades of the "balance of terror." The argument, more explicitly, is that in an emerging age of great dangers, complexities, and opportunities in global life, it is crucial that we go beyond the simple ritualized representation of Traditional theory and practice and begin to seriously question that which for so long has evoked certain irreducible images of reality for the policy and intellectual communities in International Relations.

This book will seek to explain such a necessity in terms that make the work a rather different introduction to International Relations than is commonly available—in terms, for example, that illustrate and emphasize the world-making nature of theory, of theory *as* everyday political practice.

Sometimes this explanation will concentrate specifically on the larger sociophilosophical processes by which dominant notions of "theory" and "practice" have been Traditionally framed in International Relations (e.g., theory as a cognitive reaction to a world of fact "out there"). At this level, it seeks to explain both the process by which Anglo-American societies in particular have understood the world in these dualized and dichotomized terms and the implications of the transforming of this *particular process of understanding* into the Tradition and discipline of International Relations. At other times it will speak directly to "concrete" issues and events in global political life in order to expose the theoretical/interpretive process by which we understand and give real meaning to them and so that alternative meanings might be comprehended and considered. The critical purpose of the book is bound up with this latter ambition as part of a concern for a more sensitive, sophisticated, and critically attuned perspective on global political life, concerned not just with a static image of historical necessity and grand-theorized immutable laws of action but with a continuing dynamic and changing present in which, in their many and varied sites of activity, men and women make their worlds and retain the potential to change them.

My concerns here echo those of a diverse group of scholars from across the political spectrum who have recently highlighted the dangers and inadequacies of orthodox approaches to International Relations in the 1990s. For example, the Cold War historian John Lewis Gaddis has recently expressed his disquiet with the current state of affairs. Indeed, Gaddis has illustrated how the analytical emperor of International Relations is naked after all. More precisely, the dominant perspective in International Relations, articulated latterly as neo-Realism, has illustrated that it cannot adequately explain that which it assured a generation it understood—the behavior of the Soviet Union as power politics actor in the anarchical system. This is primarily because Realism, in any of its guises, represents its knowledge of the world in terms of generalized, universalized, and irreducible patterns of human behavior, which reduces global politics to the incessant, anarchical power struggle among states and "rational" interstate activity to the simple utilitarian pursuit of self-interest. From such a perspective there can be no "rational" explanation for Soviet behavior in peacefully relinquishing its power status and systemic authority other than in Traditional power politics terms.[3] Hence the shrill triumphalism of those invoking the "victory" of the Western superpower in its power struggle with its mortal Cold War enemy. And hence the continuance of the "successful" power politics principles in the Gulf.

Like many of the more discerning observers of the post–Cold War era, Gaddis is concerned about the broader implications of this triumphalism and the impact it might have upon the capacity of the International Relations community in the United States, in particular, to comprehend and sensitively address a complex and volatile global scenario in the future. His conclusion is that the major problem emanates from a failure of "theory" at the core of the International Relations orthodoxy, which despite its claims for scientific insight has shown itself unable to adequately detect patterns of behavior at the global level and predict an event as significant as the demise of the Soviet superpower.[4] Ultimately, and disappointingly, however, Gaddis's prescription for International Relations analysis in the future represents little more than a contemporary variation on an old unity-of-science theme. It suggests, accordingly, that the pursuit of a Realist science of International Relations must remain an integral feature of theory and research but that it be brought "up to date" by utilizing the more sensitive analytical tools at the disposal of the novelist and the narrative historian.[5] This final theme is evident in much of the critically inclined literature of recent times, which seeks to ameliorate the effects of moribund thought via a mediated (social) scientific approach to knowledge and society. It is a response that predates the current crisis in International Relations scholarship and replicates a more general discursive strategy in the post-Kantian development of Western philosophy and social theory. It will, accordingly, receive more detailed attention shortly.

For now, another, more nuanced, commentary is worthy of attention, on the issue of International Relations and its contemporary failures. The commentary comes from the illustrious conservative scholar Stanley Hoffmann, and again the primary catalyst for concern is the Gulf War.[6] Hoffmann's position is that the U.S. war-fighting policy in the Gulf was derived not from a carefully formulated appreciation of the particular issue at hand, nor the long-term implications of coercive action, but primarily from Traditional balance-of-power theory and a pragmatic reformulation of collective security themes. Responding to this in critical terms, he reiterated themes central to his famous injunction of 1977 for U.S. scholars in particular to divest themselves of the discursive rigidity associated with the (behavioralist) pursuit of rational-scientific certainty.[7] The problems of the 1990s are similar, Hoffmann inferred, to the extent that again they require a more sophisticated, flexible, and incisive approach to theory and practice than is commonly brought to them by a generation immersed in the certainties of Cold War logic.

In this context, and on the issue of maintaining order and stability in the Middle East via Traditional coercive principles, Hoffmann emphasized the (at best) confusion and (at worst) cynicism of such a position, as U.S. arms sales increase in the region. He stressed more generally that, in strategic terms, the use of overwhelming force seldom works as an instrument of order in global life but more often than not gives rise to dysfunctional and dangerous consequences, which "punishes the innocent even more than the guilty."[8] The relative fate of untold numbers of Iraqi dead and that of Saddam Hussein offers poignant testament to the salience of this insight.

There is salience, too, in the proposition that even when the violence is perpetrated in the name of rational-technical "clean war," the misery is no less tangible for a society suffering in the wake of a devastated health system and the destruction of adequate water and power supplies.

Hoffmann's concern, simply put, is that unless we seriously reappraise the way we think and act in the post–Cold War era, the United States and its Western allies will become involved in a series of future conflicts that defy the kind of simplistic conceptual and strategic responses of the past generation. The related and more general problem I am concerned with in this book is that the whole pattern of thought associated with the Realism of the post–World War II period represents, at best, a dangerous anachronism in the era that has seen AIDS, global warming, and international drug cartels force their way on to the global agenda, alongside the cultural, ecological, and gendered challenges to a "reality" that for so long has defined order, security, and the common good in International Relations.

The scope and nature of this problem might be further appreciated in its relation to another dimension of the debate over the failure of orthodox International Relations theory as practice to address this expanded agenda. It concerns the broader issue of analytical and policy paralysis associated with the post–Cold War period, acknowledged by Gaddis and Hoffmann and given a generalized articulation by Lewis Lapham.[9] This paralysis has manifested itself in a variety of ways. Recent U.S. foreign policy perspectives, for example, have been likened to the "gibbering of apes" in their remoteness from the everyday situations of people around the globe in the 1990s. A more specific claim is that the mainstream U.S. International Relations community is floundering, primarily because "nobody knows the language in which to ask or answer the questions presented by the absence of the Soviet empire."[10] Rather, it is suggested, the remaining superpower continues to formulate its images of the world in terms consistent with the struggle for Cold War hegemony.

Consequently, in the 1990s, while acknowledging at one level the difficulties associated with the updated task of world "policeman," the United States continues, nevertheless, to articulate its hegemonic ambitions in terms of it retaining "the pre-eminent responsibility for addressing selectively those wrongs which threaten not only our interests, but those of our allies or friends, or which could seriously unsettle international relations."[11] This, for Lapham, represents not just the delusions of grandeur of a U.S. society seeking to buttress a threatened identity in the post–Cold War void. Rather, and more seriously, it represents the continuance of a "grotesque" general theory of International Relations that comprehends global life from within a Traditional doctrine of hierarchical conflict, characterized by fear and denial of change and "the infantile wish for omnipotence."[12]

The inadequacies and dangers of this position are articulated best in the silences of its analysis, which, in attributing the end of the Cold War to U.S. technomilitary power and deterrence strategy, implies that the collapse of the Soviet empire had little to do with domestic factors, such as a corroding social system and a mismanaged economy. It is not surprising, on this basis, that any internally generated demise of the Soviet system went undetected and unpredicted. At another level, however, this restricted perspective simply disregards many questions and conceptual issues concerning the changing nature of global affairs. It disregards, for example, the unique difficulties now associated with the fulfillment of even the most powerful geopolitical state "interests," when such interests—defined in terms of state sovereignty—are now so clearly problematic. And it disregards what for many is a fundamental question of the contemporary period, of whether the Traditional hierarchical rituals of global power relations are indeed integral to the everyday practices of the world's peoples and their various modes of life.

This theme will be addressed again more directly toward the end of the book, where attention will fall on the significance of a variety of critical social movements in contemporary global life. For now it represents a conduit into another dimension of the paralysis of post–Cold War theory and practice, this time in relation to the ethnic wars in the former Yugoslavia and in particular the plight of Bosnia. Traditional analysis of this conflict has been predictable and, in many respects, understandable and compelling. It is undoubtedly the case that with the demise of authoritarian variants of Marxism in Eastern Europe many of the political, religious, and ethnic tensions endemic to these regions have again flared, tragically so in some cases. And, in mid-1993, calls for a Traditional (military) response are increasingly resonant.

But when one ponders more carefully the events and issues surrounding this particular human disaster, it becomes apparent that there were options open to the primary decisionmakers that might have avoided, or ameliorated, the resultant carnage, and that there was nothing inevitable about the Balkan situation that led to the chaos of the present. Rather, in a situation that demanded innovative and imaginative thought and action, the Western response to the disintegration of Yugoslavia was generally characterized by the paralysis noted earlier. Consequently, at that crucial moment early on in the conflict, in June 1991, when U.S. secretary of state James Baker was confronted by Croatian and Bosnian appeals for support in their struggles for self-determination, his rejection was framed in terms that invoked Traditional notions of sovereignty, security, and order and emphasized the destabilizing effects of secession.[13] At that vital moment in post–Cold War history, accordingly, the Western superpower effectively told Serbia and the Yugoslav army that they could use any means to hold the country together—without fear of Western intervention.[14] As Tom Post has put it, from the beginning of the crisis "the West fell back on outmoded diplomacy, insisting that Yugoslavia stay together. When it didn't, the United States and most of the European Community acted like an anaesthetized patient, tuning in and out of the Balkan conflict."[15]

This is not to minimize or underestimate the complexities and dangers of the Balkan situation. Nor is it any simple appeal to hindsight, suggesting that the West, or more specifically the United States, had clearly defined policy alternatives in the Balkans and that, armed with the omnipotent powers of a new theory of "reality," it could have simply avoided the devastation that has occurred in that troubled region. There is nothing clear or simple about the Balkan war circa 1992–1993, nor is there any singular, all-encompassing grand theory of strategic action that can be applied to it in "practice." Yet this indeed is the point of the previous discussion, for integral to the problems, inadequacies, and silences in (particularly) U.S. responses to the post–Cold War crisis is *precisely this commitment* to a simplistic grand theory of International Relations, honed during the early years of the Cold War and not seriously reflected upon since then. The Bosnian example is, in this context, another illustration of the implications of often highly intelligent and compassionate people remaining incarcerated within narrowly conceived frameworks of thought when nuanced, imaginative, and flexible analysis is demanded of them.

One final commentary on the issue of post–Cold War theory as practice might provide the most explicit indication yet of why this situation continues in the 1990s and might help direct the discussion more precisely to central themes in this book. The relative positions of the Cold War superpowers are the focus of attention here. More precisely, Vaclav Havel's ruminations on this question and the contrast they evoke with mainstream Western approaches are of most significance.[16] From Havel's perspective, the demise of the Soviet empire does not, by necessity, indicate any sense of progressive linear movement toward liberal capitalist synthesis (e.g., as in the Fukuyama thesis). Rather, it is understood as having major implications for the way in which the dominant articulators of modern thought, in both the liberal West and communist societies, continue to express themselves as the "historical symbol[s] for the dream of reason."[17] Havel's position, more explicitly, is that instead of engaging in simplistic triumphalism, the Western "victors" of the Cold War must now begin to confront the aspects of their own societies that saw them bound together with the Soviet Union for so long in a

> kind of alliance *between the last citadels of the modern era* [emphasis added] making a common cause against the ravages of time and change... [in which] the two self-proclaimed superpowers propped each other up against the storm blowing from the abyss of a world dissolved.[18]

The specific proposition here is one rarely encountered in any International

Relations text, notwithstanding its significance for global life. It represents, in short, an appeal for serious critical reflection upon the fundamental philosophical premises of Western modernity. More precisely, it appeals to the most powerful Western societies (particularly the United States), at the moment of their greatest triumph, to reflect upon not just the great achievements of modern political life but also upon the dangers, costs, silences, and closures integral to it. Indeed, suggests Havel, the prospect of meaningful democratic change taking place in the wake of the Cold War depends, to a significant extent, on the capacities of the most powerful global actors to confront those aspects of their theory and practice that continue, in the 1990s, to restrict their understanding of a complex, changing global environment. Most significant, they must address the "technocratic, utilitarian approach to Being" that characterized Cold War power politics, while confronting the most profound of modernity's philosophical *illusions,* centered on "the proud belief that man, as the pinnacle of everything that exists, is capable of objectively describing, explaining and controlling everything that exists, and of possessing the one and only truth about the world."[19]

This is a significant insight in relation to this work, because in its particular representation of the dominant approach to modernity—as the philosophical pursuit of objectivity, omnipotence, and control—it adds contextual coherence to a discussion that locates the dominant Tradition of International Relations in precisely these terms. It is in these terms, accordingly, that this book seeks to explain the significance for contemporary global "practice" of that historicophilosophical process by which International Relations has framed its dominant images of self and Others in the world, in terms that continue to restrict its capacity to think and act with genuine tolerance, imagination, and flexibility. International Relations, in this sense, will be (re)introduced here as a microscopic representation of a larger process of "knowing" and "meaning" intrinsic to modern social life since images of cogito rationality became fundamental to self-identity and the rational pursuit of foundational certainty became the raison d'être of modern theory and practice.

To speak of International Relations in these terms is to recognize as integral to it the complexities and tensions of a period when, in unique technological circumstances, a narrowly based interpretation of social reality was transformed into a universal agenda for all theory and practice; when in the search for a secure (secular) foundation for understanding the modern world, the discourse of meaning associated with human history and political life was appropriated by the scientific project; when a particular image of real knowledge, centered on the natural sciences, became embedded at the core of our understanding of human society, via the influences of figures such as Hume, Kant, Comte, Dilthey, Marx, Weber, Russell, and Popper.

A critical ambition of this book, in this context, is to establish that the issues at stake in the previous discussion—faltering U.S. identity, the stilted traditionalism in thinking on Bosnia and Eastern Europe, and the predictable violence in the Gulf—are intrinsic to "theoretical" issues drawn from modern debates about the way we have come to know the world and represent that knowledge as reality. It will do so in speaking of International Relations in a way that it *has never spoken of itself,* in order that its deep silences, omissions, and points of closure be eased open and space be provided for alternative ways of thinking and acting in relation to global issues.

In this regard the book draws upon a wide-ranging literature on critical social theory that, across the disciplinary spectrum, has focused its attention on the largely taken-for-granted reference points for our understanding of the contemporary world, derived primarily from variations on liberal and Marxist themes and represented as discrete, self-contained categories of, for example, the "real," the "rational," the "scientific," and the "foundational." In this way it has sought to readdress some of the most important themes in modern philosophy—the quest for a positivist science of human society; questions of rationality, sovereignty, objectivity, and truth; relations of subject and object, fact and value, knowledge and power, theory and reality—in order that we might understand more profoundly the way we think and act in human society in the late twentieth century.[20]

This is the general context on which an emerging critical social theory literature in International Relations has focused regarding the historical and philosophical circumstances that saw positivism emerge as the foremost articulation of the Enlightenment pursuit of a rational-scientific foundation for modern human life. Hence the increasingly critical response to the dichotomized crudity of International Relations scholarship that, in the face of generations of counterargument and vibrant debate in other areas of the humanities, continues to represent its theory and practice in universalist and essentialist terms—as "corresponding" to an (anarchical) and unchanging reality—detached from and largely irrelevant to the complexities of domestic theory and practice. Hence also the growing frustration with the tendency within the discipline to fail to seriously confront the simplicity of its approach to fundamental analytical issues concerning, for example, the relationship of "knower" and "known" and the nature of individuality, of (rational) choice, of reading history, of power, and of change. Hence the attempts, in the 1980s and 1990s, to speak in a more sophisticated and insightful manner about givens such as the sovereign state, the utilitarian nature of the (anarchical) state system, and the overall closure of an approach to theory and practice rendered static by an uncritical adherence to Western, post-Renaissance historical and intellectual experience.[21]

The major target of critical social theory has been an International Relations orthodoxy—most influentially manifested in the scientific neo-Realism of (mainly) U.S. scholarship but also in its (mainly) British

Traditionalist counterpart—that continues to represent as *the* reality of International Relations a narrow, self-affirming, and self-enclosed image of the world "out there."[22] On this basis, a complex, ambiguous, and heterogeneous matrix of existence has been reduced, in International Relations intellectual and policy circles, to a simplistic, universalized image of the "real" world, which is fundamentally detached from the everyday experience of so much of that world.

I will argue here, however, that, contrary to any Realist doctrine, reality is never a complete, entirely coherent "thing," accessible to universalized, essentialist, or totalized understandings of it. Nor can the question of reality be exhausted by reference to the facts of the world or any simple aggregation of them, because reality is always characterized by ambiguity, disunity, discrepancy, contradiction, and difference. An adequate political realism, consequently, is one that above all recognizes its limitations in this regard and acknowledges its partial, problematic, and always contestable nature. Inadequacy, in this sense, is the representation of a partial, particularistic image of reality as (irreducible, totalized, and uncontestable) reality itself. The problem, as R. N. Berki suggests, is that it has been *precisely* this inadequate and "primitive" representation of reality that has dominated within the Anglo-American intellectual community, particularly that sector of it concerned with International Relations.[23]

As a consequence, two rather primitive subthemes have become integral to the question of political reality in International Relations. The first projects reality as existing "out there" and is articulated through the language and logic of immediacy. Reality, on this basis, is a world of "tangible, palpable, perceptible things or objects. . . . It is material and concrete."[24] The real world, consequently, is that which is immediately "there," around us and disclosed to us by sensory information. Realism in International Relations thus becomes the commonsensical accommodation to the tangible, observable realities of this (external) world. At this point the second primitive Realist theme reaffirms the first and, by its own logic at least, grants it greater legitimacy. This is the necessity theme, which confirms the need for accommodation to the facts of reality but accords them greater historical and philosophical facticity. Reality now becomes "the realm of the unchangeable, inevitable and in the last resort inexorable occurrences, a world of eternity, objectivity, gravity, substantiality and positive resistance to human purposes."[25]

In this manner, Realism is imbued with moral, philosophical, and even religious connotations in its confrontation with the real world "out there." It becomes moral in that it observes certain rules of conduct integral to the reality of human behavior. It can take on a religious dimension in that reality is understood as an accommodation to an inexorable destiny emanating from the realm of ultimate "necessity." Its philosophical status is established as Realists, acknowledging the need for accommodation, represent their understanding of reality in the serious, resigned manner of, for example, the scholar-statesman contemplating the often unpalatable "is" of the world. The knowledge form integral to this Realist philosophy is that concerned, above all, with *control.*

More precisely, the knowledge form integral to a Realism of this kind is positivism; its philosophical identity, as a consequence, is marked by dualism and dichotomy. At its most powerful (e.g., during the Cold War), this positivist-Realist identity is represented as the opposition between the forces of rationality, unity, and progressive purpose and an anarchical realm of danger and threat in permanent need of restraint. A genuine (positivist) Realist, in this circumstance, is the observer of the world "out there" aware, above all, of the need for the law and order proffered by the sovereign state in a post-Renaissance world of states. The Realist, accordingly, remains "heroically pessimistic," trusting only in the forces of "law and order, and their maintenance by force, as a permanent and ever precarious holding operation [understanding] peace, tranquillity, prosperity, freedom [as] a special bonus, accruing to people as a result of living in a well ordered society."[26]

As Berki suggests, this Realist approach represents logical and analytical inadequacy in that in detaching itself from theory and interpretation it effectively detaches itself from the (historical, cultural, and linguistic) context of everyday human existence—*from the social and intellectual lifeblood of reality.* Even in its most sophisticated form (e.g., Popperian/Lakatosian), a positivist-Realist approach represents an anachronistic residue of the European Enlightenment and, in general, mainstream Western philosophy, which continues the futile quest for a grand (non)theory of existence beyond specific time, space, and political purpose. More immediately, it stands as a dangerous source of analytic/policy paralysis, in the face of the extraordinary events associated with the end of the Cold War and in the face of widespread recognition that it is seemingly incapable of moving beyond its primitive intellectual agenda.[27]

Realism in International Relations, accordingly, constructs its explanatory agenda upon one variant or another of a "spectator" theory of knowledge, in which knowledge of the real world is gleaned via a realm of external facts (e.g., of interstate anarchy) that impose themselves upon the individual scholar-statesman, who is then constrained by the analytic/policy "art of the possible." In its (mainly) North American variant, infused with (primarily) Popperian insight and behavioralist training rituals since the 1960s, this has resulted in a Realism set upon the enthusiastic invocation of falsificationist scientific principles. The (mainly) British alternative, meanwhile, has invoked a species of intuitionist inductivism often more sensitive in tone to the various critiques of positivism but ultimately no less committed to its perpetuation. As a consequence, the questions asked and (historicophilosophical) issues raised by International Relations scholarship have been severely limited, to the extent that complex epistemological/ontological debates over knowledge, meaning, language, and reality—the issues of how we think and act in the world—have been largely confined to the primitive Realist framework described earlier.

In both the intellectual and policy communities, accordingly, one has seen a generation-long commitment to the power politics Realism of the postwar period, which became the Western "catechism" during the Cold War as International Relations scholars sought factual certainty about the world, verifiable via the Traditional wisdom of certain "great texts."[28] Realism, at this time, came to signify a state of mind that permeated university and government sectors and conditioned the political climate to the extent that some actions seemed "to stand to reason [while] others seem[ed] naive—by definition."[29] In this situation the real world became one in which ("out there")

> states were involved in an unending struggle with each other (because that was the nature of states in an anarchic world); power was necessary to survive in it or continue to fight; all states were potential enemies . . . but the worst might be avoided by clever diplomacy and by virtue of the fact that all alike shared a similar conception of [utilitarian] rational behaviour.[30]

The dangers of this approach were starkly illustrated in a work entirely ignored by mainstream scholarship, John Vasquez's *The Power of Power Politics* (1983), which, in the most comprehensive survey of the International Relations literature yet undertaken, indicated clearly enough the problems of understanding and explaining global life in Realist grand theoretical terms. More significant, it did so in the falsificationist terms that, since 1945, have been dominant at the (North) American disciplinary center.[31] Setting aside the quantitative idiom at the end of his study, Vasquez concluded that, as a particular image of the world employed by Realist policymakers, power politics *promotes* certain kinds of behavior and often leads to self-fulfilling prophecies. Drawing out some of the implications of this situation on the central question of war and peace, Vasquez had a chilling statement to make on the orthodox answer—the alliance system and balance of power. Here, he maintained, the most likely (statistical) outcome of Realist anarchical "theory" in "practice" is war, not peace. His findings were that

> power politics is an image of the world that *encourages behaviour that helps bring about war* . . . [thus] the attempt to balance power is itself part of the very behaviour that leads to war. . . . [Consequently it] is now clear that alliances do not produce peace but lead to war [emphasis added].[32]

Since the early 1970s, of course, a plethora of works has claimed that this crude power politics image has been superseded. In the wake of the Vietnam War in particular the scholarly literature has been characterized by a succession of claims to have gone beyond (primitive) Realism and (unreflective) positivism.[33] Indeed, it has been in this period that the discipline has understood itself as engaged in the third major stage of its (rational-progressive) development, centered on its third "great debate."

The first of these debates, according to disciplinary folklore, saw International Relations scholars responding realistically to the world "out there" in overturning the utopianism of Wilsonian liberalism in favor of the power politics format outlined in E. H. Carr's *The Twenty Years Crisis* (1939). The basic principles of power politics Realism were confirmed and rendered more systematic in the greatest of all the discipline's "great texts," Hans Morgenthau's *Politics Among Nations* (1948). The search for the objective and enduring laws of international life, spoken of by Morgenthau, was then taken up in earnest as (mainly) North American scholars sought to give modern intellectual sustenance to Carr's appeal for a mature science of International Relations.

The second developmental stage and associated "great debate" arose from this quest and a conflict concerning it within Realist ranks in the mid-1960s. Here, the (mainly) North American behavioralists, armed with (Popperian) falsificationist techniques, sought to further distance Realist scholarship from the lingering metaphysics of the (mainly) British Traditionalists and their commitments to ambiguous philosophical concepts and themes. This second "great debate" petered out in the late 1960s with both sides claiming victory as they spoke past each other in Knorr and Rosenau's *Contending Approaches to International Relations* (1969). In the period since the 1970s, the developmental story has been renewed, albeit in slightly different form. Now, it is suggested, the era of positivist-Realist dominance is effectively over and the International Relations field is, almost literally, the site of a hundred (theoretical) flowers blooming. The third developmental stage, consequently, is that of competing paradigms; of globalism, pluralism, structuralism, regime theory; of a resurgent international political economy; and of neo-Realism.[34]

This book argues that the analytical progress inherent in this disciplinary narrative is largely illusory, that while some orthodox works have illustrated a capacity for important insight (e.g., interdependence à la Keohane and Nye), they have ultimately closed off our capacity to ask more profound questions about global life in the last part of the twentieth century. Consequently, and for all its developmental claims to the contrary, International Relations in the 1990s remains fundamentally incarcerated in the positivist-Realist framework that characterized its understanding of the world "out there" in the 1940s and 1950s.

This is not to suggest that the neo-Realists of the 1990s have reverted entirely to the "high politics" scenarios of the past, or that their Traditionalism is represented, *explicitly,* in the "metaphysical" terms repudiated by behavioralism. Rather, in seeking to accommodate the criticisms of the 1960s and 1970s, the more nuanced of the neo-Realists have made selective forays into the behavioralist and Traditionalist genres in reconstructing their approach to the world in the contemporary era. The result is a fusion of Traditionalist epithets and systemic models of behavior, derived primarily from neoclassical economics, now reformulated (e.g., via Kindleberger) as contemporary reality in the age of an international political economy.

These themes will receive more substantial treatment in Chapter 6, where I take issue with the neo-Realism of the 1980s and 1990s in both its more conventional structuralist mode (e.g., Waltz) and its moderated articulations, via figures such as Stephen Krasner, Arthur Stein, and Robert Keohane. At this time I will seek to illustrate, in a number of ways, the veracity of Richard Ashley's claims, made nearly a decade ago and never seriously confronted by mainstream scholars, that neo-Realism represents an inadequate "positivist structuralism that treats the given order as the natural order, limits rather than expands political discourse, negates or trivializes the significance of variety across time and place [and] subordinates all practice to an interest in control."[35] I will argue also, again consistent with Ashley's insight in 1984, that for all neo-Realism's scientific posturing, its perspectives are predicated upon unexplained metaphysical commitments that are exempted from any analytical scrutiny. The implication of this, in a complex and changing world, is that neo-Realism remains incapable of understanding political behavior other than in the reductionist terms associated with the transplanted methodological individualism of structuralist state-centric anarchy. This is a crucial limitation upon contemporary understanding—one that effectively ignores and indeed cannot speak of the complex range of human endeavors associated with questions of class, race, gender, and religion, and forms of collectivist commitments that do not easily fit within narrow confines of neo-Realist analysis.

I will take issue also (albeit implicitly) with works not necessarily associated with mainstream neo-Realism and structuralism but that, in their "alternative" scholarship, reinforce the discursive limitations of the orthodoxy. The focus here is on a range of scholars (e.g., Beirsteker, Mansbach and Ferguson, Ruggie) whose perspectives bristle with the tensions between their "open" liberal inclinations and the closure of their behavioralist training rituals.[36] For all their differences, the contributions of these scholars and their more orthodox counterparts are dominated by a (rarely acknowledged) commitment to a positivist ontology of real meaning. Consequently, the (generally) unspoken message from the (broad) disciplinary mainstream to critical works like the present one is this: Your "theoretical/philosophical" efforts are of some value and are appreciated for the intellectual contribution they generally make to scholarship, however, we do not need another philosophical "preface" for International Relations, because the great questions have all been asked and the great philosophical conundrums all posed, and they have all been absorbed, understood, and integrated by the International Relations community, particularly by those at the apex of the discipline committed to Realist/neo-Realist approaches.[37]

My response to this perspective is that it represents another major illusion within an International Relations community that, if it has absorbed, understood, or integrated these philosophical issues at all, it has done so only in the *most shallow and superficial of terms.* The suggestion, more precisely, is that the questions and issues of ontology and epistemology—of the way we think and act in the world and understand reality—have either been ignored in International Relations or rendered marginal and barely relevant by a disciplinary orthodoxy that has interpreted the Western historical and philosophical story in a narrow, exclusionary, and inadequate manner. The result: the "backward discipline" noted by Mervyn Frost in the mid-1980s and characterized by the kind of limitation and closure at the core of the analytical and policy paralysis discussed earlier in this chapter.[38] Much of the discussion in this book will concentrate, therefore, on this disciplinary literature—not just as a site of "theory" per se but as the major site at which the reality of global political practice has been (theoretically) framed in the "backward" terms alluded to earlier. Some brief comments on the nature of this backwardness might indicate more fully why such a focus is of significance in this context.

The Backward Discipline: Some Introductory Comments

For Mervyn Frost, in 1985, the basic characteristic of the "backward discipline" was its unself-consciousness concerning its analytical and research endeavors. More explicitly it concerned the claims of Realist scholarship, in particular, to have gone beyond the intellectual narrowness of earlier times in the era of postpositivism and neo-Realism. This was not the case, suggested Frost. Instead, the discipline remains in something of a philosophical time warp with the perspectives at the apex of the discipline incarcerated within a rigid "positivist bias," determining a mode of analysis, in either Traditionalism or neo-Realism, which

> seeks to verify conclusions by reference to the "facts" which are in some sense "hard" and there for all to see (i.e., ascertaining the facts does not require an interpretative effort on the part of the investigator and the facts are ascertainable by the investigator without his having previously adopted any particular theory), and the links between conclusions and evidence (or hypothesis and verifying data) are intersubjectively verifiable. Both stress that the results of their studies do not derive from subjective, relative or conventional judgements . . . [and] common to both approaches is a radical distinction between the status accorded to factual judgements, to

> which the discipline of international relations should aspire and that accorded to value judgements.[39]

But this backwardness goes deeper into the textual heart of the discipline and is evident across its literary spectrum. It has to do, at one level, with Hans Morgenthau orienting a whole generation of scholars toward the "objective laws" of politics at the international level.[40] It concerns, too, that moment of major irony in disciplinary folklore when E. H. Carr attacked the inadequacy of interwar idealism on the basis that it was a narrow, ethnocentric approach, drawn uncritically from Western Enlightenment sources.[41] It is integral to the nominally unrelated proposition of Knorr and Rosenau in 1969 that, in the dispute between Realists of the second "great debate," one point "command[ed] universal agreement, namely that it is useful and appropriate to *dichotomize* [emphasis added] the various approaches to international phenomena."[42] It pervades Michael Sullivan's conclusion in the 1970s that one of the problems with the critiques of Realism was that perhaps "their picture of the world . . . [is] at variance with the real world."[43] It underpins James Rosenau's continuing insistence, in the mid-1980s, on "the basic tenets of empirical science which require that variables be specified and the analyst be ever mindful of the eventual need to observe and measure."[44] And it resonates through Kal Holsti's commentary, in the same period, suggesting that a new paradigm would not be unwelcome in the discipline if it passed the test that *both* scientific and Traditionalist-Realist scholarship had instigated. This test required that any new approach be characterized by "logical consistency, the capacity to generate research, and reasonable correspondence with the observed facts of international politics."[45]

More immediately, the continuing backwardness in International Relations is intrinsic to concerns expressed by Roger Tooze, in 1988, on the state of contemporary international political economy scholarship and the exclusion or marginalization of philosophical issues, in comparison with the "real-worldism" of mainstream researchers.[46] This has resulted in a state of "mutual incomprehension, if not antagonism," within the scholarly community, between those maintaining that any understanding of global life must be located in a broader philosophical context and the great majority of scholars who consider philosophical debate insignificant to their research and analysis.[47] Accordingly, in the mainstream agenda of international political economy scholarship, in the late 1980s,

> matters of philosophical interest and concern are either defined as not relevant to the individual or group producing knowledge or are left to the provenance of the theorists who inhabit a shadowy underworld of meta-everything. These theorists are [considered] inconsequential to the "real world," except to provide instrumental frameworks for the selection and ordering of "the facts."[48]

This being the case, it is clear enough that a basic unity-of-science thesis remains as dominant within international political economy circles in the present as it did in the 1960s, at the height of behavioralist influence. An integral element of positivism, the unity-of-science position consists of three interlocking propositions. The first states that the physical world is best understood in scientific terms; the second, that the social and political worlds are (therefore) in principle amenable to scientific methodology and techniques; and the third, that positivism, representing the fundamental practices of science, is the appropriate basis for social scientific analysis and research. The proposition, more precisely, is that a genuine distinction exists between "real" knowledge and (abstract) theory and that testing procedures exist that can demarcate the former from the latter, allowing for a value-free account of International Relations, via the scientific method.

The problems associated with this position will be addressed, from a number of angles, in the chapters to follow. At this point, however, with some of the themes of the "backward discipline" now in mind, it is worth summarizing where we have been in this chapter before I say something more specifically about where we are set to go, in critical terms. The summary offers another dimension to the discussion thus far in emphasizing the power of a positivist/empiricist "metaphysic" at the core of orthodox social theory and in indicating how, via an orthodox consensus within Anglo-American scholarship, it continues to cast its substantial influences within International Relations.[49]

The Power of the Positivist/Empiricist "Metaphysic" and the Orthodox Consensus

At the philosophical core of International Relations is a dichotomized ontological logic that assumes into reality a distinction between a realm of empiricist "fact" and a realm of "theorized" knowledge, derived in one way or another (i.e., either inductively or deductively) from it. The origins of this assumption arguably reside in the broader dualized tendencies of post-Platonic discourse and have, therefore, always been intrinsic to (dominant) Western philosophical images of truth, rationality, and reality. The more immediate and explicit origin of the assumption lies in the post-Cartesian age of modern rationality and, in crystalized politico-intellectual terms, in the positivism/empiricism of the period since the Enlightenment of the eighteenth century. Since this time, the fact/theory dichotomy has been the focus of widespread and damning critique, but it has remained a powerful if unstated constant at the core of much mainstream Anglo-American thought—often at its crudest within an "Americanized" International Relations discipline after World War II. The endurance of this dichotomy has little to do with the qualitative merits of its logic, as scholars since

Hume have attested and as the following chapter will illustrate. However, in an era that has seen modern Western societies represent their achievements and identities as correlative with the successful pursuit of rational-scientific certainty, this fact/theory dichotomy has legitimated politico-strategic images of rationalized interstate hierarchy and violence and theories of order congruent with them (e.g., deterrence theory).

In Ernst Gellner's terms, this dichotomy represents the most powerful articulation of an "empiricist metaphysic" at the core of contemporary social thought, distinguishing between a world of fact "out there" and a cognitive realm of theory that *retrospectively* orders and gives meaning to the factual data "not because the world is so constructed or because there is any such 'pure' data; [but] because this picture conveys so well the crucial [scientific] requirement—that of insoluble data which are independent of the theory that is being judged."[50] Gellner's commentary is particularly instructive in this context because its focus is the work of Karl Popper and the falsificationist approach to (mediated) scientific knowledge so influential within the disciplinary mainstream since the 1960s. Gellner's point concerning the "empiricist metaphysic" in Popper's work is that it represents a site of major paradox and illusion at the core of the dominant mode of social science reasoning in Anglo-American societies. The paradox, simply put, is that Popper's whole deductivist, hypotheses-testing procedure is predicated upon the very inductivist premises it sought to overcome—that is, an image of the world as constructed by sense data. The illusion associated with falsificationism is that it overcomes the crude atomism and reductionism of logical positivism, as Popper and mainstream Western social theorists in general have claimed. (This issue will be discussed in more detail in Chapter 2, where I illustrate that the negative implications of this social theory unself-consciousness were not exhausted by the discredited behavioralism of the 1960s.)

The "empiricist metaphysic" remains dominant in Anglo-American social theory. This was affirmed in 1987 by Anthony Giddens and Johnathon Turner, who affirmed also an important thematic connection between the larger interdisciplinary situation and International Relations.[51] It concerns the understanding of scholars, in both contexts, that theirs is an enterprise marked by pluralism, intellectual diversity, and theoretical tolerance in the postpositivist era. Not so, suggest Giddens and Turner. Instead, Anglo-American theory and practice remain dominated by a worldview set in logical positivist terms and characterized by "a [paradoxical] suspicion of metaphysics, a desire to define in a clear cut way what is to count as 'scientific,' [and] an emphasis on the testability of concepts and propositions and a sympathy for hypothetico-deductive systems."[52]

For Giddens, this was confirmation of an earlier judgment. In 1982 he concluded that Anglo-American social theory had not progressed, in any fundamental way, from the logical positivism of the early twentieth century but was encompassed within a disciplinary orthodox consensus.[53] This orthodox consensus represented a static impasse between an often unacknowledged but still potent positivism (e.g., expressed in liberal and Marxist terms) and an illusory "alternative" derived from the hermeneutic influences of a figure such as Max Weber, in particular.[54] Subsequently, in 1987, Giddens and Turner recorded that an orthodox consensus remained dominant (if no longer entirely secure) within Anglo-American social theory, while its mainstream remained committed to an epistemological regime that limited inquiry to questions such as "What is 'out there' in the social universe? What are the fundamental properties of the world? What kind of analysis of these properties is possible and/or appropriate?"[55]

Weber, as indicated, is an important figure in this context because, like Popper, he was a scholar who brought a sophisticated European dimension to Anglo-American thinking, effectively mediating its cruder (logical positivist) aspects on the theory/practice conundrum. As Giddens and others have indicated, however, Weber's contribution, like that of Popper, requires a more critical evaluation if its influence is to be more profoundly understood at the core of the orthodox consensus. The recent and very profound connections drawn between Weber and the exemplar International Relations scholar Hans Morgenthau (and Realism generally) make this inquiry even more significant for the present discussion.[56]

Weber sought to employ an adapted Verstehen approach in the quest for the great synthesis of the age—the bringing together in a coherent theoretical matrix of a Germanic interpretivist approach and British and French positivism/empiricism. In so doing, he reformulated the knowledge process and radically limited the capacity of the social sciences. More specifically, Weber limited his critical scientific attention to the object of inquiry, assumed to be an individual actor acting in a "rational" manner (i.e., that which is purposeful in the attempt to attain particular interests). Given this important assumption, the scientific problem associated with overcoming intersubjective meanings is effectively dissipated by a perspective that conceives of "meaning" as an irreducible quality generated through the pursuit of individual (already-given) interests.

From this theoretical position it becomes possible to calculate and predict (in a limited scientific fashion) the behavior of actors following these already-given interests. Thus, consistent with a means/ends logic, all values, ethics, or "normative" factors (e.g., theories) in either the observed or the observer are taken as given and *deleted* from useful scientific discourse. The social scientific enterprise that remains can make judgments only upon the (observed) behavior associated with already-given ends. In this way, Weber solved the modernist epistemological conundrum for contemporary social theory and Anglo-American political science in particular. And this is *precisely* the way the Weberian perspective has been utilized by Realist theorists in International Relations. Here, the behavior of the observed actors (individual states) is taken as given—that is, perceived as motivated by the rational pursuit of (national) interests.

In this way the sophisticated Weberian image of reality has, if anything, increased the tendency toward positivist closure in International Relations, for, as Susan Hekman has explained, in continuing to acknowledge fundamental ontological assumptions (e.g., the opposition of subject/object and fact/value) Verstehen approaches, like Weber's (and Morgenthau's), represent the other side of the positivist coin and lie at the heart of the orthodox consensus in the backward discipline of International Relations.[57]

To reiterate—these issues have implications well beyond their immediate "theoretical" manifestation. The issue of positivism's dominance, for example, goes to the core of the question of theory *as* practice in International Relations, for if one takes the view that knowledge is derived from activities "out there" in the real world (e.g., knowable via testing procedures designed to separate out the facts from mere interpretation) then there is little point in further reflection upon the process by which these activities are understood. One simply responds to them in ways that best serve, for example, the national interest. In regard to the Gulf War, therefore, there is little point in further contemplation of the Western policy role in the region, particularly during the Iran-Iraq War, when Saddam Hussein was provided with much of the military and psychological wherewithal for his subsequent actions. Nor is there much "practical" value in reflecting upon attitudes toward the breakup of the Soviet empire or what might have been accomplished if something other than Realist grand theory had been imposed upon the Bosnian disaster. Again, based on a dichotomized framing of such events, the (analyzing/policymaking) subject can only accede to E. H. Carr's famous dictum, that in regard to International Relations, a Realist analysis understands that "the function of thinking is to study a sequence of events which *it is powerless to influence or to alter* [emphasis added]."[58]

From my perspective, however, this represents a very powerful and highly dangerous statement of theoretical unself-consciousness, which must be confronted and questioned in a serious and sustained manner if we are to deal, in the future, with issues such as the Gulf and Bosnia in other than a crude ad hoc manner, one so costly in terms of human suffering. My own position on the theory/practice theme repudiates the notion that we can somehow detach ourselves (as subjects) from the process by which we give real meaning to an objectified world "out there." It is consistent, in this regard, with a whole range of scholarship that, over the years and the disciplines, has questioned the dichotomized simplicity of mainstream Western thought.

At the heart of the natural sciences there has long been a repudiation of this crude dichotomy. Indeed since the 1920s, in the field of quantum physics, the works of scholars such as Einstein, Bohr, and Heisenberg have effectively undermined the positivist insistence upon an objective factual world "out there" as the foundation of our (theoretical) knowledge and as the basis of *the* scientific method. The point is, of course, that theoretical physics, which deals with subatomic particles that *cannot be seen, observed, or measured,* has fundamentally reformulated the notion of scientific method in refusing to describe reality in terms of objects "out there," independent of the observing subject.[59] Heisenberg explains:

> In atomic physics observations can no longer be objectified in such a simple manner; that is they cannot be referred to something that takes place objectively or in a describable manner in space and time [thus] the science of nature does not deal with nature itself but in fact with the science of nature as man thinks and describes it.[60]

This is a position complemented from another important angle, that of Wittgenstein, who, in repudiating his logical positivist perspectives in the *Tractatus,* introduced a broader, more incisive dimension to Western philosophy and the social sciences, with the following proposition:

> There are no independent or objective sources of support outside of human thought and human action. . . . There is no standard of objective reality (always fixed, never changing) against which to compare or measure a universe of discourse . . . nothing exists outside of our language and actions which can be used to justify, for example, a statement's truth or falsity.[61]

In Chapter 6 this perspective will receive more detailed attention, but for now two brief comments can be made about it and the critical implications of it for a work of this kind. First, from this perspective there is no simple dichotomy between an observing subject and a real world "out there" that determines the way we respond to it. The argument, rather, is that at every stage of the process by which we come to know the world, we are engaged with it, to the extent that the facts of the world (e.g., historical, political, social) are always intrinsically bound up with the way we give meaning to them and accord them their "real" status. This is an interpretive process grounded in historicophilosophical, cultural, and linguistic complexity, not in some Archimedean point of ultimate reference beyond history and society. The second point that needs to made here is that for anyone even remotely aware of debates in the philosophy of science, or philosophical circles more generally, there is nothing at all remarkable about this proposition. Perspectives supporting it and contesting it have been integral to the agenda across the social theory disciplinary spectrum for many years. Indeed, it would be an unremarkable proposition in almost any other context than the present one—a discussion concerning the way that we think and act in International Relations, where a crude positivist Realism has effectively silenced such debate.

In this context, another, related, proposition has salience for the discussion to follow. It is that given the scope and nature of the problems associated with this silenced debate, there can be no simple answers to the questions it raises; nor can there be any immediate, quick-fix solutions to inadequacies so deeply embedded in the intellectual and policy sectors of the International Relations community. Similarly, there are no simple problem-solving techniques capable of overcoming ritualized images of reality, dominant in Western philosophy for four centuries and transposed, uncritically, by the "backward discipline." However, there are now a variety of alternative perspectives available to students of International Relations that provide more sophisticated, inclusive, and adequate reference points for understanding a complex world. These perspectives confront the difficult questions rather than acquiesce in Traditional simplicity. They go beyond surface-level critique and strip bare the ontological foundations upon which International Relations theory as practice has managed to reduce global life to a narrow, self-enclosed, self-affirming image of it.

For many, not surprisingly, this represents a negative, relativistic, perhaps even nihilistic approach to a world where quick answers are required to complex questions. In this book it is understood in somewhat different terms—as an entirely positive engagement with an old and very powerful set of commitments in Western social theory that insist that unless there is *certain* knowledge there can be no *real* knowledge of the world at all. Richard Bernstein has described this phenomenon as the either/or dualism integral to a modern objectivism that, since Descartes, has framed modern theory and practice in terms of the conviction that "*either* there is some support for our being, a fixed foundation for our knowledge, *or* we cannot escape the forces of darkness that envelop us with madness, with intellectual and moral chaos" (emphasis added).[62]

Once framed in this manner, of course, any perspective that questions the existence of some permanent, ahistorical framework of truth, knowledge, or reality must *by definition* be engaged in some sort of subjectivism or relativism. On the other hand, once the dichotomized framing process underlying these charges is exposed, a whole matrix of otherwise hidden logic can be opened up for scrutiny, affording the analyst/policymaker the opportunity for a more comprehensive and insightful agenda by which questions might be answered and problems might be "solved." The charge of subjectivism, for example, has a pejorative sting only if one has already framed the pursuit of knowledge in *objectivist* terms—in other words, if subjectivism, by definition, represents the negative side of the positivist subject/object dichotomy (e.g., as Realism versus idealism, scientific research versus abstract theorizing).

The charge of relativism is more commonly heard these days, particularly from a mainstream ontologically committed to Archimedean points of analytical truth, beyond history, culture, and language. The usual charge, in this regard, is that any approach that refuses to privilege a single perspective, as corresponding to reality per se, is guilty of relativism and is unable to make judgments about everyday life and political conflict. This, once again, is a valid charge only if its already-given assumption is—that decisions are made *now* in relation to some foundational (nonrelativist) realm of truth, rationality, and reality. If this assumption is not made, then the critical social theory position can be understood as no more "relativist" than Heisenberg's position, or that of Wittgenstein or Thomas Kuhn.

This position, in simple terms, is that the world is always an interpreted "thing," and it is always interpreted in conditions of disagreement and conflict, to one degree or another. Consequently, and for all our attempts to construct scientific means of solving this problem, there can be no common body of observational or tested data that we can turn to for a neutral, objective knowledge of the world. There can be no ultimate knowledge, for example, that actually corresponds to reality per se. This does not undermine one's ability to make decisions in the world. On the contrary, it allows for a decisionmaking regime based on personal and social responsibility and disallows any abrogation of this responsibility to objectified sources "out there" (e.g., the system, the government, science, the party, the state, history, human nature). This, to ventilate the point further, is an unequivocally and inevitably political basis for decisionmaking, which recognizes that all theoretical/interpretivist perspectives are grounded in a political and normative context, particularly those that deny such a context. Thus, regarding the question of on what basis a decision might be made from the position outlined earlier, the answer is, and must be, a normative and political basis—on the basis of a normative-political position in regard to other normative-political positions. This does not necessarily add up to partisanship, narrowly defined, nor does it negate the capacity for agreement, compromise, or, indeed, comparability. Instead, it locates these outcomes in a social, historical, cultural, and linguistic realm of political debate and conflict, not some idealized realm of absolute (apolitical, asocial, ahistorical) truth, evidence, or fact. Nor does this politiconormative perspective undermine the possibility of genuinely scholarly accounts of the world and its peoples. Rather, it connects the scholar directly and unequivocally to that world and imposes upon scholarship a regime of self-reflection and critical awareness sadly absent in much International Relations literature.[63]

Hence the emphasis in this book on breaking down the power of the either/or dualism and the illusory certitude and existential comfort offered therein. Hence the more general emphasis on the need to confront a social universe characterized by contingency, heterogeneity, and radical "difference" via a more sensitive, detailed understanding of particular historical, cultural, and linguistic sites of human interaction, including one's own. And hence the concern to open some "thinking space" beyond the traditions of foundationalism and simplistic appeals to objectivist truth about the world and its peoples.

It remains the case, of course, that none of this offers what a simple ritual of Realist certainty can for those seeking immediate explanatory gratification in a complex world. Rather, as Jane Flax has put it, "the more the fault lines in previously unproblematic ground become apparent, the more frightening it appears to be without ground."[64] The fear of losing foundational knowledge and the power it affords is an issue well understood in feminist scholarship such as Flax's, and in attempts to go beyond the either/or dichotomy, feminism in general has made a significant contribution to critical social theory per se.[65] Elements of this contribution might now sound rather passé, but the principle that saw feminists in the 1960s and 1970s challenge the whole notion of specific gender roles and (to some extent) change the power structures associated with those roles remains important also in the critical approaches to International Relations.

The point is that feminist scholarship confronted dominant structures of political power by challenging the powerful theory as practice that insisted that gender roles were prescribed by foundationalist dictate—be it via a foundational God figure and the impeccable truths of biblical reference, the eternal verities contained within "history" and social tradition, or the facts of a human nature that everywhere are articulated as a natural asymmetry between men and women, particularly in terms of political status and power. However, in exposing patriarchal rule, not as an irreducible fact derived from foundationalist sources "out there" but as a deeply embedded series of historicopolitical, philosophical, and cultural practices designed to maintain certain kinds of power relations, feminists were able to undermine the powerful grip of the either/or dualism and provide space for change and alternative realities in everyday life.

Moreover, and in the face of dire warnings about chaos and disorder and the implications of breaking down the natural order of things, women (and men) have illustrated that, even without (illusory) foundations, life goes on, "relativists" make decisions about their world all the time, "nihilists" engage in positive, productive activity, and conceptual/political space becomes available where none seemed possible before. And while there is always darkness and tragedy in the world, most would agree, I suspect, that any intellectual and moral chaos we might be experiencing in the 1990s has been discerned many times before, during periods when the old certainties were still firmly in place.

In the period since the early conceptual/political breakthrough, feminist literature has become a source of some of the most stimulating and acute analysis of contemporary social life. And while feminist works in International Relations represent only a small percentage of the literature generally, the contribution, in qualitative terms, is already substantial. In particular, feminist scholarship in the 1980s and 1990s has added important dimensions to critical social theory perspectives concerned to reconnect theory to practice and address the broader implications of "living dichotomously."[66] In an International Relations context this is a crucial endeavor given the virtual exclusion of gender issues and of women per se from serious concern.[67] To a greater extent than perhaps any other Other group, women have understood the necessity of exposing the intrinsic connection between theory and practice in their attempts to influence the sensibilities and political activities of the International Relations community. This is because the omission of women is absolutely integral to the "theoretical" identity of orthodox International Relations "practice." More specifically, it is integral to the Realism associated with the rule of elite men in the institutionalized forums of power and prestige worldwide.

As indicated earlier, International Relations, via its Realist perspective in particular, is a rather crude derivative of Western philosophy and Anglo-American social theory. Accordingly, it simply replicates that dominant (dichotomized) narrative of power politics, which privileges "maleness" in all its gendered splendor over a "femaleness" that, by definition, is incapable of anything more than supportive insignificance.[68] In International Relations, however, the orthodox philosophical couplings (e.g., objectivity/subjectivity, fact/value, rationality/irrationality, public/private) have a special resonance, in their integration with a similarly dichotomized frame of Traditional reference, which privileges precisely those ("male") attributes deemed necessary for dealing with a violent, anarchical world "out there." The result is a Tradition and discipline, and indeed a whole International Relations community, that has rendered women invisible as it has confronted the elite, male-defined world of the security dilemma, anarchical power relations, diplomacy, and macroeconomics.[69]

One of the concerns of contemporary feminism has been to make women visible again, often via an alternative rereading and rewriting of the Traditional "great texts" and by illustrating how, in textual terms, women were systematically omitted in the quest to represent elite male experience and images of reality, as reality per se. A more specific focus of attention has been the connection between rational-scientific approaches to knowledge and society and the simultaneous devaluation of women's lives and experiences. Here, of course, "male" attributes of objectivity, autonomy, and tough-mindedness are prized, as against the subjective, disordered world of women. Here, too, the universalized and essentialized viewpoint of the "knower" is clearly of more significance than that of the (objectified) "known." Thus, in exposing the process by which women were omitted from the scientific revolution and its triumphs, feminist literature has acknowledged the significance of positivism and has begun to engage a central bastion of (elite male) theory as practice.[70]

This has seen feminist works contributing to the postpositivist debates in social theory generally and, increasingly, to the (so-called) third "great debate" in International Relations. There is engagement, also, with some of the tensions intrinsic to this debate, as feminists move beyond the initial aim, of inclusion in an arena of exclusion, to confront the differences among women in newly opened analytical and political spaces. The traditional connection between "liberalism" and positivism is of particular significance here. More precisely, the continuing positivist commitments of "liberal" feminism are, for the more radically inclined, sources of frustration and restriction.[71] At another level, too, feminism has engaged, interestingly, with issues beyond the initial concern to illustrate the gendered nature of International Relations. Here, questions of universalism, essentialism, and the politics of "difference" are at the forefront of much feminist literature, particularly as they relate to the tensions between critical feminists in the West and their counterparts in non-Western societies.[72] Issues of race, class, and culture, consequently, have become part of the feminist agenda as it seeks to more sensitively address that complex matrix of human existence which International Relations reduces to (largely) Western, elite male images of reality.[73]

As it confronts notions of self and Others in increasingly nuanced ways, feminist literature has begun, more directly, to reformulate International Relations in explicitly gendered terms. In so doing, substantive books are now appearing that take into account the major "theoretical" issues of feminist scholarship and the major issues of International Relations "practice" that for so long have been the privileged domain of privileged males. All of the major issues and themes of the International Relations tradition and discipline are now part of a feminist agenda. The question of security, for example, is now reformulated to account for its previously ignored dimensions, including the impact of a military mind-set and violent national security practices upon poverty and family violence.[74] Dimensions have been added, also, to questions of the international political economy, which go beyond Traditional confines and speak to issues of basic needs, global patriarchy, and the preservation and reproduction of human and material resources rather than their exploitation.

In reformulating the International Relations agenda, feminists have made it clear that the process of breaking down gender barriers is not simply or exclusively about allowing women space to think and act in freer, more dignified ways. Rather, it represents a more profound way of understanding human relations and political life per se. It is in this sense intrinsically engaged with processes by which Otherness is constructed and by which women and men, throughout the world, are excluded, marginalized, or punished for their Otherness. This perspective reinforces the feminist challenges to International Relations orthodoxy and, in particular, to Realist theory as practice. At one level this is because "gender hierarchy is not merely coincidental but is in a significant sense constitutive of Western philosophy's objectivist metaphysics." At another, more tangible, level it is because

> the hegemonic ideology that treats hierarchies as natural serves powerfully to legitimate and reproduce domination through the internalization of oppression, the silencing of protest, and the depoliticization of exploitative rule and global inequalities. Thus, feminist critiques of "naturalized" subjection offer rich resources for re-envisioning, resisting and transforming social relations.[75]

Feminist scholarship, then, continues to make important and incisive contributions to the critical social theory challenge to narrow orthodoxy in the 1990s. Indeed, in many ways it is at the forefront of this challenge. In International Relations, for example, the recent contributions of Christine Sylvester, J. Ann Tickner, and V. Spike Peterson represent fully fledged feminist (re)introductions to International Relations, similar in many respects to this present work.[76]

This particular (re)introduction, however, engages International Relations from empathic yet slightly different angles, reflecting my view that, if anything, the problems of theory and practice inherent within International Relations go beyond even feminist articulations of them and require much more generalized critical attention before the significance of feminist arguments can begin to make an impact. Put another way, not only has International Relations ignored and effectively disenfranchised more than half of the world's population in gender terms, it has almost totally neglected or crudely caricatured its own (philosophical and political) Tradition, thus disallowing any genuine space for critical self-reflection and for other ways of knowing and Being. This space must be opened up, in the broadest of terms, not just for the more obvious reasons concerning closure in a dangerous world but so that the International Relations community in general might become more able to take advantage of perspectives such as feminism. Accordingly, this work brings to its critical task the kind of analytical tools that, in the broader interdisciplinary context, have seen critical social theory perspectives excavating deep within the (metatheoretical) core of orthodox perspectives in order to ventilate their points of closure and open them for debate and genuine reassessment. The two most effective critical perspectives in this regard, I suggest, are the two most influential perspectives in the transference of critical social theory themes to International Relations—Critical Theory and postmodernism—and these perspectives represent the most important influences on this work.[77]

The former has a long tradition in social theory and invokes insights from the literature of the Frankfurt School and Habermas and the sophisticated antistructuralist Marxism of Gramsci. In an International Relations context, this is where Robert Cox has made a major contribution, with his alternative perspectives on the global political economy and an approach that goes beyond the problem-solving orientations of orthodox analysis.[78] Rejecting this stance, Cox advocates a more positive, critical orientation, which explores the connections between orthodox knowledge and the power regime it supports, while opening the possibilities of thinking and acting in other than orthodox ways. This contribution, and a range of similar ones, will be discussed in broad terms in Chapter 6 and more directly in Chapter 7.

Perhaps the most significant critical social theory incursion into International Relations in recent times has been made by scholars under the postmodernist rubric. And while I have reservations about some aspects of postmodernism (discussed in Chapter 6), it is this perspective, particularly its discourse theme, that I consider of most value in this critical (re)introduction to International Relations. Accordingly, at this point a brief introductory commentary is necessary, concerning what is still for the International Relations community a rather alien approach to theory as practice.[79]

Postmodernism: (Re)Introducing International Relations as Discourse

The question of reality and realism in postmodernist literature is confronted in terms similar to the (broadly) Hegelian approach of Berki and other critical social theory approaches, including Habermas's Critical Theory. But, more unequivocally than these perspectives, postmodernists stress that reality is in a perpetual state of flux—of movement, change, and instability. This is not the common understanding of the nature of reality, of course. Social theory in general and International Relations in particular have, as noted earlier, understood reality in essentialist, unitary, and universalist terms. From a postmodernist perspective, this is not surprising, because, it is maintained, the *notion* of a singular, stable, knowable reality has been an integral part of a dominant post-Enlightenment story, in which the ascent of Western "rational man" is located as integral to the gradual historicophilosophic unfolding of the world's "real" nature.

Like all other claims to know the world and its (singular, essential) reality, this is regarded as a narrative fiction, a story of certainty and identity derived from a dominant *discursive practice* that reduces the flux of existence to a strategic framework of unity and coherence. *Discourse* in this context is not synonymous with *language* as such. It refers, rather, to a broader matrix of social practices that gives meaning to the way that people understand themselves and their behavior. A discourse, in this sense, generates the categories of meaning by which reality can be understood and explained. More precisely, a discourse makes "real" that which *it* prescribes as meaningful. In so doing, a discourse of Realism, for example, establishes the sociolinguistic conditions under which realistic theory and practice can take place, and it establishes, simultaneously, that which, by discursive definition, does not correspond with reality. Understood this way,

> to be engaged in a discourse is to be engaged in the making and remaking of meaningful conditions of existence. A discourse, then, is not a way of learning "about" something out there in the "real world"; it is rather, a way of *producing* that something as real, as identifiable, classifiable, knowable, and therefore, meaningful. Discourse creates the conditions of knowing [emphasis added].[80]

This discursive representation of reality in the world is, for postmodernism, an integral part of the relations of power that are present in all human societies. Accordingly, the process of discursive representation is never a neutral, detached one but is always imbued with the power and authority of the namers and makers of reality—it is always knowledge *as* power. A major task for postmodernist scholars, consequently, is to interrogate the conditions of knowledge *as* power. Discourse analysis seeks, in this way, to explain how power is constituted and how its premises and givens are replicated at all levels of society and to reveal its exclusionary practices in order to create space for critical thought and action.

This, simply put, is what Derrida sought to do in locating the dominant modernist discourse in the post-Enlightenment search for an essential, universal rationality. This he described as the *logocentric* process, a process of textual/social representation, derived, initially, from classical Greek scholarship, which creates identity, unity, and universalized meaning by excluding from the "meaningful" that which does not correspond to the logo (original, singular, authentic) conception of the real.[81] In this way, at the core of Western history and philosophy is a textual "past" framed in terms of a whole series of dichotomies that demarcate that which is real and that which, by its definitional relationship with prescribed reality, cannot be. This story, aggregated and institutionalized via its articulations across the contemporary social theory disciplines, is the modernist *metanarrative*—the discourse of self/other, identity/difference, realism/idealism, illusory certitude, and Realist knowledge *as* International Relations.[82]

It was in relation to this notion of a textually constructed metanarrative of the present that Foucault sought to deconstruct Western history in *genealogical* terms. The genealogical approach, derived primarily from Nietzsche, was Foucault's archaeological tool in his attempts to expose the discursive processes by which contemporary subjects and objects have been constituted in terms of a dominant knowledge form and a singular, unified meaning.[83] As Foucault put it in *Power/Knowledge,* genealogies are the stories of

> local, discontinuous, disqualified, illegitimate knowledges against the claims of a unitary body of theory which would filter, hierarchise, and order . . . in the name of some true knowledge and some arbitrary idea of what constitutes a science and its objects.[84]

Nothing in this genealogical approach to history is given, natural, inevitable, or unchangeable. Rather, the objects and subjects of history are discursively constructed via logocentric processes of framing real meaning. It is, by definition, a historical approach suspicious of any kind of determinism, universalized patterns of thought and behavior, developmental formats (e.g., stages of growth), or any grand-theorized pronouncements of essential behavior. In this regard, it rejects conservative (e.g., Realist) postulations about recurrence and repetition as firmly as it rejects radical invocations of an (already-existing) emancipatory spirit or revolutionary consciousness. It acknowledges no single, essential history but the struggle of "histories," the struggle among discursive practices.

In terms of Western modernity, thus, history is understood as the logocentrized privileging of a particular discursive constitution of subjects and objects (e.g., rational man confronted by a single knowable reality) and the marginalization or exclusion of those "histories" which do not fit within the identifiable boundaries of the modernist metanarrative. The primary suggestion is that at the heart of modernism is a philosophical illusion, derived from the Greeks, centered on the notion that there is an ultimate *foundation* for our knowledge, beyond the social construction of that knowledge. The illusion, in other words, is that beyond mere social "appearance" there is a foundational "reality," a realm of purer understanding that, once discovered, can help us unlock the essential nature of the relationship between the subjects and objects of the world.

Consequently, postmodernists have argued (since the European Enlightenment in particular), modernist history and philosophy have become a "hermeneutics of suspicion," a search for the hidden, underlying, essential meaning of life.[85] More specifically, the overwhelming purpose of modernist thinking has become the search for an Archimedean point upon which we can ground our knowledge of the real world.[86] And while belief in Archimedean points or external gods or the pursuit of ultimate foundations for reality might not be particularly dangerous phenomena, postmodern scholars (following Nietzsche's lead) have pointed to some of the dangerous dimensions emanating from such beliefs and purposes. Of particular concern is the connection between the knowledge that assumes a single foundation for reality in the world and the power regimes characterized by closure, intolerance, and the suppression of "difference." The argument here is that in the post-Enlightenment era, modernist theory and practice, set upon scientific foundations, has become more and more intolerant of Otherness, of that which cannot be "rationally" controlled.[87] Accordingly, one modern tradition after another has legitimated its own foundationalist position, by reducing nearly three millennia of discursive struggle to a series of simple oppositions in which (our) "facts" are distinguished from (their) mere "values," (our) "rationality" from (their) "irrationality," (our) identity from (their) "difference," (our) "reality" from (their) "idealism/utopianism."

Critical attention has been particularly focused on the way that the post-1945 discipline of International Relations has framed its understanding of reality in this manner, in reducing the complexities of global life through the ages to a series of simplistic dualisms (e.g., Realism/idealism, order/anarchy, domestic/international), with each coupling legitimating a range of power politics practices. This concern with the knowledge/power nexus has a number of dimensions. At one level, it focuses on discourses that define and exclude the "subversive" and the "terrorist" and that, simultaneously, legitimate their destruction on behalf of the sovereign state, the central government, the vanguard of the party. The more general concern is with a modernist knowledge form that, in its quest to master the natural and social worlds, has transformed the lives of peoples and cultures in every corner of the planet.

The modernist authority vested in "rational man," for example, has been used to liberate, to empower, to revolutionize—but at a cost. For in spreading the word of the (post-Cartesian) death of God, and in proclaiming its new secular rational-scientific substitute, Western theory as practice has, often brutally, invoked its strategies of control, its discipline, its unified frame of reference about the good life, its singular reality, its insistence on sovereignty, and its bulwarks against nihilism. It is in this quest—to impose a singular, foundational reality upon miscreants and unbelievers—that the post-Enlightenment "will to knowledge" has quite literally become the "will to power."

In confronting this aspect of modernist theory as practice in the 1990s, critical social theorists in general and postmodernists in particular have confronted the knowledge that is power politics in International Relations and have sought more sensitive, less dangerous alternatives to it. A brief comment on R. B. J. Walker's efforts in this regard might help summarize the discussion at this point and help ventilate some of the themes that are to follow.

Walker's *One World, Many Worlds* (1988) is of particular significance here, concerned as it is with the plight and the potentials of members of critical social movements around the world seeking, often in circumstances of great danger, to reclaim the power to make decisions about their lives.

Their struggles, Walker suggests, have become significant for a number of reasons, not the least being that peoples engaged in them have recognized that "it has become necessary to refuse received conceptual boundaries, to search for new forms of understanding, and to develop a clearer sense of the complex relationships between theory and practice, knowing and being."[88] Walker acknowledges as positive the localized and heterogeneous nature of these attempts to find "thinking space," perceiving in them the possibility of an alternative political future in which people might find ways of reclaiming their lives from the grand-theorized traditions that have shaped both the conservative and radical "art of the possible" in modernity. It is in this context that Walker has responded to Traditional demands that problems be solved, rather than (merely) "philosophized" about. Here, he suggests,

> [any solution] must grow out of the ongoing practices of people everywhere, not be molded by those who claim to have *a god's-eye view* of what's going on. [Consequently it] is sometimes important to resist the inevitable demand for hard-nosed, concrete solutions to particular problems.[89]

Developing the point further, he had this to say:

> Under the present circumstances the question "What is to be done?" invites a degree of arrogance that is all too visible in the behaviour of the dominant political forces of our time. It is an arrogance inconsistent with the kind of empirical evidence we have before us. This evidence requires a willingness to face up to the uncertainties of the age, not with the demand for instant solutions, but with a more modest openness to the potentials inherent in what is already going on. The most pressing questions of the age call not only for concrete policy options to be offered to existing elites and institutions but also, and more crucially, for *a serious rethinking of the ways in which it is possible for human beings to live together* [emphasis added].[90]

It is in this spirit and with these broad principles in mind that this book seeks to reconnect International Relations to the broader flow of contemporary "theoretical" inquiry, for all the "practical" reasons outlined throughout this chapter. In so doing it will bring to the forefront of contemporary debate on International Relations a number of critical and often unconventional themes, not as if in some realm of unified reality an essential/foundational Archimedean point of reality exists, in which ultimate answers can be found to the great questions of the 1990s, but in order to raise some questions that can no longer be ignored by scholars engaged, perhaps more directly than any others, with everyday questions of life and death. This questioning process will begin, at its broadest level, in the chapter to follow, which goes to the core of International Relations as a modernist discourse and which emphasizes the powerful and enduring positivist representation of it.

Notes

1. The term *International Relations* in its capitalized form refers here to the conventional way in which global life has been studied and understood in Western (primarily Anglo-American) universities and policy sectors. In this regard it represents a particular kind of theory as practice, designated as Realism by its advocates, that has become synonymous with the "reality" of International Relations for a generation of scholars and policymakers. This synonym will be addressed here in its own mainstream terms and also in critical terms that challenge its logic and validity. Challenged, in particular, will be the notion of a single reality "out there," knowable via a Realist analytical tradition. To avoid undue confusion on this issue, the term *Realism,* when capitalized, will refer to the dominant intellectual/policy perspective in International Relations, and the term *Tradition,* in capitalized form, refers specifically to this Realist perspective in its various articulations over the years.

2. There were no simple alternatives for the United States and the United Nations in a situation like the Gulf War, and this is not the point I make here. My point, rather, is that alternatives to power politics violence were not seriously addressed, nor can they be from within the orthodox agenda. For those who nevertheless would buttress their Realism by reference to U.S. "victory" in the Gulf, a number of questions remain pertinent: Did the U.S. "victory" in the Gulf really solve the problem? If not, is a quick military victory possible or desirable next time, or the time after that? Are the complex problems of global life in the 1990s merely reducible to the strategic interests of the United States and the major Western powers in general? Are there no questions raised by the end of the Cold War that require a fundamental reassessment of Traditional theory and practice?

3. See "The Cold War, the Long Peace and the Future," in J. L. Gaddis, *The End of the Cold War: Its Meanings and Implications,* p. 31.

4. This issue is discussed in more detail in Gaddis, "International Relations and the End of the Cold War."

5. Ibid., p. 58.

6. Hoffmann, "Delusions of World Order."

7. Hoffmann, "An American Social Science."

8. Hoffmann, "Delusions of World Order," p. 4.

9. The paralysis theme is most explicit in Lewis Lapham, "Apes and Butterflies."

10. Lapham, "Apes and Butterflies," p. 9.

11. Ibid.

12. Ibid., p. 15.

13. Post, "How the West Lost Bosnia," p. 60.

14. Ibid.

15. Ibid.

16. See "The End of the Modern Era," a speech given in Switzerland in early 1992 and cited in Lapham, "Apes and Butterflies."

17. Cited in Lapham, "Apes and Butterflies," p. 8. This is in contrast, for example, to the explicit triumphalism of Fukuyama, *The End of History and the Last Man.*

18. Cited in Lapham, "Apes and Butterflies," p. 8.

19. Ibid.

20. The broad notion of social theory utilized here is best articulated by Giddens in *Profiles and Critiques in Social Theory,* pp. 5–6. He suggests the following:

> Social theory . . . spans social science. It is body of theory shared in common by all the disciplines concerned with the behaviour of human beings. It concerns . . . sociology . . . anthropology, economics, politics, human geography, psychology—the whole range of the social sciences. Neither is social theory readily separable from questions of interest to an ever wider set of concerns: it connects through to literary criticism on the one hand and the philosophy of the social sciences on the other.

For good overviews of critical social theory approaches, see Bernstein, *The Restructuring of Social and Political Theory* and *Beyond Objectivism and Relativism.*

21. For a general discussion of these works see George and Campbell, "Patterns of Dissent"; Cox, "Social Forces, States and World Orders"; Ashley, "The Poverty of Neorealism" and "Living on Border Lines"; Der Derian and Shapiro, eds., *International/Intertextual Relations;* Walker, *One World, Many Worlds* and *Inside/Outside;* and Lapid, "The Third Debate."

22. This complex issue will receive more attention in Chapter 3. For now suffice to say that I do not accept that the Traditionalist or (classical) approach is fundamentally different from the "scientific" one but maintain that it is a variation on it. The Traditionalism of Martin Wight, Hedley Bull, E. H. Carr, Hans Morgenthau, or Stanley Hoffmann, for example, is a variation on a positivist theme that resonates with the influences of early British empiricism, the Humean skepticism of the Enlightenment, Comtean and Durkheimian data-gathering fetishes, and contemporary concerns for falsificationism and "research programs." But the positivist story is more complex than this, to the extent that it intersects discursively with a number of "alternative" perspectives, including the neo-Kantian and hermeneutic perspectives of a Weber or a Mannheim, which have seeped into Anglo-American social theory offering a measure of interpretive sensitivity amid the explicit search for value freedom. Traditionalist Realism in this regard represents the other side of the explicit positivist coin, repudiating the methodological orientations of the post–logical positivist era but continuing nevertheless to frame the questions it asks of the world in terms of the phenomenalist and nominalist perspectives on knowledge, which are a defining characteristic of positivist theory and practice. The result is a less harsh but no less committed rendition of a modernist ontology set in terms of a series of dualisms and dichotomies (subject/object, fact/value, theory/practice, is/ought) that afford meaning to a Realist world of order/anarchy, Realism/idealism, and domestic/international and a Realist history defined in terms of recurrence and repetition. Herein lies one of the silences and limitations of the International Relations Tradition.

23. Berki, *On Political Realism.*

24. Ibid., p. 7.

25. Ibid., p. 8.

26. Ibid., p. 16.

27. The question is broader than this, of course. As the discussion to follow will emphasize, it is not just a matter of Realism's inadequacy but the inadequacy of that whole disciplinary discourse represented as International Relations scholarship, which includes the major alternatives to a Realist perspective (e.g., conventional

Marxism, variants of systems theory, the so-called pluralist and structuralist paradigms). For a general discussion of Realism and its "alternatives," see Vasquez, *The Power of Power Politics.* On the Marxist alternative, which in International Relations has never had the kind of influences it has enjoyed, at times, in social theory generally, see Maclean, "Marxist Epistemology, Explanations of 'Change' and the Study of International Relations" and "Marxism and International Relations"; and Giddens, *The Nation-State and Violence.*

28. The "catechism" theme comes from Rothstein, "On the Costs of Realism," p. 350.

29. Ibid., p. 353.

30. Ibid., p. 351.

31. On the issue of falsificationist influence generally, see Hoffmann, "An American Social Science"; and for updated confirmation of its continuing influence, see Alker and Biersteker, "The Dialectics of World Order."

32. Vasquez, *The Power of Power Politics,* p. 220.

33. On this claim see Maghoori and Ramberg, eds., *Globalism Versus Realism;* Olson and Onuf, "The Growth of a Discipline: Reviewed"; Banks, "The Evolution of International Relations Theory"; Sullivan, "Competing Frameworks"; Keohane and Nye, *Power and Interdependence;* Keohane, *After Hegemony;* and Holsti, *The Dividing Discipline.*

34. On the first and second debates, see Knorr and Rosenau, *Contending Approaches;* Vasquez, *The Power of Power Politics;* Olson and Onuf, "The Growth of a Discipline: Reviewed"; Banks, "The Evolution of International Relations"; and Holsti, *The Dividing Discipline.* On the third debate, see Maghoori and Ramberg, eds., *Globalism Versus Realism;* Lapid, "The Third Debate"; and my "International Relations and the Search for Thinking Space." On neo-Realism, see Keohane, ed., *Neorealism and Its Critics;* Waltz, *Theory of International Politics;* Gilpin, *War and Change in World Politics;* Ruggie, "Continuity and Transformation in the World Polity"; and, most incisively, Ashley, "The Poverty of Neorealism."

35. Ashley, "The Poverty of Neorealism," p. 228.

36. The works of these scholars offer a relatively reflective brand of positivism congruent with much of the so-called postpositivist/post-Realist literature in International Relations since the 1970s. That is, it is capable of important insight and of opening up debate to the point where many of the orthodox "anomalies" are exposed, but then, suspicious of the implications of moving off from its scientific foundation, it acts to close off debate to effectively marginalize any fundamental challenge to that foundation. See, for example, Ferguson and Mansbach, "Between Celebration and Despair"; Biersteker, "Critical Reflections on Post-Positivism"; and Ruggie, "Continuity and Transformation in the World Polity." Others, such as Lapid and Vasquez, have broadly similar tendencies, but their works, I believe, are more genuinely concerned to break down the positivist orthodoxy.

37. The rejection of another "preface" is in Biersteker, "Critical Reflections on Post-Positivism," p. 266; and the attitude is very prevalent in Keohane's "International Institutions."

38. Frost, *Towards a Normative Theory of International Relations.*

39. Ibid., p. 10.

40. Morgenthau, *Politics Among Nations,* pp. 4–5.

41. Carr, *The Twenty Years Crisis,* chaps. 3 and 4 in particular.

42. Knorr and Rosenau, *Contending Approaches,* pp. 13–14.

43. Sullivan, "Competing Frameworks," p. 108.

44. This is Rosenau's view in "Before Cooperation," p. 553.

45. Holsti, *The Dividing Discipline,* p. vii.

46. Tooze, "The Unwritten Preface," p. 285.

47. Ibid.

48. Ibid., p. 286. On this theme see also Murphy and Tooze, eds., *The New International Political Economy.*

49. The debate over the relationship between empiricism and positivism is too complex to engage here. More will be added on it in the chapter to follow. The point, for now, is that the notion of positivist empiricism used here owes most to the work of Leszek Kolakowski in *Positivist Philosophy.* In this sense positivism is perceived neither as scientific methodology nor as a theory of knowledge per se. Rather it represents the major contemporary philosophical expression of an empiricist epistemology, synthesized in its most sophisticated and "skeptical" form by David Hume and articulated in a variety of forms since then. The term *positivism* will thus refer to the connected positivist/empiricist perspective. For a fuller discussion of its (often hidden) influence in International Relations see my "International Relations and the Positivist/Empiricist Theory of Knowledge."

50. Gellner, *Legitimation of Belief,* p. 175.

51. Giddens and Turner, eds., *Social Theory Today.*

52. Ibid., p. 3.

53. Giddens, *Profiles and Critiques in Social Theory.*

54. Ibid., p. 3.

55. Giddens and Turner, eds., *Social Theory Today,* p. 7.

56. Factor and Turner, in *Max Weber and the Dispute Over Reason and Value;* argue that this connection goes well beyond any generalized intersection of Anglo-American and Germanic influences in Morgenthau's approach, to the extent that every major idea in Morgenthau's power politics is derived from Weber's hermeneutic perspective. This of course to some extent explains the tensions in Morgenthau's work, which sees him crudely propound the existence of "objective laws" at one moment and at another engage in more subtle hermeneutic tones on the issue of textual interpretation.

57. On Weber, Mannheim, and the other side of the positivist coin more generally see Hekman, "Beyond Humanism" and *Hermeneutics and the Sociology of Knowledge.* The term *Verstehen* (process of understanding) refers to a range of approaches, associated (broadly) with a sociology-of-knowledge perspective, which have in their diverse ways challenged the notion that there can be objective scientific knowledge of human society akin to that in the natural sciences. The Weberian approach is part of this Verstehen tradition; more will be added on this issue in Chapter 6.

58. See Carr, *The Twenty Years Crisis,* p. 10. It is ironic that Carr was one of the few major Realists who understood the dangers of this position and in *Twenty Years Crisis* and more explicitly in *What Is History?* sought to add nuance to it. I'll say more of Carr's contribution in Chapter 3. For now, the point is that it has been passages such as this drawn from scholars like Carr (and Morgenthau) that have embedded the positivist bias at the core of the "backward discipline."

59. For a discussion of this issue in the broad social theory context, see Aronowitz, *Science as Power.* This issue is largely ignored by those in the social science still seeking scientific certainty in terms of Newtonian physics, particularly in International Relations, where the nuances of the (scientific) Realist/positivist debate have never been taken seriously (nor has the larger debate between philosophical Realism in general and positivism in the social sciences). On this see Hesse, *Revolutions and Reconstructions;* and Keat and Urry, *Social Theory as Science.*

60. Heisenberg, "Planck's Discovery and the Philosophical Problems of Atomic Physics," p. 20.

61. See Phillips, *Wittgenstein and Scientific Knowledge,* p. 30.

62. Bernstein, *Beyond Objectivism and Relativism,* p. 17.

63. It is on this basis that the Critical Theory and postmodernist perspectives are represented in this work. The latter perspective has not always been perceived in these terms, and there is undoutedly a tendency within *some* postmodern scholarship for the kind of detachment that its critics accuse it of. I discuss this issue in Chapter 6, where I argue also that to caricature postmodernism per se in this way is to misunderstand the commitment of a scholar such as Foucault to the principles espoused above, and certainly to miss the point concerning the transference of postmodern themes to International Relations. In this context, nevertheless, one hears the proposition that commitment to normative-political stances represents a "contradiction" in postmodernism, in that it represents a commitment to emancipatory themes and therefore to the very (Enlightenment) tradition it opposes. Such a charge arises from a logical positivist perspective, which designates "meaning" in singular, correspondence rule terms. If, however, acknowledging the contributions of Wittgenstein or Sassure or a generation of analytical philosophers one accepts that "meaning" is interpretively made and not given, and that terms (e.g., *emancipation*) are not restricted to a single, essential meaning, then there is nothing necessarily contradictory about its use in this context. This is an issue that postmodernism does have to confront, particularly in relation to Nietzsche and genealogical analysis, but the debate is not enhanced much by works such as Spegele, "Richard Ashley's Discourse for International Relations."

64. See Flax, *Thinking Fragments,* p. 6.

65. I appreciate the problems of speaking here of feminism "in general." My focus in this regard is on that literature which, working within space opened in the 1960s and 1970s, has represented itself as an explicit "feminist" assault upon International Relations, even while acknowledging the complexities and problems of so doing. See Peterson, ed., *Gendered States: Feminist (Re)Visions of International Relations Theory;* Sylvester, *Feminist Theory and International Relations in a Postmodern Era;* Tickner, *Gender and International Relations;* and Enloe, *Bananas, Beaches and Bases.*

66. Peterson, "Transgressing Boundaries."

67. This exclusion does not mean that International Relations is not gendered. On the contrary, it is so dominated by a single gender's perspective that questions of gender, like so many others, are simply taken for granted.

68. In general terms, see Lange and Clark, eds., *The Sexism of Social and Political Theory;* Lloyd, *Man of Reason;* Pateman, *The Disorder of Women;* and Butler and Scott, eds., *Feminists Theorize the Political.* More specifically, see Grant, "The Sources of Gender Bias in International Relations Theory"; Grant and Newland, eds., *Gender and International Relations;* and Elshtain, "Reflections on War and Political Discourse."

69. See Elshtain, "Reflections on War and Political Discourse"; and Tickner, "Hans Morgenthau's Principles of Political Realism."

70. See Flax, "Why Epistemology Matters"; and Harding and Hintikka, eds., *Discovering Reality.*

71. See Eisenstein, *The Radical Future of Liberal Feminism.* See also Peterson, "Transgressing Boundaries"; and Brown, "Feminism, International Theory and International Relations of Gender Inequality."

72. For an overview, see Goetz, "Feminism and the Limits of the Claim to Know"; Mohanty, "Under Western Eyes"; and Spivak, "Imperialism and Sexual Difference" and "Can the Subaltern Speak."

73. See Pettman, *Living on the Margins.*

74. Tickner, *Gender and International Relations,* chap. 5.

75. Peterson, "Transgressing Boundaries," pp. 202–204.

76. Peterson, ed., *Gendered States;* Sylvester, *Feminist Theory and International Relations in a Postmodern Era;* and Tickner, *Gender and International Relations.*

77. Many women have contributed to these perspectives, of course, and the works of people such as Jane Flax and Susan Hekman remain important influences on the discussion to follow. There are tensions here nevertheless, and for a discussion of some of them see Flax, *Thinking Fragments;* and Butler, "Contingent Foundations."

78. Cox, "Social Forces, States and World Orders," and *Production, Power and World Order.*

79. The term *postmodernism* will be used to designate that approach derived from a variety of contemporary Continental scholars, including Foucault, Derrida, Barthes, Baudrilliard, and Lyotard, and from Nietzsche. It is a contentious perspective for a number of reasons, particularly concerning its relationship with the modernism it seeks to critique. Some of this contention will be addressed in Chapter 6, when I will explain in more detail my view that at its best—when it is fully engaged with modern theory as practice—postmodernism represents the most acute critical perspective in the critical social theory spectrum. For a broad range of works on and by postmodernists, see Connolly, *Political Theory and Modernity;* Culler, *On Deconstruction;* Derrida, *Writing and Difference* and *Of Grammatology;* Dreyfus and Rabinow, *Michel Foucault;* Foucault, *The Archaeology of Knowledge, The Order of Things, The Birth of the Clinic, Discipline and Punish,* and *Power/Knowledge;* Lyotard, *The Postmodern Condition;* Rabinow, ed., *The Foucault Reader;* Rajchman, *Michel Foucault;* and Rorty, *Philosophy and the Mirror of Nature.*

80. This is Bradley Klein's insight in *Strategic Discourse and Its Alternatives,* p. 4.

81. See, in particular, Derrida, *Of Grammatology.*

82. This, it should be noted, does not suggest that a logocentric discursive regime disallows critical challenges to its dominance. These challenges are an ever present part of the struggle within which it exists. Its power, however, is that having established the existing historical and philosophical boundaries within which challenges take place, it continues to impose the boundaries—the framework—of those challenges. In so doing, its power is articulated through its capacity to exclude, to trivialize, to marginalize—to oppose that which is real with that (for example) which is merely "utopian," "idealist," and "irrational." But this language of exclusion is no more linguistic, in the narrow sense, than is the notion of discourse; integral to both is the power that is dominant modern knowledge.

83. For a discussion of genealogy in Nietzschean terms, see Connolly, *Political Theory and Modernity;* see also the opening pages of Ashley's, "The Geopolitics of Geopolitical Space."

84. Foucault, *Power/Knowledge,* p. 83.

85. This is a term associated initially with the critical hermeneutics of figures such as Paul Ricoeur. See Thompson, *Critical Hermeneutics.*

86. See Bernstein, *Beyond Objectivism and Relativism,* p. 16.

87. For example, the intersecting nature of the liberal "Whig" story of the march of progress, set upon universalized images of utilitarian rationality, the complex dialectical unfolding of Hegelian consciousness, and the Marxian "stages" of growth, as the class "in itself" becomes the class "for itself."

88. Walker, *One World, Many Worlds,* p. 7.

89. Ibid.

90. Ibid.

2

Discourses of Modernity: Toward the Positivist Framing of Contemporary Social Theory and International Relations

The debate over modernity is multifaceted and complex. There is, for example, a large and sophisticated literature dealing with modernity that focuses on what might be described (narrowly) as the realm of "aesthetics"—of art, literature and architecture.[1] These, however, are elements of the debate that simply cannot be addressed here except in the most superficial terms. Consequently, the primary focus of attention will fall on what Matei Calinescu has called modernism's "fifth face," that which is "broadly philosophical, including problems of epistemology, the history and philosophy of science, and hermeneutics."[2] Most explicitly, I am concerned with the way the category of the modern has been understood and articulated in the major traditions of Western philosophy, social theory, and, ultimately, International Relations.

This is still an inherently complex enterprise, but there is a useful starting point for the discussion. It relates to the tensions between two broad discursive positions on the modernity theme that, in one form or another, have been evident within social theory literature over the past century. The first, the dominant position, presents a positive and generally optimistic account of the modern world and its achievements. It represents modernity in terms of a contrast with earlier epochs, characterized by myth and superstition, in which the lives of individual subjects were suffocated beneath the uniformity and rigidity associated with the traditional objects of their worlds (e.g., gods, static social formations). Modernity, in this sense, is contrasted with traditional societies marked by an absence of democracy, individuality, and scientific orientation.[3]

A less sanguine interpretation of the modern world is also evident. It acknowledges the more obvious successes of modernity but emphasizes also its costs, perceived as an alienation from culture and tradition, from a sense of morality and spirituality, and from a "natural" social hierarchy and order. Modernity from this perspective is often presented in terms of something lost, of a world in decay and decline, of flimsy, unanchored peoples reeling under the impact of the (liberal) state and bureaucratic control. This latter position is articulated in a variety of populist neoconservative promulgations on the modern world, but it has a more substantial intellectual lineage in Western thought, encompassing the works of scholars such as Leo Strauss, Hannah Arendt, and Michael Oakeshott. It is an important theme in International Relations, too, where it has been most commonly expressed, in (ostensibly) antimodern terms, by influential Realists proffering classical or Traditionalist perspectives. This conservative modernist variant, however, is fundamental to the way that Traditionalists read their "history," interpret their "great texts," and frame their knowledge of the real world "out there." Indeed this (silenced) modernist influence in Traditionalism (and neo-Realism) is a crucial issue in any critical (re)introduction to International Relations. It is the hidden, ignored, and marginalized discursive dimension that speaks it but which it cannot speak.

This particular dimension of the International Relations discourse will be addressed, more directly, in the chapter to follow. My primary concern in this chapter is to establish the broad historicophilosophical context within which contemporary International Relations can be understood in discursive terms. My focus will be on the dominant and positive interpretation of modernity and that metanarrative of linear, rational progress integral to the Western worldview per se.

Modernity, from this perspective, is understood in developmental terms, as a progression—from the mythical to the scientific, from the barbaric to the rational/democratic, from the constrained, ordered subject to the utilitarian individual "free to choose." It is upon this image of modernity that Western philosophy and contemporary social theory have framed and responded to the perennial questions of human social life—of the relationships between subjects and objects and between humankind and the natural world, of the dilemmas of past and present, and of the possibilities for the future. The result is a narrative of modern subjects defined in terms of their distance from traditional premodern objects. In these terms, knowledge, history, and social development are interpreted as part of a sequential movement (e.g., stages of growth) in which an increasingly distanced subject confronts the problems of the natural and social worlds and, via the correct application of "rationality," overcomes them.

It is in this general context that a definition of the terms *modernity, modernism,* and *modernist thinking* is proffered here. This definition rejects the notion of the modern as a precise historical age or epoch and understands it instead as a complex set of interpretive practices, with its textual origins in the dualized and dichotomized premises of the ancient Western classics and, subsequently, in the "great texts" of post-Renaissance European culture and scientific rationalism. Two broad philosophical themes are of immediate significance here, as powerful conduits of the dominant modernist narrative. The first is centered on a post-Cartesian tradition of thought that framed Western modernity within one variant or another of cogito rationalism. The second theme, distinct yet inexorably interwoven with the first, concerns the impact upon cogito rationality of (in particular) Newtonian physics in the seventeenth century and the subsequent development of a modern philosophy of science in the post-Enlightenment period, dualistically framed in terms of "man," the rational knowing subject, responding to the vicissitudes of an (external) objectified realm of reality.

The first definitional theme, therefore—modernity as a way of discursively framing reality—highlights the interpretive continuity within Western philosophy of the attempt, via dualized and dichotomized premises, to objectify human knowledge in the search for an indubitable foundation for it.[4] It suggests that the idea of progress, integral to contemporary Western theory and practice, is set upon a particular process of interpretation in which the (historical and philosophical) ascent of rational man is framed as part of an attempt of subjects to increasingly distance themselves from the (metaphysical) objects of primitive, traditional societies. In this sense, the dominant interpretive tradition of Western philosophy is the story of the unfolding human capacity to rationalize.

A second element of this modernity definition adds an important dimension to this issue. This identifies modernist thought as the site of major paradox. The paradox in question is that which sees the celebration of an ever-increasing distance from the primitive premodern world (and its idealism and metaphysics) continually predicated upon the most basic of assumptions in "premodern" thinking—the assumption that there *is* a foundation for human knowledge, prior to and beyond history, culture, and language. In the age that has triumphantly detached itself from the legacy of such "premodern" traits, the paradox of modernity is that a faith in (premodern) *foundationalism* still reigns at its ontological core.

The paradox issue in this context is extremely complex. It is raised here not as a thematic precursor to an argument in favor of some arbitrary, synthesized notion of rationality or logical consistency to which all writing and thinking on modern political society must conform. It has a more significant role in the present discussion, as the touchstone theme of the more sinister side to modernist theory as practice. It is a paradox, in this sense, that serves its power function by seeking to deny the very existence of paradox. Or, less obtusely, the paradoxical faith in foundationalism within modernity, as scholars from Nietzsche to Adorno have noted, is at the heart of the attempt to *deny* the differences, the discontinuities, the contradictions, and the paradoxes that are an integral part of human life and reality.

This is more than some vague reference to once-liberating ideas having become ideological straitjackets; it goes to the heart of critical attempts to illustrate the other side of the dominant story of Western progress. For some, such as Habermas, the problem is manifested most clearly, and most dangerously, as knowledge forms integral to scientific control of the natural environment (i.e., positivism) increasingly become ideological mechanisms of social domination. For others, particularly postmodernists, the dangers are articulated as a homogenizing, totalizing approach to theory and practice that, in logocentric fashion, celebrates identity, unity, and sovereignty while defining as "Other," as threatening, that which is "different." Its critical emphasis, accordingly, is on that which has been excluded from the grand design, on the voices that are not heard within the cacophony of conformity, on those disciplined or punished for their difference.

To appreciate more fully the significance of these arguments and the framing and paradox themes they respond to, I want to indicate more directly now how the major traditions of contemporary social theory and, ultimately, of International Relations, were derived from a particular way of framing Western history and philosophy. Integral to this discussion, as it develops, will be the issue of positivism, the most important conduit of modernist history and philosophy across the social theory disciplines and within International Relations.[5]

The issues raised in the following discussion are inherently difficult and represent a sojourn into uncharted territory for many students of International Relations trained in the more orthodox manner. Acknowledging this, my aim is to represent some complex themes in a manner that does them interpretive justice while rendering them accessible to an audience that might then have a better opportunity to evaluate the hidden (discursive) matrix of International Relations scholarship and its implications for thinking and acting in everyday life.

From Myth to Cogito Man and Beyond

As indicated earlier, the dominant story of Western history and philosophy has been read and celebrated as an integral feature of the human trek toward modern enlightenment. On this account Western modernity is conceived of as emerging out of the darkness of primitive myth toward the brilliant light of the Greek classical age, out of the dark ages of Aristotelian and Christian speculation toward the dawning of modern consciousness in the European Renaissance and the age of science.[6] This broad framework of human progress, the story of the (philosophical) ascent of "man," has been filled out with the enduring wisdom of its heroic figures. Here, consequently, is celebrated the great poetic contribution of a Homer, the social vision of a Sophocles, the integrity and sacrifice of a Socrates, the historicopolitical insight of a Thucydides, the rationality of a Plato, and the nascent empiricism of an Aristotle. All are presented as crucially significant voices in a larger social and rhetorical process by which understanding of the world and of the conscious subject in it is slowly but surely detached from the realm of myth and the unquestioned givens of a primitive life.

Within this process are perceived some specific patterns of detachment, more identifiably modern in character. The modern individual thus comes into view, albeit faintly, as the "subject" becomes increasingly detached from the previously dominant "objects" of mythical knowledge and reality. And with the dualism between subject and object in Greek thought is glimpsed the first stirrings of modern rationality (e.g., via the Platonic duality of forms). But the modern emphasis on ego per se was held in abeyance for a while (for about a millennium), as the power of theocracy reigned over the power of scientific inquiry. Yet, even here, the sense of a forward movement was not completely assuaged, in that medieval scholars inherited a cosmology that both justified the belief in a supersensible reality and presented an elevated picture of man's ability to gain access to it.

The great dualism remained then (between the worldly sphere and the God sphere of immutability—between appearance and reality), and, increasingly, "reason" became the focus of human aspiration toward ultimate knowledge. In its most influential Christian reformulation, by St. Augustine, this dualized format was adjusted somewhat as more stress was placed on the need for those in the "inner" sphere (of human society and politics) to turn away from the ephemeral and the sensual and toward the eternal truth of the "outer" realm of the single God, of ultimate knowledge and purity.[7]

For the exemplary figure of Christian pessimism, of course, there was a fundamental impediment (human-created evil) to any reconciliation with God, at least in earthly terms. But this impediment theme has also been perceived as an important element of modernist progression, because derived from it, first in the nominalist perspective in the Middle Ages and then via the works of scholars such as Descartes, Spinoza, Kant, Freud, and Hegel, philosophical focus has fallen upon the location of the created evil—the human mind—and the classical/Christian dualisms have again been reformulated as the struggle between egoistic man and natural man, between love of self and love of God, between self-interest and social interest. In medieval Christianity therefore, for all its closure, there was space for the Greek notion of a cosmos to which a rational order applied and for scholastic training in science.

Consequently, the humanists of the Renaissance were able to propose that the Christian worldview could be gleaned not only from the holy texts but from the scientific texts of the age. In the same vein, the Protestantism of the Reformation, with its attack on institutionalized Christianity and its debunking of the miraculous, helped provide an intellectual bridge on which physics and astronomy could flourish at the expense of theological orthodoxy. This Renaissance period is often represented as a watershed in

Western history and philosophy (and particularly, via Machiavelli, in International Relations). Here, the story goes, the great classical dualisms were confronted with an emerging scientific skepticism that radically transformed the nature of Western thought. In the resulting historicophilosophical space there emerged Renaissance Man, set upon replacing metaphysics with truth, myth with fact. The classical dualisms were now reformulated to take into account an important new distinction, that between modern science and philosophy. More specifically, the philosophical purpose of the Renaissance, and the age of (scientific) revolution that followed it, centered on another attempt to *reconcile* the classical dualisms, this time via a synthesis of the scientific side of the polarity—set upon the notion of a universal law of motion—with its other side, increasingly embedded in the logic and rationality of mathematics.[8]

Two kinds of synthetic activity are particularly significant in the present context. The first concerns the geometric principles and logicomathematical deductive systems of figures such as Copernicus, Galileo, and Newton, which were to have such a direct impact upon early empiricism. The second relates to Descartes's attempt to reunify the outer "infinite" world (of the Christian God) with the inner, "finite" world of ego, of modern rational man.[9] This Cartesian synthesis is of special significance, not just because it marks a crucial juncture in the modernism story (as Western rational man accelerates away from the age of myth) but as the point where the *continuity* of Western thought is (paradoxically) systematized into a recognizably modernist form.

The crucial question here is this: How did (classical) foundationalist themes remain integral to Cartesian philosophy at the very moment when modern thinkers began to celebrate their new identity as the sovereign figures of history, the makers and shapers of their own destiny? It is a question, more pertinently, of how the foundationalist paradox, at the heart of post-Cartesian modernism, affected the European Enlightenment and the development of contemporary social theory and International Relations. Two themes drawn briefly from the complex Cartesian legacy might help to illuminate the issue. The first is integral to the (illusory) coherence of later rationalism; the second provided empiricists and positivists with their particular variation on the coherence theme.

Descartes and the Foundationalist Paradox of Modernity

Located at that margin where classical and Christian images of reality intersected with the scientific age of the seventeenth century, Descartes was confronted with a series of questions that would not be unfamiliar to a contemporary social theorist (or neo-Realist) seeking coherence and stability in a time of ambiguity and disorder. In the immediate Cartesian context these questions related to a perceived gap in the new rational-scientific logic, a space that had to be filled if metaphysical (mythical) uncertainty were not to inhibit progress toward a new kind of reconciliation between man and God. The questions, roughly, were these: (1) Given that we *are* rational, what is the exact nature of reason? (2) Does reason have "laws" that are amenable to scientific resolution? (3) If reason is "scientific," what does this imply for the relationship between man and God?

The answers Descartes proffered are extremely complex, of course, but one theme is of particular importance for the following discussions and requires at least a brief comment. It concerns Descartes's attempt to answer the great questions of the age with a "mind"-centered solution based on an immutable "external" foundation—that derived from God. This Cartesian logic is evident enough in *Meditations on First Philosophy* (1641) in which Descartes sought to throw off metaphysical thought once and for all and replace it with certainty.[10] The basis for this certainty was simply that which could not be doubted. For Descartes, on this basis, the only foundation for certainty was that "I think"—this statement is quite obviously "true" and self-verifying because even to doubt it proves it. The keystone of a new philosophy of certainty then was human rationality, the mind that thinks—cogito. This focus on the mind as the ultimate source of rational knowledge is of major significance in the modernist narrative because it marks the beginning of a systematic philosophical search for an objective (self-conscious) knowledge of reality, centered on the rational capacities of the modern sovereign individual.

But another element needs to be added to the Cartesian cogito theme if its enduring power and (paradoxical) nature is to be better appreciated. This concerns Descartes's efforts to ground cognitive certainty beyond mere subjectivity and connect rational knowledge to an independent universe of things that, in the classical/Christian tradition, could be understood only via "right reason"—a "right reason" for the modern thinker Descartes that lay in physics and mathematics.

To make this connection Descartes turned in the same direction as the classical scholars before him, to that external source of reality that for so long had provided foundational knowledge and socioethical direction. The logic was again simple enough: Because I have doubts and seek to overcome them I obviously do not have perfect knowledge. But I do have an idea of perfection, in God. However, because I do not have perfect knowledge I could not have devised this idea. It could have come only from the realm of perfection, from God. There must therefore be a God, and, more pertinently, there must be a realm of perfection, an independent reality, an immutable *foundation* for understanding the world, which via God-given rationality (and the most rational methods of science) humankind has the capacity to grasp as laws.[11]

Besides its more obvious legacy for later rationalism, this final theme is significant too for its influence on empiricism and positivism, as the cogito process of a priori reflection was increasingly connected (through God) to universal, axiomatic, physical laws and the mathematized logic associated with them. Mathematics, proclaimed Descartes, included the "primary rudiments of human reason" and, in terms of rational (God-given) knowledge, was "the source of all things." Subsequently, and as his influence grew throughout Europe, Descartes's science of universal mathematics became an integral part of a Western scientism that

> succeeded in turning all of nature into simple matter in motion. [Descartes] reduced all quality to quantity and then confidently proclaimed that only space and location mattered. . . . [This] mathematical world was tasteless, colourless and odourless. [It] represented total order, [and] successfully eliminated everything in the world which might in any way be thought of as messy, chaotic and alive. . . . [It was a] world of precision, not confusion.[12]

It was left to Newton to devise the natural laws of time and space from this universal mathematical premise; and, armed with the Newtonian laws of motion, the new modernists of the seventeenth century proclaimed what contemporary positivists (and mainstream International Relations specialists) assume as given—a fundamental distinction between objects and subjects, between mind and matter, between thought and fact.

This was an approach irresistible to the philosophers of the day, particularly in England, where the natural laws of the universe were enthusiastically embraced by bourgeois thinkers seeking to explain the progressive nature of modern society as it successfully (and rationally) detached itself from the ancien régime. It was, consequently, from within this (Cartesian/Newtonian) discourse that British empiricism developed, and it was as part of an attempt to resolve tensions within early empiricist thought that Hume synthesized it into positivism proper.[13]

This very abridged and superficial treatment of Cartesian thought requires one final summarized comment at this point. It is that, in the wake of *Meditations,* it becomes possible to speak of a uniquely modernist thought—not necessarily in terms of the questions it asks, nor in strict historical terms, nor as a break with the past (e.g., between ancient and modern), nor even in its focus on cogito man per se but in the way that Western philosophy is, from then on, increasingly captured by a *particular way of framing* its major debates. *Meditations,* in this sense, represents the textual mainspring of a (discursive) process by which the central questions, problems, and patterns of Western philosophy have been systematically framed to the present day. It has been a textual legacy with radical implications, offering emancipatory movements and a logic to overcome theological, metaphysical, and traditional prejudice on behalf of rational human creativity. It has also been a major philosophical conduit for the kind of conservative foundationalism resonant throughout the dominant tradition and discipline of International Relations.

In both cases, the Cartesian regime of discursive framing is the crucial issue, orienting modernity toward the search for irreducible foundations of knowledge.[14] Consequently, while modern thought has repudiated many of Descartes's substantive philosophical claims, it still resonates with the

> problems, metaphors and questions that [Descartes] bequeathed to us . . . problems concerning the foundations of knowledge and the sciences, [the] mind-body dualism, our knowledge of the "external" world, how the mind "represents" this world, the nature of consciousness, thinking and will, whether physical reality is to be understood as a grand mechanism, and how this is compatible with human freedom.[15]

Moreover, as Chapter 1 indicated, this Cartesian legacy has been manifested in a foundationalist anxiety at the discursive heart of modernity, which is still articulated across the social theory disciplines and at the core of International Relations. Here it is represented as a positivist objectivism, which insists that there must be an objective reality "out there," that exists independently of us and has an essential quality that we can know via rational means.

The discussion thus far brings us directly to the question of positivism and its significant influence upon Western philosophy, contemporary social theory, and International Relations. This, too, is a theme that can be dealt with only in sketchy terms here, but even in this form it is possible to understand the attraction and potency of positivism in the contemporary context. The discussion to follow seeks to explain this attraction, but it illustrates also that positivism, in its skeptical Humean form, provided a critical space for modernism that was ignored and ultimately closed off by the power of the foundationalist paradox.

The Emergence of Modern Positivist Thought

With the development of a modern physics in the seventeenth century, the rudiments of an empiricist theory of knowledge were emerging, particularly in Western Europe and Britain. Galileo, in particular, was important in this regard as the first to formulate a conception of science, based on experimentation and quantitative laws.[16] In England, moreover, Francis Bacon was pronouncing the "old" tradition of Greek philosophy as of no more value than "prattle . . . characteristic of boys" because, for all its philosophical contemplation, it had not "adduced a single experiment which tends to relieve and benefit the condition of man."[17] Accordingly, insisted Bacon, the real purpose of modern knowledge was "the building in the human understanding [of] a true model of the world, such as it is in fact, not such as man's own reason would have it be."[18] In the same vein, and in terms that bring the knowledge/power nexus more starkly into focus (particularly Foucault's focus), Bacon's search for an objective knowledge of the world was stimulated by the desire to gain "command over things natural—over bodies, medicine, mechanical power and infinite others of this kind."[19]

In this discursive atmosphere, the tensions between the early inductivist logic of Bacon, Hobbes, and, to a lesser extent, Locke on the one hand and the rationalist subjectivism of Berkeley on the other prompted the Humean attempt at synthetic resolution.[20] These tensions can only be touched on here for their significance for later debates. One theme of significance, in this context, concerns Hobbes's transference of the new physics of Galileo and Newton to a social context.[21] In the early pages of *Leviathan,* for example, Hobbes frames all human life in (Newtonian) terms of matter in motion. However, and here the Cartesian influence is evident, for Hobbes the modern capacity to control both the natural and the social worlds is understood (via rational science) as part of God's revelatory power. The capacity to create order and a unity out of an otherwise atomistic sphere of existence is, in this sense, proof of God's sovereignty and the (inexorably related) explanatory power of modern science.

Hobbes's approach to knowledge and (analogized) society resonates with these themes. Accordingly, the human world, no less than the natural one, is made up of individual, atomized entities, contingently related. The "natural order" between individuals is, consequently, a utilitarian struggle of individual (self-interested) entities, and, just as in the universe, unity and order in the human system is dependent upon a sovereign power, a leviathan.[22] Hobbes's early attempt to undermine rationalism via an empiricist theory of language is also significant. Here (foreshadowing the work of Locke, Hume, and the Vienna Circle), Hobbes sought to do away with metaphysics by denying the a priori faculty and projecting a genetic account of the origin of meaning, which rendered supersensible things "meaningless." Real knowledge, in this sense, is derived from individual sense impressions (of real things) and not from some innate "essence." In this way, Hobbes laid claim to a foundationalist knowledge and language, which identified early empiricism, literally, with sovereign authority in the sense that "the authority of the sovereign's law depends on the establishing of unambiguous proper meanings for words."[23]

John Locke's theory of knowledge generally reinforced and enhanced these Hobbesian premises in maintaining that real knowledge is derived from experienced sense data and not from some innate rationalist source. Hence the "tabula rasa" proposition.[24] Moreover, with Locke, epistemological issues became increasingly reduced to "internal" (psychological) processes of cognitive reflection and increasingly focused on the modern individual engaged in utilitarian processes of decisionmaking. The solipsistic tendencies inherent in this Lockean approach were taken to their subjectivist extreme in the work of Berkeley, who, in accepting empiricism's foundationalist premises, effectively reduced the modernist search for certainty to an exclusive "mind"-dependent process, located entirely in individual cognition.[25] And it was against this discursive background that David Hume sought to solve the problem of the rationalist–empiricist debate, bequeathed to modernity by Descartes. The end result: contemporary positivism.

The Humean Synthesis and the Development of Enlightenment Positivism

Hume's epistemological position is well enough known, set as it is upon the distinction between "impressions" and "ideas."[26] For Hume, consequently, knowledge about the world as it really "is" can be gained only from the realm of immediate sense experience or "impressions." All other cognitive activity, however complex or imaginative (including geometry and mathematics), is relegated to the retrospective/theoretical realm of "ideas." This "idea" realm does not *correspond* with reality per se, simply because as an abstract category it does not correspond with what actually (physically) exists in the universe.

This Humean distinction cannot be underestimated in any discussion on the nature and development of positivism because, upon this logic and in a more sophisticated way than ever before, Hume developed a systematic philosophical position predicated on the distinction between an objectively existing sphere of reality "out there" and a thinking subject who (passively) receives sense impressions and constructs "theoretical" images of the facts. It became possible in this context also to distinguish facts from values and to designate as metaphysical all nonfactual (normative) elements of cognition.

There are, perhaps, four defining principles of Humean positivism that remain integral to any contemporary discussion of it. The first, which privileges phenomenalist premises, states, in short, that only phenomena that can be directly experienced by the observing subject are capable of generating knowledge of the real nature of the world. This phenomenalist rule has a second element, which, in complementing the first, informs the positivist scholar of what can and cannot be regarded as legitimate knowledge of reality. This is the principle of nominalism. It proposes that general statements about the world that do not have their reference in independent, observable, atomized objects should not be afforded real knowledge status. Objects, therefore, that are not referable to the senses cannot, by nominalist logic, be assumed to exist outside of the senses. Rather, from the perspective of a phenomenalist/nominalist-based theory of knowledge, the real world, the world we can know, must be centered on individual, observable facts.

From this perspective, theorizing, however complex in nature, can only be a cognitive, retrospective enterprise. It must take place, literally, *after* the (experienced) fact. Theory or the process of theorizing is, in this sense, detached from (experiential) practice. Theoretical knowledge can thus be acknowledged only as part of a cognitive (*subjective*) attempt to organize, categorize, and give meaning to already existing reality. This leads to a third principle of Humean positivism, which continues to resonate through positivist Realism in the 1990s. It rejects all value (or normative) judgments, on the basis that their content (e.g., equity, goodness, harmony, morality, justice) refers to things that cannot be observed and verified and are thus "metaphysical" categories, not facts. The fourth principle, not surprisingly, invokes a commitment to the unity of the scientific method and indicates how the methods of the natural sciences are applicable to social and political analysis.[27]

It is on this basis that Hume stands out as the quintessential Enlightenment philosopher, intent on constructing a secular, scientifically based philosophical foundation for modern society. However, Hume's skepticism concerning the inherent inadequacies of this approach is also of significance here. This skepticism led Hume to a series of conclusions about all empiricist-based thinking that has immediate relevance for any discussion on the positivist-Realist discourse in International Relations. This is primarily because Hume's major conclusion was that empiricist-based claims for real knowledge cannot be defended, *except in metaphysical terms*.[28]

Hume's Skepticism and Critical Reflections on Positivism

Hume's skepticism centered on the question of how, precisely, knowledge of external objects is transformed into meaningful fact by the individual subject. More specifically, how do we know that our sense impressions are, in fact, derived from the physical world of reality, external to us? The empiricist's answer, of course, points to "experience." But this, Hume suggests, is not logically possible because "the mind has never anything present to it but perceptions and cannot possibly reach any experience of *their* [emphasis added] connection with objects. The supposition of such a connection is therefore without any foundation in reasoning."[29]

The point is that if we know the world only via perception, we cannot possibly know a reality, external to the mind, by perception alone. Nor can memory provide the answer, for our memory is of that which we have perceived, and a priori inference is ruled out by Hume because, as with all rationalist formulas, it refers only to relations between "internal" ideas.

What then of the basic argument of modern science—that we understand the real nature of the world via experiment and the knowledge derived from the conjunction between cause and effect? Well, here too Hume undermined the givens of his age and of those to follow. Hume's position on this issue is explained by Bruce Aune:

> To infer that A is the cause of B we must have experienced a constant conjunction between cases of A and cases of B. Hence to infer that external bodies cause our sense impressions we must have experienced a constant conjunction between such bodies and our impressions. But to experience a conjunction of two things we must experience *both* [emphasis added] things. Since we never *directly* [emphasis added] experience external bodies, we cannot experience a correlation between those bodies and the impressions they are believed to cause.[30]

The implication of this position is clear enough: *there is no logical basis, even in positivism's own terms, for the proposition that knowledge of reality is directly derived from an independent world "out there."* As the previous chapter indicated, this ought to be a crucial issue for a contemporary International Relations community that in the 1990s remains committed to the dictates of an "empiricist metaphysic," discredited in devastating fashion by arguably the greatest of all positivist empiricists in the eighteenth century. Sadly, it is not. Indeed, nowhere, to my knowledge, has this issue been raised in any serious way in a mainstream International Relations context. And nowhere is there evidence that its implications are understood by those within the disciplinary mainstream who ritually and confidently invoke their positivist-Realist dogma. Nowhere, it seems, is there cognizance of the major paradoxes at work when these scholars dismiss criticism of their incapacity as (mere) "reflectivism" or "abstract" theorizing. On the odd occasion when the question of positivism is raised, it is commonly as part of a retrospective enterprise, for example, in celebrating the "postpositivist" insights of Popper or, more trendily, Lakatos.[31] The problems with this position were touched on in Chapter 1, and I will return to the issue briefly at the completion of this chapter and in the critical discussion of neo-Realist scholarship in Chapter 5. The point for now is that whatever else David Hume's skeptical positivism represents for Western philosophy, it signifies for the International Relations Tradition and discipline in the 1990s another site of embarrassing backwardness.

But Hume's skepticism has other disturbing implications for mainstream scholarship in International Relations, because his attention was also turned, with devastating results, on the other great pillar of modernist thought—cogito rationalism. For Descartes, of course, this was the indubitable basis of certainty—that which could not be doubted. In Hume's work doubt abounded, primarily because of his insistence that it was not possible to actually know the "thing" (man) that thinks. All that is ever known, he argues, are mediated perceptions of thinking man, even of the "self" as cogitator. Consequently,

> when I enter most intimately into what I call *myself* [emphasis added], I always stumble on some particular perception or other, of heat or cold, light or shade, love or hatred, pain or pleasure. I never can catch *myself* [emphasis added] at any time without perception and never can observe anything but the perception. [Consequently] I may venture to affirm of the rest of mankind that they are nothing but a bundle of or collection of different perceptions.[32]

And in a passage that has profound implications for the confident articulations of sovereignty in Realist logic and the associated invocation of identity in a world of difference, Hume proposed the following:

> The mind is a kind of theatre where several perceptions successively make their appearance, pass, repass, glide away, and mingle in an infinite variety of postures and situations. There is properly no simplicity in it at one time nor identity in [its] differences—whatever natural propension we may have to imagine that simplicity and identity.[33]

There is then in Hume's skeptical position more than a glimmer of critical "thinking space." It is, however, a space virtually ignored by orthodox social theory and by International Relations scholars committed to the simpler, unifying features of the Humean contribution to modernism. At one level, perhaps, this is understandable, when one recalls that the critical potential in Hume's critique of empiricism and rationalism was ultimately undermined by a process of self-closure.

No work that I am aware of explains Hume's final decision to remain committed to the positivist approach he had so devastatingly undermined—other than his own, in which he suggested that finally, logic and reason must always remain secondary to "belief," to "passion." More pertinent, it seems that for all his skepticism, Hume remained incarcerated within the modernist (Cartesian) dualism of either/or, which in his case was represented *either* as the pursuit of "assurance and conviction" *or* as a situation in which "all discourse, all action, would immediately cease, and men would remain in a total lethargy until the necessities of nature, unsatisfied, would put an end to their miserable existence."[34] In this acquiescence before the foundational power of the "Cartesian anxiety" Hume was, after all, perhaps the quintessential modernist, searching even at the critical margins for assurance and conviction in the face of the "necessities of nature." Whatever the case, if there is one theme that can be said to characterize the narrative of modernity in the period since Hume, it has been the search for assurance and conviction, centered on a series of ingenious attempts to construct a scientific philosophy that avoided the paradoxical consequences exposed by Hume.

This is where the "Kantian turn" becomes an important theme in the dominant narrative of modernity. This Kantian influence will be discussed from a number of angles as the discussion develops in this book. At this point, my concern is to establish, very briefly, some discursive connections between Kant and the dominant strain of modernism located, by the eighteenth century, in the space between early Humean positivism and Cartesian rationalism.

The Kantian Turn: Toward a Modern Philosophy of Science

Kant sought to redeem philosophical thought from the skepticism of Hume, in proposing a new variation on the classical-cum-modern dualisms. Hume, as indicated earlier, ultimately advocated a positivist-empiricist approach to knowledge and society, even while the skepticism remained in his work about claims to have found the missing link in Western philosophy (i.e., between the laws of thought and reality). Kant perceived a way out of the dilemma by acknowledging the futility of all empiricist-based claims to know the world in a direct, unmediated form, via "experience." Rather, he argued, the universal axioms of science are already presupposed in empirical analysis and cannot, therefore, be logically derived from a process *of* experience, as empiricists argued. More precisely, the basis of knowledge is derived from a set of synthetic a priori categories of the mind. All knowledge involves the application of these categories (e.g., time, space, cause) *to* "experience." All objects, in this sense, require (a priori) concepts derived from the basic mind categories. This includes the objects of science. Consequently, all scientific explanation presupposes the a priori categories of the thinking subject.[35]

A new sense of rational-scientific philosophy became possible, on this basis, because it was now acknowledged that factual scientific knowledge, derived *from* "experience," must ultimately conform to the philosophical categories of mind, without which it is impossible *to* "experience." This confirmed Hume's suspicions about the theory-impregnated nature of scientific fact, but it did nothing to halt the modern pursuit of factual scientific knowledge, existing now in a dualized world of (nonpassive) thinking subjects and "things in themselves." Indeed, if anything, it accelerated this pursuit, in particular among those seeking to radically "transcend" the objective conditions of eighteenth-century modern life. In the post-Kantian period, consequently, at least three influential discursive variants have become integral to contemporary social theory. One, influenced by interpretivist themes drawn from Kant's a priori premise, has treated with some sensitivity the inherent problems of a positivist-empiricist approach to knowledge and society. Accordingly, it has centered its search for a modern scientific foundation in the realm of historically constituted social behavior and accumulated cultural experience (in the "retrospective" realm of memory, habit, and conventional wisdom). As such it has contributed to Anglo-American thinking a more critically inclined modernism with a more limited, less progressivist notion of science than that commonly associated with Enlightenment-based thinking. This tradition is described by Susan Hekman as "positivist humanism" [I will say something of its influence (e.g., via Weber) in the discussion of hermeneutic thought in Chapter 6.[36]

A second post-Kantian tendency, privileging its emancipatory dimension more explicitly, has, of course, been a major influence upon modern political radicalism, via its reformulations by Hegel and Marx. This will be the focus of attention in Chapters 6 and 7. For now, it is the third and dominant post-Kantian tendency that I am most concerned with—that which since the late nineteenth century has privileged the lingering objectivism in Kant in the search for a logical foundation for knowledge in a dualized world of sovereign subjects and "things in themselves." In this interpretive space positivist themes have been developed that pay tribute to Kantian insight but remain committed to the search for a logical foundation for knowledge, on behalf of the sovereign rational actor, able to transcend objective structures and *finally* know the self and the world. Into this space has come Comte, the Vienna school of logical positivism, Karl Popper, and behavioralism.

Logical Positivism: Framing Contemporary Social Theory

The impetus for the more "logical" orientation in Western thought came not just from the Hume–Kant debate but also from problems raised by theoretical physicists in the 1920s who found anomalies in positivist logic as they developed the areas of quantum mechanics and relativity theory. At stake were the axioms of Newtonian theory integral to modern thought since the seventeenth century. More specifically, physicists such as von Weizsäcker, Bohr, and Heisenberg confronted positivist social scientists with fundamental questions concerning the actual status of their "scientific" evidence and the validity of their experimental and quantitative methods for attaining and verifying facts.[37]

This is an important issue because it indicates why scholars, armed with nuanced Kantian perspectives, responded in such a negative and narrow manner when faced with a challenge from within scientific circles. This response saw logical positivists retreat to the "hard core" of their approach—its empiricist epistemology—and address the new challenge, not as a matter of fundamental philosophical inadequacy but primarily as a methodological issue concerning verification. The result was an even greater attempt to distance scientific rationality from the nonsense associated with ("premodern") metaphysical elements in Western philosophy. In this context logical positivism imposed a stricter regime of mathematics and formal logic upon the philosophical problems of the day, as articulated via the logical atomism of Russell, the Wittgenstein of the *Tractatus,* and the extreme phenomenalism of Mach.[38]

The general perspectives and goals of this new logical positivism were perhaps best articulated by Herbert Feigl, who stressed that the Vienna Circle scholars in particular sought a scientific philosophy of human society "in the spirit of Hume and Comte, but equipped with more fully developed tools."[39] More pertinent, the logical positivists used their new tool kit to further distance their "scientific" perspective from any association with (post-Kantian) philosophy. Or, as Giddens has put it, logical positivism sought to *redefine* philosophy as rational and scientific, by classifying "most of the traditional ontological and epistemological dilemmas of philosophy as belonging to metaphysics and hence outside the scope of rational discussion."[40] With logical positivism then, Western philosophy and, increasingly, the social theory traditions and disciplines derived from it became gripped by a systematic reductionism that correlated the study of human society with the logical structure of scientific theories and the methodology of verification. Any analytical enterprise not framed this way was deemed to be dealing in (philosophically) meaningless metaphysics. Here, of course, the foundationalist paradox was never more evident, as logical positivism celebrated its detachment from the ("metaphysical") traditions of Descartes, in exemplary Cartesian terms, and proclaimed its strict antimetaphysical stance upon the principles of the (positivist) "empiricist metaphysic." In this regard logical positivism stands as perhaps the quintessential modernist perspective. This is important in the present context because it was with the dispersal of its leading exponents, in the wake of fascism, that the logical positivist approach, in both its conservative and its more liberal form (e.g., in Neurath), became a direct and very influential feature of Anglo-American social theory and International Relations, via behavioralism in particular.

The Behavioralist Revolution and the "Americanization" of Social Theory

By the late 1950s logical positivism had become embedded at the core of social science thinking and research in the United States as part of the "behavioral revolution" sweeping through social theory in general. As David Ricci confirms, by this time "the behaviouralists [were] so persuasive within the discipline that there no longer existed any large and intellectually cohesive group of political scientists who believed in anything but behavioural work as the raison d'être for the discipline."[41] In the early years of the Cold War, consequently, the behavioralist strain of logical positivism became integral to the way that orthodox scholars understood and explained the world at the North American center of International Relations. At the core of this understanding was the dichotomy between scientific research and (metaphysical) "theorizing," a trait, as Tooze has illustrated, that still permeates orthodox perspectives in the 1990s.[42] At its most explicit, in the 1950s and 1960s, behavioralist research was associated with the "is" of the world, and its tangible, verifiable facts, while others (political theorists, traditional philosophers, theologians, Marxists, etc.) dealt with the "oughts," those aspects of existence that had no factual referents and thus could not generate real knowledge. It represented, in this regard, what it still represents—a narrow positivism, stripped of its (Humean) skeptical dimension.

Following the dictates of logical positivism, therefore, behavioralism emphasized empirical verification rather than philosophical speculation, as post–World War II social theorists sought to construct the social physics that, in earlier times, Comte had proposed as within the rational capacity of modern cogito man. And there was no doubt about the nature of the behavioralist enterprise, at least in its most basic form. In the early 1970s it was, as one advocate put it, simply concerned with "a body of systematic and orderly thinking about a determinate subject matter."[43] Some of the more direct implications of this ignorance/arrogance, for International Relations, will be canvassed in the next chapter, which speaks to the issue of behavioralist and Traditionalist Realism during the Cold War. Emphasis will be placed upon the increasingly technorationalist orientation in Realist ranks and the related issue of how Western identity was defined in terms of its superiority over a world of threatening Others "out there."

This is not to suggest that the behavioralism of the 1960s and 1970s was no more incisive than Comtean fact-grubbing or early logical positivism. One major addition, of course, was the impact upon it of Karl Popper's work and (the post-Kantian sensitivities) of critical rationalism. This Popperian influence helped sharpen at least three features of the behavioralist perspective: (1) It sharpened its cumulative, linear sense of progress and scientific discovery, as articulated via falsificationist testing procedures; (2) it gave it a more acute sense of the problems of (inductive) empiricism and the need, therefore, for the "tentative" representation of deductive science [particularly after Kuhn's critique in *The Structure of Scientific Revolutions* (1970)]; and (3) it heightened the notion of behavioralist science as a *nonideological* method for illustrating how the Western (i.e., U.S.) "open" system of politics, society, and (rational-scientific) thought was superior to "closed" ideological and interpretive regimes.[44]

At one level this led to an overwhelming concern with research methodology and scientific technique, rather than "political" analysis, and with a piecemeal approach to social issues that increased the conviction, within behavioralist circles, that any alternative approach must be committed to traditional (metaphysical) philosophy and "normative" theorizing. More pertinently, it led to a situation entirely familiar to any critically inclined observer of the International Relations community, "whereby a certain kind of political analysis was read out of the realm of respectable inquiry and then largely ignored as useless to the affairs of realistic people."[45] At another level, also of continuing significance for International Relations, Popperian-influenced behavioralism narrowed down the realm of the real and the meaningful in its social analysis, to the extent that questions of modern life could be asked and answered only in falsificationist terms. Accordingly, statements about political judgment, moral activity, and social justice were deemed "meaningful" only if couched in the language and logic of the value-free analyst responding to the data, as tested. By this criterion, the Cold War was justified "scientifically," with Western political and economic systems accorded superior status, not because of any normative commitments on behalf of the scientific testers but precisely because they were societies open to systemic testing. The behavioralist perspective on this issue was well articulated by Gabriel Almond, who proclaimed that Anglo-American societies have "some of the characteristics of a laboratory, [in that] policies offered by candidates are viewed as hypotheses, and the consequences of legislation are rapidly communicated within the system and constitute a crude form of testing hypotheses."[46] On this basis the superiority of Western (i.e., North American) societies lay in their pluaralist political systems and the capacity for objective evaluation and incremental correction of any lingering socio-ideological problems. This was undoubtedly an irresistible logic for many during the Cold War struggles between (Popper's) "open" and "closed" societies, and it was integral to the rise in status of social theory scholarship in the United States, as it celebrated the "end of ideology" and the triumph of pluralist democracy. Then came the Vietnam War, Watergate, and a crisis in confidence within U.S. social life that permeated even the logical haven of behavioralist positivism. Questions were now posed about the precise status of positivist approaches to (social) science. Behavioralists, after all, had objectively described the nature of the "new society" in the United States, where government chicanery was subject to pluralist testing procedures. And behavioralist techniques and scholarship had been integral to the policymaking sectors in International Relations, as they engaged in escalation strategies in Vietnam designed to overcome a (premodern) "traditional" Third World Other.

Much of the challenge to behavioralism in the 1970s centered on the question of how (social scientific) theory actually related to (policy) practice, in both the "domestic" and the "international" realms of life in the United States.[47] But the debate did at some points overlap with the longer and more comprehensive tradition of philosophical reflection on the

European Continent, which since World War II had been effectively removed from U.S. research agendas as "irrelevant." Consequently, questions once asked only at the margins of Anglo-American social theory were now readdressed more widely and with more critical intent. At its most profound, this challenge

> posed questions about fundamental categorical distinctions between "theory" and "practice" where "practice" is understood as the technical application of theoretical knowledge; the distinction between empirical and normative theory, where the former is directed towards description and explication of what *is,* while the latter deals with the clarification and justification of what ought to be; the distinction between descriptive and prescriptive discourse; and the distinction between fact and value.[48]

This was in many ways the catalyst for an (ostensibly) broadened agenda in International Relations circles as Realists of all hues sought to reformulate their positions. And, like their logical positivist forebears, when faced with a challenge they could not adequately counter the Realists of the 1970s began the retreat to the "hard core" of their modernism. By the end of the decade (i.e., with Waltz's *Theory of International Politics*) Realism had been regurgitated as neo-Realism—a refocused amalgam of behavioralist (scientific) predicates and Traditionalist essential wisdom in the age of U.S. hegemonic decline and politicoeconomic interdependence.

At the broader level of social theory, the post-Vietnam period saw a critical incision into Anglo-American scholarship, by perspectives previously excluded or marginalized, in a modernist discourse designed, linguistically, to deny the validity of "normative," "metaphysical," "feminine," "idealist," "relativist," "ideological," and "reflectivist" approaches. Once on the agenda, however, these previously alien approaches began to change this agenda, sometimes fundamentally, for a generation now more aware of the (silenced) other side of modernity as questions of gender, human rights, ecology, appropriate development, and political ethics were asked of social and intellectual elites.

The result—bemoaned by many, celebrated by some—is the broader, more comprehensive agenda on human society that has characterized social theory and, more recently, International Relations literature since the 1980s. As I suggested in Chapter 1, the emergence of this more comprehensive agenda is often correlated with the emergence of a more incisive understanding of it. I argued that this was a false correlation and began to explain why this was the case. The next chapter deals with this issue in more detail. But before moving on, one final related theme requires comment in this broad discussion of modernism and positivism. It concerns the claim, made for a number of years in social theory and more latterly in International Relations, that we have entered the period of postpositivism, that we have finally sloughed off the negative influences of the philosophical past, with all its foundationalist implications for modern, rational peoples.

Propositions of this kind have come from all angles. And at different times and in different disciplinary places, the claims of (among others) ethnomethodology, phenomenology, conventionalism, pragmatism, structuralism, analytical philosophy, hermeneutics, critical rationalism, Critical Theory, and postmodernism have found support. In Chapter 6 I will say something of the broad hermeneutic tradition and analytical philosophy in regard to their postpositivist claims, and the question of structuralism will figure prominently in the discussion of neo-Realism in Chapter 5. I have already indicated my empathy with elements of the Critical Theory and postmodernist perspectives, and Chapters 7 and 8 will be devoted to them. My more immediate concern is with the critical rationalism of Karl Popper and its influences upon social theory and International Relations. Some of these influences were touched upon earlier in relation to the behavioralism that became so dominant in Anglo-American circles during the Cold War and that retains its dominance, albeit implicitly, in mainstream scholarship to the present day. One more Popperian influence is of significance, in this regard—that which saw Popper convince the behavioralists they were no longer positivists. This is important not only because for a generation it enhanced the unself-consciousness of the most influential sector within the scholarly community but more specifically because it once more relieved that sector of the need for critical self-reflection upon themselves and their "scientific" analysis. These traits continue to bedevil International Relations scholarship in the 1990s.

Popper and the Postpositivist Illusion

The question of Popper's relationship to positivism is, again, a complex issue, but basically it concerns an intellectual sleight of hand on Popper's part, carried out for an uncritical audience at a time when, above all, Western scholars required confirmation of their identity as the agents of progressive "scientific" knowledge in the struggle with "ideology" and closure. This sleight of hand concerned the way Popper *defined* positivism (in a narrow and restricted way, as logical positivism) and the way that he sought to detach himself from this definition.[49] In short, Popper rejected positivism (i.e., logical positivism) on the basis that it misinterpreted the essence of the Enlightenment and the modern quest for scientific philosophy. He argued, in the process, that the (logical) positivist insistence on a dichotomy between science and metaphysics lacked logical credibility. Moreover, in confronting seriously the Humean self-critique of positivism, Popper (ostensibly) repudiated logical atomism, the extreme nominalism that underpinned it, and the inductivist methodology built upon it. Just as significant, he repudiated the phenomenalism (or sensationalism) that, via direct sensory experience, provided (logical) positivists their "protocol sentences" of real meaning.

The problem with (logical) positivism, according to Popper, was, in this sense, simple enough. Its inductivist approach fundamentally misunderstood the real and critical method of observation, which did not proceed in terms of generalizations derived from observation but as part of a procedure centered on deductive causal explanations and a regime of rigorous testing.[50] It was in this context that Popper accepted Kant's proposition about the value ladenness of the scientific process, at least as it concerned the behavioral conventions of the scientific process. Indeed, the Enlightenment tradition of scientific progress was, for Popper, bound up in these conventions, and given the (ostensible) rejection of all external foundations, these methodological conventions now *defined* science and its knowledge in sociological terms. The most famous convention was the principle of falsifiability, and it was the application of the falsifiability principle that demarcated scientific (real) knowledge from other knowledge forms (e.g., speculative, normative, ideological, religious). The pursuit of scientific knowledge in this falsifiability context was not foundationalist certainty of the Cartesian kind but a nondogmatic body of knowledge, set upon a rational procedure of "trial and error, of conjecture and refutation; of boldly proposing theories; of trying our best to show that these are erroneous; and of accepting them tentatively if our critical efforts are unsuccessful."[51] This was all wholesome stuff, of course, the stuff that the modern heroic figures of the Cold War era were made of, even if the caution, moderation, and concern for erroneous theorizing were conspicuous by their absence during the great bulk of Popper's *Poverty of Historicism* and *The Open Society and Its Enemies* (vol. 2) and its polemics on Kant, Hegel, and Marx. This, nevertheless, was the context in which Popper distanced himself from positivism, proclaiming in unequivocal terms the following:

> Throughout my life I have combated positivist epistemology. . . . I have fought against the apeing of the natural sciences by the social sciences, and I have fought for the doctrine that positivist epistemology is inadequate; even in its analysis of the natural sciences.[52]

Even from this brief outline of Popper's position, it is clear that this is not a claim easily undermined. Popper's critical rationalism echoed the skepticism of Hume concerning the problems of inductivism and solipsism and, in rejecting the axioms of nominalism and phenomenalism, he acknowledged (seemingly) antifoundationalist sociological principles. In the "behavioralist revolution" of the 1960s and since then, in the orthodox consensus in social theory and in International Relations, this Popperian position has been maintained, albeit sometimes in reformulated (e.g., Lakatosian) terms.

Popper's critics, however, have never accepted that his critical rationalism overcame the paradoxical limitations associated with positivist thought. The dispute with Popper involving both generations of the Frankfurt School is well enough known in this regard, as is Thomas Kuhn's critique, and these themes will receive attention later in the book. But criticism of Popper's position continues to flow from sources who, in other respects, would have little in common with Kuhn, Habermas et al., or, indeed, with each other.[53] As indicated in Chapter 1, Ernst Gellner, for example, maintains that Popper smuggles back into his critical rationalism the very "empiricist metaphysic" that (like Hume) he acknowledged as inadequate.[54] This is evident enough in relation to the unity-of-science theme, integral to Hume's positivism and to Popper's. Thus, while Popper ostensibly detached himself from nominalist and phenomenalist premises and acknowledged the theory-impregnated nature of observation, he (paradoxically) continued to represent social (science) knowledge in terms of a *single foundation* of understanding based on the (pure) method of the natural sciences. In the *Poverty of Historicism,* this was clearly the position taken by Popper in his support for

> a doctrine of the unity of method; that is to say, the view that all theoretical or generalising sciences make use of the same method, whether they are natural sciences or social sciences. . . . The methods always consist in offering deductive causal explanations, and in testing them (by way of predictions).[55]

This represents positivism by any other name at the core of the most influential "postpositivist" perspective in social theory. So does Popper's treatment of the issue of universal scientific laws. In *The Logic of Scientific Discovery,* for example, Popper rejected this notion on the (Humean) basis that the universal status of such laws is not empirically verifiable.[56] Elsewhere, however, this logic was itself unequivocally undermined. Consequently, and in relation to the social sciences, Popper proclaimed that "it is an important postulate of scientific method that we should search for laws with an *unlimited* [emphasis added] realm of validity [because] if we were to admit to laws that are themselves subject to change, change could never be explained by laws."[57] In Popper's major Cold War tract, *The Open Society and Its Enemies,* this theme is revisited when Popper explains the open, sociological process of understanding integral to critical rationalism, while insisting that "of course this does *not* mean that all 'social laws,' i.e., all regularities of our social life, are normative and man imposed. On the contrary, there are important natural laws of social life also. For these the term sociological laws seems appropriate."[58] The problem here, of course, is not just the implied existence of "laws" beyond and independent of the "normative" but the related and more explicit assertion concerning independent "natural laws of social life," which, by Popper's own logic of falsificationism, must be regarded as metaphysical (i.e., not empirically verifiable). This is no lapse in logic per se. Rather it is entirely consistent with Popper's futile attempt to detach positivism from the foundationalism that binds it, paradoxically, to (premodern) metaphysics and renders it incapable of speaking in dogmatic terms even when it is represented as the epitome of moderation and social sensitivity. More pertinently, it is consistent with David Hume's conclusion that, ultimately, all schemas based on the "empiricist metaphysic," including the most sophisticated positivist variants, can be defended only in *metaphysical* terms.

Whatever else this implies for contemporary social theory and International Relations, it renders mainstream (falsificationist) claims for analytical tolerance, openness, and postpositivist sensitivity effectively meaningless, because the singular, foundationalist font of positivist knowledge remains unquestioned, and beyond questioning, in scientific terms. This is a point made by Kolakowski when comparing a genuinely sociological approach with knowledge, against the Popperian perspective. The former position, suggests Kolakowski, must accept that the "data of experience always leaves scope for more than one explanation, and which one is chosen cannot be determined by experience."[59] Popper's definition of *real knowledge,* however, acknowledges as valid only an empiricist account of the *origin* of knowledge (the world of independent objects to be tested for their facticity) and it ultimately represents an extension of positivist philosophy.[60] It represents also the kind of narrow modernism that dominates in International Relations in the 1990s, to the great detriment of global understanding. Accordingly, in the following chapters this Popperian legacy, particularly at its intersections with Weberianism, will be illustrated as integral to Realist theory as practice and more explicitly to the current neo-Realist hierarchy (e.g., Waltz, Keohane, Gilpin).

To complete this discussion of the way that a modernist discourse continues, via contemporary positivism, to shape contemporary social theory and International Relations, a final commentary is worth noting. It captures nicely the significance of the postpositivist discussion and summarizes, more generally, much of the discursive ground covered in this chapter. It comes from Roy Bhaskar, who, rightly, proposes that:

> The importance of positivism lies partly in the fact that almost all post Humean, post Kantian philosophies stand in certain critical, logical and historical relations to it; partly in the fact that it is the philosophy of common sense . . . par excellence; partly in the fact that it is intimately associated, on the one hand with the most successful scientific system hitherto seen, viz. Newtonian mechanics, and on the other, with the most powerful

socio-economic order hitherto known, namely capitalism [and] partly in the fact that it continues to structure contemporary philosophy of science and social science, *even when these are formally opposed to it.*[61]

Notes

1. For an interesting overview of the issue, see Calinescu, *Five Faces of Modernity.*

2. Ibid., p. 268. My concentration on the "fifth face" is not to suggest a fundamental distinction between philosophy, social theory, and aesthetics, but except for brief and fleeting references, this is just one of the dimensions of the present debate that I cannot deal with here.

3. See Kolb, *The Critique of Pure Modernity,* chap. Connolly, *Political Theory and Modernity;* and Calinescu, *Five Faces of Modernity.*

4. This definition is influenced by Connolly's arguments in *Political Theory and Modernity,* which I want to develop a little differently here.

5. These themes warrant book-length discussion in themselves, of course, but I offer here, initially, a skeletal image of the way the story of the Western past and present have been commonly connected by philosophers, historians, and social theorists. In the discussions to follow, some of the missing nuance will be added as more emphasis is placed on particular thematic elements of this initial representation.

6. A good overview of this debate is in Findlay, *Four Stages of Growth;* see also Snell, *The Discovery of Mind.*

7. On the Augustinian dualisms, see *City of God.* For a broader discussion of Augustinian thought and influence, see Deane, *The Political and Social Ideas of St. Augustine.*

8. On this late-medieval–Renaissance period generally, see Jacob, *The Cultural Meaning of the Scientific Revolution;* Trevor-Roper, *Religion, the Reformation and Social Change;* Maxwell, *From Knowledge to Wisdom;* Aronowitz, *Science as Power;* and Bronowski and Mazlish, *The Western Intellectual Tradition.*

9. For a broad overview of Cartesian thinking, see Jacob, *The Cultural Meaning of the Scientific Revolution;* Anscombe and Geach, *Descartes, Philosophical Writings;* and Scruton, *A Short History of Modern Philosophy.* See also Gilson, "Concerning Christian Philosophy," which emphasizes the enduring connections between Descartes's new scientific philosophy and Christianity.

10. On the significance of this text, see Scruton, *A Short History of Modern Philosophy,* chap. 2; Aune, *Rationalism, Empiricism and Pragmatism;* and Bernstein, *Beyond Objectivism and Rationalism.*

11. See Scruton, *A Short History of Modern Philosophy,* for a general discussion of these themes.

12. Ibid., p. 35.

13. Without overly caricaturing the issue, I hope, it might be suggested that there was a geographic distinction associated with the spread of Cartesian influence in the seventeenth and eighteenth centuries in Europe. On the Continent, rationalism flourished, as scholars such as Spinoza and Leibniz sought to more rigorously apply the axioms of geometry and the new science of calculus to the great philosophical questions concerning the relations between God and modern "man." In

Britain, particularly England, where the theory and practice of bourgeois liberalism was at its most advanced, an atomistic, individualist brand of empiricism became dominant that was fiercely (and paradoxically) antimetaphysical and generally inclined toward epistemological reductionism.

14. This, to reiterate, is not to suggest that Descartes was the first or only Western philosopher to engage in such a search. As the earlier discussion emphasized, foundationalism, in one form or another, has been a central feature of Western thought since Plato sought to "found" real knowledge of the world in an outer sphere of truth and perfection, rather than in the inner sphere of politics and human imperfection. Accordingly, the emphasis on Cartesianism does not imply the strict ancient/modern dualism of much mainstream political theory.

15. Bernstein, *Beyond Objectivism and Relativism,* p. 17.

16. Kolakowski, *Positivist Philosophy,* p. 28.

17. This is taken from Bacon's "Novum Organum," as cited in Rifkin, *Entropy,* p. 33.

18. Ibid., p. 34.

19. Ibid., p. 34.

20. On this issue, see Cornforth, *Science Versus Idealism;* and Scruton, *A Short History of Modern Philosophy,* pp. 21–50.

21. There are, of course, many dimensions to the work of Hobbes and those whose work is discussed from now on. I am interested here in Hobbes's contribution to early empiricism and later positivist thinking centered on atomized, contingent premises. More specifically, I am concentrating on the dominant interpretation of Hobbes (in Locke and Hume, for example), which, for all its limitations, has been basically unquestioned in International Relations. For a more sophisticated recent discussion of Hobbes, see Ryan, *Marxism and Deconstruction,* chap. 1; and Connolly, *Political Theory and Modernity,* chaps. 2 and 3.

22. See Hobbes, *Leviathan,* chap. 1; and Grace, "Augustine and Hobbes." Connolly, in *Political Theory and Modernity,* illustrates that Hobbes understood the rhetorical power associated with a common faith in the idea of sovereignty in the age where God and feudal power relations were no longer obviously sovereign. Ryan develops a similar argument in his Introduction to *Marxism and Deconstruction.*

23. See Ryan, *Marxism and Deconstruction,* p. 3.

24. See *Essay Concerning Human Understanding*. For a broader debate on the close connections between the work of Hobbes and Locke often overlooked by those who would divorce the "liberal" from the "authoritarian," see Masters, "Hobbes and Locke."

25. See Cornforth, *Science Versus Idealism,* p. 43.

26. The former, Hume maintained, corresponded to the immediate sense experience of the world; the latter, to the retrospective meaning or imagination associated with such experience (i.e., the distinction between the experience of pain, sound, color, smell, and later images or memory of it). See Kolakowski, *Positivist Philosophy;* Aune, *Rationalism, Empiricism and Pragmatism;* and Scruton, *A Short History of Modern Philosophy.*

27. These themes are drawn, broadly, from Kolakowski, *Positivist Philosophy.* As Chapter 1 sought to illustrate, these are themes still entirely relevant to International Relations in the 1990s. Chapters 3, 4, and 5 will make the connections even clearer.

28. Broad overviews on the influence of positivist/empiricist thinking across the social theory spectrum are to be found in Kolakowski, *Positivist Philosophy;* Aronowitz, *Science as Power;* Stockman, *Antipositivist Theories of the Sciences;*

Giddens, *Positivism and Sociology* and *Studies in Social and Political Theory;* Keat and Urry, *Social Theory as Science;* and Ricci, *The Tragedy of Political Science.*

29. Hume, cited in Aune, *Rationalism, Empiricism and Pragmatism,* pp. 65–66.

30. Ibid., p. 66.

31. See Keohane, "International Institutions."

32. Hume, cited in Aune, *Rationalism, Empiricism and Pragmatism,* p. 67.

33. Ibid., p. 67.

34. Ibid., pp. 66–67.

35. On the Kantian argument in this regard, see Scruton, *A Short History of Western Philosophy,* chap. 10; Aune, *Rationalism, Empiricism and Pragmatism;* Aronowitz, *Science as Power;* Habermas, *Knowledge and Human Interests,* pt. 1; and from other angles, Rorty, *Philosophy and the Mirror of Nature;* and Foucault, "What Is Enlightenment?"

36. See Hekman, *Hermeneutics and the Sociology of Knowledge.*

37. For an overview discussion, see Aronowitz, *Science as Power.*

38. On logical positivism generally, see Kolakowski, *Positivist Philosophy;* Giddens, *Positivism and Sociology* and *Studies in Social and Political Theory;* Aronowitz, *Science as Power;* Suppe, *The Structure of Scientific Theories;* and Keat and Urry, *Social Theory as Science.*

39. Cited in Giddens, *Studies in Social and Political Theory,* p. 44.

40. Ibid.

41. See Ricci, "Reading Thomas Kuhn in the Post-Behavioural Era," p. 24. On behavioralism generally, see Ricci, *The Tragedy of Political Science;* Gunnell, "Political Theory"; Wolin, "Political Theory as a Vocation"; and Beehler and Drengson, eds., *The Philosophy of Society,* chap. 5. For broader discussions of positivist reductionism in an ostensibly pluralist society, see Mills, *The Sociological Imagination;* and Gouldner, *The Coming Crisis of Western Sociology.*

42. Tooze, "The Unwritten Preface."

43. This is from Evron Kirkpatrick, "The Impact of the Behavioural Approach on Traditional Political Science," p. 79, as cited in Ricci, *The Tragedy of Political Science,* p. 140.

44. Important here was Popper's *The Open Society and Its Enemies,* vol. 2, on Hegel and Marx, first published in 1945; see also Popper, *The Poverty of Historicism.*

45. Ricci, *The Tragedy of Political Science,* p. 150.

46. This is from Almond, "Comparative Political Systems," p. 398, as cited in Ricci, *The Tragedy of Political Science,* p. 159.

47. On this see Bernstein, *The Restructuring of Social and Political Theory,* Introduction.

48. Ibid., p. 21.

49. On the Popper issue in this regard, see Stockman, *Antipositivist Theories of the Sciences,* pts. 2 and 3; Adorno, ed., *The Positivist Dispute;* Habermas, *Knowledge and Human Interests;* Suppe, *The Structure of Scientific Theories,* chaps. 1 and 2; Gellner, *Legitimation of Belief,* pp. 170–176; Hindess, *Philosophy and Methodology in the Social Sciences,* chap. 7; and Chalmers, *What Is This Thing Called Science?* For a more empathic view of the affair, see Lakatos and Musgrave, eds., *Criticism and the Growth of Knowledge.*

50. See *The Logic of Scientific Discovery* on the "modern positivists" as Popper termed them, pp. 34–54.

51. Popper, *Conjectures and Refutations,* p. 51.

52. This is in Adorno, ed., *The Positivist Dispute,* p. 299.

53. On the specific dispute between critical theory and Popper, see Adorno, ed., *The Positivist Dispute;* Habermas, *Knowledge and Human Interests;* and Jay, *Marxism and Totality.* Kuhn's major critique is in *The Structure of Scientific Revolutions.* The diverse critiques I refer to can be found, for example, in Stockman, *Antipositivist Theories of the Sciences;* Gellner, *Legitimation of Belief;* Kolakowski, *Positivist Philosophy;* and Bhaskar, *Scientific Realism and Human Emancipation.*

54. Gellner, *Legitimation of Belief,* pp. 174–177.

55. Popper, *Poverty of Historicism,* p. 130.

56. Popper, *Logic of Scientific Discovery,* p. 253.

57. Popper, *Poverty of Historicism,* p. 103.

58. Popper, *The Open Society and Its Enemies,* p. 67.

59. Kolakowski, *Positivist Philosophy,* p. 158.

60. Ibid., p. 172.

61. Bhaskar, *Scientific Realism and Human Emancipation,* p. 305.

3

The Making of International Relations: From Modernist Tradition to Cold War Discipline

The aim of this chapter is to illustrate the discursive connections between contemporary social theory and International Relations. More precisely, this chapter seeks to open up for critical questioning some of the pivotal concepts, themes, and premises of International Relations effectively closed off under the narrow regime of modernist interpretation, which were discussed in the preceding chapters. Particular attention will be paid to the dominant (Realist) Tradition of International Relations and to the more recent disciplinary manifestations of this Tradition that emerged in the wake of two world wars.

Indeed, to speak of a Tradition of International Relations at all is to speak of a particular disciplinary representation of it, in embryo after World War I but at its most influential in intellectual and policymaking circles after World War II in the United States. The International Relations Tradition in this sense represents a (largely) U.S. social science reading of some of the "great texts" of Western history and philosophy. More significant, it was under U.S. social science tutelage that International Relations became focused on a disciplinary quest for (scientific) certainty, based on modernist principles of knowledge and behavioralist methodological premises.

Initially, therefore, this discussion will locate International Relations as part of a modernist way of framing—as a microcosm of the dominant Western tradition of interpretation and understanding. The focus will then fall, more generally, on the process by which the International Relations discipline has been constructed and defined in the period since its institutional inception following World War I. It will do so in a way that integrates critical social theory themes with a reformulated approach to the discipline's folklore, regarding its stages of intellectual growth and "great debates." This well-rehearsed format will be altered somewhat in the attempt to provide a broad genealogical approach to contemporary International Relations set upon four interrelated phases, which, while broadly chronological, represent not the successively greater understanding of a complex reality but, more accurately and paradoxically, the consistent repression of such understanding.

Stanley Hoffmann's insights are useful here, particularly his commentary on the development of the Realist quest for certainty in the Cold War years, discernible in "three waves" of Realist literature. The first "wave" emanated from the publication of Morgenthau's *Politics Among Nations* in 1948 and Realist responses to it until the late 1950s. The "second wave" was distinguished by a shift in Realist research orientation, from the late 1950s to around the end of the Vietnam War. This saw the discipline dominated by behavioralist approaches to Cold War strategic issues. The "third wave" saw the quest for certainty oriented toward a post-Vietnam international political economy approach, concerned with Realism's increasingly evident anomalies.[1]

With these broad themes in mind, this chapter (and Chapters 4 and 5) will add a critical edge to Hoffmann's Traditionalist-Realist perspective on this issue. Here, the quest for certainty in International Relations will be (re)introduced as various phases of a modernist regime of metatheoretical framing. These phases, are: (1) the neo-Kantian phase: most influential in the interwar years; (2) the Realist-positivist phase, centered on the E. H. Carr's "great text," which, in the Cold War years evolved into (3) the positivist-Realist phase, with its own (Americanized) "great text," a more precise positivist epistemology (rational-scientific), language mode (representational), methodology (falsificationist), and analytical orientation (problem solving).[2] Against this background emerged (4) the phase of neo-Realism, regime theory, and hegemonic stability theory; the phase of international political economy; and postpositivism. The present chapter will concentrate in particular on the first two of these phases, taking this reformulated story of the Tradition and its contemporary discipline to the early years of the Cold War. My initial concern, however, is to thematically connect this discussion of the International Relations Tradition and discipline to earlier chapters, by briefly establishing its modernist character.

International Relations and Modernism: Some Broad Discursive Connections

At its most obvious, the modernist legacy in International Relations is represented in the way the discipline has read and interpreted its "history" and framed its "philosophical" stances. Consequently, as in the broader social theory context, great texts and great men punctuate a meaning script set, unproblematically, in dualized and dichotomized terms.[3] Logocentrism is the dominant structural theme, as history is reduced to the incantations across the time, culture, and language of those whose eternal wisdom corresponds with that which is universally and foundationally real. A major characteristic of the International Relations historical narrative, consequently, is its particular reading of a "*single body of thought,* incorporating both the pre-modern work of classical Greece and the middle ages, and also writings from the 1648–1914 period."[4] It is not surprising, therefore, that what philosophical debate there has been concerning the historical development of International Relations has also been framed within classically modernist terms. More pertinent, as Chapter 1 indicated, this universalized and essentialized account of global life continues in the 1990s to underpin and direct the theory as practice of International Relations.

Textually, thus, International Relations continues to be characterized by a crude essentialism centered on a cast of caricatured historical figures. Dominating this textual monologue are Thucydides, Machiavelli, Hobbes, Rousseau, Morgenthau, and Carr.[5] Their "script," as interpreted by mainstream scholars over the years, is marked by a coherence and self-affirming logic concerning the perennial questions of power, state sovereignty, and national interest, which are underpinned by an enduring wisdom on issues of "real" human nature and political behavior. Consistent with the broader modernist narrative, therefore, the Tradition of International Relations appears as a homogenized, cumulative unfolding of real knowledge, in which certain "great texts" of Western philosophy are accorded a meaning that corresponds with the real world, while others are marginalized or dismissed altogether using logocentric strategies of exclusion.

In the Traditional narrative, for example, the Platonic contribution is considered highly problematic, not because it began the (textual) separation of subject and object in Western thought but because it *did not separate them enough.* Thus, as E. H. Carr maintained, while Platonic insight might well be significant for "domestic" theorizing, at the international level Plato's contribution was merely to "advocate highly imaginative solutions whose relation to existing facts was one of flat negation."[6] Thucydides, on the other hand, is commonly deemed to have understood the "existing facts" very well. His *Melian Dialogue* is, in particular, accorded a universal, ahistorical quality, with its enduring wisdom that "among neighbours antagonism is ever a condition of independence."[7] Later, within the millennia of theological dominance in the West, Augustine is generally perceived as having gotten it right with his pessimistic incantations on "fallen man."[8] And, in the Renaissance, modern Realism finds its exemplar scholar and text in Machiavelli and *The Prince,* as the modern world begins, in systematic form, to distance itself from the religious and social myths of its past.[9]

Leaping across cultural, historical, and linguistic voids, Hobbes's insights into the anarchical world are then usually introduced to the narrative, often via the proposition that "in all times kings and persons of sovereign authority because of their authority, because of their independence, are in continual jealousies and in the state and posture of gladiators . . . which is the posture of war."[10] Rousseau, too, is presented as a major Realist contributor to the International Relations Tradition, particularly to its understanding of the security dilemma faced by all states in an anarchical world, in which a state's "safety and preservation demand that it makes itself stronger than its neighbours [because] it cannot increase, foster, or exercise its strength except at their expense."[11] Closer to the present, various commentators are represented as carrying on the Tradition in understanding, in the contemporary world, what their forebears had so incisively understood in the past: about "human nature" (e.g., Morgenthau, Neibuhr), the structural reality of interstate competition under anarchy (e.g., Waltz, Gilpin), the "art of the possible" concerning an international society (e.g., Wight, Bull), and the enduring character of an anarchical system in an interdependent world economy (e.g., Keohane, Krasner).

The contemporary punch line to the Realist story—the post–World War II power politics approach—has been variously articulated over the years. But a number of fundamental assumptions continue to form this, the "hard core" of Realist theory and practice, and, for the great majority of contemporary scholars, they continue to define it in the 1990s. These assumptions are as follows: First, individual, sovereign states (or their official diplomatic representatives) are the most important actors on the world stage and must therefore be the primary units of International Relations analysis. Second, the international arena is the site of endemic anarchy and is fundamentally different from the domestic one (accordingly, its theory and practice must be understood in fundamentally different terms). Third, in both historical and contemporary terms, the "essence" of interstate behavior is the struggle for power. Fourth, this struggle, for all its anarchical consequences, follows a "rational" pattern, the utilitarian pursuit of (national) self-interest on the part of all actors. Fifth, while there are (societal) cooperative tendencies evident within the state system (e.g., regime behavior), these should not be understood as fundamental systemic characteristics.[12] This approach, consequently, for all its posturing toward an international political economy in recent times, has continued to represent the world in terms of

> mankind as divided into separate, sovereign states, each keeping law and order within its borders by the application of force from the centre, and also using force to keep secure against other states. Relations between states [are] conducted by diplomacy, against a background of military preparedness and alliances, and within a limited code of international law of which states, not people, [are] the subjects. The whole system of states [is] sustained against overthrow by the balance of power.[13]

The most potent metaphor in the vocabulary of the International Relations Tradition in this context is the concept of "balance" of power. Once again, however, a historically, culturally, and linguistically specific theme is accorded a timeless, universalist status. Accordingly, the most celebrated modern Realist, Hans Morgenthau, asserted in deterministic fashion that balance in the international system is a "natural and inevitable outgrowth of the struggle for power," that therefore the balance of power is a "self-regulatory mechanism."[14] This (positivist) determinism is continued in the work of one of Morgenthau's most influential heirs (and critics), Kenneth Waltz, whose structuralist positivism will receive more attention in Chapter 5, where it will be (re)introduced as the main conduit for the simplistic, albeit powerful, caricature of history politics and society that remains dominant in the neo-Realist–dominated discipline to the present.

The issue of caricature is never more pertinent, of course, than in relation to the Tradition's identifying dichotomy—that which distinguishes Realism and idealism. The crudity of this approach has been noted by Richard Cox, who has responded critically to a rather bizarre historico-philosophical perspective that groups together

> Plato, Grotius, Locke, Kant and Woodrow Wilson as "idealists," and Thucydides, Machiavelli, Hobbes, Churchill and Lenin as "realists." [Here] the idealists tend to be "rationalists" who deny or greatly underestimate the "power" factor in politics, and elevate absolutist moral principles into ultimate realities. Conversely, the "realists" tend to be pragmatists who place their emphasis on the power factor as the real basis of political action.[15]

The sheer arbitrariness of this logocentric strategy is both puzzling and troubling for Cox. He is puzzled, for example, by the oppositional regime that opposes Locke to Machiavelli but places Thucydides in the same category as Machiavelli, without (seemingly) considering the possibility that "Locke ultimately had more in common with Machiavelli than with Plato."[16] He is troubled by the analytical consequences of lumping together figures of vastly different times, places, and capacities, such as Plato and Woodrow Wilson, and of assuming that their "utopianism" was basically the same "in spite of the fact that Plato specifically makes his Socrates speak of the impossibility of making the best regime actual, whereas Wilson conceived of the actualisation of a world of democratic states as both possible and necessary."[17]

An earlier theme requires reiteration here: it is that the crudity of this dichotomized format has not, to any great extent, inhibited its influence within the International Relations discipline. Indeed, for broadly the same reasons that the Humean (self)-critique was ignored by Hume's successors (the overwhelming desire to find an irreducible foundation for knowledge of reality), the Realists of the post–World War II period in particular have constructed their own identity and the parameters of the International Relations Tradition in these dichotomized and logocentric terms. And while the problems of dichotomized thinking have been occasionally acknowledged, the general response to the problems of reading history and philosophy in this way has, to say the least, been disappointing.

Indeed, one influential response has been to suggest that the problem lies not so much in privileging a power politics reading of history and philosophy but in not privileging it enough. Thus, as Traditionalist historians have told the story, the lessons of the "great texts" (e.g., *The Prince*) and the wisdom of the "great men" have not always been heeded well enough. As a consequence, the development of a genuine Realism was somewhat diverted as other (e.g., rationalist/Kantian) influences proliferated and as early Realist thinking veered off toward reformism (e.g. in the works of the Abbe de Saint Pierre), plans for "perpetual peace" (Kant), and legalism (Grotius).[18] These utopian irritations, remnants of a metaphysical past, are in Realist narratives traced right up to the present century, in the (futile) post–World War I efforts of Western liberals to subvert the inevitable in International Relations.

This position is articulated powerfully in Hedley Bull's condemnation of those "idealists" who have sought to challenge the wisdom of Realism's insights into the universal and enduring reality of International Relations down the ages. In Bull's view,

> the "idealists" were not remarkable for their intellectual depth or powers of explanation, only for their intense commitment to a particular vision of what should happen. [However] in their disparagement of the past they lost sight of a great deal that was already known; in some respects their work represented not an advance but a decline in understanding in international relations, an unlearning of old lessons which a later generation of writers found it necessary to restate. In their assessment of the present and the future they were guided more by their hopes than by the evidence in hand.[19]

What Bull refers to here, of course, is an important element of the modernist connection in International Relations, that which connects the present broad discussion of a Tradition to the historical and intellectual circumstances surrounding the institutional establishment of International Relations as a *discipline* after World War I—or, as it is to be presented here, the neo-Kantian phase in the modernist framing of International Relations.

The Making of a Discipline (I): Neo-Kantianism and International Relations

The discipline of International Relations was institutionally formulated in the wake of World War I. It developed, accordingly, in an atmosphere charged with a fervent desire to more adequately understand and control the seemingly endemic hostility within the international arena in order, above all, to prevent war on such a scale occurring again.[20] It was in this context that International Relations scholarship was seized with a liberal reformist zeal that owed much, in tone and intellectual commitment, to the European Enlightenment and its rejection of the ancien régime.

In more explicit terms, the early years of the discipline's development saw a concerted attempt to overcome the mistakes of the past—European great power dominance, imperialism, balance-of-power strategies, and the closed, elite diplomacy of the concert of Europe. In its place the scholars and statesmen of the interwar years introduced "new world" ideas and structures set upon modern scientific-rationalist premises. The solutions proffered were often of an (Anglicized) neo-Kantian ilk, predicated as they were upon the institutionalized application of the values of democratic republicanism and the cooperative efforts of individual, sovereign states.[21]

In short, this neo-Kantian phase of the discipline's development, brief though it turned out to be, "constituted the first effort by intellectuals and statesmen alike to apply ideas of enlightened [rational] self-interest to international politics."[22] This is not to suggest that prominent scholars of the period and political figures such as Woodrow Wilson entirely rejected the strategies of power politics. Their progressivist aim, rather, was to intellectually and structurally reformulate the nature of modern relations between states in line with actual (rationally derived) "reality," as opposed to the "irrationality" of the past.

These orientations were articulated in a variety of ways. In the inaugural address of the first chair of International Politics, for example, in the early 1920s, the recipient bemoaned the lack of rational-scientific principles in the study of the state system, reflecting that if an "ordered and scientific body of knowledge did exist in 1914 . . . perhaps . . . the catastrophe might have been averted."[23] Another influential dimension to the debate was added by the U.S. president, Woodrow Wilson, advocating collective security principles and a commitment to progressivism centered on the superiority of modern democratic forms of government and the rights of individual sovereignty. Understanding world history through this dominant modernist prism, the Wilsonian approach assumed that the experiences of World War I, in sweeping away the last vestiges of the ancien régime, had brought forth the age of democratic thought and politics to the international arena. Accordingly, International Relations was now set to enter the next "stage" of its rational development, in which the language and structural principles of the domestic (democratic) realm became directly appropriate.

Integral to this postwar theory as practice was the attempt to objectify the spirit of the age via the institutionalization of democratic structural principles. The League of Nations and the International Court of Justice were, in this sense, the institutional vanguard of the postwar liberal age in international affairs, the forums in which a modern (rational) elite of sovereign states might progressively distance themselves from the inadequate theory and practice of the past. Against this background, Wilson appealed to the unfolding (universal) consciousness of the world's peoples, maintaining that, in the new objective circumstances (democracy rather than autocracy) the "conscience of the world" would decide what was "right" in postwar political life. Giving grist to the mill of those who later were to ridicule the ethnocentric arrogance of his position, Wilson propounded further that in the new age of Western rationality "a bad cause will fare ill, but a good cause is bound to be triumphant. . . . You dare not lay a bad cause before mankind."[24]

The most accomplished scholarship of the period, it is argued, emanated from the works of Alfred Zimmern, particularly his *League of Nations and the Rule of Law* (1936); a brief comment on this and other of his works indicates its modernist legacy and its consequent limitations.[25] In his discussion of the league, for example, Zimmern promoted its establishment as "in harmony with the [historical] nature of things [which] . . . in the long or the short run . . . would prevail."[26] In the same vein, the years following the first world war were understood as "a period of transition" in which the traditional resort to power politics was to be transcended in favor of the politics of cooperation and responsibility.[27]

Like many scholars of the period, Zimmern resisted the "old" power politics image of the international arena and countered it with arguments paralleling those of liberal economists of the time.[28] Zimmern, however, paid little direct attention to economic issues per se. His was a Traditionalist perspective for all its reformist inclinations. Rather, the solution for Zimmern lay in the establishment, at the international level, of the rationality inherent in the way the worst excesses of market conflict had been overcome in British law. If such a structure were in place at the international level, he argued, antagonisms might be brought to the surface for rational debate, and seemingly intractable problems could be solved.

On the question of fascism and the frailties of legal-rational solutions in this context, Zimmern explained the problem in rather predictable (dichotomized, logocentric) terms. The world, he suggested, in its "transition" period must be understood in dichotomized terms—as divided between "good" and "bad" states, between "old" and "new" systems, between "traditional" and "modern" societies, between "them" and "us." On the one hand, more explicitly, there were modern "welfare states" such as Britain, the United States, and France, where individuals ruled through democratic structures and the rule of law prevailed. On the other hand, there were "power states" such as Germany, Italy, and Japan, where individual freedom and a healthy community consciousness was still subsumed beneath the legacy of the old absolutist state system.[29] The synthesized answer to this problem, for Zimmern, lay in the transference of the value system of the "welfare states" to the rest of the world, in order that individuals in all states could control and direct foreign policy as they did in "good" societies.

In the 1930s, this kind of perspective (now resonant again in Fukuyama-type triumphalism) provoked Realist criticism of liberal idealism. Zimmern's approach, for example, was wide open to E. H. Carr's charge that it amounted to an unself-conscious avowal of Enlightenment grand theory, in that it blinded "idealist" thinkers to the fact that the "welfare states" were themselves part of the "power state" matrix. The appeal for a (universalized) consciousness of an international community based on the rule of law was, in this context, no more than the polemic of the "satisfied" allied powers of 1919 concerned to further strengthen a set of power relationships that advantaged them.[30]

Carr's critique of the neo-Kantians was designed primarily to establish the credentials of his own analysis of the actual reality of the interwar period, and I will turn to this issue in a moment. The more immediate point of the preceding discussion was to illustrate how, from its disciplinary beginnings, the International Relations discursive Tradition has been framed in modernist terms. The task now is to illustrate the specific continuity between this Tradition, its disciplinary beginnings in the idealism of the neo-Kantian phase, and the fully blown positivist-Realist phase that superseded it. This continuity theme might become more evident in the discussion to follow, which introduces the contribution of a major Traditionalist scholar, E. H. Carr, and the first (scientific) Realist "great text," *The Twenty Years Crisis*.[31]

The Making of a Discipline (II): Toward a Realist Science of International Relations

Perhaps more than any other Realist scholar, Carr, in *The Twenty Years Crisis,* confronted head-on some of the philosophical issues that connect International Relations to the broader narrative of Western philosophy. In so doing, the first "great text" of the Realist-positivist discipline resonated with a major modernist tension—between Anglo-American positivism (i.e., as in British historiography) and themes drawn from the hermeneutic tradition (e.g., Mannheim's Verstehen approach).[32] This tension was obvious enough from the beginning of *The Twenty Years Crisis,* when Carr made it clear that he sought to build upon the "science of international politics," which is in its "infancy."[33] Carr's (positivist) building-block approach was represented, however, in terms of a theory of the state set in dialectical terms. Consequently, in promoting the idea that the nature of the state and political reality in general are constructed upon the "contradictory" nature of the human actor (as both egoist individual and sociable communicator), Carr contended that "the [political] State is built up of these two conflicting aspects . . . [therefore] utopia and reality, the individual and the institution, morality and power, are from the outset inexorably linked."[34]

An adequate Realism, on this basis, must be understood as the sum of a complex dialectical interaction involving the *inexorably* linked behavior of creative individuals within a broad sociocultural context (i.e., as in a sociology-of-knowledge approach). Ultimately, however, this valuable insight was effectively neglected, with the initial dialectical format rapidly transformed into a one-sided positivist approach to knowledge and society. In *The Twenty Years Crisis,* thus, the potential for genuinely open-ended theoretical dialogue at the heart of Realist scholarship is quickly stifled, with the introduction of a series of hard-and-fast categorical distinctions set in logocentric terms. Consequently, the nature of political reality (as opposed to the "idealism" of the interwar years) is represented not in terms of inexorable links between subjects and objects, theory and practice, but rather in terms of the absolute *distinction* between "an inclination to deduce what should be from what was and what is [and] an inclination to ignore what was and what is in contemplation of what should be."[35]

Having introduced this (positivist) is/ought dichotomy, Carr then proposes that it "determines opposite attitudes towards every political problem."[36] Inevitably, then, *The Twenty Years Crisis* there appears a dazzling variety of dichotomies and dualized categories of analysis that since have afforded Realist scholars a theoretical shorthand with which to identify the "is" from the "ought" in every facet of their inquiry. In the logocentric fashion that was later to take on epidemic proportions within Realist scholarship, Carr thus shifted from an original position, emphasizing the complex dialectic of subject and object, to a power politics Realism that insisted on the factual *independence* of some "inexorably linked" aspects of existence over others. Indeed, for Carr (as it was for Weber, Popper, and Morgenthau in similar circumstances), Realist analysis was ultimately dependent for its explanation of the world upon the positivist detachment and privileging of fact *over* value, is *over* ought, and object *over* subject.

This becomes more evidently the case in *The Twenty Years Crisis* when Carr turns to the issue of Realist methodology. Here he rejects idealist/utopian attempts to transform "wish" and "need" into reality, in favor of a rigorous concentration on "the observation and collection of facts."[37] This theme is developed in explaining the theoretical bankruptcy of an idealism, identified by "its inability to provide any absolute and disinterested standard for the conduct of international affairs."[38] Carr's lurch into positivism can be gleaned also from his discussion of one of the central theoretical issues in modernity—the question of the relationship between the natural and the social sciences. On this issue, Carr's analysis (like that of Realists and neo-Realists later) promotes a crude unity-of-science thesis. Thus, in precisely the mode that Keohane was to follow half a century later,[39] Carr sought to distinguish the "natural" from the "political" sciences on the basis that the latter was dominated by the theoretical purpose and interests of the analyst (i.e., the "ought" factor) while the former, "because of the nature of the object of study," defied the corrupting influences of such analysis. Accordingly, in the study of the physical sciences,

> purpose is in the strict sense irrelevant to the investigation and separable from it. . . . [The physical scientist's] conclusions can be nothing more than a true report on facts. It cannot help to make the facts other than they are: *for the facts exist independently of what anyone thinks about them* [emphasis added].[40]

The major implication of this crude inductivist approach is that as part of the positivist notion of the scientific model it now became the basis upon which a Realist identity and analytical purpose was framed.

For E. H. Carr, accordingly, the superiority of a Realist approach was centered on its capacity to overcome (historical, cultural, theoretical/interpretivist) purpose in favor of (objective) factual analysis, the kind associated with the "natural" sciences. Carr proposed, consequently, that while in its early stages the science of International Relations suffered from idealist theorizing:

> Realism in its mature stage places its emphasis on the acceptance of facts and on the analysis of their causes and consequences. It tends to depreciate the role of purpose [value-based theory] and to maintain, explicitly or implicitly that the *function of thinking is to study a sequence of events which it is powerless to influence or alter* [emphasis added]. [Moreover] realism tends to emphasise the irresistible character of existing tendencies and to insist that the highest wisdom lies in accepting and adapting oneself to these forces and these tendencies.[41]

I referred to this theme in Chapter 1 as representative of a powerful and dangerously unself-conscious perspective in International Relations, which allows the intellectual and policy sectors to abrogate responsibility for their analysis and decisions.[42] The point, at this juncture, is that one does not need to reject Carr's critique of the neo-Kantians to recognize the paradoxical and inadequate nature of his own position, with its equally one-sided positivist determinism, which acknowledges a sphere of reality "out there," independent of the function of thinking, which the observing subject is "powerless to influence or alter."

In this way, E. H. Carr's "great text" promoted a positivist logic that David Hume, in the eighteenth century, had shown to be an entirely inadequate basis on which to understand or explain the reality of human existence. And yet, fifty years after Carr's contribution to the discipline, Realist scholars of both the British and U.S. schools continue to objectify the "irresistible" character of existing (anarchical) tendencies, while "wisdom" continues to be most associated with those who detach themselves from the theoretical process and merely adapt themselves to the external givens of an independently existing reality.

Lest my position on Carr's contribution be misunderstood, one further comment is necessary on it. It is that for all the crudity associated with its subsequent representation, there is much that is incisive and valuable in *The Twenty Years Crisis.* This is not just a matter of the more sober and cautious passages to be found there on the nature of Realism but of the more immediate analysis of the interwar period contained within its pages. Carr was, in this sense, correct to attack the one-sidedness of the neo-Kantians and their blindness to the (nonprogressivist) forces at work right at the heart of their progressivist "history." He was correct, also, to emphasize the dangers of and potential for irrationality in the neo-Kantian rational universe and to warn of the dangers of power politics behavior among European states still, in one way or another, living in the shadows of the most destructive war ever recorded. I cannot imagine any critical scholar in the 1990s who would not acknowledge Carr's insight on these issues.

The problem, however, is that those who have followed Carr in the pursuit of Realist knowledge have never seriously confronted his (or their own) one-sidedness, intolerance, and analytical silence. The result is that another potentially critical space in International Relations has been ignored, in favor of a universalist, uncritical, and dangerous "catechism." This has been the case even in Realism's more incisive moments in, for example, the Traditionalist Realism of (mainly) British scholarship. This is not to ignore the claim made by British Traditionalists that theirs is a fundamentally distinct perspective, which overcomes the positivist crudity of an "Americanized" discipline. It is to acknowledge that there are, indeed, differences of style, tone, and emphasis (e.g., international society) and that British scholarship has, on occasions, offered more sensitive insights on questions generally dismissed as "philosophical" by those at the hard edge of the behavioralist revolution. At the fundamental discursive level, however, there is no great difference between the British (and Anglophile) positions and the psuedoscientific approach of American Realism.[43]

My suggestion, rather, is that this notion of difference is another site at which the lack of serious attention to philosophical issues is evident, to the extent that the British, for all their sensitivities, have never seriously contemplated the impact upon their thinking of questions of essentialism and universalism and the logocentric structure of their philosophy in general. Accordingly, for all the professed "difference" of a Wight or a Bull, there is still the rather crude resort to the world "out there" and to essentialized, ahistorical notions of historical recurrence and repetition.

Stephen George offers a clue as to how and why this is so, with his proposal that, for British Traditionalists, "the only legitimate way to study international relations is the examination of concrete historical situations," these studies to be carried out "according to essentially subjective and intuitive procedures."[44] The paradox of this position is that it represents, for its advocates, an "antitheoretical" perspective that merely describes the world the way it "is." It is consequently an unself-conscious body of scholarship "committed to the empiricist belief that the task of the historian is to tell the story of what really happened without imposing anything of himself on the narrative."[45] The exemplar position in this regard was surely that of Martin Wight, whose unself-consciousness led to promulgations about the "recalcitrance" of International Relations to be theorized about, from a (theoretical) perspective rooted in positivist presuppositions about the distinction between the scholar (subject) and an anarchical world (of recurrence and repetition) existing objectively "out there."[46] Invoking the Traditional caricatured monologue, Wight proposed that this essential historical pattern might be understood via the textual interactions of three groupings, or categories of thinkers, within the Western "great texts"—the Machiavellians (i.e., Realists), the Grotians (i.e., rationalists), and the Kantians (i.e., revolutionaries).[47]

Whatever Wight meant to illustrate by his famous trichotomy, it is difficult to understand how "difference" can be seriously claimed for it, when all he did was to merely replicate the simplistic Realist/idealist dichotomy and then locate another universalized category in its center. The "Grotian" category might have afforded a mellower tone to power-politics Realism, but it did nothing to confront the problem of positivist dichotomy associated with behavioralist Realism. Nor did it overcome the essentialism and universalizing tendencies of positivist Realism in general. Indeed, as Wight's protégé, Hedley Bull, admitted, Wight's exemplary traditionalism was predicated on the assumption that there was a "rhythm or pattern in the history of ideas which is *there* [emphasis added], waiting to be uncovered."[48]

This did not lead Bull, or Traditionalists in general, to a critical reappraisal of a scholar who personified the "alternative" to (North) American Realism. It resulted, instead, in the impotent posturing of the second "great debate" and the continuation of a positivist bias across the Realist spectrum. In Bull's case it led to an influential and often incisive contribution to the International Relations debate that was, nevertheless, limited by Traditionalist unself-consciousness on the "theory" question. Accordingly, while seeking more sensitive answers to central Realist problems (e.g., of order and anarchy), Bull's ontological commitments saw his *questions* framed in such a way that his analytical efforts were severely undermined. Thus, in the process of providing an alternative to the explicit positivist Realism of his counterparts in the United States, Bull was drawn to the conclusion that anarchy was "the central fact of international life" and, most important, that it was the "*starting point* [emphasis added] of theorising" about International Relations.[49] This notion of an anarchical realm, beyond theorizing, the point at which theorizing "starts," is a typical example of the positivist ontological commitment at work, even when it is not acknowledged as such.

Another such example is the universalism inherent in Bull's work, which saw "time and change [as a] troublesome irrelevance."[50] Developing this theme, John Fitzpatrick has noted that, for all its (rather embroidered) historical erudition, the work of Bull and Wight is a "partisan" story that seeks to universalize a particular image of the European state system and to identify the perspectives of International Relations per se, "with the perspectives of a great power elite."[51] In this regard, the major icons of the British discipline "remained imprisoned in the restricted categories" of Wight's Eurocentric and elitist model, to the extent that the only analytical perspectives available to them were those centered on an enduring dichotomy, between the "great powers and the rest."[52] I have explained elsewhere the more direct philosophical influences upon Bull that undermined his ability to go beyond the positivist bias in his work.[53] I have argued, in this context, that if a positive critical attitude is taken to Bull's scholarship, it can pay analytical dividends for Traditionalist scholars. Too often, however, his rather insubstantial contribution to the second "great debate" has been uncritically celebrated, allowing Traditionalist scholarship an illusory "victory" and, once again, closing a potential space for critical reflection. The point is that if Bull's supporters had been a little less reverential of his argument in "International Theory: The Case for the Classical Approach" (1966), they might have noted—title notwithstanding—that Bull did not argue the case *for* the classical (Traditional) approach at all but elegantly reiterated a number of existing (classical) prejudices against positivist scienticism.[54]

Paradoxes notwithstanding, this missed the point, effectively made by John Vasquez in the 1980s, that whatever else the second "great debate" signified, it was not about a fundamental paradigm shift in International Relations but merely a (scientific) reformulation of Traditionalist certainties in the golden age of behavioralist thought.[55] More generally, as R. B. J. Walker proposes, the dispute between the British and American schools represented a low point in the discipline's development, which in an orgy of unself-consciousness saw a

> version of a more or less decrepit [British] empiricism . . . primarily inductive and idiosyncratic in orientation [pitted against] a predominantly American version of the same empiricist tradition . . . which favoured a more deductive approach and which drew upon pragmatism and logical positivism.[56]

It is toward this issue that I want to turn now, in developing further the disciplinary story of the International Relations Tradition, which by the late 1950s was increasingly captured by power politics Realism and a harder-edged modernism expressed in a more explicitly "scientific" approach to theory and research.

The Discipline Consolidated: The Cold War and the Construction of a Positivist-Realist International Relations

If the disciplinary seeds of positivist Realism were sown in the responses to the dangers of the interwar years, it was in the shadows of World War II, and more directly in the glare of the Cold War between the nuclear superpowers, that it became an integral defining feature of International Relations. In this context, thus, I want to say something about the way the Cold War has been represented in the International Relations discipline. It is, I argue, a perfect example of a modernist orthodox consensus at work, in that both orthodox *and* alternatives approaches are framed in fundamentally the same way, thus disallowing the need for either side in the dispute, or those looking on in the broader community, to seriously question the *foundations* of their discourse.

The Cold War in International Relations is most commonly represented as a clash between Realist and revisionist interpretations of the facts.[57] The Realist case, it is acknowledged, is not a homogeneous one as such. Instead, two major variants on the Realist theme are accorded significance. The first (the official U.S./Western approach) suggests that the Cold War was an inevitable outcome of the post–World War II power structure, in which the victorious democratic powers were confronted by the Soviet Union—an erstwhile ally—now ideologically committed to the destruction of liberal-capitalist principles and, ultimately, to world domination. The second Realist variant also blames the Soviet Union for the Cold War. This perspective, however, brings a slightly different emphasis to the issue, maintaining that it was not so much the ideological commitment to Marxism-Leninism that was driving the Soviets toward conflict with the Western powers but the expansionist desires inherent to great powers in the state system. This desire, according to influential Realists such as Morgenthau and Kennan, was particularly strong within Russian history and national character. And, ideologies aside, faced with the unparalleled strategic opportunities in 1945, Stalin was concerned above all to fulfill the historical/strategic ambitions of the czars.[58]

Two revisionist variants are also evident. One, associated with scholars such as William Appleman Williams, suggests that it was, if anything, U.S. desire and opportunism that was at the core of Cold War tensions, rather than Soviet expansionism. From this perspective, it was a corporate-elite-driven U.S. foreign policy, seeking worldwide market penetration, that was the keystone to Cold War conflict. The problem for U.S. ambition, of course, was the postwar existence of another superpower, disinclined to allow capitalist penetration, particularly in its newly acquired sphere of influence.[59] The second revisionist perspective had similar characteristics, but a harder, Marxian-based critical edge. Here, the Cold War is understood as part of broader developments in a worldwide class struggle, with the United States seeking, above all, to eradicate any challenge to its power from socialist states.[60]

For all their obvious differences, however, the Realists and their opponents all assumed into their analysis of the Cold War a single, external world of fact "out there," against which the reality of postwar International Relations must be understood. Both sides, in other words, were locked into positivist framing regimes, *which limited the kinds of questions they could ask* and allowed them to exclude from their analysis important self-reflective themes. Within Realist accounts this was clear enough as Soviet actions were read unambiguously as a threat to the national security of the United States.[61] For the revisionists, on the other hand, the interests of the U.S. corporate sector flowed directly and unproblematically into anti-Soviet policy.[62] Marxists meanwhile framed the whole thing as part of an objectively unfolding class struggle, at the global level.

There is, undoubtedly, valuable insight associated with all of these perspectives. The problem for the discipline of International Relations and for a generation forced to live within the confines of Cold War theory and practice is that this insight was projected in terms that saw it reduced to its most basic (ontological/epistemological) common denominator. Excluded from the Cold War debate, consequently, in both academic and more popular spheres were other insights that, while they might not have prevented conflict per se, might have alleviated its effects long before Gorbachev and his followers woke up from their particular experience of the Enlightenment dream-cum-nightmare.

The question of what was excluded from this Cold War debate has excited the interest of critical social theorists in recent times, particularly discourse scholars.[63] Of significance, from this perspective, is the process by which the Soviet "threat" became the central plank in U.S. foreign policy, after 1946, *not* because of any radical change in Soviet behavior (i.e., the external facts) but because "policy makers had found a new language, or script, for interpreting the meaning of Soviet behavior."[64] Before 1946, there was a great deal of ambivalence within the United States about the nature of the Soviet Union and an ambiguity about its future direction and strategic ambitions. As long as this ambivalence and ambiguity was acknowledged, negotiations were regarded as reasonable and necessary.[65]

After 1946, however, this ambiguity dissipated, to be replaced by the kind of foundational certainty that underlined the rise of positivist Realism in intellectual and policy circles and the often hysterical anticommunism throughout the United States. At this point, with ambiguity gone, genuine attempts at understanding and negotiation were no longer considered reasonable or necessary, particularly for a nation possessing the ultimate in modern technological achievement—the atomic bomb. At the forefront of the resultant "threat" scenario that followed was George Kennan's (initial) reading of Soviet character and intent, articulated in secret correspondence with the Truman administration.[66]

The significance of this particular example of Cold War closure was that it had little to do with any "observation" of Soviet expansionary behavior in the postwar period because U.S. intelligence in general had acknowledged that there was little evidence of either capacity or intent in this regard.[67] Rather, the foundation of Kennan's analysis was his positivist understanding of "history," especially the nature of Russian and Soviet history. Accordingly, sweeping interpretive ambiguity aside, the Soviet future was analyzed as determined both by the Soviet "past" and, implicitly, by relations between traditional and modern societies in general.

The Russians/Soviets were, on this basis, a "neurotic" people, with an "instinctive sense of insecurity" that, in the postwar era, had become heightened by their interaction with "the more competent, more powerful . . . economically advanced West."[68] Such a power could not be rationally dealt with because it was "*impervious to the logic of reason [and] seemingly inaccessible to considerations of reality* [emphasis added]."[69] On this basis, all the Russians/Soviets understood was military force—that is, power politics. With this "historical" analysis established, the Cold War scenario had its (external) factual foundation. And from this *foundation* all other Cold War logic flowed. The Soviet desire to expand was, in this discursive context, both predictable and a source of great danger, to the West in general and the United States in particular. This was because the modern attempt to alleviate Russian "neurosis" was now combined with a Marxist ideology, which preached world domination and the destruction of capitalist democracy.

Following Kennan's report, a major change in attitude occurred in policymaking circles. Now U.S. foreign policy analysts had a way of reading the Soviet Union that accorded them the *certainty* they craved. Now, backed by the wisdom of the expert, they had a language and a logic that allowed them to synthesize the ambiguity, give identity to the fragmentation, and transform mere interpretations into fact. Consequently, even while intelligence reports continued to indicate that the Soviets were not engaged in any threatening activities (or at the least that these activities could be understood in different ways), U.S. officials began the process of constructing the self-enclosed, self-affirming reality that *became* the Cold War for Western societies and for International Relations.[70]

Truman's top-ranking civilian and military advisers now lost their sense of uncertainty and a consensus emerged about the Soviets and the world "out there." The subsequent reality, complete with historical and empirical evidence, was that the Soviets

> believe that war with the United States . . . is inevitable. [The Soviets] . . . are increasing their military power . . . and are seeking to weaken and subvert their potential opponents. . . . The language of power politics is the only language which [the Soviets] understand. . . . The main deterrence to Soviet attack is the United States. . . . The United States . . . should entertain no proposal for disarmament . . . as long as the possibility of Soviet aggression exists. . . . The United States should support and assist all democratic countries which are in any way menaced or endangered by the Soviet Union.[71]

Two points require reiteration before moving on. First, I am not here seeking to dismiss as irrelevant or invalid (or "unreal") those conventional accounts of the Cold War debate outlined earlier. What I seek to do is illustrate that there were other ways of understanding the reality of the Cold War that were not encompassed within the orthodox discourse, that (just as in the Gulf and Bosnia) there were other options available *in practice* to the policymakers, at the time, which were excluded from serious consideration or marginalized by the particular discourse that framed reality for them. In the Cold War context, in other words, it was the *discursively produced reality* that the policymakers and intellectual sectors responded to, not some external world "out there" that imposed its real knowledge upon them. And while anyone aware of the literature of the period will know of Kennan's more nuanced and empathic observations in later times, Nathanson's overall point on his early contribution remains valid. It is that Kennan's "Long Telegram" of February 1946 created an interpretive straitjacket from which neither Western nor Soviet analysts could escape for forty years.

The implications of this closure were evident enough in the 1950s and 1960s, as positive assumptions and attitudes became increasingly dominant in International Relations. In this period the inherent conservatism of the power politics approach was complemented by behavioralist orientations, in the struggle with the Soviet Other. At the center of the International Relations discipline, in the United States, the result was a static framing regime articulated for the most part in behavioralist terms, which began to speak ever more confidently of its knowledge of global reality.

I want now to begin to address this issue and that period between the onset of the Cold War and (roughly) the war in Vietnam, when the modernist legacy, via a full-blown positivist Realism, framed International Relations in terms of the dichotomy between a unified, positive Western identity and the dangers of an anarchical world "out there"—the realm of the Soviet Other. Initially, at least, I will address this issue in the way that the discipline usually does when it speaks of its development—via the scholarship of its first disciplinary "heroic figure," Hans Morgenthau, particularly in *Politics Among Nations.* My treatment of Morgenthau's work, however, is concerned to open up the debate rather than close it off.

Accordingly, *Politics Among Nations* will be spoken of in terms that Morgenthau refused to speak of it—that is, in terms of Max Weber's major influence upon its basic concepts and conclusions.

Notes

1. Hoffmann, "An American Social Science."

2. The great texts were Carr's *The Twenty Years Crisis* and Morgenthau's *Politics Among Nations.*

3. On the great men/great text tendency, see Walker, "*The Prince* and 'The Pauper'"; Lijphart,"The Structure of the Theoretical Revolution in International Relations"; and George, "The Reconciliation of the 'Classical' and the 'Scientific' Approaches to International Relations."

4. Banks, "The Evolution of International Relations Theory," p. 5.

5. For examples of the monologue, see Hinsley, *Power and the Pursuit of Peace;* Clarke, *Reform and Resistance in the International Order;* Bull, "The Theory of International Politics, 1919–1969"; Holsti, *The Dividing Discipline,* chap. 2; Keohane, "Realism, Neorealism and the Study of World Politics"; and Gilpin, *War and Change in World Politics.*

6. Carr, *Twenty Years Crisis,* p. 6.

7. Thucydides, as cited in Lijphart, "The Structure of the Theoretical Revolution," p. 44. In Chapter 8 the place of Thucydides in this narrative will be problematized via a range of alternative readings of his "essential" Realist position.

8. The Augustinian influence upon Realism has been very significant, albeit implicitly so in many cases. Of the more explicit representations of a Christian pessimism, see Niebuhr, *Christian Realism and Political Problems;* and there are explicit Augustinian themes in Morgenthau's *Politics Among Nations,* particularly in its opening pages, with its perspectives on the unchanging egoistic power lust of "human nature." Waltz had some interesting things to say about the Christian reductionism of Niebuhr and Morgenthau in *Man, the State and War;* this is an issue returned to in Chapter 5. An Anglicized Augustinianism is evident also within the British Realist community, primarily via scholars such as Herbert Butterfield and Martin Wight; on Butterfield see his *Christianity, Diplomacy and War;* on Wight, see his *Power Politics.* On the more specific connection between Christianity and rational-scientific–based approaches such as positivism, see Jacob, *The Cultural Meaning of the Scientific Revolution,* chap. 4; Kolakowski, *Positivist Philosophy,* has some interesting comments on the way that Christianity made its peace with positivism.

9. The problematic nature of this particular piece of essentialism will be illustrated in Chapter 8.

10. Cited in Lijphart, "The Structure of the Theoretical Revolution," p. 44.

11. Cited in ibid. The notion of Rousseau as a Realist is perhaps most famously represented in Waltz, *Man, the State and War;* see also Clarke, *Reform and Resistance in the International Order,* where Rousseau is represented as the "pessimistic" side of a Realist/idealist dualism (with Kant on the other side).

12. I am sensitive here to the problems of providing checklists such as this, but these themes are taken from a spectrum of sources and discursive positions, including Keohane, "Theory of World Politics"; Vasquez, *Power Politics,* chap. 2; Rosenberg, "What's the Matter with Realism?"; and Banks, "The Evolution of International Relations Theory."

13. Ibid., p. 5.

14. Morgenthau, *Politics Among Nations,* p. 22. This is not the only way that the concept has been used. Indeed, it has had a variety of meanings over the years, but Morgenthau's "mechanical" one has been evident throughout Realist literature, particularly in the United States. See Vasquez, *Power Politics,* on this; and for a general discussion of the balance-of-power theme in Realism, see Claude, *Power and International Relations;* Wight, "The Balance of Power," in *Diplomatic Investigations;* and the special issue on the balance of power in *Review of International Studies* (1989).

15. Cox, "The Role of Political Philosophy in the Theory of International Relations," p. 267.

16. Ibid., p. 268.

17. Ibid.

18. See Hinsley, *Power and the Pursuit of Peace.*

19. Bull, "The Theory of International Politics, 1919–1969," pp. 35–36.

20. See Vasquez, *Power Politics,* chap. 2; Lijphart, "The Structure of the Theoretical Revolution"; Olson and Onuf, "The Growth of a Discipline: Reviewed"; and Banks, "The Evolution of International Relations Theory."

21. The reference here is to the Kant of *Perpetual Peace;* the Kant generally known to International Relations specialists. See Clarke, *Reform and Resistance in the International Order.*

22. Banks, "The Evolution of International Relations Theory," p. 8.

23. This was the view of C. K. Webster, cited in Olsen and Onuf, "The Growth of a Discipline: Reviewed," p. 6.

24. Cited in ibid., p. 52.

25. Zimmern, *The League of Nations and the Rule of Law, 1918–1935.* This is the view of Morgenthau and Thompson, eds., in *Principles and Problems of International Politics,* p. 18.

26. See Markwell, "Sir Alfred Zimmern Revisited," p. 283.

27. Ibid., p. 288.

28. Ibid., p. 289. There were in this context no fundamental conflicts between the world's peoples, but cooperation depended upon finding ways of ameliorating the struggle for scarce political and economic resources that characterized a modern state system and had resulted in the collision of the major competing actors in 1914.

29. Markwell, "Sir Alfred Zimmern Revisited," p. 286.

30. See Carr, *Twenty Years Crisis,* pt. 2.

31. On Carr's significance to Realism in this regard, see Vasquez, *Power Politics,* chap. 2; and from another angle, Evans, "Some Problems with a History of Thought in International Relations."

32. Carr's debt to Mannheim has been hinted at over the years. More work in this area might prove fruitful in explaining Carr's theoretical and historiographical approach. On Mannheim's Verstehen approach and its limitations, see Hekman, *Hermeneutics and the Sociology of Knowledge;* and on the British historiographical tradition, see Steadman-Jones, "History: The Poverty of Empiricism."

33. Carr, *Twenty Years Crisis,* p. 1.

34. Ibid., pp. 95–96.

35. Ibid., p. 11.

36. Ibid.

37. Ibid., p. 10.

38. Ibid., p. 88.

39. Keohane, "Realism, Neorealism and the Study of World Politics."

40. Carr, *Twenty Years Crisis,* p. 3.

41. Ibid., p. 10.

42. See Chapter 1, pp. 25–26.

43. For other perspectives that argue similar positions, see Vasquez, *The Power of Power Politics;* Frost, *Towards a Normative Theory of International Relations;* Walker, "*The Prince* and the 'Pauper'"; Fitzpatrick, "The Anglo-American School of International Relations"; and Berki, *On Political Realism.*

44. George, "The Reconciliation of the Classical and Scientific Approaches to International Relations."

45. Ibid., p. 34. On the broader notion of an "English School," see Jones, "The English School of International Relations."

46. See Wight, "Why Is There No International Theory?"

47. Ibid., p. 33.

48. See Bull, "Martin Wight and the Theory of International Relations," p. 111.

49. See Bull, "Society and Anarchy in International Relations," p. 35.

50. Jones, "The English School," p. 10.

51. Fitzpatrick, "The Anglo-American School of International Relations," p. 47. This is a theme taken up also by David Boucher, who has maintained that Wight's general understanding of the order issue in Western philosophy represents a highly problematic and rather simplistic reading of a complex literature. See Boucher, "The Character of the History of International Relations and the Case of Edmund Burke."

52. Fitzpatrick, "The Anglo-American School of International Relations," p. 46. On some of the other silences and omissions in Bull's thinking, see Suganami, "Reflections on the Domestic Analogy"; and Jones, "The English School."

53. George, "Some Thoughts on the 'Givenness' of Everyday Life in Australian International Relations" and "International Relations and the Positivist/Empiricist Theory of Knowledge."

54. Bull, "International Theory."

55. Vasquez, *The Power of Power Politics,* chap. 2.

56. Walker, *Political Theory and the Transformation of World Politics,* p. 29.

57. For a good discussion of this issue, see Larson, *Origins of Containment.* For another angle, see also Richardson, "Cold War Revisionism: A Critique."

58. Larson, *Origins of Containment,* pp. 7–9.

59. Ibid., pp. 10–13. On Williams, see his *Tragedy of American Diplomacy.*

60. Larson, *Origins of Containment,* pp. 11–13. See Kolko and Kolko, *The Limits of Power,* p. 109.

61. Nathanson, "The Social Construction of the Soviet Threat."

62. Ibid., p. 444.

63. See Nathanson, "The Social Construction of the Soviet Threat"; and Campbell, *Security and Identity in United States Foreign Policy.* Nathanson's work in particular draws extensively on Yergin's *Shattered Peace.*

64. Nathanson, "The Social Construction of the Soviet Threat," p. 445.

65. Ibid., p. 454.

66. This was Kennan's (in)famous "Long Telegram," which remained classified information until 1971.

67. Nathanson, "The Social Construction of the Soviet Threat," p. 459.

68. Ibid., p. 455.

69. From Kennan's "Long Telegram," cited in ibid., p. 456.

70. Ibid., pp. 445–462.

71. This is taken from a memo to the president in September 1946, as cited in ibid., p. 460.

4

The Positivist-Realist Phase: Morgenthau, Behavioralism, and the Quest for Certainty

The direct connection between Weber and Morgenthau has been rarely acknowledged by International Relations specialists. Weber's influence, nevertheless, is highly significant in an International Relations context.[1] In the early years of the Cold War this was particularly the case in regard to Morgenthau's fundamentally Weberian defense of Realism. Indeed, as Regis Factor and Stephen Turner have illustrated, Morgenthau's famous propositions concerning the difference between utopianism and Realism were derived directly from Weber. Also derived from Weber was Morgenthau's adapted notion of interests, which become a crucial theme in Realist thinking, allowing the analyst of International Relations to speak in "objective" terms about the reality of the international arena (the struggle for power defined as interests) while accounting for value-laden subjectivity.[2]

In general terms Weber gave to Morgenthau (and to a whole generation of Traditionalist-Realists) a Verstehen-based synthesis that appeared to overcome the moralism of the liberals, the progressivism of the idealists, and the crude inductivism associated with conventional scientific approaches. The resultant Weber-Morgenthau perspective was evident at two levels of Cold War theory as practice. First, at the intellectual level, it assisted in the transference of behavioralist attitudes and methodological principles to International Relations, in allowing Realists to maintain the quest for scientific analysis while (ostensibly) overcoming the problems of earlier, inductivist-based Traditionalism. And Popper's critical rationalism now intersected nicely with the power politics images of Weber and Morgenthau, with the Weberian format allowing for the possibility of "scientific" evaluation of the conflict of value-laden interests while Popperian falsificationism indicated precisely how this was to be done.

Second, Morgenthau's modified Weberianism was significant during the Cold War because of the enhanced legitimacy it afforded Realism in U.S. foreign policy circles. With its emphasis on the means/ends logic of international life and its Traditional focus on diplomatic statecraft, it signified for the policy planner and practitioner a (deceptively) simple and flattering account of who and what was fundamental to contemporary power politics existence.

These themes will be explored further in this chapter, which uses the Weber-Morgenthau connection as a point of discursive entry into a broader discussion of International Relations, in its most explicitly modernist phase. Following an initial inquiry into Morgenthau's textual legacy to the postwar discipline, some of its implications will be considered in a brief discussion of Modernization Theory, in its attempt to impose the certainties of the Western metanarrative upon the Third World. Attention will then be focused on the major mainstream articulation of Realism in the 1960s—that associated with security and strategic discourse.

Politics Among Nations: The Verstehen Dimension

The Verstehen tensions in Morgenthau's *Politics Among Nations* are, if anything, even more apparent than in Carr's earlier scientific "great text," *The Twenty Years Crisis.* Accordingly, within the opening pages of *Politics Among Nations,* Morgenthau is both classical hermeneuticist and hard-nosed positivist. In the former mode he contributed to Realism perhaps the most famous hermeneutic statement in the history of the discipline, in emphasizing that Realists must, above all,

> retrace and anticipate as it were the steps the statesman—past, present and future—has taken or will take on the political scene. We [must] look over his shoulder when he writes his dispatches: we must listen in on his conversations with other statesmen; we [must] read and anticipate his very thoughts.[3]

In this mode, Morgenthau implies that the text analogue—the world of statesmen—is the primary social and linguistic practice of power politics Realism. An adequate Realism must, on this basis, seek to understand and explain the norms, rules, ideologies, and competing interests of diplomatic statecraft. Realist analysts must attempt to get "inside" the world of the diplomat, the foreign policy maker, the strategist, and the power broker. Realism is validated, in this sense, when it has meaning for the diplomat statesman, the human agent of power defined as interest. Realist scholarship, following these broad hermeneutic principles, must do more than simply reaffirm the anarchy of the system or make more rigorous and systematic the evidence of an endemic struggle for power and influence. It is interested, rather, in a more profound kind of historical and cultural understanding of the relationship between states, emphasizing modes of (diplomatic) communication between them.

Such a task, one might argue, could be carried out only with the total involvement of the creative (and self-critical) analyst. But for Morgenthau, seeking the authority of the scientific method for the theory (and political practice) of International Relations, the value-laden scholar is magically detached from the analytical equation, via a Weberian-derived (means/ends) conjuring trick, which forty years later remains part of the Realist repertoire as expressed in neo-Realist perspectives. This Weberian influence is evident in Morgenthau's proposition that, to understand the world realistically and solve its problems, we must

> put ourselves in the position of a statesman who must meet a certain problem of foreign policy under certain circumstances and we ask ourselves what the rational alternatives are from which a statesman may choose . . . and which of these rational alternatives this particular statesman, acting under these circumstances, is likely to choose. *It is the testing of this rational hypothesis against the actual facts and their consequences that gives meaning to the facts of international politics and makes a theory of politics possible* [emphasis added].[4]

This orientation becomes more explicit in *Politics Among Nations* as Morgenthau insists that "[international] politics is governed by objective laws," the operation of which are "impervious to our preferences." In this context, consequently, the task of the Realist is to distinguish what is "true *objectively and rationally* [emphasis added] . . . and what is only a subjective judgement divorced from the facts as they are and informed by prejudice and wishful thinking."[5]

Now, even in a discipline not noted for its critical theoretical tendencies, it might be supposed that anomalies of this magnitude, within its exemplar text, would provoke serious intellectual debate. This has rarely been the case.[6] Instead, the foundationalist tendency in Morgenthau's thought has become integral to Realist perspectives per se. This is evident in relation to the debate over "theory" and the manner in which Realist theoretical statements must be judged or tested. On this issue Morgenthau insisted that Realism should meet both an empirical and a logical test. It should, he stressed, be "consistent with the facts and within itself." Consequently, the central question asked of any Realist analysis is "Do the facts as they actually are lend themselves to the interpretation the theory has put on them?" Moreover, and with the "empiricist metaphysic" looming large, Morgenthau warned that Realist theory "must be judged not by some preconceived abstract principle or concept unrelated to reality, but by its purpose: to bring order and meaning to a mass of phenomena which without it would remain disconnected and unintelligible."[7] Theory, in this sense, as it was in Weber's alternative to positivist logic, is simply a means to an pre-given end. Its purpose quite clearly is to (retrospectively) bring "order and meaning" to a (factual) "mass of phenomena" that in contingent and unique form *exist independent of the theorist.* As a result, and for all its interpretivist posturing, Morgenthau's Realism (like Carr's) is finally constructed upon a spectator theory of knowledge, which renders the subject a passive receiver of independently existing reality "out there." As such, it represents the primitive Realist understanding of reality outlined in Chapter 1.

The inadequacy of this approach has once again been no hindrance to its influence or popularity. Rather, Morgenthau's approach confirmed for the International Relations community the "realistic" response to the world "out there," thus closing off any potential openness in International Relations in favor of determinist rhetoric, reductionist method, and narrowed, Cold War focus. In this regard, the power of Morgenthau's *Politics Among Nations* was that it "provided a synthesis of what a generation had been trying to express."[8] And, while some were to reassess the more assertive elements of his approach, Realist scholars have continued to accord seminal status to Morgenthau and the positivist elements of his Cold War perspective.[9]

This was an an issue central to Stanley Hoffmann's famous article in 1977, which connected the development of a postwar International Relations discipline with the broader movement toward behavioralism in the United States.[10] Morgenthau here is, unequivocally, at the heart of scientific (positivist) Realism, primarily because in (re)invoking Carr's scientific ambitions, Morgenthau prompted an already-existing "national ideology" in the United States, set upon Enlightenment progressivist postulates.[11] Committed, at the policy level, to the crudest form of logocentrism (e.g., free world/closed ideology), the U.S. policy elite now turned increasingly to those willing to speak to the "Prince" in terms supportive of a Realist Cold War perspective and the American (scientific) way.

In this discursive context, the emerging discipline of International Relations began to speak more confidently of its (rational-scientific) knowledge and of the correct means/ends method by which the enduring Realist wisdom of Western history must be transposed to the world of nuclear weapons, deterrence, and the Third World. As part of the "can do" generation, International Relations scholars now became more explicitly connected to mainstream social theory, increasingly articulating their problem-solving perspectives at the Popperian intersection of neo-Kantianism and logical positivism. Concepts of progress and scientific method were now applied to International Relations with the kind of enthusiasm that, in the broader context, saw behavioralists attacking the (nonscientific) "metaphysics" of more traditional approaches.[12] More specifically, in the 1950s and 1960s, International Relations became committed to the "applied Enlightenment" view that

> all problems can be resolved, [and] that the way to resolve them is to apply the scientific method . . . and to combine empirical investigation,

> hypothesis formation and testing—and that resort to science will yield practical applications that will bring progress.[13]

Never was this amalgam of modernist characteristics more evident than in the literature that sought to solve the problems of the Third World by recourse to models of Western developmentalism and Modernization Theory.[14]

Modernization Theory: The Modernist Knowledge/Power Nexus Epitomized

The basic proposition of Modernization Theory in the 1960s was that modern Western industrial societies had effectively overcome most of the problems (poverty, unemployment, ideological struggle) that beset them in their "traditional" stages of development. Accordingly (and with Cold War containment themes firmly in mind), the time had come to apply Western politicoeconomic structures and rational-scientific techniques to the postcolonial societies of the Third World.

To this task Modernization scholarship brought a grand theory of development and a model of modernity concerned with a "process of change toward those types of social, economic and political systems that have developed in Western Europe and North America from the seventeenth century to the nineteenth and then have spread to other European countries."[15] Integral to this Modernization Theory was also the new rational choice orthodoxy in (neoclassical) economics, which, in Hoffmann's opinion, had already become a "dogma" in U.S. social theory circles deemed to "have met the expectations of the national ideology, and to *have become a science on the model of the exact ones* [emphasis added]."[16]

The unity-of-science theme is evident here again, of course. But another important discursive connection is signified also—between modern social theory and power politics Realism—in the form of the rational choice premise integral to Morgenthau's rational action model in *Politics Among Nations*. Consequently, at the textual core of power politics Realism is an image of (analogized) human behavior set within the conceptual boundaries of neoclassical economics and utilitarian logic. This connection is acknowledged by Robert Keohane, who considers that for Morgenthau "to say that governments act rationally . . . means that they have consistent, ordered preferences, and that they calculate the costs and benefits of all alternative policies in order to maximise their utility."[17] Keohane stresses, nevertheless, that Morgenthau was more subtle in his use of this rationality theme than it might appear, and that it was not meant to be "descriptively accurate" but rather represented, for Morgenthau, a "baseline," which could be "tested against the actual facts."[18] This indicates as much about Keohane's perspectives as it does Morgenthau's.

Keohane's updated rational choice format will receive attention in the next chapter. The point for now is that however subtle Morgenthau's thinking was on the rationality themes, for a generation of less subtle Realists the utilitarian formula *has* been understood as "descriptively accurate." Moreover, as Keohane's view illustrates, any subtlety associated with Realist thought stretches only as far as its positivist framework allows—that is, the attempt to test Morgenthau's rationality postulate "against the actual facts."

Once again, however, this limited framing regime has acted as something of an analytical magnet for those seeking quick-fix certainty in a complex world. Accordingly, this rational choice theme underlay the behavioralist certitude of prominent Modernization Theorists, such as David Apter, for whom the key to progress and modern development in the Third World was an "improvement in the conditions of choice and the selection of the most satisfactory mechanisms of choice."[19] Similarly, for Gabriel Almond the aim for scholars of development centered on the pursuit of "rational choice models of political growth."[20]

Some of the crudest, albeit most influential, work of this genre emanated from the new economics of growth, prescribed by figures such as W. W. Rostow in *The Stages of Economic Growth: A Non-Communist Manifesto.* This was a text resonant with modernist doctrines, which projected a "theory about economic growth, and a more general . . . theory of modern history as a whole."[21] The title of the work indicates its linear, progressivist tenor and, as an explicit alternative to Marxism, its Cold War orientations and disciplinary status. Rostow's modernist credentials were never more explicit than when developing his "stages" theme and propounding his theory of modern history "as a whole." Here, an essentialized history was invoked, as was the predictable logocentrism of the dominant modernist narrative. Thus, proposed Rostow,

> in terms of history . . . with the phrase "traditional society" we are grouping together the whole pre-Newtonian world: the dynasties in China; the civilisation of the Middle East and the Mediterranean; the world of medieval Europe. And to them we add the post-Newtonian societies which, for a time, remained untouched or unmoved by man's new capability for regularly manipulating his environment to his economic advantage.[22]

It is hard to imagine a more explicit celebration of Western modernity and its central sovereign figure, rational man (the user and controller of all things, natural and social), than this. Here is confirmation of Bacon's ubiquitous postulate about knowledge and power, represented as a doctrine of utilitarian "usefulness" and control, the very doctrine that continues to inform neo-Realist scholarship in the 1990s.[23] Also evident in Rostow's work is the other side of the Modernization coin, "the dark underside of the development process," which became increasingly evident as the knowledge of Modernization Theory became the power politics of Cold War political practice (e.g., as the legitimation for U.S. strategy in the Third World).[24] Integral to Modernization Theory, in this regard, was a narrow ethnocentrism and an ideological framework concerned with a "process of enforced changes, implemented from above by a secular state system, that strategically alters the social landscape and prepares the way for a capitalist, market oriented political system."[25]

Any "freedom to choose" in this Modernization Theory context was thus dependent upon, and determined by, a *particular kind* of social order, an order that in a Cold War context (Western order versus the anarchy of Soviet-inspired disorder) could be instigated and guaranteed only by adherence to the interests of the "West"—represented by U.S. foreign policy and Realist certitude. This was a theme already very evident in International Relations, well before its 1980s variation in the works of North American hegemonic theorists, explaining how and why the United States is *Bound to Lead*.[26] A more orthodox avowal of the order theme is to be found in the works of Samuel Huntington, who in reformulating some of the Modernization perspectives of the early 1960s, in less sanguine times, placed less emphasis on development as a linear, progressivist unfolding of freedom to choose and more on a minimalist Realism, in which social progress was dependent *explicitly* upon strong institutionalized order and the power of political and military elites.[27]

It might be argued, of course, that Modernization Theory, with its 1960s ethnocentricity, was itself a stage in the development of Western cultural awareness—a theoretical anachronism in an age of postcolonial innocence. After all, Rostow's theory of economic history was fairly swiftly exposed as both inadequate economics and crude ahistoricism. But to dismiss the Modernization debate in this way would be to miss an important point about it and its enduring significance for the more mainstream of International Relations literature in the 1980s and 1990s. The point, in short, is that many of the themes integral to the Modernization literature of the 1960s and 1970s—its ethnocentrism, its crude essentialist reading of history, its technorationalist bias, its positivism, and, more directly, its twin conceptual pillars of (Western capitalist) order and (individualist) choice—*continue* to be central to the way that the discipline, and its North American center in particular, has understood and legitimated its representation of global politics until the present. The order priority, for example, remains as part of the great (either/or) dichotomy throughout Realist literature (e.g., the order/anarchy theme from Bull to Waltz), while the order/choice theme remains at the heart of neo-Realist perspectives in the 1990s, which also continue to legitimate their Huntington-like advocacy of strong (hegemonic) power, via an essentialist reading of Western history and philosophy.[28]

Consequently, this discussion of the positivist-Realist phase of the

International Relations discipline now turns to that period which gave enhanced credibility to Modernization Theory and a more general projection of modernism within U.S. foreign policy. This is the period (approximately) between the early 1960s (and the enthusiasm of the "behavioralist revolution") and the early 1970s, when faith in rational-scientific Realism began to dissipate somewhat in the face of the debacle in Vietnam. More immediately, this is the period when, in Hoffmann's terms, the "first wave" of the scientific quest in International Relations gave way to a "second wave," which saw strategic and security studies scholars take up the scientific baton at the core of the Realist-led discipline.[29]

The "Second Wave" of Positivist Realism: Behavioralism and the Strategy/Security Discourse

During this "second wave" period, the discursive character of International Relations literature increasingly replicated the broader social theory debates. Consequently, behavioralist scholarship in International Relations (connecting Morgenthau via Weber and Machiavelli to Popper) did not challenge the fundamental assumptions of power politics Realism but sought instead (like neo-Realists two decades later) to make them more scientific.[30] Rhetorically, nevertheless, there was a new critical edge within the discipline as the behavioralist-inspired Realist community articulated its increasing antipathy toward Traditionalism. What the Traditionalists did not understand, insisted behavioralists, was that the inductivist empiricism of the (Traditionalist) past must give way to a more formal, systemic approach to theorizing based on Popper's falsificationist procedures.[31]

The influence of Popper is obvious enough in J. D. Singer's proclamation of the Traditional Realist approach (e.g., Carr, Bull, Wight) as inductivist and, therefore, a "prescientific" early stage of Realism.[32] Singer's proposition, consequently, was that while Traditionalist scholars had provided a great deal of "careful empiricism," this was not enough, because "these scholars have actually pinned down very little in the way of verified generalisations."[33] Thus, the scientific Realists of the behavioralist era sought to "pin down" the facts of International Relations. In particular, they sought to construct hypothesized models of interstate behavior that could be falsified against historical and contemporary fact. Important here were Morton Kaplan's *System and Process in International Politics,* which drew on a cognitive systems approach, and works by Karl Deutsch, which introduced communication theory and cybernetic approaches to the discipline.[34] Taken together, the contributions of Kaplan and Deutsch set the pattern for the behavioralist reformulation of power politics Realism during the 1960s, as International Relations turned toward its logical positivist roots in the attempt to more rigorously verify the central power politics premises of

Traditional Realism. This broadened the research scope of the discipline considerably, adding significant subfields to its power politics orthodoxy.

On the other hand, the substantive debates over global life were now increasingly reduced to the narrow logic and philosophical vocabulary of positivist Realism. The question of power, for example, was reduced to competing aspects of its Weberian reading. Was it, in this sense, "the same as capability, influence, coercion, force, or just another word for cause?"[35] Ultimately, power was represented as a national capability or resource, a representation designated as most applicable to precise explanation and predictive analysis. The works by the Sprouts in the 1950s and the Organskis in the 1960s exemplified the attempts to give operational verifiability to the power-as-capability notion.[36] Scholars such as Guetzkow, meanwhile, brought social psychology themes to bear on the issue, while Rosenau's "pre-theory" notions continued, not surprisingly, to gain influence.[37]

Another major research orientation among behavioralist scholars sought to elaborate on Traditionalist notions of the state and the nature of decisionmaking in the interstate system. Works by the Hermanns, for example, employed simulation techniques to test hypotheses on the capacity for rational decisionmaking in times of extreme crisis and (potential) nuclear war.[38] Charles McClelland studied patterns of interaction in pre- and postcrisis situations, and others developed theories of war based on perception and misperception of the "facts" under crisis conditions.[39] This line of inquiry has retained its influence in the works of Robert Jervis from the 1970s on.[40] In the 1960s, too, Neustadt's theory of bureaucratic politics emerged to stimulate later influential images of state decisionmaking based on struggles between government elites (e.g., Allison).[41]

The mechanistic and systemic orientation of the period was perhaps most obviously expressed in relation to the major Realist metaphor—the balance of power. Morgenthau, as earlier indicated, prescribed interstate balancing behavior as a natural mechanism of International Relations. Many following him sought to add more precision to the concept and, via a verifiable general theory, operationalize it. Arthur Burns, for example, sought a "pure theory" of power politics, centered on the balance-of-power principle that illuminated its transhistorical and universal applicability.[42] Kaplan, meanwhile, created complex systemic models in order to test competing explanations of the balance concept and explain change in relation to it.[43] Closely related to the attempt to scientifically theorize the balance-of-power concept was the attention paid to alliances, where coalition theory and the theory of collective goods were utilized to explain the behavior of allied partners.[44] And, influenced by game theory assumptions and techniques, scholars sought to account for systemic state behavior over time.[45] Kenneth Waltz, integral to the neo-Realism of the present, made an important contribution in the 1960s on the question of which systemic structure provided most order and stability.[46] The ensuing debate saw works employing ever more complex quantitative tools, designed to correlate and test hypotheses about balance-of-power systems through the ages.

The question of war and its causes was another theme given a more systemic treatment in this period. Whereas Morgenthau and earlier power politics scholars had been generally pessimistic (often fatalistic) on this issue, the behavioralists were buoyed by the progressiveness inherent in their approaches. This led from the mid-1960s to a "systematic effort to search for the causes of war, with the hope that in the distant future a truly empirical and scientific understanding of war (not like the normative, uncorroborated theory of the idealists) would make a world at peace possible."[47] The most significant research project to flow from this disciplinary orientation has been the Correlates of War project, which has provided a data source for scholars ever since seeking more precise models on the causes of war and how it might be prevented.[48]

Throughout the behavioralist period the issue of nuclear war loomed large. So, too, did the question of nuclear deterrence. Influential works by Herman Kahn introduced new levels of complexity to deterrence logic while prompting International Relations scholars to think the "unthinkable"—the use of nuclear weapons as an ultimate deterrent.[49] Among nuclear strategists, however, it was the rationality premise associated with game theory that proved most appealing as the basis for scientific theorizing about human behavior and decisionmaking processes in the nuclear age.

Via game theory techniques, it was argued, strategic problems could be reduced to "a manageable form in which the dilemmas and paradoxes of the age could be bared and solutions explored." At the broader level (echoing logical positivism), the aims of nuclear strategic analysis were to construct a "nuclear strategy as a science [in which, first] the logic, dynamics and management of nuclear war and its deterrence can be explained and controlled by precise, quantifiable methods and policies."[50] Throughout the 1960s, accordingly, the literature of International Relations specialists resonated with rational deductive approaches and game-theorized models derived largely from neoclassical economic theory and utilitarian assumptions about human nature and behavior.[51]

There were, nevertheless, various scholars unimpressed with the outcomes—if not the methodological inputs, or basic (positivist) philosophy—of the strategic/security discourse. Bruce Russett, for example, instigated alternative statistical studies concerned with illustrating that deterrence did not, in fact, deter.[52] Others, such as the mathematician Anatol Rapoport, also cast doubt upon deterrence logic and its assumptions, particularly its one-dimensional commitment to coercive behavior and its rigid zero-sum utilization of the rationality premise.[53] From more conventional perspectives also a range of analysts began to critically test deterrence hypotheses against historical evidence, finding the deductive logic of orthodox strategic thinking often unsound in its own (empiricist) terms.[54]

In more recent times the discipline's scientific quest has attracted broader and more profound criticism, and I want to touch on some of these critical themes before moving on to the "third wave" of the discipline's development. John Vasquez is an important figure here, and it is worth reiterating some of the conclusions his mammoth study, *The Power of Power Politics,* reached on the positivist-Realist approach between (approximately) 1950 and 1980.

On the issue of the Realist rational-actor premise, for example, Vasquez's study found that Realist scholarship at best provides ambiguous evidence in support of its claims and, at worst represents a dogmatic and narrow representation of reality, replete with danger and paradox. This is particularly the case concerning Realist presumptions that (1) decisionmakers will act in similar ways in response to a single (external) reality and that (2) these decisions can be deduced in terms of a utilitarian model of rational self-interest. This universalized and essentialist perspective is found wanting, Vasquez concluded, immediately one confronts it with a range of studies not encompassed within its narrow analytical boundaries (e.g., social psychology).[55] This concerned Vasquez in relation to the analytical/policy silences of the Cold War, but his concerns remain relevant in the age of the Gulf War and Bosnia, particularly that which suggests that under conditions of crisis, "new information that conforms to existing images tends to be emphasized, and information that is dissonant with the images is often not seen, ignored or explained away."[56]

Ultimately, Vasquez proposed, rational-actor models simply cannot explain behavior in the two situations where Realism projects its predictive power most assertively—in terms of crisis management and the onset of war.[57] This finding is particularly significant given the enormous literature that has explained issues of political crisis and war in terms of the game-theorized logic of deterrence for more than three decades. On the issue of war, more generally, Vasquez's study found that, even in relation to the behavior of the United States during the Cold War, the rational choice approach was inadequate in its own terms and, accordingly, "one cannot help but doubt its relevance for decision makers who have a different culture, history, language and ideology."[58]

The issue of war and peace, on this basis, is a much more complex phenomenon than a Machiavellian-induced power politics explanation allows. Rather, suggested Vasquez, such an explanation "does not provide a [universal] theory of world politics, but merely an image that decision makers can have of the world."[59] On alliance formation, represented as the realistic application of (power politics) "theory" to "practice," the study found that in Realism's own terms (i.e., the evidence of its literature), balance-of-power strategies and alliance aggregation generally do not prevent war but more commonly provoke it. And on the question of which (Realist) system best prevents war, Vasquez found an interesting irony concerning Realist analysis. It was that, on occasions, *both* power parity and preponderance systemic structures have been associated with peaceful relations between the major states, while at other times *both* have been associated with periods of warfare. The irony of course is that while Realist scholars might point to "factual" correlation of their hypotheses on this basis, they cannot do so in the terms that their (universalized) correspondence-rule theory demands—that is, in terms of a *general* theory of war and peace across historical time, cultural space, and interpretive practice.[60] This issue will be addressed again in the following chapter in regard to Kenneth Waltz's seminal neo-Realism; when the commitment to a utilitarian rational-actor model of behavior will be critically engaged in contemporary terms.

Vasquez's study of Realist literature ended, effectively, in 1980. But in the last decade or so, it is apparent that nothing much has changed within the strategy/security field, as mainstream International Relations scholars and policy analysts meander into the space beyond the Cold War armed with analytical tools derived from a seventeenth-century "empiricist metaphysic" and the illusory certitude of power politics modernism.

Various works have confirmed this in recent times, from a number of angles.[61] What these diverse interrogations illustrate, from the perspective of this present discussion, is that a modernist discourse continues to dominate in the current period and continues to limit strategy/security debate in significant and dangerous ways. It continues, for example, to allow analysts and policymakers to represent their perspectives in ostensibly value-neutral terms. The result, at one level, has been a familiar representation of the world "out there," effectively independent of the strategic analyst, who merely describes the anarchical reality of international affairs and explains the need for a power politics response to it.[62] Aside from the closure and paradox of this position, this has increased the systematic desensitizing of the horrors of nuclear warfare, as Carol Cohn has so vividly illustrated, and it has increased the (political, ethical) distance between the strategic "expert" and the nearly five billion nuclear hostages around the globe.[63]

This was illustrated most blatantly during the Reagan administration, with the advent of the Committee for the Present Danger to a central analytical position within the U.S. policy framework.[64] The result, aside from an enormous upscaling of the nuclear arms race and SDI, was a frighteningly simple manipulation of the strategy/security debate. In the mid-1980s, for example, the "window of vulnerability" theme was resurrected in an environment where the dominant discourse was so strong that it became official policy, even when it was clearly preposterous, even in its own terms. This scenario depicted the Soviets as having both the intent and the capacity to destroy U.S. land-based missiles in their silos. It was a scenario without credibility, given both the potency of the TRIAD defense structure and a generation-long insistence on the (power politics) rationality of the Soviet actor in the deterrence "game."

In this regard, the really preposterous aspect of the "window of vulnerability thesis" was its "expert" analytical assessment that presumed that, even in the unlikely event of Soviet success in disarming a thousand or so ICBMs, the Soviet decisionmakers would gamble on the lack of response from the fleet of B-52s and submarines, when it would have required only sixty of the former and fifteen of the latter to have effectively destroyed the Soviet Union as a functioning entity.[65] This was a preposterous scenario, then, which could be rationally defended only in a (discursive) environment where peoples have ceded their responsibility to think critically about the world to a contemporary orthodoxy offering an (illusory) certitude in complex times.

The cost of this abrogation of responsibility, even in the most basic of terms, has been borne by the global population to a staggering degree. In a five-year period alone (1983–1988), the two superpowers, for example, spent almost $3 trillion (U.S.) on weapons of mass destruction.[66] To put this in perspective for those distressed nightly by images of starving, struggling humanity around the globe, it represents the equivalent of $1 million spent every day on weapons of mass destruction for the past *seven thousand years*.[67] If one then asks precisely what was purchased in this time, the answer is simple enough: a fraction of the (approximately) fifty thousand warheads (still) stockpiled around the world, which amounts to around four metric tons of TNT for every man, woman, and child on the planet.[68]

The problem has not disappeared with the demise of either the Reagan administration or its Soviet raison d'être. Nuclear weapons will remain integral to the lives of every generation to come, and while the immediate danger of nuclear holocaust seems to have passed, the technology remains to quickly replenish depleted arsenals. Meanwhile, the major powers encourage the proliferation of increasingly destructive nonnuclear weaponry, as power politics logic makes its contemporary compromises with the dictates of a global war economy. Thus, the logic that gave the nuclear arms race its lethal legitimacy in a Cold War conflict for nearly fifty years remains integral to the post–Cold War era and at the heart of the strategy/security debate in International Relations.

The logic, for example, that invoked deterrence as the keystone strategy in containing the Soviet Other remains that which rationalizes the end of the Cold War as "victory" for Western (U.S.) technopower. The argument here is compelling, of course, once one accepts the Realist framing regime: for example, (1) we didn't have nuclear war, and the Soviets "lost"; thus (2) ipso facto, deterrence worked; and (3) the international system was ordered, because the nuclear superpowers "behaved quite prudently for three decades."[69] At least four responses are appropriate in the face of this logic. The first might ask those who simply correlate deterrence, arms racing, and the lack of a nuclear holocaust to consider the likely fate of the man who, when hurtling to the ground after falling from a hundred-story building, was asked how things were going and replied cheerily, "So far, so good!"

The second response, in contemplating what "order" and "prudence" mean in this context, might highlight a statistic not favored by orthodox scholarship. It records the deaths of forty million to fifty million of the world's peoples, killed in wars during the period of prudent "order."[70] The third response, while acknowledging the devastation wrought upon Soviet society by a permanent and crippling war economy, might also remind the "victors," in the United States in particular, of the costs of their strategic success and the actual status of their post–Cold War security. Here the advocates of American-led power politics strategies might well ponder a reality that has seen the post–World War II hegemon, the most powerful industrial society in human history, become the world's biggest debtor within a generation. Or they might be reminded of their rotting, misery-laden urban landscape; of child mortality rates and life expectancy rates worse than any other industrialized country; of their inadequate education system and social services; of their overflowing prisons; of their violence, intolerance, and cancerous racism; and of their seeming inability to move beyond their "infantile wish for omnipotence."[71] The fourth response might remind the power politics advocates of the implications of the strategy of "armed overkill," which continues to characterize U.S. foreign policy in the wake of the Cold War. From such a perspective it is perhaps both rational and prudent to incinerate thousands to "send a message" to Saddam Hussein or kill hundreds, maybe thousands, to make a single arrest in Panama. And while the post–Cold War (neo-Realist) orthodoxy continues to insist that "domestic" and "international" affairs must remain separated, there is, as Barbara Ehrenreich suggests, a rather profound connection between this kind of behavior, at the global level, and the rationale that sends a SWAT team to (brutally) subdue a single motorist in Los Angeles.[72]

Throughout this work I have emphasized that "practices" such as these do not take place in a theoretical/interpretivist void. Rather, the events and issues starkly represented here are always discursive practices, always theory as practice. They represent particular ways of framing "reality" and of responding to that framed reality. In order to effectively challenge these practices accordingly, one needs to challenge the discursive process that gives them their meaning and directs policy/analytical/military responses to them, which is why this final example of static, indeed backward, "theorizing" in the strategic/security debate is important. It comes from Stephen Walt and represents an attempt, in 1991, to illustrate how any analytical problems that might have hindered strategic and security analysis in the past have now been overcome, in the "more rigourous, methodologically sophisticated and theoretically inclined" 1990s.[73]

Walt's major aim is to establish that while in the 1960s strategic/security analysis might have suffered from the lack of "reliable information" and a paucity of "systematic evidence," this problem has now been solved by a body of scholars enjoying a renaissance in their craft centered on "systematic social science research rather than on unverified assertion or argument."[74] Acknowledging that these new perspectives still fit "comfortably within the familiar realist paradigm," Walt sought, nevertheless, to emphasize the qualitative difference between the earlier (behavioralist) Realist perspectives and the more sophisticated contemporary variant.[75] In this regard he pointed to the (perceived) fundamental changes that took place after the Vietnam War, when scholars began to abandon their "relatively simple assumptions" in favor of a new sensitivity on historical issues.[76]

Chiding earlier scholarship for its "ahistorical" tendencies, he then proceeded to represent the sophisticated alternative in typically unsophisticated terms, in celebrating the use of "historical cases as a means of generating, testing and refining theories."[77] The paradox associated with this position, which once again sees history represented as an ahistorical object in the past, generating facts that can then be tested to *create* "theory," is seemingly lost on Walt. But the limitations of Walt's position are most explicit when he turns his attention to the broader agenda in International Relations in the 1980s and 1990s.[78] The difficulty for Walt here is that his understanding of the issues at stake in the "third debate" stretches only as far as his (positivist) understanding of theory allows. Accordingly, Kenneth Waltz's *Theory of International Politics* is praised as a "powerful reformulation" of Realism, while nowhere is any attention paid to more nuanced works that have come to rather different conclusions as to its status.[79]

This omission is less surprising when one takes into account Walt's own commitment to the crude positivism that characterizes Waltz's neo-Realism. Thus, remarkably, in 1991 Walt's "new" security/strategic discourse is finally represented as a three-dimensional (positivist) project concerned initially with the process of "theory creation." This process, he explains, is all about "the development of logically related causal propositions explaining a particular phenomenon of interest." The focus then falls upon a process of "theory testing," concerning, "attempts to verify, falsify, and refine competing theories by testing their predictions against a scientifically selected body of evidence." Then there is the question of the "application" of theory, encompassing "the use of existing knowledge to illuminate a specific policy problem."[80] Summarizing this new, more sophisticated approach to security/strategic issues at the end of the Cold War, Walt invokes it as the search for "cumulative knowledge about the role of military force." This is an ambition well within the reach of the new breed of security/strategic analysts of the 1990s, because "the field [now understands that it] must follow the standard canons of scientific research; careful and consistent use of terms, unbiased measurement of critical concepts, and public documentation of theoretical and empirical claims."[81]

At the completion of the fourth chapter of this book, there is, I hope, no need for further comment on Walt's perspective, except perhaps to suggest that in itself it is a testament to the need for International Relations to take seriously the sheer backwardness of its mainstream literature in the current period. One more theme from Walt's work is nevertheless of significance here. It concerns his commentary on critical social theory contributions to the current debates in which (presumably on the basis of his close reading of such literature) he felt compelled to warn, in particular, of the threat posed by postmodernism, which

> contrary to [its] proponents' claims . . . ha[s] yet to demonstrate much value for comprehending world politics; to date these works are mostly criticism and not much theory . . . [moreover] issues of peace and war are too important for the field to be diverted into a prolix and self indulgent discourse that is *divorced from the real world* [emphasis added].[82]

On this note, with postmodernist scholarship being summarily dismissed by a primitive positivist of the Realist mainstream, the most constructive response might be to register Walt's contribution as a prime example of the continuing poverty of security/strategic discourse and as evidence of the broader continuity between modernist "theory" and International Relations "practice," which I have sought to illustrate throughout this book.

My more immediate concern in this chapter has been to illustrate why it is so important to locate the Tradition and discipline of International Relations as part of a modernist framing regime and to explain how, since World War II, Realist scholarship has been severely limited by its modernist commitments. In this regard, the chapter sought also to provide a different angle on an orthodox literature that has resounded with claims to have discovered the foundational basis of (1) the reality (i.e., anarchical) of relations between states, (2) the nature of the modern world of states and state system (with its independent, utilitarian structure and its inevitable security dilemmas), (3) the "art of the possible" (i.e., order under anarchy) associated with the "control" of modern International Relations, and (4) the correct method (positivist/empiricist) by which the world "out there" is to be understood.

Chapter 5 has similar concerns in that its focus is the replication of modernist and positivist commitments in the new orthodoxy of International Relations in the 1990s—neo-Realism. It argues that there has been nothing original or even surprising in the response of Realists to the anomalies of orthodox theory as practice in the post-Vietnam era, which undermined the certainty of their state-centric, power politics analysis. Like orthodox responses before them, across the social theory spectrum, the neo-Realist response has had all the hallmarks of a modernist discursive practice, albeit in updated and reformulated mode. There has thus been the resort to even more precise levels of certitude and a narrowing of the "meaningful" principle (i.e., rational order under anarchy), which would have done the logical positivists proud. And, in replicating earlier paradoxes associated with the postwar quest for certainty, the neo-Realism of the (full-blown) postpositivist/postbehavioralist era has been articulated in exemplary positivist terms, consistent with the behavioralist attempt to make the Tradition of International Relations Realism more scientific.

Notes

1. This is not purely because of any lack of theoretical introspection on the part of the discipline. It has as much to do with the reluctance of Morgenthau to acknowledge Weber's influence upon him until late in his life. While, therefore, Weber's ideas were to form the backbone of Morgenthau's work, and while the structure of Morgenthau's argument in his major texts was taken directly from Weber's writings, Morgenthau consciously avoided any direct association with him. Turner and Factor have explained this situation in sympathetic terms, stressing that in the 1940s and the immediate postwar years, Morgenthau was reluctant to emphasize his indebtedness to a "German theory of Politics." Consequently, Morgenthau adopted a long-term strategy, "which permitted him to present Weber's views with their full polemical force, without the disability of their origins"; see Factor and Turner, *Max Weber and the Dispute Over Reason and Value,* p. 169 and pp. 167–173. See also Smith, *Realist Thought from Weber to Kissinger.*

2. Ibid., pp. 171–173.

3. Morgenthau, *Politics Among Nations,* p. 4.

4. Ibid., p. 5.

5. Ibid., pp. 4–5.

6. When it has been as in Waltz's *Man, the State and War,* it has been on the basis that Morgenthau's Realism missed the essence of reality (e.g., the structuralist essence), not in terms of any fundamental questioning of the notion of essence or of Realist "reality." A larger discussion on Waltz and the implications of this for the discipline in the 1990s is to follow in the next chapter.

7. Morgenthau, *Politics Among Nations,* pp. 4–5.

8. Vasquez, *The Power of Power Politics,* p. 49.

9. On Morgenthau as a disciplinary icon, see ibid., pp. 16–38.

10. See Hoffmann, "An American Social Science." See also Cox, "Social Forces, States and World Orders," which, from a (broad) Critical Theory perspective, makes the same general point.

11. Hoffmann, "An American Social Science," pp. 44–45.

12. See the discussion on behavioralism in Chapter 2, pp. 69–74. In this atmosphere, as now in International Relations, those not engaged in "concrete" empirical research were attacked for their abstraction and irrelevance.

13. Hoffmann, "An American Social Science," p. 59.

14. For a useful introduction to this literature, see Higgott, *Political Development Theory;* and on the Modernization issue, from a number of perspectives, see Packenham, *Political Development: Ideas in Foreign Aid and Social Science;* Pye, *Aspects of Political Development;* Rothchild and Curry, *Scarcity, Choice and Public Policy in Middle Africa;* Moore, *Social Origins of Dictatorship and Democracy;* Frank, *Latin America;* Eisenstadt, *Modernisation, Protest and Change;* Apter, *The Politics of Modernisation;* Rostow, *The Stages of Economic Growth;* and Huntington, *Political Order and Changing Societies.* From a more contemporary angle see also Goetz, "Feminism and the Limits of the Claims to Know"; and Sylvester, ed., "Feminists Write International Relations."

15. Eisenstadt, *Modernisation, Protest and Change,* as cited in Higgott, *Political Development Theory,* p. 16.

16. Hoffmann, "An American Social Science," p. 47.

17. Keohane, "Realism, Neorealism and the Study of World Politics," p. 11.

18. Ibid., p. 12.

19. Apter, *The Politics of Modernisation,* pp. 9–11.

20. Almond, "Political Theory and Political Science," cited in Higgott, *Political Development Theory,* p. 25.

21. Rostow, *The Stages of Economic Growth,* p. 1.

22. Ibid., p. 5.

23. In Waltz's *Theory of International Politics* in particular.

24. See Klein, "How the West Was One," p. 315.

25. Ibid.

26. Nye, *Bound to Lead.*

27. Huntington, *Political Order and Changing Societies.*

28. See the discussion, for example, in Keohane, *After Hegemony.*

29. Hoffmann, "An American Social Science," p. 48.

30. Vasquez, *The Power of Power Politics,* chap. 2.

31. See the discussion on Popper and this issue in Chapter 2, pp. 61–65. Some, like Singer, wanted to distinguish his optimistic scientism from the negativity of the Popperian approach, while at the same time stating, rather strangely, that he agreed with Popper's logical argument on the problems of verification. See Singer, "The Incomplete Theorist."

32. Singer, "The Incomplete Theorist," p. 65. The reference here is to Popper's strategy in detaching himself from (logical) positivism by emphasizing its inductivism in contrast to his deductivist falsificationism.

33. Ibid., p. 65.

34. On Deutsch, for example, *Nationalism and Social Communication.*

35. Vasquez, *The Power of Power Politics,* p. 55.

36. See Sprout and Sprout, *Foundations of National Power;* and Organski and Organski, *Population and World Power.*

37. See Geutzkow et al., *Simulation in International Relations;* on Rosenau, see his "Pre-theories and Theories of Foreign Policy" and *The Scientific Study of Foreign Policy.*

38. See Hermann and Hermann, "An Attempt to Simulate the Outbreak of World War I"; and Hermann, "International Crisis as a Situational Variable." Here the social psychology work of Geutzkow was important again concerning the rational-actor model; see Geutzkow, "Some Correspondences Between Simulations and Realities in International Processes."

39. See McClelland, "The Beginning, Duration and Abatement of International Crisis." See also the works on World War I by Holsti, Brody, and North, "Measuring Affect and Action in International Reaction Models."

40. On Jervis, see *Perception and Misperception in International Politics* and "Deterrence Theory Revisited"; and Jervis, Lebow, and Rosen, *Psychology and Deterrence.*

41. See Neustadt, *Presidential Power;* and Allison, *Essence of Decision.*

42. Burns, "From Balance to Deterrence," and "Prospects for a General Theory of International Relations."

43. See, for example, Kaplan, *System and Process in International Politics.*

44. See Russett, "Components of an Operational Theory of International Alliance Formation."

45. See Kaplan, Burns, and Quandt, "Theoretical Analysis of the 'Balance of Power.'"

46. See Waltz, "The Stability of the Bipolar World"; and, more generally, Deutsch and Singer, "Multipolar Power Systems and International Stability"; and Rosecrance, "Bipolarity, Multipolarity and the Future."

47. Vasquez, *The Power of Power Politics,* p. 89. And just to reiterate the notion of an orthodox consensus once again, the peace research movement in International Relations was also largely derived from this progressivist, positivist-based approach to the evidence, as for example in the mathematical modeling of the physicist Lewis Richardson, *Statistics of Deadly Quarrels;* and the earlier pioneering work of Quincey Wright, *A Study of War.*

48. Singer, *The Correlates of War: II.*

49. Kahn, *On Thermonuclear War* and *Thinking About the Unthinkable.* On nuclear war in this era, see Brodie, *Escalation and the Nuclear Option* and *War and Politics;* Burns, *Of Powers and Their Politics;* and in more critical mode, Green, *Deadly Logic.*

50. See Kolkowicz, ed., *The Logic of Nuclear Terror,* p. 26.

51. As far as deterrence theory was concerned, the works of Thomas Schelling were perhaps the most sophisticated in their attempt to build into the equations theoretical dimensions not allowed by the more formalized approach to "gaming." See Schelling, *The Strategy of Conflict* and *Arms and Influence.*

52. See Russett, "The Calculus of Deterrence" and "Pearl Harbor: Deterrence Theory and Decision Theory." This is a tradition carried on by R. Ned Lebow and Janice Gross Stein, in "Rational Deterrence Theory: I Think Therefore I Deter."

53. Rapaport, *Fights, Games and Debates* and *Strategy and Conscience;* also, in this vein, see Green, *Deadly Logic.*

54. See Young, *The Politics of Force,* which looked at Cold War flashpoints, including the Cuban missile crisis. An updated work in this tradition is that of Alexander George and Richard Smoke, *Deterrence in American Foreign Policy;* see also Snyder and Deising, *Conflict Among Nations;* and, of course, Jervis.

55. Vasquez, *The Power of Power Politics,* ibid., p. 206.

56. Ibid.

57. Ibid., pp. 210–211.

58. Ibid., p. 212.

59. Ibid., 216.

60. Ibid., p. 221.

61. See, for example, Cohn, "Sex and Death in the Rational World of Defense Intellectuals"; Lawrence, "Strategy, the State and the Weberian Legacy"; Klein, "Hegemony and Strategic Culture"; Dalby, *Creating the Second Cold War;* Ehrenreich, "Battlin' Bill's Initiation Rite"; and Lapham, "Apes and Butterflies."

62. On this theme, see Lawrence, "Strategy, the State and the Weberian Legacy."

63. Cohn, "Sex and Death in the Rational World of Defense Intellectuals."

64. Dalby, *Creating the Second Cold War.*

65. For a discussion, see, Lawrence, "Strategy, the State and the Weberian Legacy"; Scheer, *With Enough Shovels;* and Dalby, *Creating the Second Cold War.*

66. This figure is derived from the annotated data in the annual publications of the International Institute for Strategic Studies, *The Military Balance.*

67. See Ball, "Management of the Superpower Balance," p. 217.

68. Lawrence, "Strategy, the State and the Weberian Legacy," p. 299.

69. Tucker, "Morality and Deterrence," p. 461.

70. These are figures used in Dunnigan and Nofi, *Dirty Little Secrets,* p. 382.

71. Lapham, "Apes and Butterflies," p. 15. The child mortality and life expectancy reference comes from Kennedy, *Preparing for the Twenty-First Century,* p. 303.

72. See Ehrenreich, "Battlin' Bill's Initiation Rite."

73. Walt, "The Renaissance of Security Studies," p. 211.

74. Ibid., p. 214.

75. Ibid., p. 212.

76. Ibid., pp. 216–217.

77. Ibid.

78. Ibid., p. 219.

79. Ibid. Waltz's work will be the subject of discussion in the next chapter. At this point it is worth noting Alker's and Biersteker's proposition that *Theory of International Politics* does not even represent sophisticated positivism in its pursuit of value-free timeless laws, "proposed with Olympian detachment." See Alker and Biersteker, "The Dialectics of World Order," p. 133.

80. Walt, "The Renaissance of Security Studies," p. 221.

81. Ibid., p. 222.

82. Ibid., p. 223.

5

The Backward Discipline Revisited: The Closed World of Neo-Realism

The emergence of neo-Realism as the new orthodoxy in International Relations has taken place in a period in which Realism has confronted crises on a number of fronts (e.g., the Vietnam War, the failure of Modernization Theory in the Third World, and a series of challenges to U.S. global hegemony).[1] Among more sensitive commentators at least, these crises provoked attempts to go beyond the rigidity of the post-1945 "catechism" (either Traditionalist or behavioralist) and deal with some of the more obvious anomalies in the International Relations orthodoxy. This chapter concentrates on these attempts to question and reassess Realism from within, while taking into account some of the broader critical responses to global crisis that since the early 1970s have intersected with the reformulation of orthodox theory as practice in International Relations.

This period has seen critical social theory perspectives challenging traditional orthodoxies across the disciplinary spectrum. The ensuing tensions have been replicated in International Relations. Accordingly, as conservative forces regrouped and responded to "revisionist" accounts of reality, so in International Relations the revisionism of a number of critical approaches has been countered by the neo-Realism of some of the most prominent figures in the discipline.[2] The result is that International Relations in the 1980s and 1990s has again begun to resonate with the (illusory) certitude of a reasserted positivist-Realist "catechism." It is in this context that this discussion begins, with a general overview of the discursive circumstances that saw Realism challenged, undergo metamorphosis, and reemerge as neo-Realism.

Vietnam, Interdependence, and Grotian Regime Theory: Opening Up Some Thinking Space

The debacle in Vietnam forced a reassessment of U.S. strategy/security discourse and its foreign policy perspectives in general. As part of this post-Vietnam crisis, Realists of all varieties were confronted with a range of "revisionist" critiques, highlighting the inadequacies of their approach to global affairs.[3] In the early 1970s, thus, Realism was increasingly recognized as a simplistic, ethnocentric, and ideological articulation of Western (primarily North American) interests, seemingly incapable of dealing with a complex international arena.

At least three themes, derived from the critical literature on the Vietnam War, indicate the more general concerns of Realism's critics. The first, pointing to the inadequacies of (behavioralist-based) foreign policy analysis, noted that for all the intricate modeling, mathematical posturing, systems theories, and assertions about the patterned recurrence and repetition of interstate life, Realists had no adequate theory of the state—no accurate insight into the history, culture, and sociopolitical structure of Vietnam, its peoples, or its struggle. Second, for all its proclamations of universality and its game-theorized accounts of means/ends behavior and strategic predictability, derived from the rationality principle of neoclassical economic theory, Realism had no comprehension of the North Vietnamese capacity for "irrational" behavior, in regard to levels of "acceptable damage." Third, committed to crude assumptions about the nature of power (e.g., as modern military/technological capacity), all the Realist historical and philosophical insight and its technorational predictive capacity could not account for the defeat of a modern Western state at the hands of a traditional society, utilizing premodern technological and intellectual resources.

In a rudimentary way, then, the critical responses of the post-Vietnam period prefigured the critical social theory challenges of the 1980s and 1990s. The ensuing debate saw a degree of self-reflective scholarship emerge in International Relations that (to some degree) reflected a new awareness of theoretical/interpretive issues. In this general atmosphere, in the early 1970s, scholars such as Robert Keohane and Joseph Nye began to prize open some critical space within International Relations. In their early interdependence mode they challenged Realist state-centricism with the view that actors other than sovereign states must be accorded significance in any contemporary power politics equation. To understand international order in the 1970s, consequently, was to understand a more complex matrix of power relations, not reducible solely to the crude power machinations of sovereign states but influenced also by the activities of other (multinational, transnational) nonstate actors and the politicoeconomic connections between them, at both micro and macro levels.[4]

This is not to suggest that the interdependence challenge of Keohane and Nye represented a serious effort to critically reevaluate Realism in terms of its modernist legacy, or even its more immediate positivist commitments.[5] Its purpose, as Keohane recalled, was to supplement the Realist position on state interaction with "structural models of international

Regime change" in order to "improve the ability of Realist or Neo-Realist analysis to account for [such change]."[6] For all this, in emphasizing the significance of nonstate (transnational) actors and issue-based analysis, the work of Keohane and Nye opened some space for (moderately) critical and more pluralistic analysis at the American center of the discipline that, since the Cold War, had largely recited the Realist "catechism."

It was in this space that the debate over the nature and role of politico-economic regimes became a significant theme in International Relations. The regime theme had been raised in the integrationist or functionalist scholarship of the 1950s and 1960s.[7] In the 1970s, however, when (among other things) the demise of Bretton Woods, the challenge to U.S. economic dominance by Japan, the OPEC crisis, and the catastrophe in Vietnam were increasingly represented as weakening U.S. power in the world (and in the United States in particular) as nails in the coffin of the postwar order, the regime issue reemerged as part of a reformulated disciplinary perspective on contemporary reality at the international level. Subsequently, it has become the site of various attempts to open International Relations to approaches and understandings otherwise excluded from serious disciplinary concern.

The definition of a regime is itself an issue of much debate. One influential definition emphasizes a set of implicit or explicit "principles, norms, rules and decision making procedures around which actor expectations converge in a given issue area."[8] Another represents regimes as "the set of rules, norms and procedures that regulate behaviour and control its effects in international affairs."[9] Explaining these definitional components in more detail, Stephen Krasner proposes that, in relation to regimes,

> principles are beliefs of fact, causation and rectitude. Norms are standards of behavior defined in terms of rights and obligations. Rules are specific prescriptions or proscriptions for action. Decision-making procedures are prevailing practices for making and implementing collective choice.[10]

Read positively, this approach represents an important thematic shift in emphasis for International Relations scholarship, indicating perhaps that primitive Realist notions of an anarchical world "out there" imposing its power politics essence upon passive receivers have indeed been superseded. To some degree this has been the case. Working in the "thinking space" prized open in the early 1970s, scholars such as Oran Young, Raymond Hopkins, Donald Puchala, and Ernst Haas, for example, have added interesting and useful dimensions to the regime debate. Their general perspective, designated Grotian by Realists such as Krasner, has maintained that the theory and practice of regimes largely supersede Realist understandings of the world, now perceived as too limited for explaining an increasingly complex interdependent global arena.[11]

Grotian regime theory has sought to undermine Realist orthodoxy by suggesting that Realist explanations of reality, centered upon the struggle for survival in an anarchical world, do not adequately address interstate behavior, even that involving conflicts between the major powers.[12] This Grotian approach does not dismiss Realism's power politics focus per se. Its aim, rather, is to illustrate that the reductionist homogeneity of mainstream Realism blinds it to the complex and heterogeneous nature of international behavior and to a more nuanced understanding of it. Accordingly, while it acknowledges that regime compliance is, at one level or another, based on calculated self-interest, it seeks to go beyond the obvious and investigate what *meaning* regime actors give to their calculations on the costs and benefits of particular actions. It asks, for example, how regime participants calculate moral costs and benefits in given situations. In asking these questions Grotian analysis extends the boundaries of orthodox Realism, in questioning the taken-for-granted utilitarian basis of its rational-actor model. It suggests that simplistic notions of individual self-interest are limited and inadequate in understanding global behavior and, more precisely, that notions of rational action constructed via market logic must be located in social and historical context and given normative dimensions.[13]

Another critical suggestion to come from this quarter concerns the issue of change in International Relations and the rigidity of Realist approaches to it. Thus, in acknowledging that regime change commonly comes with power shifts in the interstate system, Puchala and Hopkins have again gone beyond the obvious to propose that there are other sources and motivations for change not encompassed within the Realist frame of reference. Change can occur, they argue, via cognitive learning processes (e.g., regarding ecological dangers) and not necessarily via Traditional processes of big-power determination.[14]

Ernst Haas has added another interesting (Grotian) dimension to the debate, with the view that contemporary regime interaction represents "the interactions of *homo politicus* with nature and with culture. . . . [Moreover] it rests on the supposition that our collective understanding of our political choices increasingly depend on how we think about nature and about culture."[15] This critical tendency in Haas's approach is enhanced with the proposal that the silences of Realism, on issues such as nature and culture, require that it be superseded by a more sophisticated perspective that goes beyond its static premises and comprehends that "we cannot know the reality 'out there' because our notion of what it contains changes with every twist of the scientific enterprise."[16]

Others less Grotian in attitude and perspective have also concentrated on the regime issue in broadening the intellectual scope of their analysis. Most famously, perhaps, John Ruggie has insisted that to understand the "embedded liberalism" of the post–World War II regimes is to extend the issue beyond (orthodox) Realist boundaries and understand regimes "by their generative grammar, the underlying principles of order and meaning that shape the manner of their formation and transformation."[17] Friedrich Kratochwil has taken this theme further, emphasizing the need to conceptualize regime behavior not in traditional (social) scientific terms but as an interpretive "practice in which validity claims are scrutinized among practitioners."[18]

On the basis of contributions such as these, which acknowledge an intersubjective realm of rules and norms as constitutive of contemporary international reality, an observer encountering the disciplinary literature in the 1980s might be forgiven for thinking that Wittgenstein, Winch, and Kuhn, rather than Popper and Weber, have been most influential philosophically over the years, that International Relations is not the "backward discipline" some critics claim it to be. It might also be suggested that any crisis in Realism has been largely overcome, as International Relations scholars grapple seriously with issues integral to debates across the social theory spectrum. It could be concluded, too, that the critical social theory challenge, with its charge of continuing primitiveness, and calls for increased "thinking space," is inappropriate, exaggerated, and even churlish.

This, I suggest, is not the case. Rather, as in the broader social theory context, a discursive orthodox consensus continues to reign in International Relations, to the extent that seemingly genuine alternatives continue to be framed in modernist terms. This can be illustrated, initially, by looking more critically at the nature of the challenge offered by Grotian regime theorists and the critical linguistic dimension introduced to the debate by Kratochwil and Ruggie.[19] The discussion will then focus, more directly, on the most influential "alternative" of the post-Vietnam period–neo-Realism.

My contention on Grotian regime theory is that, for all the genuine insight it brings to the contemporary debate, it does not represent a fundamental break with the dominant discourse but rather an adaption of it (hence the unintended appropriateness of the Grotian label bestowed upon it by Realists). Ernst Haas's contribution, for example, is clearly of contemporary significance with its focus on the changing nature of international collaboration in a context of "changing self understanding."[20] Such an approach seems clearly distinguishable from the positivist objectivism that has characterized Realist analysis over the years. Yet, some rather obvious similarities remain between a Realism that rejects cooperative regime behavior on the basis of an objectified (anarchical) world "out there" and an argument that invokes the significance of regimes on the basis of an evolutionary epistemology.[21] The problem, in short, is that the insight that allows Haas to expose the limits of Realism's externalized image of the world is itself derived from the same (modernist) framework, which understands the regime-based alternative as a politics of collaboration, evolving alongside "the evolution of consciousness itself."[22] Suspicions that this useful rejoinder to positivist Realism is predicated on a rather rudimentary progressivism are confirmed when Haas sets out his intellectual position, which, he reveals, "implies the *permanent evolution* [emphasis added] of regimes and of knowledge about regimes."[23]

The contribution of Puchala and Hopkins is also intrinsically linked to the Realism it seeks to repudiate. The problems here are, if anything, more immediately evident than in the case of Haas's evolutionary epistemology. The major problem lies in the attempt to go beyond the state-as-actor focus of orthodox Realism by focusing instead on the role of elites in regime maintenance. This, in effect, is an expanded version of the bureaucratic politics model, which suffers from all the problems that have beset similar approaches over the years.[24] Moreover, while it might, as the authors intend, go beyond the "rarefied abstraction" of the state, it really only goes as far as Wight's and Bull's international society approach did—that is, to the "rarefied" world of the state elite, the world of the diplomat and statesmen, working on behalf of the state and its (presumed) national interest.[25] Consequently, while genuine analytical difference might be claimed by scholars such as Puchala and Hopkins, their basic analytical attention remains focused upon hierarchical power structures and decisions made from above by state-based actors. Richard O'Meara has come to a similar conclusion, finding, in general, that "the Grotian and traditional [Realist] approaches are not incommensurable: both rely on the analytical concepts of power and self-interest and both are ultimately concerned with describing and explaining the behaviour of states."[26]

This commensurability theme applies also to the contributions of Kratochwil and Ruggie, who, while they might blanch at the term *Grotian* as applied to their work, have introduced to recent debates some sophisticated analysis of philosophical issues, largely eschewed by the discipline in general. Here, however, the limits on critical inquiry are most clearly evident because they are self-imposed. Accordingly, having emphasized the need for insights drawn from the "interpretive sciences,"[27] they then firmly close off the discussion by stressing that their position should not be taken as "advocating a coup whereby the reign of positivist explanation is replaced by exploratory anarchy."[28]

This example of the "Cartesian anxiety" on the part of Kratochwil and Ruggie, when added to the limitations of Grotian regime theory in general, is indicative of the situation that provoked critical social theory responses to International Relations orthodoxy in the 1980s and 1990s. It indicates, primarily, that any genuinely critical space opened in the 1970s did not stay open for long. Instead, since the late 1970s, the potential for a fundamental reassessment of the theory and practice of International Relations has been overhauled by a resurgent Realism (represented as neo-Realism) concerned, at the level of "practice," with the retention of the hierarchical status quo of the post–World War II period (e.g., U.S. hegemony) and, "theoretically," with an updated discourse of Realist closure.

Closing Down the Thinking Space: Realism Resurgent

By 1977 the Realist backlash was already evident in, for example, the work of Robert Tucker, who, in reflecting upon the challenges posed by interdependence scholars, regime theorists, and "liberals" and "radicals" generally, sought to reaffirm the Traditional need for structural continuity and systemic order, albeit in terms of a basic inequality between states.[29] Tucker's logic was simple, familiar, and self-affirming. The "radicals" do not understand the reality they seek to change because they do not understand two unalterable principles of an international system—first, that the international system has always been anarchical and relations between states are oligarchical (unequal) precisely because the system has always been anarchical, and second, that order must be the dominant principle in an anarchical system and the key to order is the "self-help" principle, which is "the right of the state to determine when its legitimate interests are threatened, or violated, and to employ such coercive measures as it may deem necessary to vindicate those interests."[30] This latter principle must not be violated, Tucker insists, because while it has its drawbacks (i.e., it might create greater inequalities) it is integral to the structural reality of the international system and, as the basis of systemic order, it is the only hope for any "progressive" change or any interstate equalization in the future.

In Tucker's refurbished representation of contemporary reality, therefore, the challenge of interdependence and regime cooperation is confronted, once again, with the Realist postulate that change (in an anarchical system) is possible only when it comes from the top, when it is in the interests of the major powers, and when it does not unbalance the systemic order based on the "self-help" principle. In Tucker's terms, consequently, the dilemma of the contemporary age is that critics do not appreciate the dangers of trying to make the system more democratic and egalitarian. In particular, the critics of the post-Vietnam generation fail to appreciate the problems of change in an international structure that does not possess "the elementary conditions that . . . [make] possible the progression of equality within civil society."[31] Thus, in reinvoking the domestic/international dichotomy, Tucker emphasizes, in Traditional style, that in the absence of those conditions that make domestic society coherent "and that permit order without tyranny," any attack on the hierarchical system of states may bring increased disorder in the international realm.[32]

Those struggling to survive in domestic situations of anarchy on a daily basis might question Tucker's dichotomized view of their status, of course, as might those unconvinced that their domestic circumstances actually add up to "order without tyranny." But this is not Tucker's audience, anyway. Rather, *Inequality of Nations* spoke to those at the top of the global hierarchy about the need to renew their faith in a theory as practice that actualized and legitimated their status. In this regard, Tucker's *Inequality of Nations* is ultimately no better nor worse than any other contemporary incantation of Realist logic. Its significance here is that, published in 1977, it stands as an early testament to the post-Vietnam resurgence of the Realist dogma. It indicates that having dealt with the ephemeral anomalies of the Vietnam period, members of the International Relations mainstream were, by the late 1970s, recovering their sense of identity and analytical equilibrium, after a short period when ambiguity, ambivalence, and difference threatened. Waltz's *Theory of International Politics,* published in 1979, confirmed this, and, generally, within a few years, the potential openness of the early 1970s was effectively closed off as Realists (e.g., via Kindleberger) further integrated neoclassical economics themes with their power politics and represented their "catechism" in the moderated terms of the era of postpositivism, post-Realism, and the third debate in International Relations.[33]

The result is the modulated primitivism of neo-Realism, which has seen some of the most closed aspects of Western modernism projected back to center stage, via a resurgence of structuralist deductive modeling and rational-actor game theory, designed to scientifically insulate Realism from its interpretivist critics. All this, plus an overlay of (neoclassical) economic jargon, has seen the International Relations discipline unequivocally retain its "backward" status in the era of neo-Realism.

Neo-Realism: The New/Old Orthodoxy in International Relations

Neo-Realism is projected by its adherents as having overcome the problems of its (Traditionalist and behavioralist) predecessors and as a theoretically sensitive counterpoint to its critics in the post-Vietnam period. It is generally projected also as two variations on a structuralist theme.[34] The first is represented as a conventional structuralist perspective (e.g., Kenneth Waltz), which is explicitly conservative and, on the regime issue, for example, "rejects any significant role for principles, norms, rules and decision making procedures."[35] The second represents itself in more liberal terms, as a modified structuralism (e.g., Stephen Krasner and Robert Keohane), which, on regimes,

> accept[s] the basic analytical assumptions of [conventional] structural realist approaches, which posit an international system of functionally symmetrical, power-maximising states acting in an anarchic environment. But [it] maintain[s] that under certain restrictive conditions involving the

> failure of individual action to secure Pareto-optimal outcomes, international regimes may have a significant impact even in an anarchical world.[36]

Leaving aside the contemporary jargon ("Pareto-optimal outcomes" refers to the fulfillment of utilitarian interests), this celebration of structuralist "difference" indicates that both neo-Realist variants remain incarcerated within the restricted discursive confines of (1) the power politics Tradition, (2) a positivist/empiricist "metaphysic," and (3) an uncritical and conservative modernism. My aim, from this point on, is to illustrate how this is so, and to explore some of its implications for contemporary scholars of global politics. I will do so in terms established by Krasner, in taking seriously his proposition that the regime issue is integral to questions of contemporary world order and therefore must be addressed in a more sophisticated manner than ever before. In this context I accept entirely Krasner's proposition that "the issue is not so much whether one accepts the possibility of principles, norms, rules, and decision making procedures affecting outcomes and behaviour, as what one's *basic assumption is about the normal state of international affairs* [emphasis added]."[37] It is therefore in relation to the basic assumptions brought to images of the "normal state of international affairs," by neo-Realists of both structuralist variants, that I now turn to some of the major literary contributions of the genre. In the first instance the seminal contribution of Kenneth Waltz will receive extended attention, albeit in a rather unconventional manner. Attention will then be directed to the works of figures such as Krasner, Gilpin, Stein, and Keohane.

From Reductionism to Banality: Waltz and Neo-Realist Structuralism

Kenneth Waltz's contribution to International Relations spans four decades. In that time he has added influential dimensions to Realist scholarship. Since its publication in 1959, for example, his *Man, the State and War* has been accorded the status of a classical text in the discipline.[38] Moreover, Waltz's *Theory of International Politics* (1979) has been promoted by Joseph Nye as the work that manages to reveal the logic of power politics Realism more profoundly than any other.[39] It is difficult to argue with such a view, which unwittingly and ironically vindicates the critical attitude taken toward Realism and neo-Realism throughout this book.[40]

My own position on *Theory of International Politics* and (to a lesser degree) *Man, the State and War* is that they stand as major indictments of an International Relations community that, closed to critical reflective capacity for so long, has accorded such high status to works of so little substance. They stand, in this regard, as a testament to the continuing legacy of a closed modernist discourse in the period of Realist dominance in

International Relations. The difference between the two works is ultimately more a matter of tone and attitude than analytical quality. *Man, the State and War,* for example, had a certain charm and intellectual width, manifestly lacking from the later work, and in 1959, at the height of Realist confidence and influence, Waltz was willing to ventilate at least some of the philosophical and analytical givens of the Realist "catechism." Two decades later, however, in less favorable circumstances for U.S. foreign policy and Realist theory, his mood and ambition was narrower, more constrained, and less philosophically tolerant.

In 1959, for example, Waltz sought to confront Morgenthau's theologically based notion of human nature and its implications for Realist-based U.S. foreign policy in the Cold War years. More specifically, Waltz was concerned with the question of what causes war, a question that for Morgenthau and others (e.g., Niebuhr) was answered in reductionist terms—that is, the inherent evil of "man." In an international context, this logic flowed into another, which accorded evil intent to (some) states in the anarchical system. This Realist image of the world Waltz found unsatisfactory for a number of reasons, not the least being its connection to an idealist counterpart that based its own reductionist image on the progressive nature of the state system, in which "good" states would eventually overcome evil intent via rational processes. Both images of reality, claimed Waltz, were simplistic and one-sided, and both were bound up in a metaphysics of human nature represented as an essence of International Relations. Moreover, neither the "pessimistic" nor the "optimistic" images assisted greatly in the search for the scientific Realism that Carr had urged and (North) American behavioralists had pursued after World War II. And even here, suggested Waltz, reductionism reigned, with much behavioralist scholarship reduced to a fact-grubbing empiricism devoid of political analysis.[41]

For Waltz in 1959, therefore, Realism needed to move beyond metaphysical reductionism dressed up as analysis and engage itself with the actual reality of the state system. He sought to thus change Realism via a structuralist image of interstate conflict, derived from Rousseauian thought in particular, which illustrated that the major cause of war did not emanate from the evil in "man" or in individual states but from the state system itself.[42] Rousseau's image was crucial in this regard because it explained why, at the international level, politics is synonymous with relations of systemic *anarchy.* This, as indicated, is not because of any inherent goodness or badness at the individual level but because it is a structural determinant of interstate relations that all states necessarily respond to, whether they want to or not. Or, to put it in Rousseauian terms, just as "man, in a state of nature . . . cannot begin to behave decently unless he has some assurance that others will not be able to ruin him," so an individual state "might want to remain at peace [but] may have to consider undertaking a preventative war [because] if it does not strike when the moment is favourable it may be struck later when advantage has shifted to the other side."[43] According to Waltz in 1959, this Rousseauian insight on the security dilemma made possible a general theory of International Relations and an appreciation that all interstate behavior is characterized by a particular kind of rational self-interest, as determined by the structural facts of systemic life.[44]

This utilization of Rousseauian philosophy in *Man, the State and War* was useful also in (re)establishing two Traditional Realist givens about International Relations. First, conflict is inscribed in any social system that lacks an orderer; second, the balance of power is an integral and necessary function of the resultant anarchy of the international system. This was an approach superior to Morgenthau's, Waltz claimed, because while it acknowledged the behavior of individual states as the *immediate* cause of war, it established that, in reality, such behavior was ultimately dependent upon "the general structure that permits them [states] to exist and wreak their disasters."[45]

In *Man, the State and War,* this thesis on structural anarchy is presented in terms that allow for a modicum of interpretive space within Realist discursive boundaries. In qualitative terms, however, the Waltzian "great text" is ultimately just as limited and theoretically unself-conscious as its mainstream Realist counterparts. A Realist logocentrism remains, for example, concerning the domestic/international antimony. In Waltz's case this results in (1) the proposition that order in the international system is dependent upon a central governing authority (a leviathan) and (2) no assessment whatsoever of the anarchical nature of domestic societies that *do* have strong governing authorities. Thus, like so many Realists before him (and since), Waltz is silent on the issue of domestic anarchy, wanting only to speak about "external" factors concerning the systemic constraints imposed *upon* states. This is an important issue because it is via this silence that Realists and neo-Realists continue to demarcate an anarchical world "out there," which must be responded to in power politics terms. It is an important silence for other reasons, too, of course, in that it marks the site of Realist identity (as the "knowers" of anarchy) and of an illusory homogeneity and unity in the world, constructed and defined in relation to anarchy, threat, and disorder (e.g., during the Cold War). (These issues will be addressed in more detail and from a number of angles in Chapters 7 and 8.)

Suffice it to say for now that while Waltz's logocentric strategy might have impressed an uncritical discipline since 1959, it is less than impressive when critically examined, even in its own terms. This is particularly the case if one ponders Waltz's attempts to project his structuralist logic in game-theoretical terms. Here, Waltz acknowledges two major caveats to his theoretical enterprise that exemplify its weaknesses. The first caveat recognizes that the anarchical "systems game" is not necessarily a zero-sum game, while the second caveat allows that states are engaged in other "games," simultaneously, with the security game. The problem with these caveats is that, taken together, they fundamentally undermine the whole Waltzian schema (and structuralist neo-Realism per se). As Justin Rosenberg explains, this is because they

> concede that within certain limits (which in practice turn out to be very wide indeed) the impact of anarchy on the *behaviour of states varies according to determinations quite outside the purview of a Realist theory* [emphasis added]. [For example,] a state may choose or be forced to behave quite otherwise than predicted by the logic of balance of power: it may be prepared to countenance large scale retreat internationally in order to release resources for urgent domestic goals; it may undertake the military defence of a transnational socio-economic system which leads it routinely to exceed the requirements of the visible "national interest"; in extreme cases, where it contends with serious internal challenges, it may even fail properly to resist an external aggressor [while] certain security interests may simply be overridden because their pursuit is judged too costly in either domestic or international terms.[46]

The point here is that, even if all the "games" played by all the states are governed by the rules of structuralist anarchy, as Waltz insists, there is still nothing approaching a general explanation for why states act in the way they do, except the suggestion that sometimes they act in ways congruent with the Rousseauian security dilemma.

This, of course, begs the question of what *precisely* Waltz's early structuralist "great text" did contribute in 1959, if its anarchical premise and its balance-of-power postulate cannot account for international behavior, except occasionally and under certain circumstances and then only in retrospect. The charitable answer, perhaps, is that it provided a useful counterpoint to Morgenthau's Realist grand theory centered on original sin propositions about human nature. This, it must be said, is hardly a major contribution. Consequently, a less charitable but more accurate reading of *Man, the State and War* is Rosenberg's, which maintains that "Waltz's theoretical Realism is little more than a banality which merely reaffirms that inter-state behaviour *can* [emphasis added] be understood as a recurring Prisoners Dilemma, particularly in regard to security issues."[47]

Waltz's *Man, the State and War* thus represents little more than an embroidered representation of Realist primitivism. And like all of the Realisms that his structuralism sought to supersede, Waltz's arguments in *Man, the State and War* resonate with the metaphysics, abstractionism, and unself-consciousness of modernist discourse. This is never clearer than in regard to the lingering (and paradoxical) *individualism* at the foundation of Waltz's structuralism, as articulated, for example, via the famous "stag hunt" parable (of systemic rational action), which in *Man, the State and War* is represented in terms of Hobbesian-like actors in some presocial state of nature. This is important because it is upon this individualized parable that Waltz constructs his contemporary image of an anarchical world "out there," and indeed his whole structuralist scenario, the status of which is immediately problematic when one understands it as predicated upon the aggregated rational decisions of *individual* (presocial) actors.[48] This theme has received critical attention from a variety of sources, some of which will be considered shortly.[49] For now I am more concerned to illustrate the general discursive continuity between *Man, the State and War* and the first "great text" of neo-Realism, Waltz's *Theory of International Politics* (1979).

The continuity is apparent enough from the outset, indeed from the moment Waltz reiterates his intentions to "construct a theory of international politics that remedies the defects of present theories."[50] The basic theoretical defect is reductionism, and International Relations, he (re)asserts, must repudiate reductionist theory in favor of structuralist approaches. If the implications of Waltz's efforts were not so serious on this issue, it would be an enterprise filled with (unintended) mirth. This is primarily because from the beginning of *Theory of International Politics,* Waltz's antireductionist perspective is propounded in the most *reductionist* of terms—those associated with the singularity of the unity-of-science thesis and a Popperian analytical sleight of hand.[51]

In *Theory of International Politics,* accordingly, Waltz simply replicates the Popperian strategy, by first defining mainstream positivist Realism (Traditionalist and behavioralist) as reductionist, fact-grubbing empiricism and then contrasting this approach with his deductivist structuralism. This Popperian-induced sleight of hand allows space for three basic assumptions in Waltz's argument: (1) it is necessary and desirable for International Relations to have a structuralist general theory, characterized by the logic and rigor of deductivist theorizing in the natural sciences; (2) this general theory cannot be achieved while International Relations specialists remain committed to inductivism; and (3) this general theory is achievable because there is a systemic order in International Relations that can be "discovered" via systematic thinking about "the striking sameness in the quality of international life through the millennia."[52]

The acknowledgment of a crude empiricism at the core of the International Relations discipline is, like much neo-Realist insight (and much post positivism generally), fine as far as it goes. The problem is that this *is* as far as it goes. Thus, in Waltz's case, while (ostensibly) acknowledging the problems of an illusory real world of (independent) fact, he follows this logic anyway, in his repudiation of all "interpretative" approaches and in his advocation of a scientifically based structuralism. On the issue of theory and (scientific) laws, consequently, Waltz follows the (modernist) route laid down by Carr and Morgenthau, and by Western social theory in general, in the post-Cartesian era. Thus, he asserts, (interpretivist) "theories are qualitatively different from laws." Why? Because "each descriptive term in laws is directly tied to observational or laboratory procedures, and laws are established only if they pass observational or experimental tests." Laws, on this basis, are derived from observation and testing, as per the natural scientific model. However, "theories, [unlike laws,] contain theoretical notions [and] theories cannot be constructed through induction alone, for theoretical notions can *only be invented not discovered* [emphasis added]."[53] Anyone doubting the continuing power of positivism at the core of neo-Realism need only ponder Waltz's position here, as, like generations of positivists before him, he invokes the great dichotomy between "theory" and the "real" world—the former, the realm of "internally" generated "invention," and the latter, the "external" repository of laws that theories (retrospectively) explain, order, and systematize. Ultimately, therefore, "theory, though related to the world about which explanations are wanted, always remains distinct from that world."[54] This, it must be remembered, is a position seeking to remedy the defects in reductionist approaches to International Relations, centered on the illusory relationship between inductivist observation and a real world "out there." It represents instead another confirmation of the primitive nature of Realist/neo-Realist thinking in the contemporary period and a striking example of the continuing discursive power of a modernist regime of framing at the core of the International Relations discipline.

This primitivism is increasingly evident in *Theory of International Politics* as Waltz explains what, precisely, structuralism means in an international context and what its analytical implications are for contemporary life.[55] Here, he insists, the primary analytical task is to separate that which is essential to understanding the international system—its unchanging foundational quality—from that which is ephemeral and susceptible to historical/cultural/ideological change. This is deemed vital in order "to distinguish between causes and effects."[56] A major requirement, in this regard, is the removal of certain "vague and varying" concepts from the Realist agenda before "useful" structuralist premises can be applied to the real world. These "vague and varying" concepts include "environment, situation, context and milieu." Moreover, a whole range of questions must also be "left aside"—questions, for example, about the kinds of political leaders, social and economic institutions, and ideological commitments states may have. Also deleted are other (presumably) nonuseful questions "about the cultural, economic, political and military interaction of states."[57] The point of all these exclusions is to "establish structure by abstraction from 'concrete reality.'" And this can be achieved only "by leaving aside the personality of actors, their behaviour, and their interactions . . . [and by] ignoring how units relate with one another (how they interact) and concentrating on how they stand in relation to one another (how they are arranged or positioned)." This is absolutely crucial to Waltz's structuralist neo-Realism, because "how units stand in relation to one another, the way they are arranged or positioned, is not a property of the units. The arrangement of the units is a property of the system."[58]

The sense of ahistorical determinism engendered by a statement such as this is only increased when Waltz speaks of precisely what a structuralist approach is set to achieve. At this point, in 1979, the echoes of *Man, the State and War* and a generation of Realist conservatism rings out in Waltz's "great text" of neo-Realism, with the proposal that it is "the structure of the system [that] acts as a *constraining and disposing force,* and because it does so, systems theories explain and predict *continuity* within the system." Above all, therefore, Waltz's structuralism is system oriented because it is "within a system, [that] a theory explains *recurrences and repetitions, not change* [emphasis added]."[59]

It is at this point that the "banality" theme attributed to *Man, the State and War* by Rosenberg becomes even more relevant to the neo-Realism of *Theory of International Politics,* written twenty years later.[60] Unlike in 1959, however, there is no attempt now to embroider the structuralist argument in interesting philosophical fabric. In place of the Rousseauian parable, consequently, there is another—the parable of the capitalist market—presented as a microeconomic analogy for the endemic anarchy of the international system. In this context, Waltz insists, two questions can now be asked concerning the anarchical structure of both forums, with the answers allowing superior insight into the theory and practice of International Relations. The first question: how are markets formed? The second: how do they work? Waltz's answer to the first question is that "the market of a decentralized economy is individualist in origin, spontaneously generated and unintended." Such a market "*arises out of* the activities of separate units . . . whose aims and efforts are directed not towards creating an order but rather toward fulfilling their own internally defined interest." This begs an answer to the second question (i.e., how does the system actually work and how is order created in the system?). Waltz's answer here is as simple and unconvincing as that offered to the first—the "hidden hand." Thus "the individual acts for itself" and consequently "from the coaction of like units *emerges* a structure that affects and constrains all of them."[61]

Turning specifically to the other side of the analogy—the international market—the answers are as predictable. Accordingly, the basic insight of neo-Realism, the structuralist essence that sets it apart from its Realist predecessor, is that

> international political systems, like economic markets, are formed by the coaction of self regarding units. International structures are defined in terms of the primary political units of an era, be they city states, empires, or nations. Structures emerge from the coexistence of states. No state intends to participate in the formation of a structure by which it and others will be constrained.[62]

Rousseau thus meets Adam Smith. The result, rather incongruously represented in this context, is an ahistorical, depoliticized scenario replete with vague references to "spontaneously" generated markets and political structures that mysteriously "emerge."[63] This is the keystone of Waltz's structuralist insight. This is what he knows about the international system that is so significant as to warrant his damning critique of the disciplinary mainstream and its radical alternatives in *Theory of International Politics.*

In order that it not be thought that Waltz's more recent promulgations on the issue have been ignored here, it is worth contemplating further his position in 1990 on the theory question. Very little has changed, it seems, because as Waltz explains,

> a theory is an intellectual construction *by which we select facts and interpret them* [emphasis added]. The challenge is to bring theory to bear on facts in ways that permit explanation and prediction. This can only be accomplished *by distinguishing between theory and fact* [emphasis added]. Only if this distinction is made can theory be used to examine and interpret facts.[64]

And as a contemporary postscript to his structuralist position in 1979, Waltz left little doubt, in 1990, that the mountain has indeed brought forth another molehill, with his explanation of the fundamental difference between (state-centric) Realism and his neo-Realism. It is, quite simply, that the latter recognizes that "anarchy sets the problems that states have to cope with."[65]

Waltz's perspective has not escaped criticism, even from within the International Relations mainstream. John Ruggie, for example, has seized on the rather dramatic lapses in logic in *Theory of International Politics,* in proposing that Waltz's structuralist theory is so inadequate that not only is it unable to explain where individual states came from, it cannot explain where the contemporary state *structure* came from.[66] Ruggie's point is that, for all Waltz's protestations to the contrary, his structuralism is static and ahistorical. Accordingly, it "provides no means by which to account for, or even describe, the most important contextual change in international politics in this millennium: the shift from the medieval to the modern international system."[67] Ruggie does not question the anarchy theme at the core of Waltz's structuralism. He argues, rather, that Waltz's approach does not allow for different forms of anarchical relations, characteristic of different historical epochs during the development of the state system.[68] The claim, in other words, is that Waltz's version of the structuralist recurrence and repetition theme—relevant across space, time, culture, and linguistic practice—fundamentally misunderstands the heterogeneous and historically dynamic nature of political systems. This is a rather damning criticism of a work that seeks to remedy all that has gone before in the discipline—in systemic terms. A similar sort of criticism has come from Alexander Wendt, who has focused more explicitly on the confusion and paradox of Waltz's approach to the agent/structure conundrum.[69] Waltz's argument, suggests Wendt, fails to deal adequately with this crucial issue because it is ultimately about a one-sided structuralist determinism, which sees Waltz simply ascribe ontological priority to (individual) states without explaining their precise relationship to the structure as a whole.[70]

As the discussion above sought to illustrate, this is precisely the way Waltz deals with the state-as-agent issue. Indeed, this is precisely the way his paradoxical individualism was represented in *Man, the State and War* in 1959. In *Theory of International Politics,* in 1979, it represents a continuing backwardness at the apex of the International Relations discipline, manifested in the inability of its structuralist "great text" to explain the structural existence of states! Or, as Wendt puts it, "systems structures cannot generate agents if they are defined exclusively in terms of those agents in the first place."[71]

For all the saliency of Wendt's and Ruggie's criticisms of Waltz, there is in Wendt's structuration perspective and Ruggie's perspective, influenced by analytical philosophy themes, a continuing commitment to a unity-of-science thesis and the pursuit of a theory of international reality based on positivist basic assumptions. Their critical "alternatives," in other words, reinforce the discursive power of the (modernist) orthodox consensus in International Relations and remain of limited value in alleviating the "poverty" of neo-Realism.[72]

Gilpin and the Hegemonic Image of International Political Economy

Even when attempts are made to explicitly rehistoricize the neo-Realist primitivism, the modernist discursive legacy continues to dominate proceedings. In Robert Gilpin's *Political Economy of International Relations* (1987), for example, this legacy is evident within a work presented in the tolerant, moderated tones of the postpositivist age in International Relations. However, the underlying positivism of Gilpin's approach limits, and ultimately renders paradoxical, his attempts to add historical and philosophical sensitivity to neo-Realism. Stephen Gill has explained, more precisely, why this is so in (correctly) characterizing Gilpin's understanding of the world as derived from a discursive amalgam of

> institutionalism, utilitarian rational choice analysis and a Realist framework of international relations, which is built upon the insights of Thucydides, E. H. Carr and Hans Morgenthau. . . . [Accordingly] he is a methodological individualist who separates "politics" and "economics" and his ontology emphasizes states and markets.[73]

It is on this basis, and utilizing a Traditional rational-actor model, that Gilpin reduces behavior in the state system to the kind of simplistic utilitarian calculus (e.g., cost/benefit analysis) that Grotians and more nuanced mainstream scholars alike recognize as inadequate.[74] The end result, inevitably, is an anarchic scenario in which the focus of attention is order and the given interests of all (rational) states are calculated as support for institutional mechanisms that produce this order (e.g., World Bank/IMF) established by the United States, the hegemonic orderer.[75]

In this manner Gilpin constructs his theoretical defense of hegemonic stability, in an era when, for many, the United States is in structural decline. And it is via this hegemonic position that Gilpin's "theory" is intrinsic to the power politics "practice" of U.S. foreign policy in a period that has seen an "armed overkill" strategy invoked in Grenada, Panama, Somalia, and the Gulf.[76] More generally, it is via this knowledge/power nexus that Gilpin, like Waltz, and neo-Realism overall, observes the world from the perspective of the largest capitalist states and seeks the kind of structural stability and political order that serves the interests of this sector of the global community. Thus, Gilpin's narrative of world history represents a cyclical pattern of hegemonies and balance-of-power systems, in which the contemporary period fits perfectly as the story of stability (postwar U.S. hegemony) overturned by a disorderly global structure in the post-Vietnam period. For Gilpin, accordingly, and for other neo-Realists of the "declinist" variety, the crucial issue of International Relations in the 1980s and 1990s has been the resuscitation of U.S. hegemonic power and, by definition, the resuscitation of international order and stability.

The problem with Gilpin's perspective is not just its narrow U.S.-centered worldview but the silences and omissions associated with it. In *The Political Economy of International Relations,* consequently, there is no serious attempt to deal with arguments that challenge the notion that Traditional order is, by definition, a "public good." Nor is there any serious concern to debate the proposition that, for all its problems, the post-Vietnam period represents for many a more progressive, more egalitarian phase in global life in which the voices of the previously unheard have begun to resonate in forums where previously the hegemon dominated. The former challenge is summarily dismissed by Gilpin (and Tucker, Waltz, etc.) as "ideological," the latter (more commonly) as "Grotian."

Moreover, in Gilpin's explanation of contemporary reality, the analytical silences are deafening. The EEC, for example, is not analyzed at all, while the USSR (as it was) and Eastern Europe are virtually ignored and China hardly rates a mention. The reason for this is a Traditional one. It has to do with the restricted and inadequate representation of the world at the discursive core of Gilpin's Realism, which orients his thinking toward Traditional notions of static systemic hierarchies and simple calculations about the relativities of power. This, as indicated earlier, is only one dimension of the problem, because the modernist characteristics that continue to hinder the work of conventional structuralists like Waltz (and "historians" like Gilpin) are just as evident in the literary contributions of the self-proclaimed modified neo-Realist structuralists. And it is to the contribution of these scholars that I now turn, in taking up Krasner's invitation to investigate the "basic assumptions" of some of the most prominent neo-Realists of the current period.

Probing Some "Basic Assumptions" in Modified Neo-Realism: Krasner, Stein, and Keohane

Stephen Krasner's proposition that the keystone of neo-Realism lies at the level of its basic assumptions was presumably made in line with his understanding of the new theoretical sensitivity of the postpositivist age. Whatever Krasner's motivation, this proposition invites a critical investigation of his own basic assumptions and, once accepted, finds them wanting, particularly on the central regime issue.

The first problem, in Krasner's case, arises when one ponders again the (modified) structuralist position he associates himself with. This position, as Krasner makes clear, does not accept that regime behavior is the fundamental organizing principle of the international system, even in an interdependent world of international political economy. Rather, for Krasner, as it has been for Realists down the ages, "power-maximizing states acting in an anarchical environment" remain the foundational element of international reality.[77] This being the case, and if regimes, defined by Krasner as "principles, norms, rules and decision making procedures," are *not* fundamental to international life, the question of what *is* fundamental becomes significant in Krasner's scenario.

More precisely, Krasner's position begs two questions. The first, simply put, is this: if contemporary state interaction is not about principles, norms, and decisionmaking procedures, what, precisely, does affect "outcomes and behavior" in the international system? On Krasner's own account, principles are "beliefs of fact, causation, and rectitude." Norms of behavior, meanwhile, relate to a set of social "rules and obligations." Rules relate to "specific prescriptions or proscriptions for action," while decision-making practices are defined as the "prevailing practices for making and implementing collective choice."[78] In light of this, the proposition that these are *not* the fundamental issue in everyday international life becomes more problematic. Indeed it is hard to imagine, theological images aside, how one does come to an understanding of regimes or of anything else if not through a process such as this. Putting the question a little differently would be to ask of Krasner this: if understanding is not derived via "beliefs of fact and causation," if it is not formulated in human societies with "rules and obligations" that mediate, define, and police understanding in terms of sociointellectual "prevailing practices," what on earth is it derived from? *If, in other words, understanding is not derived from human social interaction and knowledge construction, where* is *it derived from?* The answer, in Krasner's terms, is already given—from one's "basic assumptions" about the normal state of international affairs. Which, of course, only serves to beg the second, obvious question, concerning the derivative source of these basic assumptions if they do not emanate from the historical, societal, and philosophical experiences encompassed in regimes.

For Krasner, and for those neo-Realists so confidently asserting the "concreteness" of their approach to the world, it is at this point that their paradoxical commitment to the "empiricist metaphysic" is exposed. Exposed also at the core of neo-Realist structuralism, again, is a modernist ontology that is paradoxically reductionist and reliant upon positivist premises concerning the anarchic structure that *just exists* (beyond explanation) "out there." This becomes more evidently Krasner's position when he reflects that, for modified structuralists, the prevailing explanation, for regime behavior, and indeed all other behavior at the international level, is "egoistic self-interest . . . [which is] the desire to maximise one's utility function where the function does not include the utility of another party."[79]

In short, then, the basic assumption of Krasner's kind of structuralist neo-Realism is the Traditional, interstate anarchy assumption, the very same (unexplained) assumption that has informed Waltz and Gilpin, Carr and Morgenthau, Wight, Bull, Kaplan, and Tucker of the "normal state" of International Relations, down the ages. For all the structuralist and (neoclassical) economics jargon, therefore, and for all the updated behavioralism of its representation, this remains the highly problematic basis of neo-Realist wisdom in the 1990s.[80]

Arthur Stein is explicit enough in this regard, arguing that, for all the talk of a changing international environment, nothing has changed concerning the fundamental nature of International Relations, and nothing can change in terms of its fundamental problem of analysis, which is "to describe and explain patterns of order in the anarchic world of international politics."[81] When it comes to articulating his basic assumptions concerning this Traditionalist perspective, Stein is just as explicit, proposing, on the regime issue, that "the same forces of autonomously calculated self interest that lie at the root of the anarchic international system also lay the foundations for international regimes."[82] Consequently, when Stein applies his neo-Realist insight to the issue of regimes, he does so in precisely the same discursive manner as his neo-Realist counterparts and a whole generation of his Realist peers. The way he compares neo-Realist structuralism with its Grotian challengers is particularly interesting in this regard, if only because it confirms again the rather parlous state of mainstream thinking in International Relations in the 1990s.

Stein's argument here is familiar, self-enclosed, and, as usual, authoritatively stated. Thus a neo-Realist structuralism is superior because it is "rooted in the classic characterization of international politics as relations between sovereign entities dedicated to their own self-preservation, ultimately able to depend only on themselves, and prepared to resort to force."[83] The great value of this approach is that it provides an image of interstate behavior that *corresponds* to reality per se, because it understands that

> the [systemic] outcomes that emerge from the interaction of states making independent decisions are a function of their interests and preferences. [Consequently such] independent behaviour and the outcomes that result from it constitute the working of *normal international politics—not of regimes* [emphasis added].[84]

The implication of this argument is that "normal" International Relations takes place where actors make independent decisions in a free market of anarchical power politics. And this is precisely Stein's point. He explains, accordingly, that regimes exist where "the interaction between the parties is not unconstrained or is not based on independent decision making."[85] Again, and just as incongruously as in other neo-Realist scenarios, Rousseau (or Thucydides or Machiavelli) is joined in unholy union with Adam Smith (or Charles Kindleberger) and, just as in Waltz's case, the old dichotomies are trotted out to add Traditionalist credibility to the new international political economy of neo-Realism. For Stein, thus, the most common regime is "domestic society" because

> even the freest and most open [domestic] societies do not allow individualism and market forces full play [therefore] . . . domestic society, characterised by the agreement of individuals to eschew the use of force in settling disputes, *constitutes a regime* [emphasis added] precisely because it constrains the behaviour of its citizens.[86]

The definition of *regime,* utilized here by Stein, owes something to another modernist theme that over the years has intersected with positivist utilitarianism (i.e., social contract theory), a perspective that David Hume found unconvincing when it was first used to project a set of bourgeois interests as a grand theory of human behavior in the eighteenth century. The more immediate problem of this definition of domestic society is that, as the opposite of the international realm, it designates the latter as the site of the kind of crude laissez-faire atomism that even liberal political economists have repudiated. Indeed, Stein's image of an unconstrained rational universe of competing (state) actors—"free to choose"—represents not a return just to Traditionalist Realist reductionism but to the crudest "billiard ball" articulation of it.

Not all modified structuralists represent their position in quite the way that Stein does, even if their basic assumptions remain fundamentally the same. Robert Keohane, for example, takes a more measured approach to the regime issue as befits an erstwhile liberal interdependence scholar of the 1970s. Speaking in the mid-1980s about the neo-Realist approach in general and his own assumptions in particular, Keohane is the model of the new breed of theoretically sensitive Realist, gently chiding the policy analyst for perhaps thinking that theory is irrelevant to the real world of International Relations.[87] Not so, soothed Keohane, because theory can be "useful" in understanding the real world. Indeed, he suggests, "theory does have implications for practice."[88] Outlining some of these implications, Keohane is particularly concerned to distinguish between the "theories of world politics on which policymakers and commentators rely" and scientific theories, such as Newtonian physics. The distinguishing factor here, he proposes, is that while the latter provided "powerful, value-free explanations of outcomes," the former are invested with the "scholar's values, and their own personal experiences and temperaments."[89] It might be expected that in the 1980s the odd policy analyst who had read Thomas Kuhn or pondered Heisenberg's conclusions about the interpretive nature of quantum physics might have wanted to question this particular rendition of the modernist story. But this aside, the positivist primitiveness of Keohane's theoretical understanding becomes increasingly evident, as he turns to the question of the relationship between theory and reality.

Again the tone is moderate and impeccably 1980s, even if the substance reeks of eighteenth-century empiricism. Thus, intones Keohane, on the question of understanding reality, "even if one could eradicate theory from one's mind it would be self defeating to try." Why? Because "reality has to be ordered into categories, and relationships drawn between events."[90] For Keohane, then, as for so many in the line through Descartes, Locke, Hume, Comte, and Popper, "theory" is represented as a *cognitive reaction to reality* rather than as integral to its construction. Theorizing, consequently, is understood as the the retrospective process by which reality is ordered into (interpretive) categories. Theory, in this context, takes place *after the fact.* More explicitly, theory helps us understand the "relationship between events" that are *prior to theory.*

From this position, of course, the really meaningful question becomes that framed by logical positivism: how do we test or verify whether our theories of reality are, in fact, congruent with reality as it is "out there"?[91] It is not necessary to call upon the work of critical "reflectivists" for confirmation that this is Keohane's position; Stephen Krasner has confirmed it. He proposes that, for Keohane, international reality is framed in terms of two basic assumptions about the nature of the real world—two a priori "facts" against which the scholarly (theoretical) enterprise must *start.* The first, echoing power politics Realists from Morgenthau to Waltz, is that International Relations is all about "a world of sovereign states seeking to maximise their interest and power." The second, echoing marketplace logic from Smith to Kindleberger, is that the fundamental determinant of behavior (including regime behavior) is "egoistic self-interest."[92]

Consequently, for Keohane, taking his cue from the logical positivists, the issue (in this case the nature of regimes and the contemporary international arena) becomes essentially a matter of methodology—a process of theorizing and falsifying the facts, of explaining their "implications for practice." Given that the major facts are already framed, as the site of egoistic individualism and market anarchy, there is not much question of which methodology is the appropriate one. Keohane, accordingly, takes a position on regimes "that relies heavily on rational choice analysis in the utilitarian social contract tradition."[93]

The analytical results are predictable and disturbing in their simplicity and narrowness. Thus, because the world "out there" is made up of sovereign states, following selfish interest, two conclusions must logically flow from this: (1) the cooperative/communitarian impulse within the state system, recorded by regime theorists, is in reality an illusion; and (2) all "meaningful" international behavior is, in essence, the pursuit of individual self-interest on the part of sovereign states, following Traditional "self-help" principles. Regime behavior, on this basis, can be understood *only* as the pragmatic (rational-actor) response of self-seeking actors to conditions in which utility maximizing is sometimes best served by some sort of collective decisionmaking scenario. Moreover, as the Realist Tradition has always insisted, change can come *only* from above—from the rational action of the major powers following rational self-interest. The change to regime institutionalism in the post–World War II period, celebrated by some as fundamental change, is consequently no more than a pragmatic readjustment of power politics behavior. Realism, in short, still corresponds with the world "out there," and the Tradition and discipline is saved from the horrors of critical self-reflection by neo-Realism.

Many, however, remain unconvinced by this logic. Richard O'Meara is one commentator who has voiced his dissatisfaction at the "shallow" and "sterile" attempt of neo-Realists, such as Keohane, to integrate their newfound concern with (neoclassical) economics with their deeper commitments to conservative Realism.[94] This only increases the paradox and incoherence of Keohane's structuralism, which, like Waltz's, ends up as a reductionist doctrine, centered on crude utilitarian premises. Thus, for all his posturing toward sophisticated structuralism, Keohane must apply his microeconomic analogies in terms of "[individual] states as coherent units which alone comprise the world political system. Although elsewhere Keohane has described states as 'multifaceted, even schizophrenic' he now assumes that states are not only 'billiard balls,' but rational utility maximisers as well."[95]

Throughout this chapter my intention has been to illustrate that this kind of unself-consciousness and analytical primitiveness continues to dominate in International Relations in the era of neo-Realism. The broad context for the discussion was the period between the end of the Vietnam War and the present. The more specific focus was the challenge to International Relations posed by, among others, Grotian regime theorists seeking to add a long-overdue critical dimension to Realist images of the world. The aim was not to argue for Grotian perspectives per se but to illustrate, in a specific way, the closure and dogma associated with neo-Realist responses to them.

Integral to these responses, I argued, has been the theory of structuralist anarchy invoked by Kenneth Waltz and the (modified) structuralism of figures such as Keohane, Krasner, Stein, and Gilpin. The discussion sought to critically evaluate their positions in their own terms and from a variety of perspectives, some generally supportive of neo-Realism. The result was not very comforting, to say the least. Any sense of a new, more sophisticated understanding in Realist ranks was found to be illusory the moment one critically examined the textual contributions of leading neo-Realist scholars. On behalf of antireductionist structuralism, for example, the crudest reductionism was seen to flourish (e.g., in Waltz and Stein). At the center of a discipline that dismisses its critics as abstract "reflectivists," the "empiricist metaphysic" was seen to reign, the hidden font of intolerance and rigidity. The picture got bleaker. Leaving aside the problems of structuralists who can't explain structure (e.g., Waltz, according to Ruggie and Wendt) and analysts of an interdependent world who leave the EEC, China, and the Soviet Union (as it was then) out of their analysis (e.g., Gilpin), the neo-Realist worldview was shown to be as narrow, silent, and caricatured as it ever was on questions of power, change, and human complexity. Or, as Susan Strange has put it, neo-Realism, no less than its Realist predecessor, "deals predominantly with the status quo, and tends to exclude hidden agendas and to leave unheard or unheeded complaints, whether they come from the underprivileged, the disenfranchised or the unborn, about the way the system works."[96]

In the following chapter I will begin to address some of the ways scholars in the broad social theory context have begun to address the silences associated with a situation like this and move beyond it. These critical interdisciplinary debates have been the wellspring of the major critical social theory approaches in recent years, and the discussion now seeks to explain some of the major debates, themes, and issues that have underlain the critical challenges to International Relations since the 1980s.

Notes

1. For a broad overview of this period, see Maghoori and Ramberg, eds., *Globalism Versus Realism.*

2. The interdependence position at this time is associated primarily with the work of Robert Keohane and Joseph Nye; see their *Transnational Relations and World Politics* (1971), which they edited, and *Power and Interdependence* (1977); see also *Power and Interdependence* (2d ed., 1989). The latter works reflect the shifting attitudes of the authors away from the (relative) liberal openness of the period after Vietnam and the crises of the 1970s and toward the resurgent (neo)Realism of more recent times. There were others, too, working in this interdependence area; see, for example, Cooper, *The Economics of Interdependence* and *A Reordered World.* The "Grotian" designation is that of neo-Realists such as Stephen Krasner toward the works of figures such as Donald Puchala, Raymond Hopkins, and Ernst Haas; see Krasner, "Structural Causes and Regime Consequences." The term *Grotian* has a broader connotation, of course, designating a via-media position between Realist and revolutionist positions in Martin Wight's "Why Is There No International Theory?"

3. See, for example, Blum, *Drawing the Line;* Yergin, *Shattered Peace;* Halberstam, *The Best and the Brightest;* Gelb and Betts, *The Irony of Vietnam;* Kalb and Abel, *Roots of Involvement;* Kattenburg, *The Vietnam Trauma in American Foreign Policy, 1945–75,* and Ellsberg, *Papers on the War.*

4. See Keohane and Nye, *Transnational Relations and World Politics.*

5. Though for some the interdependence approach "transformed the American discipline of international relations." Gilpin, *The Political Economy of International Relations,* p. xi.

6. This is Keohane's view of the purpose of *Power and Interdependence* as articulated in *Neorealism and Its Critics,* p. 160.

7. See, for example, Haas, *Beyond the Nation State;* Deutsch, *The Analysis of International Relations;* and from a European perspective, Mitrany, *A Working Peace System.* In this period, others, such as John Burton, were also developing alternative perspectives that did not center on Traditional state-centric analysis. Burton's alternative stressed integrative behavior among a variety of actors, and it was presented in terms of social psychology premises and with "systemic" ambitions. It has remained an influential approach in Britain in particular. See Burton, *Systems, States, Diplomacy and Rules* and *World Society.* Vasquez's insight needs to be noted on this issue regarding the discursive continuity of this early regime (or integrationist) theory. Vasquez's point is that the work of Deutsch and Haas, for example, was always conducted "within the context of the [R]ealist paradigm," with neither Deutsch's communications and cybernetic theory nor Haas's functionalism, violating the "fundamental assumptions" of power politics Realism; Vasquez, *The Power of Power Politics,* p. 115.

8. Krasner, "Structural Causes and Regime Consequences," p. 1.

9. Nye, "Nuclear Learning and US-Soviet Security Regime," p. 374.

10. Krasner, "Structural Causes and Regime Consequences," p. 2.

11. Ibid., p. 8.

12. See, for example, Puchala and Hopkins, "International Regimes."

13. Ibid., p. 90.

14. Ibid.

15. Haas, "Words Can't Hurt You," p. 24.

16. Ibid.

17. Ruggie, "International Regimes, Transactions and Change," p. 196.

18. Kratochwil, "Regimes, Interpretation and the 'Science' of Politics," p. 281.

19. A good general critique of liberal/Grotian regime theory is to be found in O'Meara's "Regimes and Their Implications for International Theory." O'Meara's

article includes commentary on contributions not covered here (e.g., by Oran Young).

20. Haas, "Words Can't Hurt You," p. 24.

21. Ibid.

22. Ibid.

23. Ibid., p. 25.

24. On these problems, see the discussion in Vasquez, *The Power of Power Politics,* p. 76.

25. Puchala and Hopkins, "International Regimes," p. 63.

26. O'Meara, "Regimes and Their Implications for International Theory," p. 257.

27. Kratochwil and Ruggie, "International Organization," p. 771.

28. Ibid., p. 768.

29. Tucker, *The Inequality of Nations.*

30. Ibid., p. 4.

31. Ibid., p. 172.

32. Ibid., p. 175.

33. The influences of the economist Charles Kindleberger have become evident in the neo-Realism of scholars such as Keohane, Gilpin, Krasner, and Stein. Kindleberger, via the rational-actor model associated with collective goods theory and a game-theorised "history" of the last century or so, has provided much of the discursive raw material for the enhanced interest in "economic" themes in recent years (and for hegemonic stability theory). His basic argument is that economic stability at the international level is, by definition, a collective or public good, in that all actors benefit from the ordered and stable nature of international trade in such circumstances. The problem with the international "market," however, is that many actors will "free ride" in the pursuit of national interest rather than the public interest of the system as a whole. Accordingly, the goal of order and stability at the international level is dependent upon the power and public-spirited motivation of the strongest power—a hegemon—who can underwrite and maintain the conditions under which order and stability can characterize the "market." Integral to this theory of order, for Kindleberger, is the need for a hegemonic power regime based on Western liberal premises of market openness and (capitalist) freedom to choose. See Kindleberger, *The World in Depression, 1929–1939* and "Dominance and Leadership in the International Economy."

34. Krasner, "Structural Causes and Regime Consequences," p. 1.

35. Ibid.

36. Ibid., pp. 1–2.

37. Ibid., p. 10.

38. Ibid., p. 292.

39. Nye, "Neorealism and Neoliberalism," p. 235.

40. The "Reductionism to Banality" theme is taken from Rosenberg's "What's the Matter with Realism?"

41. Waltz, *Man, the State and War,* pp. 42–80.

42. Ibid.

43. Ibid.

44. Ibid.

45. Ibid., p. 185.

46. Rosenberg, "What's the Matter with Realism?" pp. 293–294.

47. Ibid.

48. The Rousseauian parable goes like this: Five hunters agree to join together to hunt a stag and share the proceeds in order that their general hunger program can

be overcome. However, as they wait for the moment of cooperative action, a hare runs by and one of the hunters grabs it, thus startling the stag, who runs off. Rousseau's point was that it was just as logical and rational for the hunter to take the hare as to leave it—because he could not be sure that someone else would not do the same. For Waltz, the parable was used to represent the security dilemma of states seeking cooperative relations in an anarchical system. It leads, of course, to a conclusion that all states must follow the "self-help" principle and the proposition that individual intentionality is not the basis of interstate behavior.

49. I refer here not just to Ashley's commentary in "The Poverty of Neorealism," which will be discussed in Chapter 8, but to the critiques of Waltz's updated structuralism in *Theory of International Relations* (1979); by Ruggie in "Continuity and Transformation in the World Polity"; and by Wendt in "The Agent-Structure Problem in International Relations Theory."

50. Waltz, *Theory of International Politics,* p. 1.

51. On the unity theme, see the discussion of positivism in Chapter 2, pp. 60–78. On Popper, I refer to the strategy utilized during the positivist dispute of the 1960s, when Popper defended his critical rationalism as nonpositivist by (re)defining positivism as the narrow inductivism of logical empiricism. On this Popperian strategy, see Popper, *The Logic of Scientific Discovery,* pp. 34–54. For an overview discussion, see Stockman, *Antipositivist Theories of the Sciences.*

52. Waltz, *Theory of International Politics,* p. 66.

53. Ibid., p. 5.

54. Ibid., p. 6.

55. Ibid., chap. 4.

56. Ibid., p. 78.

57. Ibid., p. 80.

58. Ibid.

59. Ibid., p. 69.

60. In Rosenberg, "What's the Matter with Realism?"

61. Ibid., p. 90.

62. Ibid.

63. The point here is that like many neoconservatives seeking to fuse a minimalist reading of Smith with a rigid conservative traditionalism, Waltz does no justice to either discourse by depoliticizing and dehistoricizing them.

64. Waltz, "Realist Thought and Neorealist Theory," p. 22.

65. Ibid., p. 36.

66. Ruggie, "Continuity and Transformation in the World Polity."

67. Ibid., p. 141.

68. Ibid., pp. 140–148.

69. Wendt, "The Agent-Structure Problem in International Relations Theory."

70. Ibid., pp. 342–344.

71. Ibid., p. 342. This Waltz does in 1979 via the logic that sees markets *arise* out of the activities of separate units.

72. In the following chapter, something will be said about analytical philosophy influences upon contemporary critical scholarship such as Ruggie's. Wendt's perspective is perhaps better understood in relation to the scientific realism of scholars such as Mary Hesse and Roy Bhaskar in the philosophy of science field and in more popular mode in Anthony Giddens's structuration theory. For a discussion that acknowledges the insights of this approach while illustrating its lingering structuralist one-sidedness, see Hekman, *Hermeneutics and the Sociology of Knowledge.*

73. Gill, "Two Concepts of International Political Economy," p. 369.

74. Ibid.
75. Ibid., p. 372.
76. Ehrenreich, "Battlin' Bill's Initiation Rite."
77. Krasner, "Structural Causes and Regime Consequences," p. 2.
78. Ibid.
79. Ibid., p. 11.
80. For an updated example of Krasner's basic assumptions at work, see "Realism, Imperialism and Democracy," where the neo-Realist structuralist seeks to detach himself from the (foreign policy) implications of his discursive position.
81. Ibid., p. 115.
82. Stein, "Coordination and Collaboration," p. 132.
83. Ibid., p. 116.
84. Ibid.
85. Ibid., p. 117.
86. Ibid.
87. Keohane, "Realism, Neorealism and the Study of World Politics."
88. Ibid., pp. 1–2.
89. Ibid., pp. 4–5.
90. Ibid., p. 4.
91. This raises the specter of positivist paradox once again, of course, given that Keohane is seeking to *distinguish* his theory from the scientific model derived from Newtonian physics. This, however, is an issue that presumably does not warrant the attention of a "real world" researcher.
92. This is Krasner's view of Keohane in "Structural Causes and Regime Consequences," p. 11.
93. Keohane, "The Demand for International Regimes," p. 141.
94. O'Meara, "Regimes and Their Implications for International Theory," p. 255.
95. Ibid., p. 255.
96. Ibid., p. 338.

6

Critical Social Theory: Thinking Beyond the "Orthodox Consensus"

In previous chapters my aim was to illustrate the intrinsic connections between an orthodox consensus in Anglo-American social theory and the dominant Tradition and disciplinary protocols of International Relations. Emphasizing the inadequacies and limitations associated with this connection, I also indicated why it is so important that the resultant positivist-Realist discourse be critically challenged. This chapter is concerned more directly with the questions of what such a challenge might encompass and what an alternative critical agenda might look like. It focuses initially on general critical social theory themes that seek to facilitate such a broadened agenda; it then concentrates more specifically on the two most influential critical perspectives in this regard—Critical Theory and postmodernism. This discussion will address the critical concerns shared by these perspectives and the significant tensions between them, particularly on the modernity question. Finally, I will indicate my reservations about aspects of both perspectives before returning to the broader issue of a critical social theory agenda in International Relations.

The style and tone of this discussion is inevitably more reminiscent of Chapter 2, with its "philosophical" orientation, than of Chapters 3, 4, and 5, which dealt explicitly with conventional International Relations themes, albeit in an unconventional way. However, just as Chapter 2 represented a broad intellectual conduit between the larger Western historicophilosophical narrative and the more recognizably International Relations themes of the following chapters, so this chapter is intended as something of an intellectual bridge, between that which has gone before in this book and that which is to come in Chapters 7 and 8. It is, in this sense, never detached from issues of war and peace and sovereignty and power politics, which are the stuff of International Relations. Rather, it speaks to them in different ways and in order that the dominant theory as practice associated with them be opened for critical scrutiny in an era that demands a more inclusive, less dogmatic approach to the world and its peoples.

Prizing Open the Orthodox Consensus: Some General Perspectives

The critical social theory challenge to orthodox theory as practice has centered generally on the proposition that there are major silences and dangers inherent in the way that we ask our questions of the modern world and construct our (rational-scientific) answers. Examples of this critical perspective have come from a whole range of intellectual locations in recent years. The two examples to follow have particular thematic significance in a critical social theory context, given their explicit concern with the crisis of modern thought and post-Enlightenment political practice.

The first comes from Robert Bellah, who in 1985 spoke of some of the paradoxes of modern life, in these terms:

> There is a widespread feeling that the promise of the modern era is slipping away from us. A movement of enlightenment and liberation that was to have freed us from superstition and tyranny has led in the twentieth century to a world in which ideological fanaticism and political oppression have reached extremes unknown in previous history. Science, which was to have unlocked the the bounties of nature, has given us the power to destroy all life on earth. Progress, modernity's master idea, seems less compelling today when it appears that it may be progress into the abyss. And the globe today is divided between a liberal world so incoherent that it seems to be losing the significance of its own ideals, an oppressive and archaic communist statism, and a poor, often tyrannical third world reaching for the first rungs of modernity.[1]

These themes have been taken up even more profoundly by Jane Flax, who has captured the sense of the critical social theory challenge to modernity with her proposition that

> something has happened, is happening to Western societies. The beginning of this transition can be dated somewhat arbitrarily from after the First World War in Europe and after the Second World War in the United States. Western culture is in the middle of a fundamental transformation: a "shape of life" is growing old. The demise of the old is being hastened by the end of colonialism, the uprising of women, the revolt of other cultures against white Western hegemony, shifts in the balance of economic and political power within the world economy, and a growing awareness of the costs as well as the benefits of scientific "progress." [Moreover] Western intellectuals cannot be immune from the profound shifts now taking place in contemporary social life.[2]

For Flax this is a crisis of contemporary society that reflects a growing recognition that the Enlightenment dream is over, that peoples everywhere are becoming increasingly awakened to the dangers of the Enlightenment narrative of reason, knowledge, progress, and freedom. This is an important theme in a critical social theory context concerned to open up closed theory and practice, in that it allows for (effectively) silenced voices to be heard again, including those associated with anti-Enlightenment sentiments, such as Nietzsche. It is important also because it connects the broader social theory debate starkly and directly to an International Relations context. It does so when the progressivism of the post-Enlightenment period is confronted with some of its more sinister dimensions, concerning, for example, the connection between the rational modern subject and the experiences of Hiroshima and Auschwitz.

The point here, of course, is that a celebration of the age of rational science and modern technological society cannot simply be disconnected from the weapons of mass slaughter and the techniques of genocide. Nor can the language and logic of liberty and emancipation be easily detached from the terror waged in their names by, for example, the major Cold War foes, each proclaiming itself the natural systemic heir to the Enlightenment dream. And while many in the 1990s celebrate the end of the Cold War—as the victory of one Enlightenment-based economic doctrine over another—the other side of this particular coin must also be confronted, in the poverty of so much of the world and in the growing underclasses in First World societies, where neoclassical and neo-Marxian "scientific" approaches have dominated the economic debates.

It is worth pondering, too, in this context, that the issue of ethnic cleansing, rightly condemned by the Western powers in the 1990s (and resisted in the 1940s), is an *integral part of modern Western history,* particularly via its Realist narrative, which celebrates the process of state making, of the triumphant march of modern, rational man. Ethnic cleansing is in this sense an integral feature of the story of modernization and Western triumph over "traditional" ignorance. Even a rudimentary appreciation of silenced histories implies as much—the histories of, for example, the Huron, the Oglala, the Mandika, and the Pitjantjatjara, all victims of ethnic cleansing for the greater good of a unified, homogeneous state system and the eradication of (anarchical) difference.

For all this, there can be no resort to simplistic responses on the part of critical social theorists seeking to deal with the other side of the modernist story. Hence the reluctance of a scholar like Flax to simply condemn the Enlightenment (or more precisely its dominant scientific project) in favor of some ready-made alternative Realism, unfettered by its distorting influences. The alternative she offers, consequently, is predicated on a positively ambivalent approach to a complex, often paradoxical world, which recognizes that we cannot simply separate the terror that is modernity from the liberty that is modernity, no more than we, the products of modernity, can detach our (modern) selves from alternatives to it.

This theme has been integral to critical social theory challenges to modernity and positivist social theory in recent years, as scholars from a range of disciplinary backgrounds have sought different ways to understand the world and speak of change within it. It has been an attitude evident, for example, in debates over contemporary philosophy, where critical social theory perspectives have prompted a significant reassessment of some intellectual and institutional sacred cows.

Questioning the "Perennial Questions": Reassessing Contemporary Philosophy

The critical social theory challenge to philosophical orthodoxy is exemplified in a number of recent works.[3] The overall thrust of these works, simply put, is that the foundations of mainstream philosophical inquiry are now under more severe challenge than at any time since Cartesian influences framed modern philosophical rationality. The general tone of these works is perhaps best summed up in the proposition that, for many in the contemporary period, "philosophy is at a turning point, that things philosophical cannot simply go on as they have."[4]

At the core of the criticism is a widespread dissatisfaction, not just with the obvious manifestations of post-Enlightenment philosophy (e.g., Popper's critical rationalism) but also with influential approaches that have critical and postpositivist credentials. Two of these approaches warrant discussion here—the broad analytical philosophy approach and the hermeneutic tradition of interpretivist analysis. The significance of these approaches is twofold. First, their influences have been evident in some of the more sophisticated of recent International Relations scholarship (e.g., Ruggie and Kratochwil); second, claims to have gone beyond the Realist orthodoxy in International Relations often emanate from scholars utilizing these perspectives.[5] The brief commentary to follow illustrates the problematic nature of these claims and indicates why Critical Theory and postmodernism have excited the most interest among those seeking to transfer critical social theory themes to International Relations.

Beyond Modernism and Positivism? Analytical Philosophy and the "Linguistic Turn"

The analytical philosophy approach emerged as a critical counterpoint to the crude inductivism associated with logical positivism. The works of two figures in particular epitomize the analytical position in this regard—those of W. V. Quine and the "later" Wittgenstein, whose recantation of the logical atomism of his *Tractatus* sparked off a "linguistic turn" in Western philosophy.[6]

Quine repudiated the twin pillars of (post-Kantian) empiricist-based philosophy: (1) the notion of a fundamental distinction between analytic and synthetic statements (between logically true knowledge received via experience and that produced via verificationist procedures) and (2) the nominalist principle, which reduces the conditions for real knowledge of the world to a universe of atomized contingent "things." Instead, Quine pronounced all knowledge "synthetic" in the sense that all knowledge, including scientific knowledge, was derived from "man-made fabric." Accordingly,

> the totality of our so called knowledge or beliefs, from the most casual matters of geography and history to the profoundest laws of atomic physics or even of pure mathematics, is a man-made fabric which impinges on experience only along the edges. . . . But the total field is so undetermined by its boundary conditions, experience, that there is much latitude of choice as to what statements to reevaluate in the light of any single contrary experience. *No particular experiences are linked to any particular statements* [emphasis added].[7]

Wittgenstein, in his later works, made a major contribution to the analytic position in instigating a fundamentally revised understanding of the nature and role of language in constructing social reality. In explaining his shift in thinking, Wittgenstein acknowledged that "my notion in the *Tractatus Logico-Philosophicus* was wrong . . . because I too thought that the logical analysis had to bring to light what was hidden (as chemical and physical analysis does)."[8] The significance of this statement is that it goes beyond the question of whether, via protocol sentences, one can "discover" the real knowledge of modernity and society. It questions the whole notion of a reality "out there" waiting to be discovered. This led, in *Philosophical Investigations,* to a broad critique of the reductionism and essentialism associated with the positivist approach to language, particularly the proposition, dominant since Hobbes, of an atomized, contingent, linguistic universe in which words were accorded singular, essential meanings that corresponded to real things. This view was repudiated by Wittgenstein in terms that emphasized not the homogeneity and singularity of language but its heterogeneity and social diversity. In short, he rejected the essentialism of language in favor of a notion of socially constructed and applied "language games," which emphasize the way that language was actually used, in different times and places, and how it constructs reality as part of a speech act.[9] It is in this sense that, following *Philosophical Investigations,* for many within Anglo-American philosophical circles the search for reality became the attempt to understand the way that grammatical rules are used in various societies to give meaning to their (linguistically constructed) real worlds. Thus, on the centuries-old notion of an objective correspondence between reality and language, Wittgenstein had this to say: "Grammar is not accountable to any [external] reality. It is grammatical rules that determine meaning (constitute it) and so they themselves are not answerable to any meaning and to that extent are arbitrary."[10]

In this way Wittgenstein undermined the positivist correspondence rule regarding language and reality at its metatheoretical core—its empiricist epistemology. More specifically, he undermined its phenomenalist logic, which takes as given the atomistic nature of the relationship between the objects of the world as expressed in elementary linguistic propositions. Wittgenstein argued instead that to understand reality through language is to engage in complex social practices that defy positivist explanations of the empirical moment in understanding. In this context, it is necessary to concentrate not on the logical independence of things, but on the systemic relationship *between* them that invests them with social meaning.[11]

Accordingly, the meaning of a term/word/symbol cannot be assumed to correspond to some essential (and externally derived) foundation or object but is dependent upon the particular constitutive role it has in particular sociolinguistic systems.[12] To conceive of language in this way—not as an exclusively descriptive medium but as a form of life, a process intrinsic to human social activity—is, in effect, to convert nouns into verbs. To "speak" in this sense is to "do": to engage in a speech act is to give meaning to the activities that make up social reality. Language no longer describes some essential hidden reality—it is inseparable from the (necessarily social) construction of that reality.

The insights of Quine and Wittgenstein, therefore, have acted as a catalyst for much of the critical reassessment of Anglo-American thinking in the contemporary period, prefiguring the critical social theory perspectives of the present. This begs the question of why the voices of Habermas and Foucault have had the most impact upon Anglo-American critique and not the more direct heirs of Quine and Wittgenstein (i.e., why not Davidson or Dummett or Putnam or Searle?). The answer, simply put, is that for all its critical potential and insight, analytical philosophy has not broken free of the repressive impact of modernism. This is evident, at one level, in the lingering conservative tendencies within the seminal works of figures such as Quine and Wittgenstein.

Quine, for example, "did a Hume" in the sense that, having effectively illustrated the inadequacy of positivist approaches, and indeed any notion of realism based on empiricist principles, he then continued to advocate an empiricist basis for logical analysis. Thus, in terms that reemphasise the power of the "Cartesian anxiety," Quine (and many who followed him in the analytical philosophy school) decided ultimately to hold on to the "boundary's edge" of science and the traditional logic of language rather than confront the possibilities beyond that boundary.[13]

Wittgenstein's conservatism was articulated in another way. In *Philosophical Investigations,* for example, in discussing the purposes of his new philosophy of language, Wittgenstein proposed that "philosophy may in no way interfere with the actual use of language; it can in the end only describe it. For it cannot give it any foundation either. It leaves everything as it is."[14] Consequently, while post-Wittgensteinian scholarship in general has stressed the meaningful and social character of human action, it effectively disregards issues such as "power and repression, history and social change."[15] The problem, in short, is that the language-based analysis of the analytical philosophy variety does not always ground its inquiry, unequivocally enough, in the everyday practices of political society. Accordingly, on the question of why Habermas and Foucault (and not analytical philosophers) are at the forefront of critical social theory in the 1980s and 1990s, the answer perhaps lies in the (modernist) conservatism of a "postpositivist" claimant that does not emphatically enough connect *knowledge* to *power.*

In this regard, analytical philosophy has largely betrayed any critical potential that scholars such as Quine and Wittgenstein gave it, and has become

> one more variant of Kantian philosophy, a variant marked principally by thinking of representation as linguistic rather than mental, and of philosophy of language rather than "transcendental critique" or psychology, as the discipline which exhibits the "foundation of knowledge."[16]

From this perspective, analytical philosophy, whose claim to postpositivism and postfoundationalism is centered on its notion of reality as sociolinguistically produced, is instead paradoxically committed to the modernist search for a permanent, neutral, ahistorical framework for inquiry. Hence my reservations in the previous chapter about the otherwise insightful contributions of a scholar such as John Ruggie.

The issue of analytical philosophy's ahistoricism is also of significance in a postpositivist context because of its relationship to the broad hermeneutic tradition, which has sought, explicitly, to historicize social understanding and which, via Weber in particular, has been an important influence on Realist scholarship. Having already indicated my position on this Weberian influence, it is worth adding something more general on an approach that continues to stimulate analysis in the contemporary era.

Beyond Modernism and Positivism? The Hermeneutic Tradition

The hermeneutic approach has a long and distinguished pedigree in Western philosophy. It was integral to both Greek and Roman attempts to interpret reality in the ancient world. In the post-Reformation period in Europe it was articulated most commonly in philological texts, in jurisprudence, and increasingly as part of a German-based Protestant reformism, which maintained that the new world of scientific rationality could be understood, most profoundly, by reference to historical and cultural tradition (e.g., as interpreted through the Christian scriptures).[17]

During the Enlightenment, however, the gap between scientific approaches and the hermeneutic philosophy of textual interpretation began to widen as logical calculation and empirical analysis gained ascendancy over cultural tradition and scriptural exegesis. The Enlightenment, nevertheless, was the catalyst for a new form of philosophical hermeneutics, which understood itself as a humanist alternative to "mechanical" modernism. By the nineteenth century, this hermeneutic perspective was articulated as part of that broad Romanticist movement which held significant sectors of the central European intellectual community in its grasp. Consequently, in the atmosphere of the (antimodernist) new aesthetics of Fichte, Schelling, and the Schlegels, German thinkers such as Schleiermacher and, later, von Humboldt began to reformulate (interpretivist) themes from Kantian thought into an approach to knowledge and society that focused on human rationality in the sociocultural process of understanding (Verstehen).

From this perspective, we come to know and give meaning to the world not through some passive encounter with external sense data but through a creative social process in which the human mind is shaped by, and shapes, cultural reality in language. Meaning, argued von Humboldt (and Gadamer and Habermas later), is a matter of active linguistic competence (Sprachkraft) that arises from the human social process, the dialectical interaction of mind, and the social use of grammar. On this basis, hermeneutic scholarship countered Comtean influences in philosophy and the increasing tendency to objectify history as a thing in the past. Rather, it was argued, the historian deals with the things of the past (ideas, institutions, texts, practices) in the *present,* and the interpretive practices of the present can never be detached from the "objective" happenings of the past.

For nineteenth-century hermeneutics, this was the basis of an alternative science of social interpretation, centered on a historical understanding of temporally and geographically diverse language forms, which, in a nonpositivist sense, existed independently of time and space (in sociocultural meaning, art, and literature), and were susceptible, therefore, to social scientific inquiry. This rather problematic claim was rendered even more problematic in the mid-nineteenth century (e.g., via Droysen), with a shift in hermeneutic orientation that saw the attempt to counter positivism's "external" scientific focus with a mind-centered rationalism and an interpretivist perspective grounded in psychological, emotional, and spiritual themes.[18] This "internalized" focus characterized Wilhelm Dilthey's perspective, which insisted that the knowledge of the human sciences was independent of that of the natural sciences. Thus the positivist quest was an illusory and inappropriate one.

The result, however, was an approach resonant with modernist influences that stressed an extreme form of individualism (albeit of the psychic rather than the utilitarian kind) with major solipsistic tendencies. The extreme psychologism of Dilthey's approach was mediated somewhat in his later works, where, in a manner similar to (the later) Wittgenstein, Dilthey acknowledged that reality is not independent of cognition but that to interpret social meaning is to engage in a process by which reality is constructed and reconstructed across time and culture.[19]

It was via this later perspective of Dilthey that the hermeneutic approach began to influence Anglo-American, particularly British, scholarship in the first quarter of this century. Its impact upon Collingwood, Oakeshott, Greenleaf, and the British history of ideas school has been documented by David Boucher, who has identified the hermeneutic approach in this way:

> Its central concern [was] with the search for the author, for the understanding that historical actors had of the situation in which they found themselves. It concerned itself with the integrity and autonomy of cultures and the authors who wrote within these confines. It assumed that the meanings which individuals hoped to convey were somehow fixed in the artifacts they produced, or in the languages they used. Sensitive intelligent research exegesis, it was believed, guided by hermeneutic principles, would enable the student to recover, re-enact, or even re-experience the original meaning, or at least come very close to this ideal.[20]

This Anglo-American hermeneutic approach has had a checkered history in relation to social theory in general and International Relations in particular. At one level—as expressed in Collingwood's work—it has had only a moderate influence on either. At another level—via Weber (and to a lesser extent Mannheim)—it becomes a significant, albeit silenced, issue for International Relations. The impact of Weber's thinking upon the exemplar Realist, Hans Morgenthau, was discussed in Chapter 3, and it really requires only one more summarized comment here, in this more general context. Weber's particular hermeneutic perspective owed much to the influences of neo-Kantian scholars, such as Rickert and Simmel, who sought to shift Verstehen scholarship away from its psychological emphasis (*Geisteswissenschaften*) to a more specific study of cultural issues (*Kulturwissenschaften*). This shift in emphasis was characterized by a more thorough attempt to integrate social and psychological factors than had been the case even in Dilthey's later work. Its aim was to overcome the narrow egocentrism associated with Dilthey's approach while retaining his basic distinction between the "cultural" and "natural" sciences.[21]

Weber's ultimate perspective, as we have seen, was a classically modernist one in which the old philosophical questions of epistemology and methodology were reduced to an instrumental relationship between a scientifically deduced "is" and a culturally derived "ought." Its impact, also recorded earlier, has been a model of rational behavior for International Relations in which, in an objectified realm, the motives of actors (e.g., individual states) are given the rational pursuit of culturally determined ends or interests and further analysis of them is considered logically unwarranted in any scientific judgment as to the nature of the system "out there." In this way the sophisticated Weberian contribution to social theory has, if anything, increased the tendency toward positivist closure in International Relations. And while, at one level, this has to do with the crude reading of such a contribution in an Americanized Cold War context, there are more profound issues at stake here concerning the hermeneutic tradition per se. In particular, in seeking to distinguish a human science of interpretation, it fails to confront the foundationalism that affords positivism its objectivist logic. Approaches such as Weber's, accordingly, for all their critical insight on the problems of objective knowledge in the *social* sciences, remain effectively uncritical on the objectivity question in the *natural* sciences.

Indeed, in continuing to accept the validity of the (natural) scientific model for *all* knowledge (even while repudiating positivism's applicability for the knowledge of human society), Verstehen approaches, like Weber's, represent the other side of the positivist coin. This point is well made by Roy Bhaskar, who proposes that

> hermeneuticist and neo-Kantian philosophies of social science tacitly presuppose positivism—first in their acceptance of it as the essentially unquestioned truth about the world known by natural science; second in their reproduction (in transposed forms) of characteristically positivist philosophical positions in their accounts of the knowledge of the social world.[22]

The point, to reiterate it, is that the mainstream hermeneutic Tradition in Anglo-American social theory remains, like so many of its counterparts in the postpositivist debate, discursively committed to the modernist regime of framing so effectively represented by positivism across the disciplines. And this, of course, is precisely what Mervyn Frost was getting at with his proposition that Traditionalist Realist scholarship in International Relations remains, for all its historicophilosophical sensitivity, captured by the positivist bias at its metatheoretical core.[23] This is so even in the most sophisticated of hermeneutic-based works (e.g., by Kratochwil).

It is for this reason that approaches seeking to go beyond the modernist legacies of analytical philosophy and the orthodox hermeneutic tradition have gained most support in critical social theory circles. This has been the case also in critical International Relations scholarship, where a paramount concern has been to reconnect (Realist) knowledge to power and theory to practice. The contribution of Hans Georg Gadamer has gained influence in this context, and Gadamer's critical hermeneutics is replete with themes to be found also in the major critical social theory approaches—Critical Theory and postmodernism.

Gadamer and a Critical Hermeneutics of Praxis

Gadamer's hermeneutic approach differs from those that preceded it in a number of important ways. It shares a legacy with Schleiermacher and von Humboldt, but it draws its influence also from figures such as Heidegger and from classical Greek scholarship. Gadamer, in *Truth and Method,* for example, defines his critical hermeneutics as a universal approach to understanding that comes to know the world through the interpretation of texts in history, as they express their *"Dasein"*—their "basic being in motion . . . [a] being that can be understood as language."[24] From this perspective, Gadamer pronounces the modernist story a particular image of the world derived from the "unbroken tradition of [Western] rhetorical and humanist culture," which has been metamorphosed into a universalized and objectivist framework of understanding, via positivist scienticism in particular.[25] In this way, he suggests, a latent Cartesianism has generally transfixed hermeneutic thought, trapping it within a dichotomized metatheory that dichotomizes culture and (universal) reason. However, in terms that link him to Habermas, post-Wittgensteinian thought, and (with qualifications) postmodernism, Gadamer insists on a historically and culturally situated reason that, in its various language traditions, exhibits its essentially human quality.

In this context, Gadamer has sought to overcome the legacy of foundationalism. This, strange as it might seem, is where he returns to the Greek classical texts in order to reconvene a practical philosophical perspective set in terms of *praxis* rather than *techne.* This *praxis* is closely identified with the Aristotelian notion of *phronesis.* For Aristotle, and for Gadamer (and in modified form for Habermas), the importance of *phronesis* is that it represents an alternative knowledge form to both episteme (scientific knowledge) and *techne* (technical knowledge). *Phronesis,* in contrast, is concerned with practical-ethical knowledge, with understanding the human world and learning how to live in it.[26]

Phronesis is also about difference rather than unity, about diversity rather than homogeneity. Whereas scientific and technical knowledge forms deal with foundations, with independent "things" and formulas of given means and ends, *phronesis* knowledge is about concrete, particular knowledge of social situations. By pursuing *phronesis* knowledge, therefore, the "scientific mystification" of modernity might be broken down and the "false idolatry of the expert" reassessed in favor of a critical hermeneutics of *praxis* concerned with a knowledge of human society, which is

> not of a general kind of knowledge, but of its specification at a particular moment. This knowledge also is not in any sense technical knowledge. . . . The person with understanding does not know and judge as one who stands apart and unaffected; but rather, as one united by a specific bond

> with the other, he thinks with the other and undergoes the situation with him.[27]

This, for Gadamer, is a more profound process of understanding than any derived from an objective knowledge or even that which seeks "empathy" between individual minds in history. It is the basis of all genuine understanding, which sees a fusing of horizons between the interpreter and that which is interpreted. And it is not a foundationalist position, for while the text and its language contain "universal" human themes, texts are not given, to be understood "as such and only afterwards used . . . for particular purposes." Rather, the interpreter is never detached from the concrete hermeneutic situation, for it is in the fusion of time and mind that we become conscious of the "I" as the "thou."[28]

Nevertheless, in Gadamer's concept of *Dasein* there are obvious influences of Hegelianism and the historical movement of consciousness. There is also a sense of holism and suggestions of a universal process of understanding in Gadamer's fusion notion. But Gadamer emphasizes the distinction between the dialectic of the *Geist* and his dialectic of historical fusion, maintaining that in the former the Hegelian movement of consciousness heads toward an absolute knowledge, while in the latter it is oriented toward ever opened dialogue, never ultimate closure. Gadamer's notion of hermeneutics, accordingly, represents a "dialectic of experience [which] has its own fulfillment not in definitive knowledge, but in the openness to experience that is encouraged by experience itself."[29]

For obvious reasons, Gadamer's critical hermeneutic perspective has been taken seriously in critical social theory circles. Much of its influence, however, has been indirect, in modified form, for example, via Habermas.[30] And it is toward Habermas (or, more precisely, Critical Theory in general) that I turn my attention now to introduce one of the foremost critical social theory perspectives of recent years.

Confronting Modernity (I): The Critical Theory of the Frankfurt School

To help locate the Critical Theory approach, it is necessary to briefly touch on that complex theme in Marxist literature concerning the question of whether there was an early "philosophical" Marx and a later "scientific" one. Both interpretations have held sway within Marxist literature in the years since Marx's death. For the majority of that time, however, Marxist orthodoxy has been gripped by a rigid ("scientific") materialism, set in dialectical terms.[31] There has, nevertheless, been another prominent approach to the issue, which insists that Marxism is an antiempiricist, antipositivist perspective that understands "objective" reality and the post-

Kantian emancipatory project in social and interpretivist terms. Relations between objects and subjects, in this sense, are intrinsic to the dominant relations of power at a given historical period. In a modern class context, therefore, that which appears external to social consciousness (scientific fact) is regarded, rather, as a reified expression of the ruling ideas of the class that rules, an ideology of bourgeois scientism designed to alienate modern peoples from an understanding of their (class) reality by detaching the story of power politics from its human source.

This was a theme integral to the attempts of Frankfurt School Critical Theorists, from the 1920s on, to shift emancipatory thinking away from the reductionism of its scientific orthodoxy (particularly its tendency toward a determining economic sphere) and recapture the philosophical kernel of Marxism in human society and culture.[32] The argument, broadly put, is that social progress is not dependent upon the scientific discovery and application of universal laws but on concrete social practice associated with critical reflection on dominant knowledge/power relations. Positivism becomes an important factor here, in transforming a particular knowledge form (scientific empiricism) into a sociopolitical force with universal application. In this way, critical reason is reduced to instrumentalist ends. Thus, *techne* is reified while *praxis* is denied, and social power is ceded to the "objective" knowledge of the expert. Knowledge, in this sense, is very definitely power, and the language of bourgeois power is the language of instrumental rationality, the language of natural science (e.g., positivism) applied uncritically to social life. In particular, the logic and language of the post-Enlightenment philosophy of science is, on this basis, deeply implicated in the subjugation of the potential for self-reflective social emancipation, upon which modern progress depends.

The early Critical Theorists acknowledged that this was so in "revolutionary" societies (e.g., the USSR) as well as in the liberal states of Western Europe and North America. The problem they faced, in the 1930s, was that they perceived this scenario throughout the Western heartland of industrial capitalism, where the ideology of instrumental-rationalist knowledge had become *the* (illusory) reality for the industrial working classes, the supposed proletarian agents of progressive change.

Consequently, in the works of Adorno and Horkheimer in particular, there was little left of the optimism that characterized earlier Marxist analysis.[33] Indeed, the whole modernist tradition, set upon linear notions of progress and emancipatory consciousness, was now perceived in a different, more somber, light. Gone was any faith in the revolutionary potential of the industrial proletariat, as the welfare state and mass consumerism gave material sustenance to the claims that ideological struggle was indeed at an end. If there was space for difference, for questioning, for emancipation, it was at the margins of modern society among the artists, writers, and creative avant-garde. Hence the shift in Critical Theory literature toward "cultural" themes and away from traditional Marxist concerns with proletarian class struggle.[34]

But for all the pessimism associated with the works of the first generation of Frankfurt School scholars, they bequeathed a "thinking space" to those who followed them, which framed the possibility of an emancipatory *praxis* with implications beyond the dichotomized logic of a positivist-dominated modernity. This, as Horkheimer explained in a passage that remains integral to the contemporary debate, is because

> the intervention of reason in the processes whereby knowledge and its object are constituted, or the subordination of these processes to conscious control, does not take place . . . in a purely intellectual world, but coincides with the struggle for certain real ways of life.[35]

This principle, which asserts the historical and political nature of all knowledge *as* power and understood "theory" as inexorably connected to "practice," has remained at the core of the contributions of the second generation of Frankfurt School scholars in the years since the death of Adorno and Horkheimer et al. The most prominent figure in Critical Theory in this period has been Jurgen Habermas, and Habermas's influence has been integral to the critical social theory challenge of recent years and to its transference to International Relations.

Jurgen Habermas and the Emancipatory Project Revisited

A central feature of Habermas's wide-ranging analysis of contemporary society has been the attempt to resuscitate the emancipatory project within the theory and practice of modernity.[36] But the Habermasian project—emerging in the Cold War years, developing in the brief and heady days of new left radicalism, and maturing during an age that has seen something of a flight from Hegelian-Marxism among European scholars—has, by necessity, differed in important respects from earlier Frankfurt School approaches.

Habermas has, for example, rejected the pessimistic tendencies in earlier Frankfurt School scholarship as a one-sided and negative interpretation of the dialectical legacy of Hegelian and Marxist thought, which has resulted in a negative modernism that is a "left counterpart to the . . . theory of totalitarian domination."[37] In order, thus, to rekindle the positive emancipatory element in Critical Theory, while rejecting its universalist totalizing tendencies, Habermas has engaged in a long-term restructuring of Hegelian-Marxist thought in terms of a radical communicatory rationalism.

In particular, and here his response has been aimed at both (early) Critical Theorists and postmodernists, Habermas has argued that there is nothing conceptually or historically *inevitable* about the suppressed nature of the critical capacity in modern societies. Rather, for Habermas, the potential for radical democratic resistance still remains in post-Enlightenment modernism, beyond the restrictions placed upon it by a particular (positivist) knowledge form in its association with capitalist social relations. Habermas's Critical Theory project, accordingly, is aimed at resuscitating the (modernist) critical faculty in the face of those who no longer acknowledge such a possibility.

The problem with earlier forms of Critical Theory, he insists, is that they misunderstood the emancipatory task in seeking to overcome the power of instrumental reason in *all* spheres. Critical Theory's pessimism and sense of resignation (and its resort to Hegelian totalism) were inevitable because it sought the transformation not only of social relations but also of relationships with nature and its productive forces. The point, argues Habermas in *Towards a Rational Society,* is that scientific rationality per se is not an ideological force, nor the instrumental action it produces. What is repressing emancipatory thinking and action is the power of social theories such as positivism, which transfer the logic of instrumental rationality from its *appropriate sphere* to the sphere of everyday communicatory activity, where it distorts the categories of practical social life and reduces questions that ought to be open to political and ethical discussion into closed issues of technical formula.[38]

In these terms, Habermas has sought to go beyond the Critical Theory of the original Frankfurt School and acknowledge, more broadly, some of the omissions and silences in Marxism. His argument, in this regard, is that a contemporary Critical Theory requires something more than a blanket and indiscriminate rejection of modern scientific knowledge as ideological or of appeals to some form of Hegelian totalized consciousness as an emancipatory alternative. It requires, for example, an appreciation that it is no longer just the (traditionally) oppressed parts of society that are ideologically pacified. Instead the focus of Critical Theory attention must be on those spheres of humanness that are excluded from, and repressed by, the transference of scientific principles into social life. It must, in this regard, "penetrate beyond the level of particular historical class interests to disclose the fundamental interests of mankind as such, engaged in the process of self constitution."[39]

Leaving aside for the moment the notion of the fundamental interests of mankind "as such," this perspective of Habermas has prefigured an important theme in a critical social theory context, in that it led him to a concern with language and the emancipatory possibilities therein. This theme was evident in his work well before his "linguistic turn" in the 1980s. As he explained in *Towards a Rational Society* (1976), the problem with modern scientific ideology, as articulated in positivism in particular, is that it

> violates an interest grounded in one of the two fundamental conditions of our cultural existence: in language, or more precisely, in the form of socialisation and individuation determined by communication in ordinary language. This interest extends to the maintenance of intersubjectivity of mutual understanding as well as to the creation of communication without domination. Technocratic consciousness makes this practice disappear behind the interest in the expansion of our power of technical control.[40]

This passage draws together many of the concerns, themes, and issues of the large and complex Habermasian project. Here, for example, is a concern about the legacy of logical positivist linguistic analysis and its association with the modern urge for social control. Here is a hermeneutic concern for a humanness, derived from a discourse of intersubjective communication; and here, too, albeit in different form, is a concern of the Frankfurt School to overcome technocratic consciousness in favor of a rational mode of communication free from (ideological) domination.

These themes were evident also in *Knowledge and Human Interests* (1972), a work that more than any other has assisted in the transference of Habermasian themes to International Relations, a work that exemplifies the ambition (and the problems) of Habermas's contribution to critical social theory.[41] This work sought to establish an open-ended dialectic of communicative rationality (a contemporary *praxis*) upon a series of socially grounded "cognitive interests." The first of these interests—the technical-cognitive interest—reflects the fundamental human interest in survival and material existence. It promotes a knowledge form aimed at more effectively manipulating and controlling an objectified environment. In the modern period this interest has found its foremost philosophical expression in positivism, via which it had become reified into an object in itself, constituting a reality beyond socially based communicative knowledge.

Habermas acknowledges this knowledge form as important but stresses that it represents only one aspect of human social life. Just as important, though effectively marginalized in modernity, is a practical-cognitive interest in social understanding, interpretation, and communication. This is associated with the (broad) hermeneutic knowledge form, which emphasizes the need for inquiry into the way that social and cultural meaning became transposed into (scientific) fact. The third "interest," in many ways the most important in the Habermasian schema, constitutes the generative capacity for change. This, the emancipatory-cognitive interest, is associated with the most repressed knowledge form in modern society, the critical knowledge form inherent in the post-Enlightenment urge to question, to reflect, to reason.[42]

To gain emancipation from the ideological structure of modernity is, therefore, for Habermas, to reconnect (rational) knowledge to human interests, to regenerate the critical potential of modernity in terms of an ideologically unhindered communicatory process. In this quest Habermas has drawn upon a variety of intellectual sources in the 1980s in his quest for a theory of communicative action. Two principal influences upon this theory have been the hermeneutics of figures such as Gadamer and elements of the broad analytical philosophy approach inspired by Wittgenstein.[43] And for all the conflict of the Habermas-Gadamer dispute, Habermas has integrated into his reformulated Critical Theory the Aristotelian distinction between *techne* and *praxis,* which underpinned the refusal of Gadamer to reduce politics to administrative technique, or to reduce power to force. Moreover, in accepting (albeit with reservations) the Aristotelian concept of *phronesis* as the basis for social communication, Habermas has sought to uncover what he regards as the "universal conditions that are presupposed in all communicative action."[44] In short, in the 1980s, Habermas has continued to insist that there are dimensions, possibilities, and potentials inherent *within* the Enlightenment tradition of modernity that offer opportunities for critical reflection and political dissent and must not be dismissed in an age that has lost its faith in the human capacity for radical thought and action.

For a whole range of reasons, however, there are many within the critical social theory community who feel decidedly uneasy about Habermas's attempts to resuscitate this rational dimension of post-Enlightenment philosophy. Notions of universal conditions of communication and human interests associated with rational theory and practice have obvious and negative connotations for contemporary scholars seeking to break free of the power of the modernist framing regime, of foundationalism, and of the "Cartesian anxiety." Consequently, Habermas and contemporary Critical Theory in general have come under concerted attack, from postmodernists in particular, perceiving in the new rationalism of the 1980s and 1990s the old rationalist illusions (and dangers) of the modernist "metanarrative."[45] This tension between Critical Theory and postmodernism is an issue I regard as crucial for the future of critical social theory scholarship, particularly in International Relations, and I will return to it shortly, after making some general remarks about postmodernism that develop further the introductory comments in Chapter 1.

Confronting Modernity (II): The Postmodernist Perspective

It is difficult to speak of postmodernism in general terms without violating what is perhaps its primary characteristic—its concern for heterogeneity and difference. For all its diversity, however, it is possible to discern a corpus of attitudes, themes, and concerns (values even) shared by scholars as different as Foucault, Derrida, Kristeva, Lacan, Lyotard, and Rorty. Framed as a series of questions asked by scholars such as these, a postmodern critical agenda includes (1) the question of modern Western society and culture, or, more precisely, the question of the legacy of Western modernity for contemporary understandings of the real world and the real self; (2) the question of knowledge and power, in particular the *how* question concerning the sociolinguistic conditions of the construction of dominant knowledge forms and their disciplining and representation in contemporary life; (3) the (more precise) question of history and philosophy—of the Western metanarrative, the impact of the Enlightenment and the subsequent pursuit of a modern scientific philosophy; (4) the question of the modern subject—of the sovereign rational actor of modernity; and (5) the question of closure, exclusion, power politics, and life on the margins—the question of dissent and resistance.

Derived from these major headings are various analytical subthemes that give meaning to the postmodernist critique of modernity. Important in this regard is the notion that reality is not a unified, systemic whole, understandable in objectivist terms. Rather, from a postmodern perspective, the objects and subjects of reality are sociolinguistically constructed, and their meanings are not given but made and remade by people in different times and places, representing themselves and their world as part of discursive practices. As indicated in Chapter 1, a discursive practice is not reducible to a single "great text" or even (necessarily) to a dominant Tradition or discipline. It represents, rather, the embodiment of a *particular way of framing questions and answers,* of distinguishing truth and reality in social and political institutions, in the dominant technical processes, and in the general behavior of people in their societies. This connects language and society in a way that defies dichotomized representations of their relationship, in the sense that it is the discursive practices that construct the subjects and objects about which language speaks. Any discursive inquiry, therefore, is simultaneously an investigation of the sociohistorical conditions under which language, meaning, and social power intersect. As the preceding chapters have sought to show, this has obvious implications for some of the most revered themes in post-Enlightenment philosophical folklore: the notions of modern rational man, history, scientific knowledge, power, and a reality "out there."

Perhaps the most controversial aspect of the postmodern critical agenda in this regard is its proclamation of the (metaphoric) "death of man." The target here, of course, is not humankind per se—postmodernism is not an antihuman perspective—but the particular idea of "man" or "human nature" that has been privileged in modern Western philosophical discourse. The proposition here is that because human Being and nature are social, historical, and linguistic constructions—not the mirrored reflections of some external realm of pure essence; there can be no essential "man" whose fundamentally transparent character can be known via the correct knowledge/language form. Hence the proclamation of the "death" of, or, more commonly, the decentering of, the modern heroic figure of Western philosophy (e.g., the author, the sovereign individual, the class-conscious citizen).[46] Hence the (Nietzschean-inspired) suspicion of a modern story of "man" set upon the unfolding capacity for rational thought and action and increasingly enlightened structures of power. Hence the genealogical approach to history, derived from Nietzsche, which aims to expose the power/knowledge connection in modern theory and practice by critically analyzing the ways we have constructed the knowledge of ourselves as modern subjects and objects.

Postmodern scholarship has also been at the forefront of the critiques of modernist philosophy (at least in "big-P" institutionalized terms).[47] The argument here is that because knowledge is not a homogeneous entity but discursively produced and legitimated, there can be no foundational (Philosophical) knowledge that underpins all other knowledge forms and that can act as a criterion of truth and meaning for them (e.g., as in analytical philosophy). Accordingly, the notion of a Philosophy of language that can arbitrate on truth claims is repudiated by postmodernists. Knowledge (including philosophical knowledge) is socially and historically constituted; there can, therefore, be no neutral, transparent (realm of) philosophical knowledge, or language, against which philosophy can make rational judgments concerning the reality of its meanings.

This critical insight is applied also to the rational-scientific knowledge of social theory in general. Thus, while acknowledging the moderated tones of contemporary knowledge claims (the notion of "lawlike" descriptions of laws rather than laws per se), this, from a postmodernist perspective, disguises an important dimension of the modernist power/knowledge nexus. The point is that the "descriptive" knowledge of mainstream social theory is always inherently and powerfully prescriptive, in that it is the knowledge form that gives (rational-scientific) meaning to the decisionmaking procedures, policy formulations, and general rules of thought and behavior in the modern world. Consequently, those who deviate from this meaning or question and disregard official decisions and policies do so in the face of a knowledge form and its procedural techniques that are, by definition, rational, ordered, and corresponding to the reality of human nature and society.

From a postmodernist perspective, this is just one example of the relations of power that emanate from the struggle of discursive practices. Power in this context cannot be reduced to its traditional sites (class, gender, the state system). Rather, power operates in every site. It cannot, as such, be ultimately overcome—not by revolutionary means nor by the freeing up of modern emancipatory potentials (e.g., as in Habermasian Critical Theory). Power, instead, is integral to all discursive practices, to the way we think and act, to the way that we are *defined* as thinkers and actors. The discursive politics of power, consequently, is at its most reprehensible for postmodernists in societies that understand reality in the most homogeneous, unified, and orderly of ways, for here the subjugation of difference, of heterogeneity, of alternative discourses of reality, have been most successful—and thus most brutalizing of both mind and body.

A postmodernist politics of dissent, accordingly, seeks to disrupt and erode the theory and practice of these power regimes, which, in celebrating the ascent of *some* in the post-Enlightenment period have, for the sake of identity, unity, coherence, and order in their world, suppressed the (human) difference, ambiguity, and Otherness integral to it. Postmodernism, in this regard, seeks to illuminate the positive as well as repressive elements of power relations by exposing the process by which they are constituted and represented and opening space for resistance to them. This it does in relation to the "woman" who, from Aristotle to Freud, has been represented as the negative side of "man" to the people of the Third World, defined and named as the negative side of the (developmental story) of the First (and socialist) World. This it does not in absolute terms but in support of approaches to knowledge and society that disrupt the closure associated with all forms of absolutism.

In Chapter 8 I will return again to this postmodern politics of dissent as it has been articulated in the critical social theory literature in International Relations. At this point, however, I want to say something about another dimension of the critical social theory agenda—that concerning the tensions between Critical Theory and postmodernism on the question of modernity. Here the conflict between postmodernists and Habermas in particular has provided some stimulating and occasionally vitriolic exchanges.

Habermas Versus Postmodernism

There are perhaps two phases in the Habermasian contribution to the modernity debate with postmodernism. The first, which takes in the period up to and including *Theory of Communicative Action* (1984), is characterized by a rather uncompromising approach to postmodernism as neoconservatism.[48] In the second period, since the early 1980s and including Habermas's *Philosophical Discourse of Modernity* (1987), there has been a more measured response to postmodernist thought, though some major differences clearly remain. Indeed, in a recent debate with his critics, Habermas reflected on this early antipathy toward postmodernism in a way that continued to represent his distaste for "theories of totalitarian domination," derived from Nietzsche in particular.[49]

Habermas has two important statements to make to his contemporary critics on the postmodernism issue. On the one hand, he acknowledges that, to a substantial degree, they are engaged in a shared project, that of exposing logocentrism and opposing "the ontological privileging of the world of beings, the epistemological privileging of contact with objects or existing states of affairs, and the semantic privileging of esoteric sentences and propositional truth."[50] On the other hand, however, Habermas rejects the broad conclusions reached by French scholars such as Derrida and Foucault and their Anglo-American counterparts such as Rorty. Just like the early critical theorists, suggests Habermas, and even more ironically, these thinkers have become victims of the totalizing tendencies within modernity, which has seen a "single thread of propositional truth and theoretical reason . . . stylized into the monopoly of humanity."[51] His point is that postmodernists have seized on a single thread of post-Enlightenment experience—its pessimistic dimension—and have transformed it into an inevitable and all-encompassing "counternarrative," which inevitably dissolves into violence, negativity, and terror and systematically excludes any space for creative, radical change.

Consequently, Habermas reiterates that the Enlightenment tradition does still offer such space—the space for critical reflection and democratic resistance. He proposes, therefore, that in the face of a logocentric metanarrative,

> instead of following Nietzsche's path of a totalising and self-referential critique of reason, whether it be via Heidegger to Derrida, or via Bataille to Foucault, and throwing the [modernist] baby out with the bathwater, it is more promising to seek this end through the analysis of the *already operative potential* [emphasis added] for rationality contained in the everyday practices of communication.[52]

Postmodernists confront Habermas and the modernity question on somewhat different premises, in rejecting either the possibility or the desirability of retaining the emancipatory spirit of the Enlightenment dream. Or, more precisely, postmodernists emphasize that the emancipatory spirit of the Enlightenment was always *nothing more* than a dream, that notions of a universal emancipatory theory and practice, capable of freeing people from the ideas and structures that oppressed them, was always and inevitably the "will to power" of certain actors, in a power matrix designed to privilege certain discursive practices. The rationality of the Enlightenment, from this perspective, is always, simultaneously, the power and domination of (for example) the Western imperialist, the Stalinist apparatchik, the Modernization Theorist, the Cold War technician and nuclear strategist, the (humanist) agent of power politics.

This theme has been addressed, in incisive fashion, by Mark Poster, as part of his general discussion of the dispute between Habermas and postmodernism in the 1980s.[53] Habermas, suggests Poster, disturbs postmodernists most with his insistence that the modern critical project should seek to resuscitate those elements of (genuine emancipatory) reason in contemporary bourgeois society. The problem with this proposition is that it misses the point about the relationship between knowledge as power and theory as practice, the point being that postmodernists "do not dispute that there are elements of reason in liberal culture. What they dispute is the lens that discerns reason in law and democracy but not in gas chambers and atom bombs."[54] The point, to reiterate it in terms of Jane Flax's concerns in *Thinking Fragments,* is that Habermas seeks to privilege the positive aspects of a modernist discourse while silencing its negative, oppressive dimensions. In seeking, therefore, to resuscitate the emancipatory potential in modern human life, Habermas effectively promotes its potential for mass destruction, for social control, for domination at all levels. Summarizing the postmodernist concern on this issue, Poster proposes that

> when Habermas defends with the label of reason what he admires in Western culture, he universalises the particular, grounds the conditional, absolutizes the finite. He provides a centre and an origin for a set of discursive practices. He undermines critique in the name of critique by privileging a locus of theory (reason) that far too closely resembles society's official discourse.[55]

But there is another dimension to the postmodernist critique of Habermas and modernity that needs to be emphasized if the profundity of its challenge to modern theory and practice is to be appreciated. This concerns the earlier Critical Theory perspectives of, in particular, Horkheimer and Adorno. Their *Dialectic of Enlightenment,* for example, was marked by a deep sense of pessimism about the nature of modernity and disenchantment, in particular, with the emancipatory promise of Enlightenment rationality in either its liberal or Marxist guise. In this regard, accordingly, there are obvious and significant thematic similarities between part of the first generation of Frankfurt School scholarship and contemporary postmodernism. The differences, however, are more important in the present context. They relate to the reasons for the disillusionment felt by Adorno and Horkheimer that, for them, centered on the demise and "distorted" nature of the post-Enlightenment emancipatory project.

Postmodernists do not share this disillusionment. Instead, and following Nietzsche's view of modernity rather than that of Kant, Hegel, and Marx, the emancipatory project is perceived as distorted *in the first instance.* There is from a postmodernist perspective, therefore, no sense of once great liberating ideas and practices becoming agencies of repression and domination. The proposition, rather, is that all discourses centered on unified notions of humankind and society, privileging given subjects and objects (the autonomous individual, the class, the tradition, the religion, the developmental process), are already and inexorably implicated in relations of domination, control, and power. Thus, while it might be suggested that the (scientific-rationalist) foundations of modernity have been undermined or "distorted," a postmodernist approach maintains that it is this very *foundationalism* that is at the core of the problems of modern theory and practice in the first place.

This is why the question of rationality becomes for postmodernism an integral feature of modern theory *as* practice, because since Descartes the rational voice has been the universal voice, the voice of the autonomous subject of modern life that "knows" itself, that speaks of, and for, universal reality. The voice of reason, thus, is never innocent. The voice of reason—of modern truth—is also the voice of modern biology, chemistry, and physics, of technocracy, of multinational capital, of warfare, of the power politics state. It is, as such, the institutional voice of both freedom *and* oppression, of liberation *and* domination, of openness *and* closure. To theoretically privilege one side of modern rationality, in this situation, is to engage in the practice of exclusion (and sometimes terror) that is the experience of the other side—that which has no (rational) voice.

Postmodernism: Some Reservations in a Critical Social Theory Context

Having said all this and accepting the significance of it, I want now to go against the grain of the discussion a little and argue that, nevertheless, postmodernism must remain engaged with the Critical Theory perspective of Habermas, and indeed with the critical social theory enterprise in general, if it is to have the critical impact upon International Relations that its insights warrant. I take this position for two reasons. First, for all the emphasis placed on the problems of a Habermasian position, outlined earlier, there are dimensions of the Critical Theory project (and other modernist approaches) that might not necessarily add up to foundationalist closure in the traditional sense. There are, in other words, critical opportunities and tensions in modernity, and particularly in Critical Theory, that should not be dismissed in any critical social theory enterprise. The second reason for raising this issue in this way concerns my reservations about some elements of postmodernist scholarship and a tendency within it for simplistic dismissal and for the kind of detachment that renders it no more connected to political practice than the positivist objectivism of so much modernist literature.

In this latter context I have in mind the work of Jean-François Lyotard and *The Postmodern Condition* (1984).[56] More precisely, it is the tendency within this work to "escape" modernity that is of concern. David Kolb has made the point well in his commentary on Lyotard's proposal that, like the great modernist artists (e.g., Joyce, Schoenberg, and Cézanne), we must seek to counter modernity's repressive features by "starting new language games . . . new forms of life."[57] The problem with this position, for Kolb, is that it "pictures the modern world as more unified than it is, with the consequence that the postmodern gesture becomes too stereotyped."[58] Kolb might have reflected on a more profound problem here, that associated with a postmodern perspective that creates a dichotomy between one hermetically sealed unity (modernity) and another (postmodernity). But his point is nevertheless an important one. It suggests that Lyotard's postmodernism is effectively detached from the modernity it seeks to counter, in seeking "new language games" (in analytical philosophy style) rather than taking advantage of the multiplicity of tensions already constituting modern knowledge and society.

The point, more generally, is that this tendency toward avant-gardism, this sense of detachment within some postmodernist scholarship, is, as Habermas suggests, a conservative and stultifying aspect of its character.[59] It is this tendency, I suggest, that it must confront and overcome if it is to remain the most potent voice within a critical social theory attempt to open up the theory and practice of modernity. It must, in this regard, acknowledge that modernity, for all its closure, is also a complex matrix of tensions and critical potentials with the capacity for something other than unreflexive complicity.

This does not require compliance with a (unified) metanarrative, as a Lyotard would have it, nor is it a simple "hermeneutics of suspicion" position, assuming deep within the Western philosophical tradition some essential, transhistorical, transcultural theme (individualism, rationality, logic, emancipation, spirit, alienation) just waiting to be recovered and applied to the problems of the age in grand-theorized form. It does require, however, that in recognizing the problems of modernist thinking, one recognizes also that the complex "interpenetration" of ideas, themes, and concepts acknowledged by Hegel, or the "intersection of narratives" recognized by Derrida, or the multiplicity of "language games" described by Wittgenstein, or the *"Dasein"* perspective outlined by Gadamer, represents space for something more than a unified conformist set of modernist practices. It represents space also for critical dissent, the potential for resistance. It is in this space, and upon this potential, that postmodernism must expose closure and confront the exclusionary repressive aspects of modernity.

This, it seems to me, is a position congruent not only with Habermasian attempts to refocus a disillusioned radicalism on the potential for rational thought and communicative practice but with a Foucauldian concern to locate a Nietzschean resistance in a rationalized world. This perspective is articulated powerfully by the Foucault of "What Is Enlightenment?" (1984), who in moderating much of the earlier vitriol against all aspects of modernism emphasized that while he retained a deep suspicion of Enlightenment rhetoric and ambition, it was important to understand that "the thread that may connect us with the Enlightenment is not faithfulness to doctrinal elements, but rather the permanent *reactivation of an attitude*—that is, of a philosophical ethos that could be described as a permanent *critique* of our historical era [emphases added].[60] My suggestion in this regard is that it is worth taking seriously Foucault's insight concerning the potential for something other than "faithfulness to [the] doctrinal elements" in the modernist tradition, and that a genuinely critical social theory must continue to explore this possibility, albeit on the excluded and often silenced margins of modernity.

This is not just to acknowledge the historically and culturally obvious—that we cannot simply detach ourselves from the Enlightenment and its influences. It is to acknowledge that we cannot simply disengage our alternative critical perspectives from it. It is to acknowledge that a scholar such as Berki might have something more to offer than Hegelian totalism. It is to suggest that an Adorno, a Gramsci, and a Robert Cox represent something other than conventional Marxist closure. It is to think seriously about the proposition that dialectical logic need not be teleological. It is to critically, rather than dismissively, confront the complex Habermasian claim that there still might be space within modernity for a more open critical theory and practice, that the modern metanarrative is not bereft of the potential for nonfoundationalist theory and practice. It is, in short, to reject the paradox associated with some postmodernism that, projecting the spirit of tolerant critical theory and practice, engages in the clichéd, polemical closure that characterizes so much of the modernism it eschews. It is to define a postmodern politics of dissent as the attempt to go beyond the dominant meanings and practices of modernity, *not* as detachment from modernity per se.

This is not to ignore the problems (and dangers) of a Habermasian perspective, it is to take seriously those elements of his thinking that defy simplistic categorization. There is, for example, the question of the subject in Habermas (and in Hegelian Marxism in general) that might easily be dismissed in "hermeneutics of suspicion" terms—thus closing off any useful conversation. And yet there is clearly something more than this going on in Habermas's thinking, as is evidenced in his reflections on Hegelianism in *Theory and Practice.* Here, concentrating on the notion of spirit, in Hegel's *Philosophy of Mind,* Habermas stresses that Hegel's perspective is unequivocally the product of human social interaction as mediated through language (symbolic representation), labor (control of nature), and the struggle for "recognition."[61] Consequently, in stressing the interpenetration of these elements in the social construction of the subject, Hegel explained that

> Spirit is not the fundament underlying the subjectivity of the self in self consciousness but rather the medium *within* which one "I" communicates with another "I," and *from* which, as an absolute mediation, the two mutually form each other into subjects [emphases added].[62]

The point of course is that this interpretation of Hegel (or more precisely of Hegel's reading of Kant) problematizes the notion of a unified (transparent) ego "I" that comes to know its "objective" self through self-reflection, in favor of a heterogeneous, historicosocial notion of the subject in which knowledge, of self and other selves, is grounded in the (constructed) reality of social interaction. Accordingly, Habermas goes on to conclude that

> Kant proceeds from the identity of the "I" as an original unity of transcendental consciousness. In contrast to this, Hegel's fundamental experience of the "I" as an identity of self consciousness is not an original one, but can only be conceived as one that has developed. . . . The (Hegelian/Marxist) critique of knowledge . . . consists precisely in relinquishing the viewpoints of a "ready made" or "completed" subject of knowledge.[63]

And there is the question, too, of Habermas's universalism, again a seemingly obvious aspect of a modernist "metanarrative" of the Kantian emancipatory variety. But is it? It certainly did not appear so in *Communication and the Evolution of Society* (1979), where Habermas stressed his opposition to the teleological tendencies in Kant, Hegel, and Marx and argued for a progressivist approach that privileged "neither unilinearity nor necessity, neither continuity nor irreversibility."[64]

The point here is not that it is possible to find passages in the work of a sophisticated scholar like a Habermas (or a Foucault) that problematizes the general categorization of them. The point is rather that a postmodernism engaged with a world of complexity, paradox, and ambiguity should never be engaged in simplistic categorization and closure but must always be open to critical conversation, particularly with those it opposes. This, to reiterate, is not an argument *for* Habermas, as it were, nor is it in any way an argument in favor of some sort of synthetic fusion between Critical Theory and postmodernism. It is an argument *for* openness and positive, constructive theory and practice over polemic, detachment, and closure.[65]

This is an issue far too complex for any comprehensive treatment in this book. It is introduced at this point because I believe it is a crucial aspect of the contemporary debates in critical social theory and International Relations, which must take seriously the questions raised in the conversation *between* Critical Theory and postmodernism. My concern is that this has not been a trait evident in International Relations, where, to this stage at least, there has been no equivalent to the works of scholars such as Mark Poster, Michael Ryan, or Jane Flax.[66]

Generally, however, the postmodern scholarship in International Relations has not been guilty of the Lyotardian overstatement and avantgardism. For the most part, the tendency has been toward a kind of intellectual apartheid, with Critical Theorists and postmodernists invoking strategies of exclusion or marginalization similar to those that have had such a detrimental effect upon debate in International Relations, generally, in the era of Realist dominance. The tendency toward dismissal and closure is evident, nevertheless, in otherwise very powerful and sophisticated postmodernist works. In his "Living on Border Lines" argument, for example, there are times when Richard Ashley's rather cavalier attitude to modernist philosophy sees him come very close to the Lyotardian perspective. In this work, consequently, as part of a Foucauldian-inspired reading of Kant and the emergence of modern "sovereign man," the contribution of Habermas is simply lumped together with that of Christian humanists, liberal notions of the "rights of man," and a Marx who, it is claimed, appealed to something called "dialectical materialism."[67]

I have indicated my reservations about treating Habermas in this simplistic way, and nothing of value can be achieved by developing the point further here, except perhaps to suggest that to dismiss Habermas on the basis of *Knowledge and Human Interests* (and I know of no postmodern work in International Relations that seriously confronts any other of his works) is surely contradictory to the spirit and critical integrity of the postmodernist enterprise set down by a Foucault. Similarly, there is more at stake than mere pedantry on the issue of Marx as a "dialectical materialist." For anyone even sketchily aware of the complexities and controversies associated with Marx's work on this point (i.e., its relationship to Engels's later works), this issue goes to the heart not only of the scientific debate in Marxism but to the question of whether Marx's *historical* materialism was ultimately foundationalist, in a modernist sense, or whether it was emphatically grounded in human history and society. A more sensitive approach would surely have left space open for this question. Likewise, an approach concerned with openness over closure would surely take more care with the issue of totalized history in Marx. For Ashley in "Living on Border Lines," however, Marx's sketchy image of a future communist society is effectively reduced to a simplistic "end of history" scenario. Thus, approaches such as Marxism, it is contended,

> can imagine the end of the state only when the sovereign subject it invokes finally achieves total knowledge and total freedom—only that is when history is totally subordinated to man's sovereign will. It can imagine the end of the state, yes, but only at the end of time.[68]

The point here is that while it might well fit a (rather overstated) Foucauldian argument to read Marxism in this way, a very serious doubt remains as to whether Marx really did see a communist society as the "end of time," as the moment of "total knowledge and total freedom." It would be just as simple, and just as inappropriate, to reduce Nietzsche's insights on modernity to a grand theory of the human psyche, a "hermeneutics of suspicion" concerning the taken-for-granted inadequacies and blindness of the "herd." It could mean this, but it could (and does) mean a great deal more, and it is in that space—beyond the simplistic, beyond the polemical—that critical social theorists and postmodernists, in particular, must be engaged.[69] A postmodernist politics of dissent, in this regard, is *post*modern in the sense that it seeks to confront, at every level, those aspects of modernity that undermine any potential people might have to produce, in their everyday lives, resistances to power relations that silence, demean, and oppress them. To achieve this, a postmodernist approach cannot become a negative philosophy of "disintegration," as some critics perceive it, nor dare it close off the possibility that, within postmodernism, there are the very modernist tendencies that its own critical insights expose so starkly.[70]

I will return to this issue again in Chapter 8, primarily in regard to R. B. J. Walker's *One World, Many Worlds,* which represents a rudimentary statement of a postmodern politics of dissent, of the engaged, constructive kind alluded to earlier. For now I want to take the route taken by critical scholars in the 1980s, which saw them transfer Critical Theory and postmodernist critiques directly to the Traditional agenda of International Relations.

Notes

1. Bellah, as cited in Kolb, *The Critique of Pure Modernity,* p. 273.
2. These are Jane Flax's insights in *Thinking Fragments,* p. 5.
3. For example, Rorty, *Philosophy and the Mirror of Nature;* Rajchman and West, eds., *Post-Analytic Philosophy;* Baynes, Bohman, and McCarthy, eds., *After Philosophy.* Another in this idiom is Dunn's *Western Political Theory in the Face of the Future.*
4. Baynes, Bohman, and McCarthy, *After Philosophy,* p. 2.
5. See, for example, Kratochwil, "Regimes, Interpretation and the Science of Politics"; and Ruggie, "Continuity and Transformation in the World Polity."
6. Quine, "Two Dogmas of Empiricism"; and Wittgenstein, *Philosophical Investigations.*
7. Quine, "Two Dogmas of Empiricism," pp. 59–60.
8. Wittgenstein, *Philosophical Grammar* (1974), p. 210, cited in Thompson, *Critical Hermeneutics,* p. 14.
9. Wittgenstein, *Philosophical Investigations,* section 23.
10. Wittgenstein, *Philosophical Grammar,* cited in Thompson, *Critical Hermeneutics,* p. 23.
11. Wittgenstein, *Philosophical Investigations,* section 65.
12. Ibid.
13. For a discussion, see Aronowitz, *Science as Power,* pp. 242–243.
14. Wittgenstein, *Philosophical Investigations,* p. 49.
15. Thompson, *Critical Hermeneutics,* p. 4.
16. This is Rorty's view in *Philosophy and the Mirror of Nature,* p. 9.
17. On the hermeneutic tradition generally, see Mueller-Vollmer, *The Hermeneutics Reader.* This summarized discussion is drawn primarily from this source. Other useful overview works include Outhwaite, *Understanding Social Life;* Dallmayr and McCarthy, eds., *Understanding Social Inquiry;* Hekman, *Hermeneutics and the Sociology of Knowledge* and *Weber, the Ideal Type and Contemporary Social Theory;* Giddens, *Profiles and Critiques in Social Theory;* and Boucher, *Texts in Context.*

18. Mueller-Vollmer, *The Hermeneutics Reader,* p. 19.
19. Ibid., pp. 23–25.
20. Boucher, *Texts in Context,* p. 5.
21. Dallmayr and McCarthy, eds., *Understanding Social Inquiry,* pp. 1–25.
22. Bhaskar, *Scientific Realism and Human Emancipation,* p. 306.
23. In *Towards a Normative Theory of International Relations.*
24. Gadamer, *Truth and Method,* pp. xxii–xxiii.
25. Ibid., p. 23.
26. Ibid., pp. 283–290.
27. Ibid., p. 288.
28. Ibid., p. 485.
29. Ibid., p. 319. The term *experience* used here is not that used by empiricists. Rather it relates to the Hegelian use of the term denoting the movement of consciousness. A more appropriate term in German is *Erfahrung.*
30. The relationship between Habermas and Gadamer is a social theory debate in itself, of course; see McCarthy, *The Critical Theory of Jurgen Habermas,* pp. 187–193; and Jay, "Should Intellectual History Take a Linguistic Turn?"
31. Given the actual revolutionary circumstances that Marxist theory and practice confronted, it was not surprising, perhaps, that highly complex and ambiguously presented positions were simplified and sloganized. But as other Marxist scholars have noted, there is plenty of scope for the view that in the "great texts" of Marx and Engels it is possible to find crude positivist understandings of knowledge and society. In Engels's work this is less ambiguously the case, particularly in his *Anti Duhring,* published during Marx's life and containing a chapter from Marx. It was *Anti Duhring* that, according to Plekhanov, gave "final shape" to a Marxist philosophy of science that directed orthodox Marxist thinking until perhaps the 1960s. This is Plekhanov's view in *Fundamental Problems of Marxism,* p. 23. It is also the view of Lukacs in *History and Class Consciousness,* p. 3; Lukacs spoke of the "decisive influence" of *Anti Duhring* upon the later course of Marxist theory.
32. I refer here initially to the first generation of Frankfurt School scholars, such as Max Horkheimer, Theodor Adorno, and Herbert Marcuse. For a good overview of their works, see Arato and Gebhardt, eds., *The Essential Frankfurt School Reader;* Jay, *The Dialectical Imagination* and *Marxism and Totality;* and Held, *Introduction to Critical Theory.* More specific contributions include Horkheimer, *Critical Theory;* Horkheimer and Adorno, *Dialectic of Enlightenment;* Adorno, *Negative Dialectics;* and Marcuse, *One Dimensional Man.*
33. See Horkheimer and Adorno, *Dialectic of Enlightenment;* and Adorno, *Negative Dialectics.*
34. And hence the attack on "Western" Marxists by more orthodox Marxist scholars like Perry Anderson in *Considerations on Western Marxism.*
35. Horkheimer, *Critical Theory,* p. 245.
36. Works by Habermas include *Knowledge and Human Interests* (1972); *Theory and Practice* (1974); *Legitimation Crisis* (1975); *Towards a Rational Society* (1976); *Communication and the Evolution of Society* (1979); *Theory of Communicative Action* (vol. 1) (1984); *Theory of Communicative Action* (vol. 2) (1988); and *The Philosophical Discourse of Modernity* (1987). For discussions on Habermas, see McCarthy, *The Critical Theory of Jurgen Habermas;* Jay, *Marxism and Totality* and *The Dialectical Imagination;* Held, *Introduction to Critical Theory;* Thompson, *Critical Hermeneutics;* Held and Thompson, eds., *Habermas;* Bernstein, ed., *Habermas and Modernity;* and Poster, *Critical Theory and Poststructuralism.*
37. Habermas, *Communication and the Evolution of Society,* p. 72.
38. Habermas, *Towards a Rational Society,* p. 112.
39. Ibid., p. 113.

40. Ibid.

41. The primary transference of Habermasian themes has been by Richard Ashley in "Political Realism and Human Interests" and "The Poverty of Neorealism."

42. For Habermas's discussion of these "cognitive interests," see the Appendix to *Knowledge and Human Interests.* The point of Habermas's argument here, of course, is to reground (critical) theory in practice (human interests). This, however, for Habermas's critics, is the weakness of the argument, with many of them unhappy about the actual status of the "interests" in question. In the Postscript to *Knowledge and Human Interests,* Habermas confronted his critics. For an interesting discussion of this issue see Jay, *Marxism and Totality,* chap. 15.

43. For a discussion of this, see Jay, *Marxism and Totality;* McCarthy, *The Critical Theory of Jurgen Habermas;* Thompson, *Critical Hermeneutics;* and Bernstein, *Beyond Objectivism and Relativism.*

44. Bernstein, *Beyond Objectivism and Relativism,* pp. 40–48, 185.

45. For an overview, see Whitebook, "The Problem of Nature in Habermas."

46. Most famously perhaps by Roland Barthes in *Mythologies.*

47. On the problems of "big P" philosophy, see Rorty, *Philosophy and the Mirror of Nature.*

48. See Habermas, "Modernity Versus Post-Modernity." For a general overview of this debate, see Bernstein, ed., *Habermas and Modernity;* and Poster, *Critical Theory and Poststructuralism.*

49. See Habermas, "Questions and Counterquestions." There are clear biographical and historical reasons for the shift in tone and subtlety over this period. Until "Modernity Versus Postmodernity," there is little evidence that Habermas had seriously grappled with the post-1968 shift in French social theory. This had to do with the (perhaps understandable) aversion of a German leftist to the German forerunners of postmodernism (e.g., Nietzsche and Heidegger) and his primary interest in emancipatory post-Enlightenment theory.

50. Ibid., p. 197.

51. Ibid.

52. Ibid., p. 196.

53. Poster, *Critical Theory and Poststructuralism.*

54. Ibid., p. 22.

55. Ibid., p. 23.

56. See Lyotard, *The Postmodern Condition.*

57. Kolb, *The Critique of Pure Modernity,* p. 258.

58. Ibid., p. 259.

59. See Richard Rorty on this in "Habermas and Lyotard on Postmodernity."

60. Foucault, "What Is Enlightenment?" p. 42.

61. See the debates in *Theory and Practice* and *Knowledge and Human Interests* in particular.

62. Habermas, *Theory and Practice,* p. 145.

63. Ibid., p. 156.

64. Habermas, *Communication and the Evolution of Society,* p. 140.

65. It is in this context, and for all that has gone before in this chapter, that I regard Foucault's work and that of a scholar like Habermas as aspects of a broader shared project, as indicated in the discussion of critical social theory in Chapter 1. For all their differences, I suggest, theirs is a positive attempt to open up the closure in modern Western theory and practice in order that its reflective, critical potentials for resistance be explored and utilized. This is not, of course, the common reading of the relationship between the most influential Critical Theorist of the age and the

most illustrious of his postmodernist counterparts. More often than not the two are presented as two ends of a modernist spectrum: Habermas, the German heir of Kant, Hegel, and Marx, desperately seeking to retain an Enlightenment faith in rationality, progress, and emancipation; Foucault, the heir of Nietzsche, and a post-1968 pessimism in French intellectual circles, propounding an extreme antipathy to modernity in all its dimensions, particularly its rationalist/emancipatory one. This is a position easily enough defended. Within the works of both scholars over the years many passages suggest that the popular reading is the most accurate. My point, simply, is that simple conclusions of any kind are singularly inappropriate in relation to projects as complex and contentious as these, and much work is still necessary in the space between them.

66. This is not to suggest that postmodernists are unaware of the issue. Der Derian, for example, makes this clear in his "Boundaries of Knowledge and Power in International Relations," pp. 3–11.

67. Ashley, "Living on Border Lines," p. 266.

68. Ibid., p. 269.

69. This has been the space where Ashley has worked, almost exclusively, over the years, and no one has contributed more to a critical social theory perspective of the kind advocated here. His "Living on Border Lines" argument, for example, will be featured in Chapter 8 as a major example of postmodernist scholarship, which opens up previously closed space on the sovereignty issue. My point here, critically made in relation to aspects of that work, is a more general one. It is, simply put, that postmodernism cannot afford closure in its own works while exposing it in others.

70. On the disintegration theme, see Dews, *The Logic of Disintegration.*

7

Thinking Beyond International Relations: The Critical Theory Challenge

This chapter and the one to follow are concerned with the way the issue of theory as practice, dealt with throughout this book, has been directly confronted in the 1980s and 1990s in the new critical literature of International Relations. The two chapters seek, more explicitly, to say something of the various ways the Tradition and discipline of International Relations, framed in modernist terms and articulated primarily within positivist-Realist principles of understanding, have been rewritten, respoken, and reconceptualized in recent years. The major conduits of critical social theory analysis in this context have been Critical Theory approaches and post-Kantian emancipatory perspectives in general and, in more recent times, various approaches invoking postmodernist principles of critique. This chapter will concentrate on that literature invoking (broadly) Critical Theory concerns, which has been at the forefront of the challenge to the neo-Realist orthodoxy since the early 1980s and which has brought to the orthodox agenda a range of alternative suggestions for thought and action, beyond International Relations. It concentrates on dimensions of the critical theory perspective on International Relations, as articulated in the contributions of scholars such as Richard Ashley, Robert Cox, Andrew Linklater, Mark Hoffman, and Nick Rengger.

This Critical Theory perspective has, since the early 1980s, highlighted discursive tensions connecting power politics Realism to the post-Enlightenment pursuit of a science of human society, in order that the emancipatory potential of such tensions be ventilated and positively invoked within the International Relations community. The Habermasian influence on this literature is most explicit in Richard Ashley's "Political Realism and Human Interests," which in 1981 employed concepts from *Knowledge and Human Interests* to illustrate how, since the Cold War, Realism had systematically reduced understanding and explanation in International Relations to a single knowledge form (scientific rationalism), a single methodology (deductive empiricism), and a single research orientation (problem solving). Realism, in this sense, has reduced International Relations to a single "cognitive interest"—in a technical knowledge and the methodology of control. In rejecting this knowledge/power nexus, Ashley did not simply seek to condemn or dismiss Realism per se but, in Habermasian terms, sought to expose some of the critical tensions within Traditional Realism, which made *it,* at least potentially, an open, interpretivist approach to the world.

This could only begin to happen, argued Ashley, if International Relations scholars turned away from the analytical cul-de-sac of structuralist neo-Realism and rediscovered the interpretivist route traversed, however rudimentarily and sporadically, by a "practical" strain of (Traditionalist) Realist thought that sought a knowledge of International Relations not in order to more effectively control an objectified environment but so that notions of power and national interest could be understood as historically, politically, and culturally derived. It was in this sense, and in concentrating on the political interests of human actors rather than the mechanical operation of systems or structures, that a Traditionalist-based Critical Theory of International Relations offered an approach to global life "freed from unacknowledged constraints, relations of domination, and [the] conditions of distorted communication that deny humans the capacity to make the future through free will and consciousness."[1] These were themes taken much further in Ashley's most powerful contribution to the emancipatory genre: "The Poverty of Neorealism" (1984).[2] This work quickened the pulse of the critical challenge to the disciplinary orthodoxy perceptibly and became something of a catalyst for the extended critical agenda of the past few years.

Critical Theory, the Emancipatory Impulse, and the Poverty of Neo-Realism

In "The Poverty of Neorealism," Ashley set his sights on the elite of the neo-Realist mainstream in proposing that, in the name of scientific scholarship, they had "betrayed" the dialectical potential of Traditionalist Realism in the same way that positivist structuralists (e.g., Althusser) had purged the emancipatory legacy of Marxism, reducing it to an ahistorical and depoliticized understanding of politics.[3] Borrowing some vitriol from E. P. Thompson, Ashley branded this neo-Realist approach "an orrery of errors" that, for all its scientific posturing, effectively immunized its state-as-actor premise from any process of falsification and generally excluded from its agenda any perspective that challenged orthodox perspectives.[4] This limited neo-Realist understanding to the extent that alternative behavior (e.g., transnational regime behavior, class relations) could be comprehended only when reduced to the logic of methodological individualism.

Neo-Realism, accordingly, represented a normative, biased, and ideological perspective that, in the more critically attuned atmosphere of the post-Vietnam period, presented the Realist hierarchy with a serious challenge to its logic and legitimacy. Hence the post-Vietnam attempt to relocate the Realist Tradition more securely within the realm of scientific objectivity via a highly problematic variant on the structuralist theme. Ashley focused on the "poverty" of Kenneth Waltz's structuralism, in this regard, maintaining that since Waltz's *Theory of International Politics* neo-Realism has suffered the worst of both theoretical worlds, encompassing "atomism's superficiality combined with structuralism's closure."[5]

As my earlier discussions sought to illustrate, this projection of neo-Realism's limitations is relevant not only to Waltz but also to many of those who have sought to detach themselves from his "conventional" structuralist approach. This was Ashley's general conclusion also. Accordingly, in 1984, the work of Waltz, Keohane, Krasner, Gilpin, Tucker, and Kindleberger et al. was represented in (broadly) discursive terms as a "collective movement or project," underwritten by the (unacknowledged) impact upon it of positivist principles of knowledge.[6] More precisely, and in more direct Habermasian terms, the problem was perceived as neo-Realism's commitment to a technical-rationalist mode of knowledge that professed its concern to "demystify all forms of romanticism, [and] dispense with atavistic myth" while ultimately endorsing "a metahistorical faith in scientific-technical progress that positivist science itself cannot question."[7] This was the basis of neo-Realism's "betrayal" of the Realist revolt against idealism and metaphysics. It was a "betrayal" in the Frankfurt School sense in that it betrayed an entire Weltanschauung (emancipatory democracy) in favor of the closure and rigidity of positivist scientism.

In the broader International Relations context, argued Ashley, this has resulted in the post-1914 quest for a sensitive, enabling knowledge of International Relations being increasingly reduced to the ritualized dogmas of a particular economic logic and power politics ideology. Neo-Realism, in this sense, is a microcosmic expression of the "totalitarianism" of Anglo-American modernity, an ideological hybrid that has taken from Traditional Realism "only an interest in power" and from post-Enlightenment science "only an interest in expanding the reach of control."[8]

The major implication of all this remains the effective exclusion from International Relations discourse of any reflective self-inquiry into questions of knowledge construction and the complexities of understanding the world in Realist terms. In Ashley's terms these implications include (1) the denial of history as an indeterminate social process in favor of a singular, universalized "history," (2) the denial of social practice in favor of an essentialized sociopolitical reality, set upon the behavior of an "idealized homo economicus," (3) a narrow and self-serving comprehension of power, reduced to the calculation of "means" (interests), and (4) an inadequate understanding of politics, reduced to utilitarian struggle and represented as the structural "is" of the world.[9]

In 1984, as indicated, Ashley's critical perspectives were still framed in emancipatory terms drawn primarily from Habermasian Critical Theory. However, other influences were becoming apparent in his thinking, most particularly those of Bourdieu and Foucault. It was from this (rather problematic) intellectual trinity that Ashley constructed his alternative to positivist neo-Realism. This he described as a "dialectical competence model" approach, which, he maintained, represented the genuine fusion of theory and practice that is necessary in any project designed to adequately understand the complex world of the 1980s. Offering interpretive, hermeneutic-based insight, this model allows for enhanced reflection upon neo-Realism's status, not just as a "theory" concerned to explain, interpret, and organize the facts but as a deeply embedded regime of theory as practice, which helps *create* and reinforce the facts of modern global hegemony. Once understood this way, different questions might be asked of neo-Realism and the process by which it constructs its knowledge of the hegemonic patterns of power "out there." Similarly, different analytical/policy perspectives might become available, based not on images of structuralist inevitability nor some irreducible anarchical "essence" but in terms of a dominant world order "among a multiplicity of mutually interpenetrating and opposed world orders some of which might escape the logic of the modern global hegemony and assert alternative structuring possibilities."[10]

The emancipatory connections between Ashley's 1981 article and the "Poverty" arguments of 1984 were most explicit when he outlined the rudiments of his alternative "dialectical competence" model. This is primarily because in 1984, as in 1981, he reiterated his earlier proposition that such an alternative was already present, in embryo, in the Traditionalist Realist approach that neo-Realism sought to make scientific. A major critical purpose of the "Poverty of Neorealism," accordingly, was the attempt to "recover" from Traditional Realism those insights into political practice that neo-Realism had purged with its narrow scientism. And while Ashley was not unaware of the complicity of Traditionalist scholarship in the global hegemony of neo-Realism, he insisted that its broad hermeneutic approach to understanding was resistant to the frozen categories of neo-Realism and its rational choice premises.

In 1981, consequently, Ashley sought to utilize the sensitive Traditionalism of John Herz as an example of this hermeneutic difference. In 1984 it was Morgenthau who was projected as the personification of Traditionalism's "practical" cognitive interest. In "The Poverty of Neo-realism," thus, a series of quotations from Morgenthau are presented, all indicating his distaste for the post-Enlightenment "scientific" approach, all invoking a historical and interpretivist alternative. Indeed, maintained

Ashley, on many occasions Morgenthau stressed the "unhistoric and apolitical" nature of the utilitarian, positivistic, and rationalist commitments characteristic of neo-Realism, and, therefore, "given a chance to speak, [Morgenthau] would be among neorealism's sternest critics."[11]

Ashley's important critique of neo-Realism is, in this regard, an attempt to reinvoke Morgenthau's voice on behalf of a silenced interpretivist insight at the core of neo-Realism. It is an attempt to emancipate International Relations by emancipating Realism's repressed critical dimension. This particular element of the work, however, stands as its most obvious point of weakness, not necessarily because of its attempt to illuminate a critical potential within Realism, effectively silenced by its dominant reading. As stated earlier, I have some empathy with such an ambition. Rather, the problems for Ashley, as his critics were quick to discern, concerned the implications, for his general argument, of the "recovery" theme.

Kratochwil, for example, in a spirited defense of (scientific) interpretivism, landed some telling and valid critical blows on Ashley's characterization of Morgenthau as the exemplar Traditionalist, repelled by the positivism of neo-Realism.[12] Kratochwil countered by simply selecting from Morgenthau's writings famous passages that emphasize Morgenthau's (at times) crude positivism. Kratochwil, moreover, accused Ashley of blindness in relation to Morgenthau's influence in transferring rational-actor premises to contemporary Realism. He stressed, too, the intellectual insensitivity associated with Ashley's lumping together of critical influences drawn from diverse sources, such as Habermas, Foucault, and Bourdieu, in his "dialectical competence model." These were the kind of issues raised by others also. Gilpin, for example, though generally out of his depth with the intellectual issues at hand, was able to highlight the problems of Ashley's tendency toward dichotomy in his representation of the relationship between Traditionalism and neo-Realism, on behalf of an otherwise dialectically informed approach to knowledge and society.[13]

These criticisms, to some extent at least, are justified. Ashley in 1984 seemingly did not comprehend (or at least did not acknowledge) that the repression of critical potential in Realism is not due to the impact of neo-Realism's positivist scientism per se but to the modernist framing regime at the core of Traditionalism that establishes, at the metatheoretical level, the discursive conditions for *both* Traditionalism and neo-Realism. Nor did he acknowledge what Stanley Hoffmann understood in 1977, that Morgenthau is the "father" of scientific neo-Realism and integral to the transference of economic rationalism at the core of the discipline of International Relations.[14] Moreover, in 1984 Ashley did not acknowledge what this book sought to illustrate in its early chapters: (1) that positivists can repudiate scientific rationality on positivist grounds (e.g., Popper, Lakatos), (2) that an anti-Enlightenment approach proclaiming historical/philosophical knowledge can be advocated in terms of the essentialist, universalist principles of positivist rationalism (e.g., Wight, Bull, and the British School), and (3) that Verstehen-based interpretivist perspectives (e.g., Morgenthau via Weber) are the other side of the positivist coin.

My own view is that Ashley's "Poverty" article represents the contribution of an outstanding and creative thinker who in the early 1980s personified the restlessness and frustration of a liberal sector within the U.S. International Relations community, which perceived the promised openness of the post-Vietnam period rapidly being closed off by the neo-Realist hierarchy. The restlessness, creativity, and frustration are very evident in the "Poverty" article. The result, for the most part, is a stimulating and sophisticated critique of neo-Realism, pitched at an intellectual level generally alien to an International Relations audience, a critique that prefigured much of the critical social theory literature that was to follow. At the same time, there is in Ashley's wide-ranging attack on the orthodoxy an occasionally cavalier approach to complex issues (e.g., the connections between Habermas, Bourdieu, and Foucault), which leaves his arguments vulnerable to a critical audience only too pleased to pick up on some obvious flaws.

In concentrating on the more obvious problems of logic in "The Poverty of Neorealism," Ashley's critics were able to ignore or marginalize those elements of his argument which exposed the limitations of neo-Realism in general. Moreover, in missing the point on the Morgenthau issue in particular, Ashley allowed the neo-Realist hierarchy to sidestep the broader questions of Realism and modernism and the broader inadequacies of their Tradition and discipline. Consequently, while Ashley's emancipatory insights in "The Poverty of Neorealism" opened up important "thinking space" for many within the International Relations community, those who were its major targets were able to effectively close it off. Indeed, there is little evidence to this day that neo-Realists have even begun to address the substantive issues raised in Ashley's exposition of their "poverty."

Since the mid-1980s, Ashley has shifted considerably, from an explicit emancipatory approach to a postmodernist perspective and to a position that does acknowledge the larger modernist location of the issues at hand in 1984. More will be added later on his important contribution to the critical social theory literature in this genre. At this point, however, another important contribution to emancipatory scholarship requires attention, one that raises these issues again, albeit in a slightly different form—the contribution of Robert Cox, who throughout the 1980s confronted neo-Realism with an emancipatory perspective influenced by Habermas but also by Gramsci and antistructuralist Marxism in general.

Cox, Gramsci, and International Political Economy from the Bottom Up

Cox's essay "Social Forces, States, and World Orders" (1981) is an early example of his contribution to the critical social theory literature.[15] This work, like Ashley's, sought to "recover" from Traditionalist Realism an open-ended interpretive nuance, which for Cox was located in the historical scholarship of figures such as E. H. Carr and Ludwig Dehio. And, like Ashley, Cox developed his arguments in terms of a major tension—between a latent Critical Theory perspective at the core of Traditionalism and a "problem-solving" approach, dominant since the Cold War and the Americanization of the discipline. This "problem-solving" category generally complemented Ashley's (Habermasian) concept of "technical" Realism. Cox's argument diverged significantly from Ashley's, however, when it came to the question of Morgenthau's role in the discipline's development. On this issue Cox stressed that Morgenthau was integral to the objectification of Realism and to a concern, above all, with "the defence of American power as a bulwark of the maintenance of order."[16] This ideological form of Realism, he proposed, continues to underpin and direct neo-Realism, to the detriment of International Relations in general.

In Cox's "Social Forces" article, consequently, a major emancipatory task is the attempt to "recover" for contemporary global understanding some basic philosophical principles of critical interpretation that the neo-Realist orthodoxy has effectively ignored. The first and most important of these principles is that which rejects any notion of an independent reality "out there," accessible via objective empirical observation. Rather, Cox insists, knowledge of reality is always intrinsically connected to social practice and to the ways human affairs are organized in particular times and places. Consequently, "theory is always for someone and for some purpose" and always, therefore, socially and politically located.[17] His point, more precisely, is that neo-Realist hegemonic theories are historically and politically located in the history and politics of the Cold War and the Traditional problem of how to control and manage an apparently enduring superpower conflict. This is an inadequate perspective, he maintains, because in focusing its attention upon a frozen objectified image of the world "out there" and not reflecting upon the larger process by which that image is theoretically constructed, it effectively blinds neo-Realism to the prospect of a changing reality, generated by the dialectical interaction of theory as practice.

A Critical Theory approach is necessary, in this context, because it *does* reflect upon the process of theorizing, thus reconnecting knowledge, human interests, and the everyday practice of power and opening up a previously foreclosed debate about reality. It is an approach that does not accord existing institutions and power relations the status of given facts but "call[s] them into question by concerning itself with their origins and how and whether they might be in the process of change."[18]

It is in these terms that in 1981 and in subsequent works, Cox has introduced a definably Gramscian tone to his Critical Theory arguments.[19] This he has done in confronting neo-Realism's approach to international political economy and the hegemony question with a series of counterhegemonic propositions, centered less on Traditional state-centric analysis and more on the emancipatory potentials of "social forces." The notion of social forces represents an attempt to go beyond the conventional Marxist notion of the social relations of production, although this clearly is its conceptual source. As Cox explains, a social-forces approach is concerned with the interconnection of three dimensions of power: (1) that concerning the productive process, (2) that concerning the relations between classes—social power, and (3) that encompassing political power—control over the state. It is from this power matrix, he argues, that particular constellations of social forces emerge in the world. Thus, in the contemporary period, with an increasingly interdependent global economy and an internationalized production process, there is the possibility for genuine change around the world as new constellations of social forces emerge, seeking greater political and economic participation and social freedom.[20]

This is a distinctly different perspective from that dominant in International Relations, which addresses the world in terms of hegemonic structures and a power matrix reflecting the dominance of an "orderer"—the most powerful state (i.e., the United States)—over the "ordered." Consequently, when the issue of change is addressed from the orthodox perspective, it is framed negatively (e.g., change as the demise of hegemonic order in the state system). From a Critical Theory perspective, this is a myopic and dangerous approach to a complex and volatile global situation. Hence the need to reconceptualize contemporary international political economy in Gramscian terms, which understands hegemonic power regimes more dynamically—as dialectically energized and as always in the process of change.

From this Gramscian perspective, neither the structure of interstate interaction nor the question of hegemony is necessarily understood in power politics terms. Rather, systemic and hegemonic power is understood as the "temporary universalisation in thought of a particular power structure, conceived not as domination but as the necessary order of nature."[21] In other words, the power of ideology—the power that transforms particular global structures into the "necessary order of nature"—is just as important as politicostrategic power, which buttresses the "necessary order." Since the nineteenth century in Anglo-American societies, the "necessary order of nature" notion has been articulated in relation to the correctness of capitalist market relations and associated social formations. The role of the state (and the state system) in this hegemonic scenario is to ensure that the necessary conditions exist, at the global level, for the universalization of capitalist relations to take place.

Thus, at the pinnacle of the hegemonic formation (the United States after 1945), the ideological tendency has been to herald international capitalism as consistent with the "natural order" of modern social existence (e.g., Modernization Theory). Any challenge to this order is then interpreted as "unnatural" interference in the process of universalization, which must be resisted for the common (systemic) good. This is where Realist theory as practice becomes a vital ideological factor in this hegemonic context, with its concern to reduce the complex realities of contemporary International Relations to a concern with (U.S.) hegemonic order, an order now represented as in the interests of the state system as a whole. In this scenario (capitalist, market) economics is accorded a given, taken-for-granted status within Realism and throughout its hegemonic territory. The emergence in the 1970s of a neo-Realist structuralism (based on microeconomic theory) and a hegemonic stability theory is, in a Critical Theory context, merely the *explicit* representation of a deep ideological commitment in International Relations per se.

The current, multifaceted challenge to this hegemonic structure does not represent an immediate threat to the universalization of capitalist relations per se, nor, in the short term, to the state system built upon them. Rather, as Cox argues, the hegemonic crisis for the United States is to a large extent a crisis of ideological legitimation. It represents the crisis of a dominant power no longer able to effectively articulate its hegemonic logic to a global community increasingly able and willing to question such logic.[22] In Gramscian terms, this represents a significant historical moment, when the hegemon can no longer project its domination as in line with the "necessary order of [politico-economic] nature." This is not solely or primarily because of the demise of institutions (e.g., Bretton Woods) that acted as major agencies of U.S. hegemonic power. Nor is it due directly to the end of the Cold War. It has more to do with broader structural changes in the international political economy. And these are changes that neo-Realism cannot adequately deal with because they are not reducible to simple models of individual state interaction. Rather, they concern changes in social forces brought on by an internationalized production process and the international division of labor associated with it.

These changes have provoked significant responses in societies both favorably incorporated in the world economy and increasingly marginalized by it, with both sets of responses placing pressures upon the post–World War II hegemon. In the case of First World industrial societies, for example, the costs have largely been borne by labor forces engaged in traditional industries (e.g., manufacturing, agriculture). This has produced increased tension in recent years regarding issues of protectionism and socioeconomic restructuring and increased conflict between small, indigenous capitalist sectors and multinational capital. It has also given rise to an increasing global cynicism toward calls for free trade on the part of the hegemonic power (the United States) and the development of alternative politicoeconomic blocs, constructed to compete with U.S. hegemonic power.

In the marginalized societies of the Third World the response to contemporary global hegemony has been somewhat different, with the political and social conflict more direct and more violently articulated. In general terms, there has been increased conflict between elites seeking to control (in one way or another) the consequences of the internationalization of production upon their societies and the (often) disenfranchised masses seeking (in one way or another) to confront the everyday misery of their existence. In this context, too, the United States has found it increasingly difficult to project its image of the benign hegemon, ordering International Relations in favor of the market and "natural" (Western, modern) political structures.[23]

This scenario is likely to continue in the foreseeable future, suggests Cox, because there is little evidence that the intellectual/policy community in the United States understands that its politicoeconomic power is dependent upon something other than its power politics capacity to "deter" and keep the world in its "natural" (free-trade) state. From a Critical Theory perspective, it does not understand that there is

> a world order . . . founded not only upon the regulation of interstate conflict, but also upon a globally conceived civil society, i.e., a mode of production of a global extent which brings about links among the social classes of different countries. [It is] the global structuring of [these] social forces [that] shapes the different forms of state, while states in turn influence the evolution of the regulatory pattern of the global hegemony.[24]

This is an important affirmation of Cox's Critical Theory position. It is what he was getting at with his distinction in 1981 between an ahistorical "problem-solving" Realism and a Critical Theory approach that refuses to take existing power relations as given. It is an important dimension of the critical perspective that Cox has brought to his examination of the emancipatory potentials of new social forces and new state formations that might emerge with contemporary changes in global production processes.

From this perspective, change is not explained from the top down (at the behest of the major states), as in Realism, but it occurs as part of a more complex matrix, as changes in social forces at all levels help restructure world order and the pattern of global hegemony. It becomes possible, consequently, to think of stability, order, and hegemony not necessarily in terms of the dominant state or as a recurring factor in some determined historical structure but as part of a dialectic between social and material forces mediated through the political/institutional agencies of the state. Moreover, from this Critical Theory perspective, when the question is asked about a future beyond U.S. hegemony, the answer does not have to be the ungovernability of the system, as in neo-Realism. Instead, space becomes available for examining the emancipatory potentials of social forces emerging in the present and for the possibility of alternative state formations in the future.

In *Production, Power and World Order* (1987), Cox concentrated on this latter issue in particular in developing a complex sociohistorical explanation of the different kinds of social forces associated with particular politicoinstitutional structures, in the period between 1945 and 1980.[25] In this period, he argues, there was an ongoing tension between variants of the "redistributive" state formation, based on a command economy and single-party control (e.g., USSR and China), and "neoliberal" states, derived from the welfare-based states of the post–World War I era. By the 1970s, the "redistributive" state formations were generally in decline, while some of the most powerful "neoliberal" states had been transformed into the "hyperliberal" systems associated with the United States under the Reagan administration and Britain under Thatcherism. Within "hyperliberalism," emphasis is placed on possessive individualism, patriotism, and a strong military profile, while in both international and domestic policy there is an antipathy to issues of, for example, welfare statism and human rights.

It is with the emergence of this kind of state formation and associated ideologies (e.g., economic rationalism) that the marginalization of the Third World and conflict between the marginalized and the major productive states is set to worsen and pressure on the hegemon is set to increase. Unlike his neo-Realist counterparts, however, Cox perceives this hegemonic crisis as pregnant with potential for progressive social change, a historical moment with the potential for counterhegemonic response. His point, in short, is that if one understands the contemporary situation, in Critical Theory terms, there are no (anarchical) structural determinants at work, "out there," that must prevent changes in global productive processes nor changes in social forces worldwide.

Cox's broader intellectual point, consistent with his philosophical discussion in 1981, is that there is nothing determinate about the real world "out there." Accordingly, it can be examined and understood from a perspective other than the dominant hegemonic perspective, its answers being effectively shaped by the (metatheoretical) questions asked of it. For Cox, thus, asking questions framed in the critical modernist tradition of the Frankfurt School and antistructuralist Marxism, the answers, at least, allow for the possibility of something other than recurrence and repetition or the necessity of U.S. hegemony. Above all, they allow for a serious analytical inquiry of international political economy along Critical Theory lines.

Cox's Critical Theory approach is not without problems, of course. Like every other mode of inquiry discussed in this book, it is replete with them. His major work, *Production, Power and World Order,* for example, really only covers the period until the end of the 1970s. Since that time, some of its empirical analysis has been rather overtaken by the extraordinary events of the past decade, particularly in Eastern Europe. In this regard, as Stephen Gill suggested in 1990, the new state formations that seem to be emerging might not be characterized by greater capacity for dissent at the international level but by a consolidation of "hyperliberalism," which will see

> a new identity of interests between established workers and transnational productive capital, between certain financial and trading interests, consumers, service workers, and even the leaders and some workers of the previously communist states (perhaps eventually in the USSR).[26]

In the context of this work, of course, there is another level at which Cox's Critical Theory requires critical attention. This concerns its location in modernist discourse. Or, more precisely, it concerns the question of whether its critical value is undermined by its modernist emancipatory commitments. My position on Cox's contribution, in this regard, is that it represents something other than vulgar Marxism and that, analytically, it has a great deal more to offer than the narrowly framed image of international political economy projected by figures such as Gilpin, Krasner, and Keohane. I do, however, take seriously the postmodernist position on this issue, and there *are* themes in Cox's work that could be interpreted as consistent with a metanarrative reading of historical materialism and the historical development of a repressed critical rationality. On close reading, however, Cox's *Production, Power and World Order* is a more sophisticated argument than this, with its detailed discussion of the relationships between production, social class, and political power, warranting serious and sustained study before any conclusion is reached regarding Cox's modernist status.[27]

Critical Theory and the Tendency Toward Progressivist Synthesis

The modernist commitments and limitations of some other Critical Theory contributions are less difficult to evaluate. The work of the Anglo-Australian scholar, Andrew Linklater, for example, is characterized by an explicit Kantian progressivism and, in more recent years, by arguments oriented toward an actual synthesis of Traditionalist Realism and Critical Theory. In two editions of *Men and Citizens in the Theory of International Relations* (1982 and 1990), Linklater's commitment to Kantian philosophy is expressed in attempts to establish, for contemporary International Relations, notions of "a moral progress, universality, human subjectivity and autonomy."[28] In the interim this has led to some rather strange conclusions regarding the post-Vietnam reformulation of the International Relations orthodoxy.

In 1986, for example, Linklater proposed that the interdependence literature of the 1970s represented a liberal counterpoint to Realism, which "inevitably paved the way" for a more systematic appreciation of Marxist-based perspectives on international political economy.[29] The claim, more specifically, was that interdependence scholars

> combined their critique of realism as an empirical account of world politics with a challenge to its adequacy as a guide to political practice. This challenge began to *recover the concept of progress for the theory of international relations* [emphasis added], and encouraged the belief that the purpose of international theory was not to understand "recurrence and repetition" in the international system but to identify and strengthen alternative historical possibilities immanent within it.[30]

The most charitable response to a proposition such as this is that it might have relevance to *some* interdependence scholarship, but it is clear that, for Linklater, major interdependence works, such as those of Keohane and Nye, contributed to the (perceived) post-Realist search for "progress" and "alternative historical possibilities" in international political economy.[31] This, as Keohane has affirmed (and Chapter 6 illustrated, in some detail), is assuredly not what such works were about. Indeed, it is difficult to imagine how they could be so interpreted, unless one is committed to an overwhelming modernist image of history as the unfolding of a progressive human rationality, most powerfully "immanent" at the core of the dominant ideology (i.e., as liberalism gives way to its "higher form").

This is, I think, the discursive keystone of Linklater's progressivist optimism and the philosophical catalyst for his broader project, outlined in *Beyond Realism and Marxism: Critical Theory and International Relations* (1990). Here his primary concern is the construction of "a philosophical defence of the notion of universal emancipation, and a practical inquiry into the measures which may be capable of advancing this ideal."[32] This ambition, as the title of his work suggests, is bound up with an attempt to incorporate and supersede Realism and Marxism. It is, in effect, an argument in favor of dialectical synthesis that goes far beyond the emancipatory themes to be found in either Ashley's or Cox's work. While Ashley and Cox sought to expose a tension within Realism that represented a (hermeneutic) potential for any Critical Theory perspective, Linklater's approach is built upon more orthodox modernist foundations. Consequently, Linklater's dialectical approach has a totalizing dimension to the extent that its "thesis" (Realism) and "antithesis" (Marxism) are represented in antinomized form—a form capable of generating a "real" meaning from both—which might then be utilized as the basis of a synthetic "transcendence."[33]

This perspective is articulated in *Beyond Realism and Marxism* from a position rooted in Enlightenment rationalism. Consequently, Linklater's reading of Realism and Marxism, in International Relations, acknowledges their limitations but seems oblivious to, or uninterested in, those critiques *of both* which stress the dangers of modernist universality and the imposition of essentialist meaning in theory and practice. Thus, in *Beyond Realism and Marxism,* Linklater couches his arguments in terms of Habermasian Critical Theory and seeks his synthesis with Realism on this basis.[34] He is aware, of course, of Realist antipathy to such a connection and the added difficulties, therefore, of any synthetic position in this context.[35] This, however, is no insurmountable problem for a scholar of the British/Australian school who, in time-honored fashion, turns to Martin Wight for a Traditional answer to the problem.

The value of Wight here, of course, relates to his (in)famous trichotomy of 1966, which categorized International Relations thought in terms of Realist (Machiavellian), rationalist (Grotian), and revolutionist (Kantian) perspectives.[36] For scholars such as Hedley Bull, this second category allowed space for Realist analysis of an international society rather than merely a system of anarchic states. For Linklater, the final two categories allow space for an analysis that "shifts the emphasis from systemic forces to systemic principles."[37] The systemic principles at issue, in this case, are those of universal morality and universal community, the principles of a universalized emancipatory project, which now via Wight can be encompassed within a single synthetic schema involving elements of (Traditionalist) Realism.

As my previous comments have indicated, I have some empathy with a project that confronts neo-Realism with insights drawn from a sophisticated historical materialism, à la Robert Cox. However, while Linklater's contributions over the years have been characterized by high-quality analysis and a thoughtful, critical disposition, his perspective is more problematic in terms of its modernist limitations. It is one thing, for example, to develop a counterhegemonic argument on Gramscian and Habermasian grounds; it is quite another thing to seek to combine "elements of Realism and Marxism within one conceptual framework," particularly if that conceptual framework is dependent upon the "recovery" of universal moral norms and notions of universal moral communities.[38] It is in this sense that Linklater's work is highly susceptible to the metanarrative critiques of postmodernists concerned about the dangers of continuing to think and act in terms of (Western, modernist) universalist schemas for emancipation of the species.

In a postscript to the second edition of *Men and Citizens,* Linklater began to address this issue, and he did so with some sensitivity to the differences and potential points of contact between Critical Theory and postmodernism. But in *Beyond Realism and Marxism,* also published in 1990, the sensitivity toward postmodernism is effectively absent to the extent that when alluding to the new critical debates in International Relations it is virtually ignored. There are obtuse references, however, that say much. For example, when discussing the theoretical agenda of the 1980s, Linklater reduces the issues at stake to the tension between positivism and hermeneutics, claiming that the debate in general has overlooked "the possibility of a critical theory of international relations which analyses the prospects for universal emancipation."[39] This really is an extraordinary statement, given the focus upon this very question in almost all postmodernist scholarship, but it does indicate the attitudes and perspectives of some Critical Theorists in the larger critical social theory debates and in the contemporary critical literature of International Relations. It indicates, more generally, that, as I suggested in the previous chapter, there is a need for a more tolerant and incisive approach to issues raised by Critical Theorists and postmodernists if the contributions of both are to be utilized effectively in the challenge to conservative orthodoxy in International Relations.

Probing the Space Between Critical Theory and Postmodernism: The Hoffman/Rengger Debate

The tensions between Critical Theory and postmodernism are confronted in a useful way in the final example of emancipatory scholarship for discussion here, which centered on the mini debate of the late 1980s between two British scholars, Mark Hoffman and Nick Rengger.[40] Hoffman ignited the debate in 1987 with an article highlighting the significance of Critical Theory approaches for the interparadigm debate, which for British scholars centered at the London School of Economics in particular represents the current state of the disciplinary art in International Relations.[41] Hoffman's proposal, complementing the Traditional view of the discipline's development, was that following the critical challenges of the 1970s and the new international political economy surge of the 1980s, Realism had lost its status at the core of theory and research, and the International Relations discipline was now characterized by paradigmatic diversity.[42] Hoffman emitted one cheer for this diversity, and his response (like Linklater's) was to seek to overcome any sense of intellectual insecurity brought on by this situation by restructuring the discipline in favor of a new dominant paradigm—Critical Theory. Indeed, in Hoffman's view, Critical Theory represented "the next stage in the development of International Relations theory," a stage with

> the potential for creating a new focus within the discipline of International Relations that is post-realist and post-Marxist . . . [which] provides the basis for the reintegration of International Relations into the broader traditions and concerns of social and political theory.[43]

In more specific emancipatory terms, this new Critical Theory paradigm was set to establish for International Relations thinking its fundamental purpose, which is "not to alter the way we look at the world, but to alter the world."[44]

Responding to Hoffman's article, Nick Rengger affirmed his general agreement with its concerns but questioned some of Hoffman's assumptions about his Critical Theory paradigm and its status in the contemporary debate.[45] He did so in terms that brought the tensions within critical social theory to the surface in a valuable way. Rengger proposed, for example, that Hoffman's notion of a radically inclined paradigm, set to lead International Relations into the next stage of its development, missed two important points intrinsic to the issue. The first is that much of the critical literature of the 1980s seeking a reintegration of International Relations and social theory does so from positions that are, in other respects, incompatible with Hoffman's Critical Theory (e.g., postmodernism).

The second point, a more substantive one in relation to Hoffman's argument, questioned the nature of his Critical Theory and its relationship to the paradigms it seeks to supersede. The argument here was that Critical Theory, as propounded by Hoffman, sounded uncomfortably like the orthodox perspective it opposed.[46] The connection point, as Rengger noted, is the rationalism inherent to both. In Hoffman's approach (like Linklater's), this rationalist legacy is represented in terms of the search for elements "universal to world order." In neo-Realism, of course, it is represented in terms of an unambiguous and reductionist rationalism, integral to problem-solving theory.[47] On this basis, suggested Rengger, Hoffman's Critical Theory appears to be (paradoxically) committed to the very foundationalism and positivism that it is constructed to overcome. In this sense, it is part of a dominant modernist discourse, articulated in terms of a conventional Marxist dialectic and encompassing "a fixed terminus: a telos to aim for and to bring about."[48]

Hoffman's reply to Rengger was pitched at a significantly higher level than his original article, and it introduced to the debate some themes that are crucial to the debate between (broadly) emancipatory approaches and postmodernism in International Relations.[49] On the question of rationality, for example, Hoffman invoked Habermas in rejecting the notion of a single, already-existing rationality deep within modernism awaiting rediscovery in Critical Theory. Acknowledging the obvious Enlightenment legacy within Critical Theory, Hoffman maintained, nevertheless, that it represented "the most self-reflective outpost of the radical tradition of the Enlightenment," and it was in this context that its rationalist commitments needed to be understood.[50] In this context Critical Theory emphasis is oriented not toward human rationality per se but toward "the universalisation of a single form of rationality, namely instrumental, economic and administrative reason." Consequently, Critical Theory

> retain[s] a concept of reason which asserts itself simultaneously against both instrumentalism and existentialism, which is exercised in conjunction with normative concerns and which is critically applicable to itself. The essence of rationality, in the context of critical theory, entails a limitless invitation to criticism. In consequence a complacent faith in rationalism is ruled out.[51]

The issues of foundationalism and universalism received similar treatment. On the former, Hoffman reiterated Critical Theory's antipathy to all kinds of certain knowledge, derived from "external" sources. Rather, he countered, Critical Theory "points to open ended knowledge which is continually subject to critical assessment."[52] It is in this sense that a Critical Theory approach to dialectics resists the teleology of a "fixed terminus" approach, such approaches entailing "a determinism of outcomes which critical theory specifically seeks to counter."[53] This principle, Hoffman suggested, flows over to the question of universality in Critical Theory, which it always confronted in a "cautious and contingent" manner. What Critical Theory provides, in this circumstance, is an approach that both "recognises the problem [of universality] and acknowledges its own limitations."[54] Hoffman did not directly address the issue of postmodernism in his reply to Rengger, but implicit throughout it is an attitude rather similar (unfortunately) to Linklater's, which effectively dismisses postmodernism as dispassionate and detached commentary, rather than as a genuinely concerned, critical engagement with the contemporary world.[55]

This aside, the Hoffman-Rengger conversation has added a useful, if rudimentary, dimension to a discipline unused to the art of philosophical reflection on the way we come to know and give meaning to the world. And, in its British context, it brought some interesting contemporary social theory themes to bear upon a disciplinary sector bereft, generally, of such discourse.

More precisely, the Hoffman-Rengger interchange illustrates both the potentials and the problems of the Critical Theory perspective, derived from the post-Kantian emancipatory impulse in Western philosophy and the more specific influences of Hegel, the Frankfurt School, and antistructuralist Marxism (e.g., in Gramsci). This was a theme central to this chapter in general, which sought to give a sense of the critical potentials and diversity associated with the Critical Theory perspective while indicating, again, some of the difficulties of an emancipatory approach in its attempts to overcome the closure of neo-Realism in the 1980s and 1990s. Ashley's contribution remains an important one in this regard, not only for the intellectual breadth and insight it brought to the debate but because of the tensions it exposed in the Critical Theory quest to "recover" from modernity its emancipatory dimensions. Ashley's critique of neo-Realism stands as perhaps the most devastating indictment of orthodox unself-consciousness yet recorded in the critical International Relations literature. Yet there was enough slippage in Ashley's argument to allow for counterresponses that had a measure of validity.

Cox's contribution also illustrated the "poverty" of neo-Realism but in a slightly different, and more cohesive, manner. In 1981, for example, in applying some relatively orthodox Critical Theory principles, Cox was able to locate neo-Realism's "problem-solving" approach as an updated variant of a conservative (Cold War–oriented) Realism, committed above all to a retention of the status quo in theory and (foreign policy) practice. Moreover, from his Gramscian-oriented perspective, in 1987, he illustrated the static and limited nature of neo-Realist analysis again, this time by providing an alternative analysis of the world political economy that is inclusive, wide ranging, and theoretically sophisticated.

The contributions of both Ashley and Cox have added significant critical dimensions to the debate in raising questions about issues effectively silenced by the neo-Realist orthodoxy (e.g., power, hegemony, change, ideology). Linklater's attempt to synthesize Realism and Critical Theory has also added a measure of sophistication and insight to the International Relations agenda, but its totalizing tendencies undermine its validity as an approach concerned to open a closed modernist discourse. The tendency toward synthesis and progressivist grand theory, in Critical Theory, was a theme central to the Hoffman-Rengger debate that represents a useful and long-overdue attempt within the critical literature of International Relations to explore the space between Critical Theory and postmodernism. The chapter to follow enters that space for the more specific purpose of introducing the postmodernist contribution to a critical social theory of International Relations.

Notes

1. Ashley, "Political Realism and Human Interests," p. 227.
2. The "Poverty" article is reprinted in *Neorealism and Its Critics* (1986).
3. Ashley, "The Poverty of Neorealism," p. 228.
4. Ibid.
5. Ibid., p. 256.
6. Ibid., p. 249.
7. Ibid., p. 251.
8. Ibid., p. 228.
9. Ibid., pp. 258–260.
10. Ibid., p. 279.
11. Ibid., p. 281.
12. See Kratochwil, "Errors Have Their Advantage." On the issue of Morgenthau's positivist statements and the ambiguity surrounding his position generally, see Chapter 4, pp. 111–113.
13. Gilpin, "The Richness of the Tradition of Political Realism." Gilpin's response, though pertinent on this point, perhaps best illustrated how correct Ashley was in his projection of neo-Realists as limited and unself-conscious in their understanding of the world they speak so confidently of. Gilpin's response was generally dismissive of Ashley's, chiding Ashley for the "needless jargon" of his argument, p. 289. It was on this issue of Ashley's jargon, however, that Gilpin revealed the narrowness and superficiality of his response to serious criticism. Gilpin, for example, complained that he couldn't respond to some of Ashley's arguments because

"*International Organization* failed to send an English translation with the original text," ibid., p. 289. This was, presumably, intended as a humorous comment meant to further convince the mainstream readers of *International Organization* of the tortuous and ultimately insignificant nature of Ashley's thinking and writing. The joke, though, is on Gilpin and indeed on the discipline, because the passage that most offended him indicates only that his reading regimen remains incarcerated in the caricatured debates of the past. The offending passage came as Ashley was seeking to distinguish other approaches than the positivist one for understanding the world. In this vein, his point was that "for eschatological discourse (evident in phenomenology, ethnomethodology, and some hermeneutical sciences) the objective truth of the discourse lies within and is produced by the discourse itself" ("The Poverty of Neorealism," p. 249). Gilpin's response was simply to pronounce that while he was sure this statement "and many like it throughout the article are meaningful to Ashley, I [Gilpin] have no idea what it means," p. 289. There is no attempt to understand Ashley's point, which after all, in 1984 and after years of postbehavioralist debate on the hermeneutics issue and the "theory impregnated" nature of the facts, is not that difficult to understand. But it is not just the arrogance of Gilpin's response that is its most disturbing feature—such arrogance is almost to be expected in a discipline that has been so uncritical of its "heroic figures." The more disturbing point is the indication the response gives of the shallowness of Gilpin's understanding of the issues he deals with in his work, remembering that Gilpin engages explicitly in theoretical debates and speaks with authority on theoretical issues. It was Gilpin, after all, who bemoaned the fact that Traditionalist scholars (unlike neo-Realists) were "not well grounded in social theory" (see Ashley, "Poverty of Neorealism," p. 231), and it was Gilpin in *The Political Economy of International Relations* who invoked Thomas Kuhn as an influence and who was confident enough to take on the complex issue of Marxist ideology. Yet, in relation to Ashley's criticism of his theoretical position, he suddenly doesn't know what all this "means." This, unfortunately, is a response not restricted to Gilpin, but in general attitudinal terms it represents the response of mainstream scholarship to the attempt to open its closed discursive boundaries of meaning.

14. In "An American Social Science: International Relations." This was acknowledged also by Robert Cox in 1981 in "Social Forces, States, and World Orders," and by Robert Keohane in "Realism, Neorealism and the Study of World Politics," pp. 11–12.

15. Cox, "Social Forces, States, and World Orders." This has been reprinted with an important postscript where Cox discusses the distinction between positivist and historicist forms of knowledge in *Neorealism and Its Critics.* On his Gramscian connection, see Cox, "Gramsci, Hegemony and International Relations."

16. Cox, "Social Forces, States, and World Orders," p. 131.

17. Ibid., p. 129.

18. Ibid.

19. See "Gramsci, Hegemony and International Relations."

20. See "Production and Hegemony" and *Power, Production and World Order,* chaps. 1 and 10 in particular.

21. Cox, "Production and Hegemony," p. 38.

22. Here the influence of Habermas is evident also in terms of his arguments in *Legitimation Crisis.*

23. More often than not, consequently, its one-dimensional perspective on the issue has seen it drawn toward cruder articulations of order maintenance in the Third World.

24. Cox, "Production and Hegemony," p. 45.

25. See Cox, *Production, Power and World Order,* chaps. 6 and 7.

26. Gill, "Two Concepts of International Political Economy," p. 379.

27. There are some other high-quality works of this genre also. They include Gill, *American Hegemony and the Trilateral Commission* and "Historical Materialism, Gramsci and International Political Economy"; Gill and Law, *Global Political Economy;* and most of the chapters in Murphy and Tooze, *The New International Political Economy.*

28. Linklater, *Men and Citizens,* p. 209. References here are to the second edition.

29. Linklater, "Realism, Marxism and Critical International Theory," p. 301.

30. Ibid., p. 302.

31. Ibid., pp. 301–302.

32. Linklater, *Beyond Realism and Marxism,* p. 7.

33. Ibid., p. 5.

34. Ibid., p. 7.

35. Ibid., chap. 1, especially pp. 9–15 and Conclusion.

36. See Wight, "Why Is There No International Theory?" See also the comments on this strategy in Chapter 3.

37. Linklater, *Beyond Realism and Marxism,* p. 17.

38. Ibid., p. 165.

39. Ibid., p. 4.

40. See Hoffman, "Critical Theory and the Inter-Paradigm Debate" and "Conversations on Critical International Relations Theory"; and Rengger, "Going Critical?"

41. For an influential articulation of this theme, see Banks, "The Inter Paradigm Debate," in *International Relations: A Handbook of Current Theory.*

42. Hoffman, "Critical Theory and the Inter-Paradigm Debate," p. 231.

43. Ibid., p. 247.

44. Ibid., p. 244.

45. Rengger, "Going Critical?"

46. Ibid., p. 82.

47. Ibid.

48. Ibid., p. 83.

49. Hoffman, "Conversations on Critical International Relations Theory."

50. Ibid., p. 92.

51. Ibid.

52. Ibid.

53. Ibid., p. 93.

54. Ibid.

55. Ibid.

8

Thinking Beyond International Relations: Postmodernism—Reconceptualizing Theory as Practice

The nature of the postmodernist challenge to the Tradition and discipline of International Relations is quite literally spelled out in the title of James Der Derian's and Michael Shapiro's *International/Intertextual Relations: Postmodern Readings of World Politics.*[1] The explicit influences on this work—those of Foucault, Derrida, Lacan, Kristeva, Barthes, and Baudrillard—are, in more than the obvious sense, "foreign" to a discipline dominated from its Anglo-American center. The influences, more generally, are those of discourse analysis, genealogy, deconstructionism, and textuality, and it is in this context that postmodernists have sought to question, critique, and reconceptualize the "reality" of International Relations.

The "foreignness" of the postmodern approach is epitomized in the inclination to read the social world as a text, an inclination integral to Derrida's deconstructive philosophy aimed at logocentric framing practices and Foucault's concern with discursive practices generally. The central questions asked by scholars such as these concern notions of "meaning" and "knowing," fundamental concepts in Western philosophical discourse. Or, more precisely, they concern the implication for our orthodox ways of understanding the world, if the processes integral to the construction of a text are indeed analogous to the process by which social and political reality is constructed. From a postmodernist perspective, the critical tasks are to illustrate how the textual and social processes are intrinsically connected and to describe, in specific contexts, the implications of this connection for the way we think and act in the contemporary world.[2] In this way, postmodernism refocuses contemporary analysis on the power/knowledge nexus and, to a greater extent even than Critical Theory, on theory *as* practice.

In the postmodernist contribution to International Relations, consequently, there has emerged an alternative way of understanding and articulating reality, one focused on intertextuality and sociolinguistic practice rather than monological literary convention and positivist objectivism and foundationalism. Whatever else this alternative approach achieves, it problematizes the dominant modernist commitment to a world of given subjects and objects and all other dichotomized givens. In so doing, it reformulates basic *questions* of modernist understanding in emphasizing not the sovereign subject (e.g., author/independent state) or the object (e.g., independent world/text) but instead the historical, cultural, and linguistic practices in which subjects and objects (and theory and practice, facts and values) are constructed.

In this way, postmodernist scholars have begun to challenge the dominant orthodoxy in International Relations. In the final phase of this book, consequently, I want to address some of the most significant of these postmodernist works and indicate more generally their contributions to a critical social theory of International Relations.[3] The discussion will be organized around four broad concerns of postmodern scholarship in particular. The first emphasizes the concern to open up to critical interrogation the "great texts" of the International Relations Tradition and discipline; the second focuses on challenges to fundamental Realist concepts such as sovereignty, anarchy, and the construction of Otherness; the third looks at some of the ways postmodernists have confronted strategy and security issues in the post–Cold War era; and the fourth touches on the nature of and prospects for a postmodern politics of resistance in International Relations.

Textualizing International Relations: Rereading the Tradition and Its Discipline

One of the major postmodernist incursions into alien International Relations territory has sought to disrupt the discursive certainty derived from the Traditional "great texts." The aim here has not been to dismiss the dominant readings but to illustrate that they are, indeed, *readings*—that they can be read in different ways and that their status is derived not from any correspondence with an essential (real) meaning but from a discursive strategy intrinsically connected to the dominant form of (sociohistorical) knowledge and power. This marks a repudiation of the positivist reading rules characteristic of International Relations scholarship, in which reading is understood as a largely unproblematical enterprise, a natural, neutral activity whereby an interested individual enters into some sort of imaginative encounter with a (literary) text, reading it respectfully on its *own* terms and drawing real meaning from it. The contrary position is that this approach to reading is far from neutral but rather congruent with a particular modernist discursive practice that objectifies the text and detaches the reader from it.

The necessity for an alternative reading of the major Realist texts has been enhanced in recent times, as neo-Realists have confronted the uncertainty of the age by calling again on "heroic figures" such as Thucydides and Machiavelli to grant their updated scientism a measure of Traditional credibility.[4] This has prompted critical responses from a range of scholars who have assisted postmodernists in undermining neo-Realism on this issue. Michael Doyle, for example, has noted that while a particular reading of Thucydides might be consistent with a "minimalist" form of Realist power politics, it is entirely incompatible with a neo-Realist approach that reduces human interaction to a (structuralist) variant of rational choice theory.[5]

Daniel Garst has also illustrated the problematic nature of neo-Realism's textual foundations in concentrating on the problems associated with the way figures such as Gilpin, Waltz, and Keohane seek to appropriate Thucydides as the first scientific Realist.[6] The primary problem, suggests Garst, is that it disregards the emphasis placed by Thucydides on the significance of human actors as the conscious initiators of events and his antipathy to structuralist principles that posit the foundation of an anarchical world in the (external) power distribution of actors.[7] Indeed, in *The History of the Peloponnesian War* Thucydides specifically rejects the notion of general (structuralist) laws capable of explaining international conflict. Rather, and contrary to neo-Realist readings of him,

> Thucydides reminds us that power and hegemony are above all bound to the existence of political and social structures and the intersubjective conventions associated with them. [Thus nothing] could be more foreign to Thucydides' way of thinking than neorealism's ahistorical treatment of these concepts. And nothing could be more pernicious to Thucydides than neorealism's insistence that the quest for power is an underlying and enduring systemic imperative that exists independently of social structures created and maintained by human agency.[8]

Another dimension to this issue has been added by Hayward Alker, who has emphasized the significance of dialectical logic in Thucydides's work.[9] Utilizing a formal dialogical approach to textual inquiry, Alker has illustrated how the *Melian Dialogue* in particular has been appropriated by neo-Realism in ways that have severely limited the consideration of political options in the contemporary period. As Alker illustrates, if the *Melian Dialogue* is read in its dialectical and dramaturgical context, the "Thucydides" of the Realist narrative becomes something other than the caricatured precursor of conservative scientism. If anything, he represents the kind of classical scholar who Gadamer located as integral to the *phronesis* tradition and to a critical hermeneutic approach to political society.[10] In Alker's terms, Thucydides's legacy, ignored by Realism, is that of a scholar seeking to invoke "contextually appropriate practical-normative standards of just conduct and institutional worth," not a universalized, ahistorical "truth" about interstate conduct.[11]

These critiques are significant for the manner in which they undermine the textual foundations of International Relations. In so doing they bring into question the literary font of Realist eternal wisdom, upon which scholars from Wight to Waltz have legitimated their ahistorical images of reality. They create ambiguity at the core of Keohane's philosophical certainty concerning the fundamental connection between the ancient and contemporary worlds, now flowing through neo-Realism.[12] And they render ironic Gilpin's proposition that "everything that the new realists find intriguing in the interaction of international economics and international politics can be found in *The History of the Peloponnesian War*."[13]

This point is not lost on postmodernist scholars, of course, who have engaged themselves in this debate in the most thorough and detailed fashion to further disrupt Realist textual certainty and illustrate the discursive connections between neo-Realism and modernist theory as practice. R. B. J. Walker, for example, has critically reassessed the significance of Machiavelli in this regard, finding that, as with Thucydides, Machiavelli has been reduced to a figure of parody and caricature by those seeking philosophical certainty for their image of the contemporary world of states.[14]

As a leading Realist icon, Machiavelli appears in Traditional folklore on one side of the great logocentric divide, between Realists and Others (idealists, "domestic" political theorists, ideologues, etc.). This has provided the discipline with its dialogue of eternal wisdom on questions of human nature, structural necessity, gender, power, the state, and national interest. Sometimes, as indicated in earlier discussions, this dialogue is reformulated somewhat to include a via-media notion, as in Wight's work, or to take account of Weberian sensibilities, as in the contributions of a Morgenthau or a Stanley Hoffmann. But this has not in any fundamental way challenged either the boundaries or the (power politics) premises of the dominant textual Tradition. Accordingly, crucial to all Realists—be they Humean Tories such as Wight and Bull or North American structuralists such as Waltz, Keohane, and Krasner—is the figure of Machiavelli, or at least the Machiavelli of the dominant Realist disciplinary reading.

This "Machiavelli" is vital to contemporary Realism because he affords a linear credibility to its homogenized image of history, with Machiavelli located along the way as the Renaissance voice of Thucydidian wisdom concerning the eternal vicissitudes of a world in which power reigns over ethics, ends justify means, and all behavior is rationalized in terms of *raison d'état.* However, as Walker illustrates, at least two significant silences are evident in the dominant Realist reading.[15] The first concerns *The Prince,* the exemplar text of Machiavellian Realism. Here, Realists have accorded essentialist status to those passages in which Machiavelli appears to distinguish between power and ethics, privileging the former over the latter. But to represent this as Machiavelli's essential position and, more significant, as an element of some essential Realist wisdom is to engage in the kind of exclusionary textual strategy that is replicated in the dominant knowledge forms and power relations of modern social life.

In the case of *The Prince,* for example, the dominant reading is rendered entirely problematic the moment one includes that which is excluded or marginalized in Traditional discourse—that is, the issue of virtú, and the problem of violence in the pursuit of a life of virtú, which is the major focus of *The Prince.* Moreover, when the question of virtú is read into *The Prince,* it becomes apparent that the text revered by Realists as integral to the Tradition of state-centric Realism is, more accurately, a work concerned with the specific problems of the new Renaissance states. It is not surprising that this theme is virtually ignored by Realists because, once it is accounted for, Machiavelli becomes not the Renaissance heir of Thucydides but a thinker in specific time and space dealing with his world in terms of the discursive categories available to him.

Further, for those still seeking to unproblematically connect Machiavelli via some linear textual chain to the contemporary world of International Relations, there are other problems clearly evident when the second major silence of the Realist Machiavelli is opened up for inquiry. This is the silence concerning works other than *The Prince,* also effectively ignored by Realists, which, when consulted, contain another "Machiavelli" and a series of questions that the International Relations Tradition cannot ask from within its essentialized reading practices. The point, in short, is that the Machiavelli who emerges from the *Discourses on Livy, The History of Florence,* or the *Art of War* is not the arch-Realist of International Relations at all but a complex Renaissance scholar concerned not with the anarchic state system per se, as the Tradition and discipline must insist, but with the classical (Greek) conception of the (domestic) polis—part of the very realm (dichotomously) separated from the "international" by the Tradition that proclaims Machiavelli as its own.

These problems are extenuated when one takes into account Machiavelli's antipathy to all universalist schemas and notions of transhistorical structural laws, which, like that in Thucydides, is once again ignored by Realists. Here it is the question of fortuna and the classical notion of time that problematizes any appropriation of Machiavelli as an early voice of structuralist determinism. Rather, Machiavelli can be seen to draw on classical philosophical notions of time that rebut any Christian-derived notions of determinate "externalities" and modern notions of time, which fit some chronological pattern or structure. Machiavelli's notion of time and political life was instead dominated by the notion of temporal flux and contingency, in which the vicissitudes of fortuna rendered inappropriate and dangerous any philosophy of certainty, order, and control.

As in the case of Thucydides, then, the Tradition of International

Relations, legitimated to the present by the textual certainty of power politics and structural anarchy in Machiavelli, is found to be highly problematic and uncertain under alternative critical inquiry. As Walker concludes,

> Structural accounts of the international system draw upon ontological (and thus political) commitments that are significantly different from those to be found in Machiavelli's writings. [Moreover, contrary] to some translations, there is no clear statement to the effect that the end justifies the means. There is no clear notion of national interest defined as power.[16]

An important analytical point is worth reiterating here: the deconstruction exercise seeks to illustrate that the Tradition and discipline of International Relations are constructed upon a highly contestable terrain of textuality and representation, *not* politicoeconomic certainty, *not* historical "fact." In an era in which hermeneutic insight and contextualist approaches have become rather passé in Anglo-American social theory, this might appear a rather insubstantial point to be making (or remaking) at this stage. However, as Chapter 1 emphasized, this remains an issue of real significance in International Relations because it goes to the heart of the primitive positivist Realism, which for a generation has legitimated its power politics perspectives in terms of textual certainty and continues to do so in the 1990s.

Illustrating that the "great texts" of International Relations can be read in ways entirely contrary to their ritualized disciplinary treatment is, consequently, to open up space for other ways of reading *global life,* effectively and powerfully blocked off under a foundationalist textual regime. More precisely, it is to undermine the notion of a single, irreducible reality of contemporary global life, against which conflicting interpretations and theories can be evaluated for their truth content. It is, in this sense, to bring into question the very Tradition that *is* International Relations and to cast doubt upon the discipline that sets its boundaries and establishes its rules of thinking and research.

For all this, it is not at all surprising that Realists of all hues should continue to privilege a caricatured reading of their great-man history. Indeed, a caricatured Machiavelli, in particular, is vital to neo-Realism's contemporary pursuit of certainty, identity, and control, primarily because

> it was only after Machiavelli that the principle of state sovereignty came to be framed within the context of the Euclidean-Galilean principle of absolute space rather than the complex overlapping jurisdictions of the medieval era. [And] . . . it was only after Machiavelli that it became possible to pretend that the state is a fixed form, a pretence expressed initially in the legal codes of territorial sovereignty, and found more recently in the reifying categories of so much of the socioscientific analysis of "balances of power" and "foreign policy decision making."[17]

This is an important insight in that it returns the discussion squarely to the issue of modernism and the discursive process underlying the framing of International Relations. More precisely, it takes International Relations into a space where its orthodoxy cannot go, that space beyond its disciplinary training rituals and Traditionalist protocols in which alternative ways of thinking and acting are systematically excluded and displaced and a narrow, inadequate grand theory of human society is proclaimed "real" per se. It is in this space that postmodernist scholarship is concerned to open up other closed regions of the discursive empire that is International Relations. The narrow world of diplomacy is one arena that has received attention in this regard, given its significance for Realist theory as practice since Morgenthau's *Politics Among Nations* and given the embedded nature of a (particular) diplomatic culture within the contemporary International Relations community.

Rereading Diplomatic Theory as Practice

James Der Derian has confronted the diplomacy issue in his attempts to reconceptualize the diplomatic process at a time when sensitive and sophisticated global interaction has never been more necessary.[18] Utilizing a (broadly) Nietzschean genealogical approach in *On Diplomacy* (1987) and *Antidiplomacy* (1992), Der Derian's narrative of diplomacy does not add up to the Traditional story of an essential body of statecraft historically unfolding to the present via the rationality inherent in power politics logic. Rather, it adds a provocative dimension to the power politics idiom, which explains diplomatic history and practice in discursive and genealogical terms.

This genealogy of diplomacy explores questions effectively ignored by Realist scholars, including the question of how a (Western) diplomatic culture was constructed and continues to be projected as universally and unproblematically applicable in the last quarter of the twentieth century. In this context, and acknowledging the limitations upon what can be achieved in the short term, the aim is not to provide a new grand theory of diplomacy so superior to the reigning model that it can immediately solve the problems of the day. The task, rather, is to open up theoretical and political space in order that a crucial aspect of global politics be imaginatively and seriously reassessed, critically reflected upon, and empirically evaluated in complex and dangerous times.

The primary foci of critical attention in *On Diplomacy,* consequently, are the "great texts" of diplomatic discourse, written almost exclusively by former diplomats and those captured by the orthodox teleological narrative. To this literature Der Derian brings etymological sensitivity while remaining critically attuned to that which is not said, that which is strategically excluded in the processes of state making, the diplomatic exchange, and the great-man anecdote. In broadening this agenda, the orthodox diplomatic literature is interrogated, via Nietzsche and via the (Hegelian) concept of alienation, which provides a working definition of diplomacy—as a process of mediation between estranged (alienated) individuals and groups.[19]

In this way, the orthodox story of diplomacy is reconceptualized as the attempt to mediate an estranged and alienated international realm. This provides a historical rather than an ahistorical dynamic for the diplomatic process, which sees changes in the theory and practice of mediation (diplomacy) occurring as part of a broader agenda of change associated with changing relations of estrangement. From this perspective, diplomatic reality is not a phenomenon derived from an eternal wisdom integral to diplomatic training manuals or some objectified textual past. It arises, rather, from a particular discursive matrix that designates as legitimate certain practices (e.g., Western, Realist, rational) while rejecting others as threatening to the ordered nature of global interaction.

To understand diplomacy, thus, and to begin to problematize its givens regarding the state system, it is necessary to focus not on the closed, narrow world of the diplomatic elite but on that much broader historicopolitical process by which diplomacy is discursively constructed and its rules and boundaries are legitimated. In this way—in explicitly reconnecting diplomacy with its historical, cultural, political, and linguistic practices—it becomes more possible to question its universalized (power politics) image of reality and open up its practices to those, for example, who suffer by their estrangement from them.

The result, in Der Derian's case, is a genealogy of diplomacy that includes rather than excludes historical themes and ideas that challenge the uniform identity of the Realist narrative. More precisely, he contributes to a rather mundane literature a broad-ranging and incisive historical argument illustrating at least six different ways the contemporary reality of diplomacy can be understood, all of which question the simple story of the "true" Tradition. The first and second themes stress the impact of Judeo-Christian perspectives upon diplomatic discourse and the significance of the struggles of an estranged Christianity both within the Holy Roman Empire and outside it, in its confrontation with its hated Other (Islam). The third and fourth themes emphasize that increasingly complex period associated with the breakdown of Christendom and the emergence of a modern state system. The fifth concentrates on the dramatic impact upon diplomatic culture of both the French and the Russian revolutions. The sixth theme, encompasing the present period, investigates the transformation of Traditional diplomatic practices in the age of "technodiplomacy."[20]

Whatever else this genealogical perspective achieves, it effectively undermines the Traditional proposition that "realistic" diplomatic practice must conform to some essentialized past, some universalized common sense, or simple historical precedent. It confirms, rather, that at every moment of its development, diplomacy is shaped by the matrix of tensions, ideas, and conflicts that gives its dominant discourse its knowledge and power. In the contemporary period, this remains the case. Hence Der Derian's efforts to speak to a contemporary diplomatic community—which in the 1990s faces an interdependent world economy, massive social inequality, unique ecological dangers, and exploding historicocultural tensions, with a diplomatic culture constrained by the illusory certainty of modernist universalism and power politics logic.

In *Antidiplomacy* this theme is more explicitly developed, particularly via a discussion concerning the independence struggles of the Baltic states amid the breakup of the Soviet empire.[21] Here, no easy quick-fix solutions are proffered, but an alternative course of action is proposed that allows for something other than the Traditional diplomatic "art of the possible." Indeed, contrary to traditional diplomatic wisdom but congruent with his suspicions of it, Der Derian suggests that in the quest for self-determination and global justice "one [alternative] historical lesson should have been learned by all Balts: balance of power politics will not do it."[22] This connects a broader postmodernist theme with an immediate issue of political practice, in signifying that once the conflict is *framed* in power politics terms the only recourse for a small power "is to leave the court of international law and human rights behind and enter the international free market of threat exchange."[23] From a postmodern perspective, the "free market of threat exchange" is the contemporary power context in which international diplomacy operates. It is from within these discursive boundaries that it asks its questions of the world and propounds its (predictable) answers about the enduring reality of the interstate anarchical struggle.

The vulnerability of small states, in this situation, is a predominant postmodernist concern. Accordingly, in relation to the Balts, Der Derian stresses the continuing dangers of engagement with dominant diplomatic practices, warning that if the Baltic peoples do not find alternative means of representing their case, any long-term aspirations concerning self-determination are likely to be dashed, as they were in the past (e.g., at Yalta via a secret diplomatic protocol). In this scenario the dominant powers would once again celebrate the repression of culture, language, and life opportunity, in the name of systemic order, stability, and diplomatic rationality.

On the other hand, in the 1990s there are possibilities for marginalized actors outside the narrow boundaries of diplomatic "reality," once its arbitrary nature is recognized and its power is confronted with appropriate strategies of resistance. One possibility associated with the future of the Baltic peoples concerns a process of antidiplomacy, a process of "détente from below."[24] In this alternative détente scenario, connections must be increasingly developed between peoples in the old Soviet empire and independent, nonaligned movements in the West, in order that, in the future, there might be other sources of pressure to apply to ruling elites, in Eastern

Europe in particular, who might again seek to replicate old-world orders in Traditional terms. Acknowledging the current asymmetries of power in this new/old diplomatic conflict, Der Derian points, nevertheless, to the increasing success of groups such as the Britain-based European Nuclear Disarmament movement and the U.S. Campaign for Peace and Democracy, East/West in reformulating some of the traditional realities of global life in recent years, most particularly in "demystify[ing] the demonology of the Cold War and . . . opening a discursive space in which alternative strategies for defence and human rights might freely develop."[25] The concern to help facilitate a politics of resistance among the globally disenfranchised is a theme becoming more explicit in postmodernist scholarship, and it will receive more direct attention shortly. At this point, however, I want to illustrate, from another angle, how postmodernist scholarship has assisted this project, in generally implicit terms, by demystifying the given conceptual framework of International Relations and rendering illegitimate its Traditional knowledge concerning the irreducible reality of global politics. In this case it is the concept of sovereignty that is the issue at hand, a concept absolutely integral to Realism's image of a state-centric, anarchical reality "out there."

Deconstructing Sovereignty: Toward a New Genealogy of International Relations

The concept of sovereignty in International Relations is commonly (Traditionally) perceived as synonymous with that of state power, the legitimate use of state violence, legal/territorial legitimacy, and, in Hobbesian terms, a supreme and necessary authority in a leviathan-less world. For those articulating their Realism in more explicitly systematic terms (e.g., neo-Realism), the sovereign rational actor (the state) engaged in an analogized politics of the market is the primary focus of attention.

Postmodernist concerns on the sovereignty issue, however, are generally focused on the connections *between* these articulations of sovereignty and the taken-for-granted status of the sovereignty theme within Realism, which renders it an effectively ahistorical, universalized component of an "art of the possible" bounded by power politics logic. It is in this sense that the issue of sovereignty represents another point of closure in International Relations in an era in which the need for openness and flexibility of thought and action are vital. In postmodernist literature, accordingly, the issue of the sovereign state is now understood in radically different terms and with a radically different sense of its nature and role in contemporary global life.[26]

To appreciate this difference on the sovereign state issue is to appreciate its relocation as part of that much larger discursive agenda (discussed in

Chapter 2), which saw the emergence of post-Kantian sovereign man, the modern rational figure invested with the capacity and will to emancipate humankind from those objective forces that were traditionally thought to determine reality. This is a historical moment of great significance for modernism. From some liberal perspectives it represents an important moment of political autonomy, marking the rationale for civil society. For Marxists it marks a crucial moment of radical potential in the face of growing ideological and institutional oppression. For the conservative Tradition in International Relations it represents one of the major problems to be solved in a modern world of states—the problem of how to reconcile the principle and practices of individual sovereignty at the state level with peaceful relations at the interstate level. More specifically, it represents the rationale, in Hobbesian terms, for a leviathan in an anarchical world.

For postmodernists, the post-Kantian modernist narrative represents something else again; it represents that moment when logocentrism became systematically embedded in Western modernity, when a privileged, singular, interpretive orientation became dominant within the major philosophical traditions invoking a unified, rational meaning to history, politics, and social reality. At one level, therefore, as conflicts grew among modern liberals, radicals, and conservatives, at another (discursive) level the great ideological debates became increasingly *framed* in similar terms, in terms of a fixed regime of meaning in which the myriad complexities of human experience were reduced to a singular, linear narrative centered on a sovereign figure (e.g., the "individual," the "class," the "Tradition," the "state"). Understood this way, the Kantian moment represents not just Enlightenment progress, potential, and openness but also devastating closure, the closure of critical, historical, and social reflection upon critiques, histories, and societies.

This closure has been particularly (and paradoxically) severe in relation to the central figure of Enlightenment openness—sovereign man—the maker of history, the modern source of real meaning in the world. It is in response to this closure that scholars such as Richard Ashley have reconnected the larger sovereignty theme to its derivative in International Relations.[27] Bringing a Foucauldian reading to the sovereign state issue, Ashley emphasizes the silenced other side of the narrative of modern sovereignty. This concerns a tension within modern man, who after the "death" of God is bequeathed God's omnipotence, along with the knowledge of the limitations upon human objectivity and the powers of transcendence. Consequently, upon exercising his powers of reason, modern sovereign man

> sees plainly that he is enmeshed in language and in history, indeed that he is an object of language and history. [Further,] if man is the transcenden-

> tal condition of the possibility of all knowledge, he also knows himself to be an empirical fact among facts to be examined and conceptualized. If he is a potentially lucid cogito, he knows himself to be surrounded by domains of darkness and ambiguity that resist the penetration of his thought.[28]

This is the dilemma of the modern man/god, the creator of knowledge and its meaning who, knowledgeable of his limitations, must seek to overcome them and fulfill his potential as the maker of history, the shaper and controller of human and material destiny. This, too, is a foundational theme in a Western metanarrative framed in relation to the figure of sovereign man, seeking to deal with the constraints upon his capacity to remake the world in his image. For market-centered liberalism, this framing regime records the efforts of the possessive individual of civil society to break down constraints upon free choice and natural competition (in the general/national interest). For Marxism, it records the struggles of the oppressed classes fighting to overcome the constraints upon their potential as fully conscious human beings. In each case, however, the narrative is framed in terms of a given sovereign subject, privileged, via logocentric reasoning, over a world of objectified limitations and constraints.

But it is with the modern *fusion* of sovereign man and the sovereign state, argues Ashley, that the modern "will to knowledge" and "will to power" are connected, most powerfully, in an institutionalized forum. The (sovereign) state, in this sense, becomes the most potent site of reasoning man's knowledge and power, representing the major resource by which the constraints upon rationality must be controlled, disciplined, and punished. This is a crucial theme in a Foucauldian-based rereading of the sovereign state issue because it prefigures the modern logic of power politics and the state-centric view of an anarchical world of Otherness. It gives identity to the sovereign state, as the site of modern reason, in opposition to a world of anarchy "out there," always threatening to undermine rationality and truth, with its false beliefs and counterpractices. It offers an (alternative) explanation, too, as to why, from a Realist perspective, the fundamental questions of International Relations (war, peace, security, power, hegemony, justice) must remain framed within a dichotomized logic, which opposes a realm of reasoned understanding against a realm of anarchical, threatening Otherness. And it has something quite profound to say about the Realist construction of identity in International Relations, which must retain an anarchical specter "out there" in order to represent the Traditional *self* in privileged terms. As Chapter 6 illustrated, this anarchy theme is indeed of special significance for neo-Realism in the 1990s, and it is not surprising that it has been the focus of critical attention also for postmodernists, such as Ashley in his interrogation of what he calls the anarchy problematique.[29]

The Anarchy Problematique: Framing Identity in International Relations

On this anarchy question, Ashley has reconvened his critical stance toward the poverty of neo-Realism, reexamining it in Foucauldian terms and in terms of the strategy by which the narrative of sovereign man is transformed into the narrative of the sovereign state in an anarchical system. This strategy is apparent enough if one reads Waltz's *Man, the State and War* through a Foucauldian rather than a Realist prism. Read this way, Waltz invokes his three images of Realism in the search for that space in which man's modern quest might be fulfilled, for the essential logic by which the restraining forces of anarchy might be overcome. Morgenthau's crude individualist image is rejected in this context, so too the more general Traditionalist state-centric perspective. Ultimately, Waltz concludes that only his third (structuralist) image is valid because, in its conservative fixity, it understands that the whole Kantian promise is illusory, that modern man *cannot* transcend the objective forces that impose their meaning upon him. In this way, for the "father" of neo-Realism, the focus of all understanding is unequivocally shifted from the sovereignty of reasoning man to the (objectified) sovereignty of the anarchical system..

With *Theory of International Politics* in 1979, it becomes clearer that the anarchical structure is now *the* sovereign voice of International Relations, *it* is now the shaper and maker of history, of political power, of human potential. Anarchy, thus (made by man but beyond his transcendental powers), is now the foundation of real meaning in relations between states, and Realist knowledge is now centered on a pessimistic, fatalistic determinism that, in its (structuralist) certitude, requires no further critical questioning. Instead, the neo-Realist task is to accommodate to the necessities of an anarchical structure while seeking, via scientific knowledge, its systemic intricacies. Unquestioned, of course, in all of this is the hidden figure of modern sovereign man, the philosophical catalyst of Waltz's (ostensibly) antimodernist Realism.

There is no more explicit example of International Relations theory as practice than this anarchy problematique. It was, after all, upon these premises that a Cold War logic was articulated for a generation on both sides of the East/West divide. It was the logic of anarchical struggle that gave coherence to the most costly arms race in human history. It was on the basis of the anarchy "out there" that people's aspirations were brutally repressed in the name of revolutionary socialism, and the same logic, albeit it in reformulated fashion, continues to legitimate the truncheon in the hands of the "world's policeman." In the 1990s, it is via the anarchy problematique that a sovereign presence (the state) is still identified as *the* principle of neo-Realist interpretation, establishing for International Relations a hierarchical distinction between that which is rational and meaningful (i.e., which can be known scientifically and whose behavior can be mediated) and that which is "outside" the realm of rational, meaningful discourse and is a danger to it. Moreover, it is the anarchy problematique that ensures that when neo-Realists ask the central questions of the contemporary agenda (e.g., How can there be governance without an international government? How can there be order without an orderer? How can there be lasting regime cooperation in a situation of endemic anarchy?) the answers are *already given*—at the (hidden, unspoken) core of its logocentric discourse. And it is the anarchy problematique that allows neo-Realist problem solvers to assume as axiomatic the problems of an anarchical world of states they purportedly seek to solve.

The state, in the contemporary equation, is not privileged as it once was, of course. Rather, the state is now projected as one sovereign actor among a multiplicity of sovereign actors (including nonstate actors), and the new reality of neo-Realism is calculated (in Weberian terms) as the sum of the rational decisions made by all (recognized) sovereign actors. However, while the state is no longer explicitly represented in Traditional terms, in the age of interdependence and regime interaction it remains, like all other actors, conceptually imbued with the kind of rational, sovereign identity and utilitarian decisionmaking impulses that characterize the dominant narrative of modern sovereignty. Accordingly, when newly recognized actors (e.g., regimes) are examined, it is on the basis that they are essentially individual, rational-choice-making objects in the world "out there," transparent to the similarly endowed subjects of International Relations. As indicated in earlier chapters, this leaves the dominant approach within the International Relations community effectively mute on a whole range of human activity that does not easily fit the discursive patterns of knowledge associated with sovereign man *become* the sovereign state.

For postmodernists this has implications not just for the immediate post–Cold War struggles of Realism to reinvoke its inadequate images of reality but for modernity in general faced with widespread challenges to the narrative of sovereign rational man. Contemporary challenges to the sovereign state, in this sense, mark a crisis in International Relations to be sure, but more broadly they mark a crisis of modern representationalism starkly evoked. This is why, in recent times, postmodernists have been concerned to critically reevaluate foreign policy theory as practice in these terms, perceived as it is—a major site of the anarchy problematique, the sovereignty narrative, and the politics of representation.

Foreign Policy as the Politics of Representation

These are themes now central to postmodernist works on U.S. foreign policy. Michael Shapiro, for example, has asked questions of the politics of representation in relation to the way that the United States has represented Central America, specifically Guatemala, as part of that threatening realm of Otherness intrinsic to U.S. security discourse.[30] There are at least two themes here that require comment, both of which are important in understanding postmodernism's interpretivist approach and its analytical potency. The first reflects the capacity of intertextualist premises to open some of the closed dimensions of International Relations theory; the second concerns the "practical" implications for a state such as Guatemala of dominant representational practices in International Relations.

The first theme is raised by Shapiro in the context of Todorov's *Conquest of America* (1984), which problematizes the conventional notion of "discovery" and shifts attention to a representational practice of Spanish imperialism.[31] This is regarded as a valuable historical analogy with the way Guatemala is constituted within U.S. foreign policy discourse, on the basis that, like Spain in the sixteenth century, the United States simply treats Otherness with the contempt of the conqueror, reducing a complex social existence to an objectified threat "out there," which must be disciplined and made acquiesent. Disregarded here is any nuance integral to the social and political history of Guatemala (e.g., of colonial and class relations) in an approach that depoliticizes and dehistoricizes the whole practice of state making in Central America by which "Guatemala" was made. On the other hand, this simplistic analytical reductionism allows U.S. foreign policy to locate Guatemala as a knowable part of a power politics agenda of meaning, centered on the anarchy problematique and a world of threat "out there."

This still begs the question of what precise danger a small state like Guatemala could possibly pose to the United States and its way of life. The answer is intrinsic to the modernist constitution of the identity/difference dichotomy. Accordingly, if the self is construed in terms of contemporary security discourse (the anarchy discourse), then *all* other actors in the discursive system will be located somewhere within this threat agenda. Moreover, if, as in the case of the United States, the self is identified in terms of a worldwide security dilemma, then states such as Guatemala are identified as indirect threats whose *potential* for disorder must be disciplined and controlled.[32] And if identity is also imbued with a (Realist) sense of morality and natural hierarchy, then there is an added (Western, ethnocentric) dimension to the reality of this threat scenario, "to the extent that the Other is regarded as something not occupying the same natural/moral space as the self, [thus] conduct towards the Other becomes more exploitative."[33] In discursive terms, therefore, to understand how the Guatemalan Other is represented as a threat in U.S. foreign policy is to understand the representation of the U.S. *self* in International Relations. Or, more precisely, it is to appreciate how the "United States" has come to be represented as a sovereign actor in the Realist security/strategic discourse.

To illustrate how this representational process works textually, Shapiro focused attention on the *The Kissinger Report* (1984), regarded as an exemplary document in the construction of U.S. identity in relation to a world of threatening Others.[34] In this vein it reinvokes the cultural contempt of the conquistadors in their "discovery" of the Indian peoples, insisting, for example, that for Guatemala to become a stable, less threatening factor in the world, it must become like *us,* it must seek to replicate *our* identity. The *we* here are, of course, the champions of foreign private investment, of multinational penetration of another Central American economy. In the mid-1980s, while there was some awareness that *they* might resist *us,* in these ambitions, some other conquistadorian tendencies remained discernible, particularly on the issue of "realistic" responses to any attempted nationalization of U.S. companies by a noncompliant Central American government. In such circumstances, it is asserted, the United States would be forced to defend an irreducible principle of its identity, which insists that, above all, property rights must be protected. Just to make sure the message was clear enough, and in preempting any (idealist) propensity toward accommodation in these matters, the Report warns that "Congress usually exerts pressure to proceed firmly against the small brother who has disregarded his big brother's rights."[35]

Even when a more sensitive tone is evident in the *Report*'s findings, the dominant security discourse remains integral to the U.S. location of Guatemala as a potential threat to order in the post–Monroe Doctrine sphere of influence. This is never more evident than in the *Report*'s attitude to the question of human rights in Central America generally. On this issue there is some acknowledgment of the need for land reform but no acknowledgment at all of the incompatibility between U.S. strategic interests in the region and the possibility of its peoples acquiring such reform. In particular, there is no mention of U.S. involvement in the overthrow of Guatemalans actually engaged in land reform.[36] Instead, the question of human rights is subsumed within the debate on the possibility of U.S. intervention to protect its security interests. Thus, summing up U.S. involvement in Guatemala, and the region in general, the *Report* recognizes that

> on the one hand, we seek to promote justice and find it repugnant to support forces that violate—or tolerate violation of—fundamental U.S. values. On the other hand we are engaged in El Salvador and Central America because we are serving fundamental U.S. interests that transcend any particular government.[37]

From a postmodernist perspective, there are at least two conclusions to be drawn from this interrogation of one of the most sensitive and volatile issues in U.S. foreign policy. The first is that the discourse approach is a valuable critical counterpoint to conventional perspectives when it comes to understanding the process by which the political figures, academics, journalists, and others associated with *The Kissinger Report* framed their "reality" of Guatemala and Central America. The second is that, more explicitly than ever, foreign policy "theory" is better understood *as* power politics "practice." Consequently, in refuting the proposition that the findings of *The Kissinger Report* were based on a reality "discovered" during its inquiries, Shapiro argues that, on the contrary, they were framed in accordance with a discursive representation of Guatemala and Central America that was *already there* in the colonial mentality of European culture and literature and in the unquestioned premises of modernity corresponding to U.S. identity in the world. Consequently, *The Kissinger Report* (and the larger U.S. security discourse that its findings replicated), "failed to understand both its own discursive practice and to attain a grasp of what Central America could be if it were approached in a less-appropriating form of knowledge/practice."[38]

The *Report* illustrates, moreover, that at the core of its thinking on Central America, U.S. foreign policy remains constricted within the static confines of a security discourse bounded by the anarchy problematique and modernist notions of sovereign self and threatening Other. This being the case, there are some frightening implications for the region in the future if U.S. policymakers, failing to reflect upon the way they construct the reality of Central America, continue to "respond" to that reality in Traditional fashion. Indeed, as Shapiro concludes, the representation of Guatemala and Central America in U.S. foreign policy in the late 1980s "provides the general rationale for the already-in-place policy of active economic and civilian/military intervention to help the not-yet-perfected Central American Others."[39]

David Campbell has developed these themes from a different angle in looking at some of the implications of U.S. foreign policy continuing, in the 1990s, to conceptualize the world in terms of modernist sovereignty and the anarchy problematique.[40] Here the focus is on issues introduced in Chapter 1 concerning the demise of the major Cold War Other and the tendency toward triumphalism on the part of the "victors." In Campbell's view, any self-congratulation is entirely misplaced, and even to speak of "victory" in proclaiming a new (democratic) world order not only trivializes the great dangers following the breakdown of the Soviet empire but ignores the plight of the majority of the world's peoples facing a future as bleak and undemocratic as ever.[41]

These concerns aside, a more immediate danger is the primary focus of Campbell's critical attention—the danger of continued U.S. incarceration within a Cold War discursive identity centered on notions of modernist sovereignty and the anarchy problematique. His critical project, accordingly, is to illustrate that U.S. foreign policy is constituted by dimensions other than "external" necessity and to reconceptualize U.S. foreign policy in discursive terms, as a derivative of the anarchy problematique, which limits conventional foreign policy discourse to a narrow analytical agenda and Traditional geopolitical practices.

Of particular concern in this regard is the continuing propensity to conceive of security in terms of (sovereign) territorial integrity, while ignoring or treating as epiphenomenal issues of culture, ideology, representation, and interpretive ambiguity at the core of the sovereign state. As this book has emphasized from its beginning, these are themes that must be explored if we are to begin to confront the policy paralysis of the present and enhance the possibilities for sensitive and more appropriate foreign policy options in the future.[42] Hence the value of Campbell's contributions to the debate that locates U.S. foreign policy not just in terms of the danger *between* states, in orthodox terms, but as part of a much larger regime of framing concerned with the disciplining of dangers *within* the state. The proposition here is that a logocentric framing regime that opposes, for example, inside/outside, self/other, identity/difference, is intrinsic to the process by which the United States has been constructed in International Relations. In this sense,

> the practices of [U.S.] foreign policy serve to enframe, limit, and domesticate a *particular meaning of humanity* . . . it incorporates the form of domestic order, the social relations of production, and the varying subjectivities to which they give rise.[43]

The "particular meaning of humanity" privileged in the United States is that centered on political pluralism, capitalist economics, and the modern sovereign individual, (ostensibly) "free to choose." These have been the identifying characteristics by which the United States has framed its identity in global life and designated its enemies. However, when this narrative of self-identity is questioned, reread, rehistoricized, and politicized, it becomes clear that a number of other narratives have been excluded in order that a *particular kind* of self is here represented as the "United States." Necessarily excluded, for example, are the narratives of genocide, expansionism, dispossession, extraordinary state surveillance, and the struggles of gender, sexuality, difference, contingency, ambiguity, and domestic anarchy, which are also part of the United States.

The point, of course, is that if one includes these (generally) silenced readings, as Campbell and other postmodernists do, and if one *then* ponders the orthodox representation of the United States in International Relations, another "reality" is discernible concerning the circumstances in which the Western superpower has confronted the forces of anarchy in the national and International interest. It is that "the boundaries of the state [system have] . . . long been the result of domesticating the self through the transfer of differences *within* society to the inscription of differences *between* societies" (emphasis added).[44] Reconceptualized in this manner, the Cold War, for example, can be understood not as the only "realistic" response to anarchical necessity but as another site at which the anarchy problematique has been invoked to provide a sovereign, foundational presence, from which the threat of anarchy and Otherness *within* states could be rendered unified and controllable. Western analysts have been willing to ascribe such a scenario to the Soviet empire over the years, but as Vaclav Havel has noted, and postmodernists have insisted, it is very relevant also to the "democratic" side in the modernist regime of knowledge and power.[45] In the U.S. context it has been a strategy articulated simply, "through the invocation of anarchy and disorder as problems that threaten the United States and via a concern with the 'individual' as a defining moment of being 'American.'"[46]

This is not to suggest some simple cause-and-effect scenario, nor any conventional class/elite-based design at the core of U.S. theory as practice. But what Campbell's contribution suggests, as did Shapiro's, is that questions of representation, systematically excluded from foreign policy discourse, must be included if the United States, and the International Relations discipline centered therein, is to be more capable in the future of understanding itself and the world in which it lives. What it suggests, more generally in relation to the present discussion, is that modernist "theory" is intrinsic to the "practice" of International Relations and that postmodernist critical perspectives have something important to contribute to the opening of that theory *as* practice, in the post–Cold War era. This is particularly so in relation to the discourse of strategy and security. Accordingly, I want to turn briefly to some postmodern scholarship that seeks to reconceptualize the dominant security/strategic discourse in the era that has seen the demise of its Cold War raison d'être.

Reconceptualizing Strategy and Security in the Post–Cold War Era

The discussion on strategy and security in Chapter 6 illustrated that while there were always reflective and sophisticated tendencies within this field, it was (and remains) an exemplary arena of positivist Realism, technical rationality, and modernist discursive practices in general.[47] This being so, postmodernists have sought to reconceptualize the strategic/security discourse by opening it to questions that its Traditional agenda continues to ignore or marginalize. Attention, for example, has been focused on the growing sense of *insecurity* concerning state involvement in military-industrial affairs and the perilous state of the global ecology. Questioned, too, has been the fate of those around the world rendered insecure by lives lived at the margins of existence yet unaccounted for in the statistics on military spending and strategic calculation. And, for those concerned to open a closed intellectual/policy realm to greater democratic participation, a critical target has been the (technical-rational) language of exclusion integral to a strategy/security discourse to the extent that complex questions of politics, ethics, and social life have been reduced to the illusory certainties of rational-actor models, game-theory, and systems analysis.

It is in this context that postmodernists have insisted that the dominant (Realist) notions of strategy and security be reconceptualized to include debates on a discursive process that has privileged the major powers in their manipulation of violence and threat as legitimate instruments of policy. The point of critique, in this regard, is to divest power politics "practice" of its legitimacy by undermining its "theoretical" foundations. More succinctly, in Bradley Klein's terms, its aim is "to give power no [theoretical] place to hide."[48] This, it is acknowledged, is no easy task given the embeddedness of a discourse that, since the Cold War, has successfully projected a Traditional (modernist) narrative as synonymous with Western strategic interest.

Nevertheless, when strategy and security issues are read in representational terms and located in their discursive context, the detached, technorationalist naturalness of orthodox analysis largely dissolves into a modernist framework of pseudoscientific privileging. It is this narrow representation of global life that is now under challenge in a postmodernist scholarship intent on relocating the discourse of strategy/security as part of a larger process of identity construction, which continues to represent a particular "meaning of humanity" *as* International Relations in the post–Cold War era. Scholars such as Bradley Klein and Michael Dillon have located the crisis of identity in NATO as both a microcosm of this contemporary problem and a potential space for change.[49] At one level, NATO has become the victim of its own success in this regard. This success was not so much in deterring the Soviet Union but in having constructed a Cold War identity for itself and its allies that was worth dying for. At another level, the demise of the Soviet Union has significantly undermined NATO's success by undermining the primary reason for its existence and by opening up some space for critical reflection, effectively closed down during the Cold War.

The most obvious implications of this opened space are already to be seen and heard on the streets of those states once unified by the threat narrative of the Warsaw Pact security discourse. But it is in the West that the implications of the challenge to NATO's identity are perhaps even more profound, given that organization's connection with, and articulation of, modernist representational practice. In this context the crisis of strategic identity exposes Cold War knowledge and power to a different logic, one that repudiates any (positivist) sense of detachment integral to the success of the International Relations orthodoxy, and stresses instead that

> knowledge in doubt radically problematises the exercise of power, because the one is the principal medium of the other [and] Power prob-

> lematised, of course, threatens the character and constitution of political order, for without the inscriptions of power there is no order, because all order is an effect of power.[50]

What is at stake here, then, is not just the future of NATO as the strategic mainspring of Western power politics for almost half a century but the very framework of knowledge that has defined reality in International Relations in that period. This, of course, is why the issue is exciting so much attention among postmodernists, because the space opened now is that which leaves exposed and vulnerable the discursive process that for so long has represented a particular "meaning of humanity" as reality in International Relations, the unifying, sovereign presence that *we* must defend, to the point of genocide if necessary, against *them.*

For postmodernists such as Dillon, Klein, Walker, Ashley, Campbell, Shapiro, and Der Derian (and for a critical theorist such as Cox), none of this evokes concern over hegemonic decline and the restoration of Traditional order. On the contrary, it stimulates a sense of long-overdue "thinking space" and invocations of alternative political formations, of more tolerant, more inclusive forms of human society. This perspective suggests that while the sudden devaluation of the dominant discourse has obvious dangers, it provides us with a unique opportunity to comprehend the process by which we ask our questions about strategy and security and begin to go beyond that process. This, it must be stressed, is no paradoxical invocation of Traditional progressivism in postmodernist literature. The intellectual legacy of Nietzsche and Foucault eschews such a position. What it represents, rather, is the acknowledgment of the space for resistance to power politics and imposed subjectivity in Europe in particular, which is now engaging every day in the actual process of remaking its "real" meaning. It is a celebration, in this regard, of the enhanced potential for creative reformulation as a generation-long regime of strategic unity and reality dissolves into a site of unique reconstitution (e.g., in Germany) and the reconceptualization of self and others.[51]

All this, of course, needs to be kept very much in perspective. The war in the Persian Gulf (1990–1991) is evidence enough of the continuing capacity of the erstwhile Cold War superpower to invoke the Traditional meaning of the strategy/security discourse for its own interests. Nevertheless, emerging tendencies within (often) marginalized communities around the world to question the meanings and boundaries of their lives are of obvious significance for postmodernism. To conclude this discussion, therefore, I want to address this issue in relation to R. B. J. Walker's *One World, Many Worlds,* a work that explores many of the major themes of the postmodernist genre—sovereignty, textuality, representationalism, the anarchy problematique, and the limitations of strategic/security discourse—from the vantage point of the marginalized, the silenced, the omitted, those whose lives, cultures, and histories have for so long been read out of the power politics narrative.[52]

One World, Many Worlds: *Toward a Postmodernist Politics of Resistance?*

The immediate loci of Walker's attention are those critical social movements around the world working to more fully understand, resist, and change oppressive power structures in their specific sites and under a diversity of cultural circumstances. Movements of this kind range from the more conventional social movements in Western industrialized societies organizing to resist nuclear weapons, militarism, environmental degradation, and gendered politics, to the movements in Eastern Europe and throughout the Third World engaged in similar struggles, those over specific issues of ecology (e.g., pollution, deforestation), and broader struggles for a more secure, peaceful, and dignified life. The significance of these movements is that while they are inevitably part of a global struggle in one (interdependent) world, they represent also a politics of difference, the articulation of the many worlds of people's experiences and aspirations, which cannot and should not be constrained by the dictates of a particular "meaning of humanity" as projected in the Traditional discourse of International Relations.

Their significance is enhanced, in this latter regard, by many of their practices, which defy traditional grand-theorized strategies of revolutionary thought and behavior in favor of creative, innovative resistance, established and carried out in specific sites of struggle. They are, in this sense, activating in their everyday lives and struggles the concerns of critical social theorists seeking to challenge dominant discourses of closure and intolerence in the academy. In their different locations and circumstances, thus, the struggles of critical social movements represent an important critical dimension for postmodernists, suspicious of all Traditional claims for emancipation, on behalf of *the* people, *the* class, *the* common interest and skeptical of all singular, homogenized images of "reality," "liberty," "freedom," and all "isms" proclaiming post-Enlightenment visions of *the* good life.

This is not a perspective that denies the desirability of traditional struggle for a more meaningful democracy and security. Rather, it is a perspective that cares enough about the possibility of such conditions not to endanger them by abrogating responsibility for them *again* to another vanguard, another Realism, another Tradition, another religion, another Philosophy, another rational-scientific panacea for a self-satisfied, disempowering, bourgeois ideology. Accordingly, while there is no reification or idealization of critical social movements, their struggles and aspirations are perceived as indications of what a postmodern politics might look like, as a counter to the Traditional theory as practice of International Relations.

It is acknowledged, consequently, that critical social movements will, and must, continue to struggle against the most obvious and reprehensible injustices and dangers in the one world (e.g., against nuclear arms, apartheid, and brutal military repression in Africa and Central and South America). But these struggles, while connected to a broader sense of radicalism, will be energized, directed, and articulated by a process of understanding derived not from some sovereign center, some privileged omnipotent presence, but from the creativity and critical capacities of people learning about their world in their own ways and through their own struggles. In this way, a broader, more profound potential for "meaning" and "knowing" might be realized, in which

> people learn to recognize not only the authoritarian state "out there"—the identifiable events of armoured vehicles and dawn awakenings, of censorship and beatings, of propagandistic images and inaccessible decisions—but also the authoritarian state "in here"—the routines taken for granted, the conveniences of forgetting, the capitulation of apathy.[53]

It is in this regard that the diversity of challenges to International Relations is indicative of a broader reconceptualization of contemporary life beginning to emerge at all levels of society as the other side of the modernist agenda is increasingly exposed. The appreciation, for example, that issues of war, peace, and security cannot any longer be reduced to rational-scientific certitude is regarded as part of a more general appeal for a non-Traditional agenda, including newly formulated developmental, ecological, gender, and cultural themes and new levels of democratic participation in decisionmaking processes.

The experiences of a range of critical social movements have, for example, illustrated the dangers of the Traditional insistence on secrecy and exclusivity concerning security/strategy issues and invocations of the "national interest." In Central America, for example (as Shapiro has indicated), the connections between "national interest" and "security" are at best highly problematic for the great mass of people struggling to survive under military regimes and the influences of U.S. foreign policy. Consequently, as many indigenous movements have insisted, any meaningful notion of security must be reconnected to an open social agenda and participatory politics. In the West, too, the space opened by antinuclear movements, for example, has resulted in challenges to the antidemocratic nature of strategic/security thinking and policymaking in International Relations generally. This is a positive and necessary incursion into closed space because it challenges the habit of abandoning responsibility for thinking on security issues in particular to a Traditional elite (the diplomat, the strategist, etc.) and a closed Traditional discourse.

The question begged here—about what a more democratic process might entail—is, of course, of major significance for postmodernists concerned with the ways powerful emancipatory themes can impose themselves as oppressive practices. It is acknowledged, for example, that formal political democracy is often connected to life experiences dominated by bureaucratic stultification, authoritarian state rule, elite-sponsored apathy and cynicism, and conditions in which most people are still excluded from decisionmaking processes. Thus, in confronting the question of democracy in contemporary times, critical social movements, like critical social theorists, have become engaged in a broader agenda involving the reconceptualization and rearticulation of emancipatory concepts and practices, such as democracy and progress.

This tendency is particularly evident when Traditional issues of strategy and security are connected to questions of economic development. Here, there is an increasing acknowledgment that, in the age of monopoly capitalism and a worldwide transformation in productive processes (as described by Cox, for example), the rhetorical power of Traditional theory is shown to be increasingly incoherent in practice. Under challenge, in this regard, is the Modernization discourse, still dominant at the core of the Realist image of a world of sovereign states hierarchically located in power politics terms. In countering this with alternative developmental strategies constructed at the level of specific communities, critical social movements have simultaneously challenged the modernist historical narrative and its associated philosophical wisdom. Consequently for many in the 1990s, there is a renewed respect for much dismissed as (prescientific) and "traditional" in the rapid ascent of Western progressivism, and it is in this expanded context that reconceptualized development strategies become part of an inherently democratic process "in which people participate in the making of their own communities, one in which economic life is intrinsically connected to the social, environmental, and cultural processes that are essential to a sustained and meaningful way of life."[54]

More explicitly than anything else in the postmodernist contribution to International Relations, Walker's *One World, Many Worlds* articulates this challenge to modernism and Realism as part of an emerging politics of postmodern resistance. It is *post*modern resistance in the sense that while it is always directly (and sometimes violently) engaged with modernity, it seeks to go beyond the repressive, closed aspects of modernist global existence. It is, therefore, not a resistance of traditional grand-scale emancipation or conventional radicalism imbued with the authority of one or another sovereign presence. Rather, in opposing the large-scale brutality and inequity in human society, it is a resistance active also at the everyday, community, neighborhood, and interpersonal levels, where it confronts those processes that systematically exclude people from making decisions about who they are and what they can be. In this regard it resists "any autocratic presumption of the right to rule, whether this presumption is defended with crude force or by appeal to some natural superiority given by gender, race, class or expertise."[55]

It is often at this level that power politics operates most insidiously and potently. Yet, as peoples around the planet have illustrated in recent times, given the opportunities to understand the processes by which they are *constituted* (as, for example, subjects in an objective world of anarchical power politics), it is possible to change power relations and overturn irreducible "realities." In these circumstances it becomes possible also to say *no,* to ask *why,* to understand *how.* A range of resistances can flow from this. People can, for example, resist the dangers of extreme nationalism, the illusory certainty of nuclear deterrence theory, the transformation of global life into the construction of Otherness; they can help prevent their social and environmental structures being destroyed in the name of, for example, economic rationalism; they can oppose racism and sexism and the exploitation of the marginalized and "different"; and they can insist on participating in decisions that define and determine their life opportunities and the fate of those most brutalized by dominant regimes of stability and order "out there" in the real world. In this way, a politics of resistance is possible that "extend[s] processes of democratization into realms where it has never been tried: into the home, into the workplace, into processes of cultural production."[56]

Throughout *One World, Many Worlds,* Walker rightly stresses that neither critical social movements nor postmodernist perspectives on them have any monopoly of wisdom when it comes to understanding and responding to the complex issues of global life. Critical social movements are nevertheless of particular importance because their practices deal with the world not as "a future abstraction but as a process in which to engage wherever one is."[57] This, it seems to me, is a principle integral to any sense of what a postmodernist politics of resistance might be because, be it articulated at the dissenting margins of academic life or as part of a more direct social movement of change, it must be engaged with the language, logic, and power relations of modernity, not (somehow) detached from the modern world, part of the philosophy of the avant-garde.[58]

It is this engagement that makes Walker's contribution an important and incisive one, and it is this engagement, more generally, that characterizes the postmodernist contribution to a proliferating critical social theory challenge to the Tradition and discipline of International Relations in the 1990s. It is via this engagement with neo-Realism in particular that, to a greater extent than other critical social theory approaches, postmodernism has exposed International Relations for what it is: a textual Tradition *become* "reality"; a particular reading of (Western) philosophy and history *become* transhistorical/transcultural "fact"; a way of framing "meaning" and "knowing" shaped by Newtonian physics and Cartesian rationalism *become* meaning and knowing in the world of nuclear weapons, AIDS, and ozone depletion. What postmodernism has exposed, more directly, is International Relations as a discursive process, a process by which identities are formed, meaning is given, and status and privilege are accorded—a process of knowledge *as* power.

This is what is at stake in the postmodernist challenge to the Tradition and discipline of International Relations. This is what is at stake when those whose identities (literally and figuratively) are dependent upon the Traditional knowledge *as* power seek to exclude postmodernism from serious analysis, marginalize the significance of its arguments, and ridicule its attempts to go beyond the boundaries of Traditional concepts and language. In short, at stake in the postmodernist politics of resistance in International Relations is that "something" that is happening in the modern world that Jane Flax pointed to in *Thinking Fragments.* It is the acknowledgment—positively endorsed by some, lamented and resisted by others—that "a shape of life is dying," that a profound shift is taking place in contemporary social life as a generation understands that the Enlightenment dream (and the unquestioned hegemony of its modernist discourse) is over.[59] At a more prosaic level, it is the acknowledgment, in Kal Holsti's terms, that a "three centuries long intellectual consensus" has broken down in International Relations, leaving exposed the narrow assumptions and inadequate premises upon which a Tradition, a discipline, and a "reality" were constructed.[60]

This final chapter has sought to illustrate how postmodernist scholarship has responded to this crisis in International Relations and to the broader "something" that is happening in the contemporary world. It has done so in terms consistent with my view that, in the exciting and dangerous spaces now opening up, postmodernism is the most exciting and least dangerous way of understanding and participating in a changing world.

Notes

1. See Der Derian and Shapiro, eds., *International/Intertextual Relations.*

2. Derrida, for example, sought to do this by illustrating how the logocentric process of construction in modernist philosophy is intrinsic to the way that contemporary social reality is constructed in terms of a hierarchy of sociopolitical meaning, centered on a sovereign voice (e.g., of reason, reality, systemic interest) and a marginalized, excluded regime of otherness. Foucault sought to further historicize these dualized processes by illustrating how, via dominant discursive practices, we have come to know ourselves as modern peoples and how, in this discursive context, we give (subjective) meaning to the (objectified) world. See, for example, Derrida, *Of Grammatology,* and Foucault, *The Archeology of Knowledge.*

3. Postmodern scholars have been extraordinarily prolific in recent years. This, added to the complexity of their arguments, means that I can't claim the fol-

lowing discussion to be comprehensive as such. My aim, rather, is to select what I consider to be some of the major contributions of recent times, works that establish some of the larger philosophical principles of postmodern scholarship in dealing with quite precise topics and issues. My aim on the complexity issue is the same as that throughout the work: to do justice to sophisticated themes while representing them in the most accessible and concise way I can.

4. Kenneth Waltz, for example, has maintained that *The Peloponnesian War* represents a fundamental account of the "anarchic character of international politics." As an early Realist, claimed Waltz, Thucydides understood the timeless axioms of international life and consequently remained a thinker relevant to the contemporary age of nuclear arms with his insights into the "striking sameness of the quality of international life through the millennia"; see *Theory of International Politics,* p. 66. Robert Keohane, meanwhile, in discussing the latest (structuralist) reformulation of Realist thought, acknowledges a linear connection between Thucydides, Morgenthau, and Waltz. Indeed, he suggests, in Thucydides there is to be found the three fundamental assumptions of Realism that in *Politics Among Nations* formed the basis of Morgenthau's contribution to the theory and practice of U.S. foreign policy in the Cold War years and in *Theory of International Politics* underpinned the structuralism or neo-Realism that is "at the center of contemporary international relations theory in the United States" in the 1980s and 1990s. See "Realism, Neorealism and the Study of World Politics," pp. 2–11.

5. Doyle, "Thucydidean Realism," p. 235.

6. Garst, "Thucydides and Neorealism," pp. 3–27.

7. Ibid., p. 6.

8. Ibid., p. 25.

9. Alker, "The Dialectical Logic of Thucydides' Melian Dialogue."

10. In *Truth and Method.* An explanation of this *phronesis* perspective is in Chapter 6.

11. Alker, "The Dialectical Logic of Thucydides' Melian Dialogue," p. 817.

12. In "Realism, Neorealism and the Study of World Politics."

13. Gilpin, "The Richness of the Tradition of Political Realism," p. 308.

14. Walker, "*The Prince* and 'The Pauper'."

15. Ibid., pp. 30–40.

16. Walker, "*The Prince* and 'The Pauper'," p. 40.

17. Ibid., p. 42.

18. For example, see Der Derian, *On Diplomacy* and *Antidiplomacy,* in which the influences of Virilio are increasingly evident. See also "Spy Versus Spy" in *International/Intertextual Relations* and "The (S)pace of International Relations."

19. See ibid., p. 6. The discussion of alienation in *On Diplomacy* goes far beyond its common articulation in Hegelian-Marxian terms. But it does deal with a modernist concept in a sensitive and interesting way, one that does not see central modernist concepts as entirely incongruous in a postmodernist idiom. The relationship between Hegel and Nietzsche is a connection that requires more serious study than it has, as yet, received in postmodernist circles—so, too, the larger issue of nonteleological dialectics, which I associate with a scholar like R. N. Berki and, more broadly, with Heraclites.

20. Ibid., p. 203.

21. *Antidiplomacy,* chap. 7.

22. Ibid., p. 155.

23. Ibid.

24. Ibid., pp. 153-154

25. Ibid., p. 155.

26. See Ashley, "Living on Border Lines" and "Untying the Sovereign State." For another interesting perspective on this issue, from a different angle, see the discussion of Anthony Gidden's views in Rosenberg, "A Non-Realist Theory of Sovereignty?"

27. Ashley, "Living on Border Lines."

28. Ibid., p. 265.

29. Ashley, "Untying the Sovereign State."

30. Shapiro, "The Constitution of the Central American Other." See also Weber, "Writing Sovereign Identities"; Escobar, "Discourse and Power in Development"; and Dubois, "The Governance of the Third World."

31. Todorov, *The Conquest of America.* The genre, if not the specifics, is that of Edward Said's *Orientalism.* The term *discovery* here refers to the notion of finding something that was not previously there, either via isolated scientific experiment or in anthropological terms, as in this case. The postmodern counter, of course, is bound up with Barthes's intertextualist notion and the general argument concerning representation as opposed to "experience." For a discussion of the difference between experience and representation in this context see Shapiro, "The Politics of Fear" and Connolly, "Identity and Difference in Global Politics."

32. Ibid., p. 102.

33. Ibid.

34. More formally, *The Report of the President's Bipartisan Commission on Central America.*

35. Ibid.

36. For example, in the intervention of 1954, which overthrew the Arbenz government.

37. Cited in *The Report,* p. 120.

38. Ibid., p. 122.

39. Ibid.

40. Campbell, *Writing Security* and "Global Inscription."

41. Ibid., p. 263.

42. On the paralysis issue, see Chapter 1.

43. Ibid., p. 272.

44. Ibid., p. 273.

45. See Havel's insights in Chapter 1.

46. Campbell, *Writing Security,* p. 278.

47. Even in the most thoughtful contemporary outposts of the genre, in, for example, the work of Barry Buzan, the focus of analytical attention remains firmly focused on the Traditional geopolitical framework of reference and a privileged state, the sovereign voice of national security, albeit now as part of an updated levels-of-analysis approach. This is not to trivialize Buzan's contribution. There is much to applaud in his thoughtful approach, but it remains an example of "repressed" modernist critique. See Buzan, *Peoples, States and Fear,* and more recently, "The Case for a Comprehensive Definition of Security." In these works his level-of-analysis approach is indicative also of the legacy of Traditional thinking. Thus, while acknowledging the importance of other actors and levels than the state, the argument on national security remains rooted in the notion of a distinction between the state and civil society on the one hand and between individual states and the state system on the other. The point is that such a position tends to reify the liberal notion of a special relationship between individuals and civil society in the "domestic" realm while understanding as fundamentally different those relations outside this realm. As the discussions above have sought to show, this stance, however sensitively presented, excludes from serious critical questioning relations integral to both "inside" and "outside."

48. Klein, *Strategic Discourse and Its Alternatives,* p. 5.

49. See Klein, "How the West Was One"; and Dillon, "The Alliance of Security and Subjectivity" and "Modernity, Discourse and Deterrence."

50. Dillon, "The Alliance of Security and Subjectivity," p. 117.

51. In this vein, also see Joenniemi, "The Social Constitution of Gorbachev" and "The Post Cold War Warsaw Treaty Organization"; and Dalby, "Dealignment Discourse" and *Creating the Second Cold War.*

52. Walker, *One World, Many Worlds;* see also Walker, *Inside/Outside.* A range of interesting works of this genre are also appearing now. See, for example, Chaloupka, *Knowing Nukes,* especially chap. 5; Walker and Mendlovitz, eds., *Contending Sovereignties;* Manzo, *Domination, Resistance and Social Change in South Africa;* and the diverse contributions to Sylvester, ed., "Feminists Write International Relations."

53. Walker, *One World, Many Worlds,* p. 154.

54. Ibid., p. 131.

55. Ibid., p. 159.

56. Ibid., p. 160.

57. Ibid., p. 157.

58. Dews, *The Logic of Disintegration.*

59. Flax, *Thinking Fragments,* p. 7.

60. Holsti, *The Dividing Discipline,* p. 1.

9
Conclusion

This book began with a discussion outlining my concerns about the contemporary state of global politics, with particular attention paid to the conflicts in the Gulf War of 1990–1991, the tragedy that is Bosnia, and the more generalized anxieties associated with the breakup of the Soviet empire. It ends in the same vein, with the United States, in mid-1993, again firing cruise missiles into the suburbs of Baghdad to deter Saddam Hussein from acting in the manner it once encouraged in the name of balance diplomacy, and with the UN, in Somalia, engaged in another vicious, confusing, and bloody conflict with a people it initially sought to save from the ravages of starvation. As I explained at the outset, there are no easy, ready-made solutions for situations like these, nor do such situations easily fit the patterns of understanding and explanation by which we have traditionally confronted the vicissitudes of global existence.

Rather, as this work has sought to illustrate in a number of ways, events such as these, occurring in that space beyond the Cold War, expose ever more starkly the inadequacies and dangers of Traditional thinking and behavior within the International Relations community, particularly among the "victors" of the Cold War. More precisely, the theory as practice of violence, dichotomy, and global containment that defined the post–World War II world and gave coherence, meaning, and identity to a generation in the West, is now exposed as a serious impediment to dealing with a complex, changing, global environment in the 1990s. The point, simply put, is that the deep, multifaceted problems of the Middle East region, of warlordism and famine in the Horn of Africa, of exploding ethnic hatreds in the Balkans, of culture, gender, transmigration, and global economic crisis, cannot be "solved" by recourse to crude power politics dogma, nor even the most fear-inspiring display of contemporary technorationalist savagery, for all its laser-directed fascination for some sectors of the community.

The challenges of the post–Cold War era defy the simplistic reductionism, universalism, and essentialism that has provided illusory certitude for so long and which, sadly, continues to characterize orthodox approaches to International Relations to the present. Hence this critical (re)introduction to International Relations, which sought to explore the crisis of theory and practice of the current age in a manner that, in acknowledging its dangers and tribulations, acknowledged also its opportunities and potentials. In this latter context, this book brought a positive and wide-ranging critical social theory dimension to the International Relations debates of the 1990s. It emphasized the need for a serious and sustained reassessment of the way we think and act in relation to global politics, not just in its more immediate (Cold War/Anglo-American political science) context but in terms of a broader and more profound discursive commitment, which has seen a particular "meaning of humanity" become International Relations per se. More specifically, it emphasized the need to critically reassess the social and intellectual processes by which (modern) images of a singular, irreducible reality, privileging a particular knowledge form, cultural experience, and mode of life, has framed our understanding of the world "out there" and determined our analytical and politicostrategic responses to it. In this way, and in recognizing the intrinsic connections between theory and practice, interpretation and action, and knowledge and power, we might begin to address the problems and potentials of the present in something other than the narrow, intolerant, and caricatured terms of a Realist-dominated International Relations Tradition and discipline.

This book, consequently, (re)introduced International Relations by relocating its dominant ways of understanding, its analytical protocols, and its normative-political commitments in terms of a more inclusive historical and philosophical agenda, in order that its major silences be spoken, its closures be exposed and opened for questioning, and space be facilitated for thinking and acting beyond its boundaries of "possibility" and "meaningfulness." The primary suggestion, in this regard, was that to begin to understand the silences and dangers of International Relations, we need to understand it in discursive terms, as a way of framing the basic categories and experiences of modern social life in a manner that represents a particular knowledge/power matrix as universally and irreducibly "real." Here, emphasis was placed upon the discursive connection between the dominant Anglo-American social theory perspective—positivism—and the dominant Tradition of International Relations—Realism/neo-Realism. This connection represents the most powerful contemporary articulation of a much larger philosophical theme, which (discursively) binds together orthodox readings of the modernist historical narrative and the disciplinary rituals of contemporary International Relations scholarship.

This theme, integral to the attempts of the Greeks to (rationally) distance themselves from the traditional objects (Gods, static social formations) of their world, was articulated, more explicitly, in the wake of the "death" of God, as Cartesian rationalism accelerated the modern search for a secular foundation for certainty in an increasingly uncertain world. In the European Enlightenment it became more intrinsically associated with the pursuit of an indubitable social reality, independent of the distortions of specific time and place but imbued with laws of thought and behavior analogous to the axioms of natural science. From the nineteenth century on, it has energized the more precise quest for a social theory purged of (traditional) metaphysics, from which analytical protocols might be gleaned and scientific, lawlike statements invoked about modern human life. This theme—the projection of reality in terms of a (rational) separation between that which is foundational, irreducible, and eternal and that which is prejudiced by history, culture, and language—remains at the ontological heart of modernist social theory and the dominant (Realist) Tradition and discipline of International Relations.

In its various positivist-Realist guises (e.g., as Traditionalism, behavioralism, or neo-Realism), this theme has had some crucial implications for the way International Relations scholars and practitioners have framed their questions of global life and applied their answers to its complex problems. This, in general, has been a site of discursive primitivism, which has seen knowledge of global humanity reduced to a singular, self-affirming narrative of Western (primarily Western European) eternal wisdom, derived (crudely) from the scattered textual utterings of the Greeks, Christian theology, and post-Renaissance Europe. Articulated in logocentric terms, this narrative remains, in the 1990s, rigidly state-centric and centered on the opposition between a realm of (domestic) sovereign identity, rationality, and social coherence and a realm of (international) anarchy, fragmentation, and threat "out there," which must be disciplined, ordered, and controlled for the common, systemic good. Under this discursive regime an "us" is easily identified and opposed to a "them"; a homogeneous "self" confronts a threatening Other; a free, open, pluralistic social system can be distinguished from its closed, totalitarian counterparts; and a particular (Western, rational-scientific) way of knowing the world can be intellectually and institutionally legitimated in its struggle against the forces of ideology, irrationality, distortion, and untruth. The point, more precisely, is that this particular discursive representation of human life at the global level has *become* International Relations, the positivist-Realist image of the world "out there" has *become* reality, and the foundationalist approach to knowledge has become the *only* legitimate way of understanding global human society.

Accordingly, in (re)introducing International Relations as discourse, this book sought not only to speak of it as it has never spoken of itself but to illustrate some of its limitations and dangers and indicate how they might be resisted. It did so in confronting a range of "concrete" events and issues, not only in their own terms but in terms of the silenced discursive agenda that has produced their real meaning for International Relations down the years. In relation, for example, to the definitive event of recent history, the Cold War between the two superpowers and their alliance blocs, it indicated how crucial analytical and policy options were irrevocably and systematically closed off within an International Relations community constrained by the discursive practices it left unquestioned. Unable to think and speak outside a primitive logic of (objectified, externalized) reality, it could not question the discursive process that saw a range of alternative perspectives—all articulating empirical facts about Soviet capacity and intent—reduced to an unambiguous, singular narrative of "fact," which gave unity and identity to Western scholars and policy practitioners and a simple self-affirming meaning to the Cold War.

The inability of mainstream analysis to predict the demise of the Soviet superpower is intrinsically connected to the interpretive silences and inadequacies at the core of the Realist discourse of International Relations in the 1950s. The point is that, for all their professed knowledge of Soviet thought and behavior, Realists actually knew very little about the primary Cold War Other beyond the restricted boundaries of their discourse of Otherness. From this (objectified/demonized) perspective, there was indeed no strategic or humanitarian value in seeking a more sensitive dialogue with the Soviet enemy, nor was there any other rational choice for Western policy planners than arms racing, proxy war fighting, deterrence strategy, support for neofascist thuggery, and Vietnam. And from this perspective, an internally generated, largely voluntary process of self-destruction by the Soviet people was never part of the predictive agenda. Consequently, that doctrine which for nearly half a century represented its god's-eye view of the world in the most authoritative of (positivist-Realist) terms is now increasingly exposed for what it always was—a discursive emperor at best, only scantily clad.

It is troubling, therefore, though hardly surprising, that commentators across the political spectrum in the post–Cold War period are expressing their concern at the lack of understanding, sensitivity, and incisive behavior within elite sectors of the International Relations community. This, after all, is the scholarly/policy elite that, via its ethnocentric arrogance, the (illusory) certainties of its technorationalism, and its crude ideological bias, sought to impose its developmental Realism (i.e., as Modernization Theory) upon an objectified Third World in the 1960s. It was, moreover, from within this sector that, in the "golden age" of positivist-Realist strategic thinking, questions of human security were reduced to simplistic and inadequate modeling techniques and pseudoscientific representations of (utilitarian) rational action. And it was in line with the eternal power politics wisdom of (the great majority) of this sector that the United States got its political, ethical, and strategic orientations so tragically wrong in Vietnam.

The major concern in the 1990s is that nothing much appears to have changed. Thus, the crudity and analytical silence of the erstwhile "Wizards of Armageddon" is now replicated in the false (scientific) rigor of neo-Realism's updated advocation of U.S. hegemonic rule. Thus, in the new/old age of structuralist Realism, arrogant unself-consciousness abounds as those who disallow, disavow, and decry "reflection" illustrate their overwhelming need for it. Consequently, neo-Realist arguments designed to provide antireductionist and structuralist explanations of the world are invoked in the crudest of reductionist and atomized terms (e.g., by Waltz). Likewise, proposals for a sophisticated postpositivist (neo-Realist) theory, detached from the traditional premises of Newtonian physics, are advanced in terms derived directly and crudely from Newton (e.g., by Keohane). In the age of internationalized processes of production, explosive nationalist reawakenings, globalized drug cartels, and the potential perils of the greenhouse effect, the neo-Realist mainstream continues to represent its analytical insight in terms of anarchical state-centric conflict, the "billiard ball" logic of the 1950s, and simple utilitarian models of economic behavior. Meanwhile, large-scale works on the international political economy are projected in mediated power politics terms that predictably ignore and marginalize the impact of global capital upon the lives of the great majority of humans (e.g., by Gilpin). In summary then, and for all its jargonized appropriation of (neoclassical) economic insight, neo-Realism, the dominant representation of global life in the 1990s, retains its Traditional interest in status quo order and patterns of domination and control and, more specifically, at the end of the Cold War, in the foreign policy interests of the United States, as world hegemon.

It was in this discursive context that this book turned to the interrogative perspectives of critical social theory approaches (and postmodern perspectives in particular) to engage the silences and probe the unreflected inner sanctums of International Relations discourse. It sought in this way to counter a crude Tradition and a generation-long disciplinary ritualism by opening up some analytical possibilities beyond the positivist-Realist boundaries. It did this in a variety of ways, in easing International Relations into those spaces where it is forced to confront the silences of its "theory" as "practice." Here, in its quest to foundationalize, to squeeze diversity into unity and heterogeneity into homogeneity, it is confronted by the sovereign presence (autonomous individual, state) that cannot be defined in other than social terms, the independent object that is simultaneously subject, the irrefutable word that goes beyond its singular meaning, the absolute truths that are always interpretations, the pluralism that is reductionist, the science that is sociology, the rationality that is metaphysics, the relentless differences that are intrinsic to patterned social life. Here, more generally, a critical social theory perspective gives power politics no "theoretical" place to hide.

Rather, such a perspective challenges those assumptions that have become "fact," it questions those assertions that have become "reality," and it undermines the Traditional and disciplinary foundations that have been the major conduits of the International Relations discourse since World War II. Accordingly, particular attention was paid here to some of the primary strategies by which International Relations represents its narrow regime of exclusivity as global reality (e.g., its dominant disciplinary reading of international history and the "great texts") as evidence for the retention of a conservative status quo. Feminist scholars have illustrated just how narrow and exclusive this dominant representational strategy is, in exposing its systematic gender bias and its lack of concern for the experiences of women globally. From a number of different angles, its biases, silences, and dangers were further exposed, in this work, via a critical spectrum, including Vasquez's Kuhnian-based indictment of Realism's inadequacies, Ashley's Habermasian-induced articulation of the "poverty" of neo-Realism, Cox's Gramscian-inspired critique of mainstream "problem-solving" techniques, Wittgenstein's insights on the social construction of language, Gadamer's reformulated hermeneutics centered on *phronesis* principles of *praxis,* and a whole range of works influenced by Nietzsche and Foucault.

In their different ways, all of these critical perspectives helped undermine the Realist proposition that its knowledge corresponds to a universal, essential reality of global political life, which must be adhered to if the forces of anarchy and systemic disaster are to be kept at bay. In so doing these diverse approaches illustrated that those at the apex of the International Relations community do not understand the implications of the questions they ask of their (objectified) history, nor do they comprehend the meanings generated by their own historical/textual "fact." Specifically, what a critical social theory perspective illustrates is that power politics behavior is not endemic in global history, nor is the cause of "peace" greatly assisted by the Traditional solutions (balancing strategies and alliance formations) when it does occur. Rather, the dominant historical narrative in International Relations is both inaccurate, in its own terms, and highly dangerous, in anyone's terms, given that by Realism's own literary account the Realist "solution" to warlike activity in an anarchical world is to effectively accelerate the likelihood of war.[1]

It is evident also that the textual basis of a neo-Realist approach in the 1990s—the Tradition's "great texts"—represents nothing more than a highly contestable terrain of discursive reading protocols articulated as foundational knowledge. To emphasize this point, and to put the narrowness of the dominant reading practices of International Relations in its proper perspective, it is worth recalling Isiah Berlin's proposition that there are at least twenty-eight major interpretations of Machiavelli's textual legacy acknowledged by political theorists.[2] International Relations continues to insist on only one—the power politics interpretation—which, as the discussions here have shown, is little more than a crude and opportunistic caricature of a complex and sophisticated body of work. In this regard it is but the exemplar case within a larger caricatured agenda in which Thucydides, Augustine, Hobbes, and Rousseau meet a similar representational fate. The broader point is that the silences, omissions, and basic inadequacies of mainstream International Relations become much easier to understand in a representational context, particularly if one reflects that there is *no* historical, philosophical, or textual foundation to its dominant Realist perspective, other than that constituted by a post-Cartesian assumption about the existence of modern foundations and a crude positivist reading regime that makes this assumption "fact."

The power of this foundationalist illusion is most apparent in relation to two of the core concepts of Realism and neo-Realism—the concepts of sovereignty and anarchy—which remain effectively unquestioned at the heart of mainstream theory as practice. Both, however, under critical social theory investigation, are revealed for what they are—discursive derivatives of a modernist framing regime that provides an (illusory) foundation and simple, coherent meaning to a world of diversity and difference. Both, consequently, represent powerful sites of conceptual closure on the International Relations agenda. The sovereignty theme—articulated, for example, as *the* state, *the* individual, *the* system, *the* facts, *the* class, *the* (analytical/behavioral) model, *the* method, *the* Tradition, and *the* discipline—has acted to close off a particular and vital question of human discourse intrinsic to an "open" Western philosophical tradition otherwise celebrated by International Relations. The question, simply put, is this: How is it that this sovereign voice/theme/figure became sovereign? Or, more precisely, how is it that some voices/concepts/perspectives have been accorded sovereign status while others have been ignored or marginalized (e.g., gender, culture, race, ethnicity, religion, interpretive, normative, non-Western).

This is a question considered unnecessary, of course, from a self-enclosed logic set in foundationalist terms. But, having undermined any sense of foundationalist certainty in International Relations, a critical social theory perspective insists that the sovereignty question must be asked and, indeed, that its asking is crucial in the current global environment. Questioned, too, must be the anarchy principle, which has been a foundational feature of International Relations discourse since Realists proclaimed it so on the basis of their reading of the "great texts" (i.e., of Thucydides, Machiavelli, and Hobbes) in the late 1930s. Since then it has continued to represent a point of unreflected foundationalism for Realists, the point at which "theory starts" for a Hedley Bull or a Martin Wight, the keystone of the structuralist security dilemma for a Kenneth Waltz, the irreducible "basic assumption" of an interdependent political economy for a Stephen Krasner or a Robert Keohane. It has been integral also to a generation of strategists and policy planners who have effectively abrogated responsibility for their actions in merely "responding" to that ever present anarchical environment "out there." In the wake of the Cold War, this framing regime remains in strategic, political, and intellectual circles as a new/old anarchical scenario emerges on the discursive horizon to threaten the Traditional order (e.g., in the form of Islam, Third World terrorism, protectionism, "reflectivism," etc.).

Thus, in the 1990s, an anarchical world "out there" remains contrasted to the rational, ordered model of domestic life, even while the experience of so many at the domestic level is incontrovertibly and terrifyingly "anarchical." Meanwhile, the enormous complexity and indeterminacy of human behavior, across all its cultural, religious, historical, and linguistic variations, continues to be reduced to the simplicities of reading/writing protocols elsewhere discredited long ago. There is, to reiterate, nothing surprising about this, for as postmodernists in particular have illustrated, the representation of an anarchical world "out there" is, simultaneously, a strategy of identity formation that in International Relations gives meaning and foreign policy legitimation to the "self" (e.g., as national interest). This is not an original theme. Western analyists have recognized it as vital to Soviet propaganda strategies and their attempt to gain citizen support for a corrupted system in the struggle against the encircling forces of capitalist anarchy. Rarely, however, has the Western construction of identity been understood in these terms, and even rarer has been the attempt to seriously consider the implications of the self/other, identity/difference issues for the global future.[3]

This is now part of the critical agenda, however, as critical scholars have begun to confront the modern "self" in a positive, constructive manner, aware of both the extraordinary achievement and the colossal brutality that is their heritage but now no longer willing to celebrate the former while remaining blind to the latter. This has meant more than a surface-level consciousness of the need to think and act in more sensitive and tolerant ways. It has meant a more profound willingness to critically confront the way we think and act, to strip bare the very basis of thinking and acting, to reinterrogate its meaning and the ways we legitimate the social and intellectual givens that for so long have been reality—the way the world is, "out there."

This has some quite obvious implications for political theory and practice at all levels of experience—from the personal to the global. In an International Relations context it has some immediate implications for a discursive agenda that offers no space for genuinely critical reflection and political change. And while it would be a mistake to underestimate the problems of theory and practice that we face in the current period, there are indications that, in the 1990s, the discursive conditions for critical debate and enhanced understanding might be changing on questions of global political life, despite the Tradition and discipline of International Relations.

This is evidenced in the proliferation of critical literature emanating from a generation of scholars no longer willing to acquiesce in "theoretical" simplicity but willing to confront their complicity in modernist (e.g., power politics) "practice." Thus, in the process of giving Realism no theoretical place to hide, its narrowness and inadequacy is increasingly contrasted to the potential richness of approaches that explicitly connect theory to practice in order that the often destructive implications of the latter be always open to the critical reflection of the former. Moreover, in retaking responsibility for their own thoughts and actions, critical scholars are exposing the inadequacy and ethical nihilism of positions that seek merely to "describe" and interpret the facts of global hegemony (e.g., neo-Realism).

In this (marginally) changed environment, the resort to simple, sloganized rhetoric and power politics crudity is perhaps less effective than it once was, as alternative images of hegemonic power relations, market structures, cultural and gender politics, and human capacities begin to make analytical incisions into a previously closed arena of discourse. This can only be encouraged in order that when, for example, a Robert Cox illustrates, in great detail, a whole matrix of social, political, and economic behavior in the contemporary world that defies representation in neo-Realist terms, it might receive a careful and serious investigation of its immediate and long-term implications, rather than some ritualized resort to foundationalism articulated in exclusionary terms.[4]

It is in this more tolerant context, and despite Traditional attempts to dismiss and trivialize its perspectives (e.g., as mere "reflectivism"), that postmodernist insights on issues of theory and practice and knowledge and power are beginning to resonate among those who, at all levels and in their different ways, refuse the imposition upon them of preposterous certainty, of ritualized hierarchy and the language and logic of closure. In this space a more inclusive research orientation and questioning regimen is developing, in which questions are asked not only of the immediate circumstances of power politics but of the whole process by which a discourse affording identity, influence, credibility, and power to some among the global population is represented as universally and unproblematically "real" for all (e.g., the national interest, the new world order, state security, common sense, the revolutionary manifesto).

Here, the focus of critical attention is turning toward those effectively excluded from Traditional analysis but integral nevertheless to a volatile, changing world that defies grand-theorized representations of it. Included in this enlarged and enriched agenda of global politics must be the voices and aspirations of the nonelite, the nonwhite, the non-Western, the non-Christian, and those who in their repossession of culture, history, and language, in their challenges to rigid developmental models, in their insistence on political participation, in their questioning of the "expert," in their dissent against gendered and class givens, and in their confrontations with systemic "big brother" have illustrated their desire to think and speak for themselves, to face their worlds as creative, imaginative human beings capable of both understanding the processes that "objectively" define them and changing those processes.[5]

This critical (re)introduction to International Relations has sought to make a contribution to this developing agenda of global politics. It has done so not on behalf of any traditional invocation of emancipatory consciousness nor any radical manifesto of change. The answer to self-affirming grand theory is not self-affirming grand theory, however sympathetic one might be to emancipatory ideas and the struggles for change. Rather, as I have emphasized throughout this work, any agenda of global politics informed by critical social theory perspectives must forgo the simple, albeit self-gratifying, options inherent in ready-made alternative Realisms and confront the dangers, closures, paradoxes, and complicities associated with them. The option advanced in this work is a more difficult, complex, and uncertain one, which reflects the difficulties, complexities, and uncertainties of modern social life rather than the unreflective certitude of some within its elite sectors.

Consequently, it offers no final, synthesized conclusions that tie up the loose ends, smooth out the ragged edges, and provide straight-line direction for all thought and behavior. It offers, instead, the opportunity to think and behave in those spaces beyond the arbitrarily constructed boundaries of the final, the concluded, and the synthesized and to explore, at every level, the possibilities for something other than the Traditional "realistic" ways of knowing and Being. This has been the context in which two critical perspectives—the (broad) Critical Theory approach and postmodernism—were accorded special attention in this work. Both were addressed in critical terms, and I stressed my reservations about both as agencies of enhanced "thinking space" in global politics. Both, however, allow space for something other than metanarrative closure and Realist conclusion. Lingering doubts remain about much Critical Theory analysis in this regard, but there is much, in sophisticated Habermasian and neo-Gramscian approaches in particular, that deserves analytical respect and critical exploration.

Postmodernist perspectives, I believe, have most to offer in that space beyond International Relations. Accordingly, it has been from this source that this book has drawn its major analytical orientations and its concern to avoid speaking on behalf of some sovereign, unimpeachable ritual of understanding so as to better facilitate the means by which an audience reading this book might better think for itself. In this regard, it has taken seriously Foucault's injunction against "universal intellectuals" who have traditionally detached themselves from the larger struggle for freedom, openness, and enhanced human dignity while ostensibly and loudly propounding their commitment to these principles. Foucault's point, of course, was that traditionally those who have spoken for the "people," the "state," the "national interest," the "state system," the "free world," the "marginalized," and the "oppressed" have done so in universalized, essentialized, and ultimately exploitative terms.[6] The other option, Foucault argued, is to disavow one's (modernist) Godlike status and seek not to speak for others but to utilize one's capacities to help others speak for themselves.

This is no paradoxical reinvocation of the notion of free-floating intellectuals selflessly articulating knowledge for the good of humankind. It is precisely the opposite. It is an acknowledgment that none of us can "float" above or detach ourselves from a global political existence that is for so many unremittingly bleak and terrifying. It is to recognize that, to one degree or another, we as modern peoples are intrinsic to the problem as well as crucial to any solution. It is, more precisely, to accept that as the major recipients of modernity's triumphs we stand at a historical moment of great danger and great opportunity, when the narratives and political practices of International Relations that have served some of us so well must, for all our sakes, be reconnected to the unspoken, unwritten, unreflected narratives of the dispossessed and silenced. This is the challenge that faces us in the space beyond International Relations.

Notes

1. See Vasquez, *The Power of Power Politics,* for the most explicit evidence of this.

2. Berlin, cited in O'Brien's *The Suspecting Glance,* p. 21.

3. When it has been, by Marxists, for example, the answer has been represented in traditional sovereign terms—in terms of the universal overthrow of the (objectified) bourgeois "self," by the (equally objectified) proletarian Other.

4. The point here is not that Cox's position would be beyond criticism in this changed discursive situation; it would, on the contrary, be subject to a more profound critical scholarship than ever before in International Relations. The point, rather, is that Cox's important contribution could not be dismissed in crude Traditional terms—as "irrelevant" to the "reality" of an international political economy whose essence can be understood only in power politics terms—and as mere (Marxist) "ideology" in contrast to the Traditionally informed and falsified knowledge of mainstream scholarship. It is not just Cox's contribution that is under discussion here but a whole range of works that in a more tolerant and less intimidating context might help illuminate a complex world from Critical Theory perspectives. This is an important generalization to make because Cox's work per se is rarely the direct focus of a neo-Realist community, which really isn't equipped to deal with its nuance.

5. An example of the changing times, in this regard, is the journal *Alternatives* and the "Other" dimension it has brought to the scholarly literature on global political life.

6. Foucault's statements on "universal" and "specific" intellectuals are scattered through his works, particularly those devoted to interviews. See his comments in *Power/Knowledge.*

Bibliography

Adorno, Theodor. *Negative Dialectics.* Trans. by E. B. Ashton. New York: Seabury Press, 1973.

———. ed. *The Positivist Dispute in German Sociology.* Trans. by G. Adey and D. Frisby. London: Heinemann, 1976.

Alker, H. R., Jr. "The Dialectical Logic of Thucydides' Melian Dialogue." *American Political Science Review* 82 (1988): 805–820.

Alker, H. R., and T. Biersteker. "The Dialectics of World Order: Notes for Future Archeologist of International Savoir Faire." *International Studies Quarterly* 28 (2) (1984): 121–142.

Allison, Graham. *The Essence of Decision: Explaining the Cuban Missile Crisis.* Boston: Little, Brown and Company, 1971.

Anderson, Perry. *Lineages of the Absolutist State.* London: New Left Books, 1974.

———. *Considerations on Western Marxism.* London: New Left Books, 1976.

Anscombe, G. E., and P. T. Geach. *Descartes, Philosophical Writings.* London: Nelsons University Paperbacks, 1970.

Apter, D. *The Politics of Modernization.* Chicago: University of Chicago Press, 1965.

———. *Choice and the Politics of Allocation.* New Haven: Yale University Press, 1971.

Arato, Andrew, and Eike Gebhardt. *The Essential Frankfurt School Reader.* New York: Urizen, 1978.

Arendt, Hannah. *The Human Condition.* Chicago: University of Chicago Press, 1958.

Aronowitz, S. *Science as Power: Discourse and Ideology in Modern Society.* Minneapolis: University of Minnesota Press, 1988.

Ashcraft, Richard. "Rethinking the Nature of Political Theory." *Journal of Politics* 44 (2) (1982): 577–585.

Ashley, Richard K. *The Political Economy of War and Peace: The Modern Security Problematique and the Sino-Soviet-U.S. Triangle.* London: Frances Pinter, 1980.

———. "Political Realism and Human Interest." *International Studies Quarterly* 25 (1981): 204–236.

———. "The Poverty of Neorealism." *International Organization* 38(2) (1984): 225–286. Reprinted in *Neorealism and Its Critics,* ed. by R. O. Keohane. New York: Columbia University Press, 1986.

———. "The Geopolitics of Geopolitical Space: Towards a Critical Social Theory of International Politics." *Alternatives* 12 (1987): 403–434.

———. "Untying the Sovereign State: A Double Reading of the Anarchy Problematique." *Millennium: Journal of International Studies* 17 (1988): 227–262.

———. "Living on Border Lines: Man, Poststructuralism, and War." In *International/Intertextual Relations: Postmodern Readings of World Politics,* ed. by James Der Derian and Michael J. Shapiro. Lexington: Lexington Books, 1989.

Ashley, Richard K., and R. B. J. Walker. "Reading Dissidence/Writing the Discipline: Crisis and the Question of Sovereignty in International Studies." *International Studies Quarterly* 34 (3) (1990): 367–416.

———. "Speaking the Language of Exile: Dissident Thought in International Studies." *International Studies Quarterly* 34 (3) (1990): 259–268.

Augustine, St. *City of God.* Ed. by R. Taskar, trans. by J. Helay. London: J.R. Dent, 1945.

Aune, Bruce. *Rationalism, Empiricism and Pragmatism.* New York: Random House, 1970.

Austin, J. *Philosophical Papers.* Ed. by J. Urmson and G. Warnock. Oxford: Oxford University Press, 1970.

Ayer, A. J. *Language, Truth and Logic.* London: Gollancz, 1962.

Ball, Desmond. "Management of the Superpower Balance." In *International Security in the Southeast Asian and Southwest Pacific Region,* ed. by T. B. Millar. St. Lucia: Queensland University Press, 1983.

Ball, Terrence, ed. *Idioms of Inquiry: Criticism and Renewal in Political Science.* Albany: State University of New York Press, 1987.

Banks, Michael, ed. *Conflict and World Society: A New Perspective on International Relations.* Brighton: Harvester Press, 1984.

———. "The Evolution of International Relations Theory." In *Conflict and World Society: A New Perspective on International Relations,* ed. by M. Banks. Brighton: Harvester Press, 1984.

———. "The Inter-Paradigm Debate." In *International Relations: A Handbook of Current Theory,* ed. by A .J. R. Groom and Margot Light. London: Frances Pinter, 1985.

Barthes, Roland. *Mythologies.* New York: Hill and Wang, 1973.

Baynes, Kenneth, James Bohman, and Thomas McCarthy, eds. *After Philosophy: End or Transformation?* Cambridge, Mass.: MIT Press, 1987.

Beehler, R., and A. R. Drengson, eds. *The Philosophy of Society.* London: Methuen, 1978.

Bellah, R., ed. *Habits of the Heart: Individualism and Commitment in American Life.* Berkeley: University of California Press, 1985.

Berki, R. N. *On Political Realism.* London: J.M. Dent, 1981.

Berlin, Isiah. "The Originality of Machiavelli." In *Studies on Machiavelli,* ed. by J. M. Gilmore. Florence: G.C. Sansoni, 1972.

Bernstein, Richard. *The Restructuring of Social and Political Theory.* London: Methuen, 1976.

———. *Beyond Objectivism and Relativism: Science, Hermeneutics and Praxis.* Oxford: Basil Blackwell, 1983.

———, ed. *Habermas and Modernity.* Cambridge, Mass.: MIT Press, 1985.

Bhaskar, J. *A Realist Theory of Science.* 2d ed. Brighton: Harvester Press, 1978.

Bhaskar, Roy. *Scientific Realism and Human Emancipation.* London: Verso, 1986.

Biersteker, T. J. "Critical Reflections On Post-Positivism in International Relations." *International Studies Quarterly* 33 (3) (1989): 263–267.

Blum, Robert. *Drawing the Line: The Origin of the American Containment Policy in East Asia.* New York: W.W. Norton, 1982.

Boucher, David. *Texts in Context.* Dordrecht: M. Nijhoff, 1985.

———. "The Character of the History of the Philosophy of International Relations and the Case of Edmund Burke." *Review of International Studies* 17 (1991): 127–148.

Brodie, B. *Escalation and the Nuclear Option.* Princeton: Princeton University Press, 1966.

———. *War and Politics.* New York: Macmillan, 1973.

Bronowski, J., and B. Mazlish. *Main Currents of Western Thought.* New York: Alfred Knopf, 1952.

———. *The Western Intellectual Tradition.* New York: Harper Bros., 1960.

Brown, Sarah. "Feminism, International Theory and International Relations of Gender Inequality." *Millennium: Journal of International Studies* 17 (3) (1988): 461–473.

Bull, Hedley. "Society and Anarchy in International Relations." In *Diplomatic Investigations,* ed. by Herbert Butterfield and Martin Wight. London: George Allen and Unwin, 1966.

———. "International Theory: The Case for the Classical Approach." *World Politics* (April 1966): 363–377. Reprinted in *Contending Approaches to International Relations,* ed. by K. Knorr and J. Rosenau. Princeton: Princeton University Press, 1969.

———. "The Theory of International Politics, 1919–1969." In *The Aberystwyth Papers: International Politics 1919–1969,* ed. by B. Porter. London: Oxford University Press, 1972.

———. "Martin Wight and the Theory of International Relations." *British Journal of International Studies* 2 (2) (1976): 101–116.

———. *The Anarchical Society: A Study of Order in World Politics.* London: Macmillan, 1977.

Burns, A. L. "From Balance to Deterrence: A Theoretical Analysis," *World Politics* 9 (1957): 494–529.

———. *Of Powers and Their Politics: A Critique of Their Theoretical Analysis.* Englewood Cliffs, N.J.: Prentice Hall, 1968.

———. "Prospects for a General Theory of International Relations." In *The International System,* ed. by K. Knorr and S. Verba. Princeton: Princeton University Press, 1968.

Burton, John. *Systems, States, Diplomacy and Rules.* Cambridge: Cambridge University Press, 1968.

———. *World Society.* Cambridge: Cambridge University Press, 1972.

Butler, Judith. "Contingent Foundations: Feminism and the Question of Postmodernism." In *Feminists Theorize the Political,* ed. by Judith Butler and Joan Scott. New York: Routledge, 1992.

Butler, Judith, and Joan Scott, eds. *Feminists Theorize the Political.* New York: Routledge, 1992.

Butterfield, Herbert. *Christianity, Diplomacy and War.* London: Epworth Press, 1953.

Butterfield, Herbert, and Martin Wight, eds. *Diplomatic Investigations.* London: George Allen and Unwin, 1966.

Buzan, Barry. "The Case for a Comprehensive Definition of Security and the Institutional Consequences of Accepting It." *Arbejdspapirer Working Papers* 4 (1990): 1–17.

———. *People, States and Fear: An Agenda for International Security Studies in the Post–Cold War Era.* Boulder: Lynne Rienner, 1991.

Calinescu, Matei. *Five Faces of Modernity.* Durham, N.C.: Duke University Press, 1987.

Callinicos, A. "Post-modernism, Post-structuralism and Post-Marxism." *Theory, Culture and Society* 2 (1985): 85–101.

Campbell, David. "Global Inscription: How Foreign Policy Constitutes the United States." *Alternatives* 15 (1990): 263–286.

———. *Writing Security: United States' Foreign Policy and the Politics of Identity.* Manchester: Manchester University Press, 1992.

———. *Politics Without Principle: Sovereignty, Ethics, and the Narratives of the Gulf War.* Boulder: Lynne Rienner, 1993.

Carr, Edward Hallett. *The Twenty Years Crisis, 1919–1939: An Introduction to the Study of International Relations.* 3d ed. New York: Harper and Row, 1964.

———. *What Is History?* Middlesex: Penguin, 1964.

Cassirer, J. E. *The Individual and the Cosmos in Renaissance Philosophy.* Trans. by M. Domandi. New York: Harper and Row, 1963.

Chalmers, Alan. *What Is This Thing Called Science?* Brisbane: University of Queensland Press, 1976.

Chaloupka, William. *Knowing Nukes: The Politics and Culture of the Atom.* Minneapolis: University of Minnesota Press, 1992.

Charlesworth, James, ed. *The Limits of Behaviouralism in Political Science.* Philadelphia: American Academy of Political and Social Sciences, 1962.

Clarke, Ian. *Reform and Resistance in the International Order.* Cambridge: Cambridge University Press, 1980.

Claude, Inis. *Power and International Relations.* New York: Random House, 1962.

———. *Swords into Plowshares.* 4th ed. New York: Random House, 1971.

Cohn, Carol. "Sex and Death in the Rational World of Defense Intellectuals." *Signs* 12 (Summer 1987): 687–718.

Connolly, William. *Political Theory and Modernity.* Oxford: Basil Blackwell, 1988.

———. "Identity and Difference in Global Politics." In *International/Intertextual Relations: Postmodern Readings of World Politics,* ed. by James Der Derian and Michael Shapiro. Lexington: Lexington Books, 1989.

Cooper, Richard. *The Economics of Interdependence: Economic Policy in the Atlantic Community.* New York: McGraw-Hill, 1968.

———. *A Reordered World: Emerging International Economic Problems.* Washington, D.C.: Potomac Associates, 1973.

Corcoran, Paul. "Rousseau and Hume." In *Comparing Political Thinkers,* ed. by R. Fitzgerald. Sydney: Pergamon Press, 1980.

Cornforth, Maurice. *Science Versus Idealism.* London: Lawrence and Wishart, 1946.

Cox, Richard. "The Role of Political Philosophy in the Theory of International Relations." *Social Research* 29 (3) (1962): 261–293.

Cox, Robert. "Production and Hegemony: Towards a Political Economy of World Order." In *The Emerging International Economic Order,* ed. by H. Jacobsen and D. Subyanski. Newbury Park, Calif.: Sage, 1982.

———. "Gramsci, Hegemony and International Relations: An Essay in Method." *Millennium: Journal of International Studies* 12 (2) (1983): 269–291.

———. "Social Forces, States and World Orders: Beyond International Relations Theory." *Millennium: Journal of International Studies* 10 (2) (1981): 126–155. Reprinted in *Neorealism and Its Critics,* ed. by R. O. Keohane. New York: Columbia University Press, 1986.

———. *Production, Power and World Order: Social Forces in the Making of History.* New York: Columbia University Press, 1987.

Cragg, G. R. *The Church and the Age of Reason.* London: Hodder and Stoughton, 1962.

Craib, I. *Modern Social Theory: From Parsons to Habermas.* Sussex: Harvester Press, 1984.

Culler, Jonathon. *On Deconstruction: Theory and Criticism After Structuralism.* Ithaca: Cornell University Press, 1982.

Dalby, Simon. "Geopolitical Discourse: The Soviet Union as Other." *Alternatives* 13 (1988): 415–442.

———. "Dealignment Discourse: Thinking Beyond the Blocs." *Current Research on Peace and Violence* (1990): 140–155.

———. *Creating the Second Cold War: The Discourse of Politics.* London: Pinter Publishers, 1990.

Dallmayr, Fred. *Beyond Dogma and Despair: Towards a Critical Phenomenology of Politics.* South Bend, Ind.: University of Notre Dame Press, 1981.

Dallmayr, Fred, and Thomas McCarthy, eds. *Understanding Social Inquiry.* South Bend, Ind.: University of Notre Dame Press, 1977.

Deane, Herbert. *The Political and Social Ideas of St. Augustine.* New York: Columbia University Press, 1963.

Der Derian, James. *On Diplomacy: A Genealogy of Western Estrangement.* Oxford: Basil Blackwell, 1987.

———. "Philosophical Traditions in International Relations." *Millennium: Journal of International Studies* 17 (2) (1988): 189–193.

———. "Spy Versus Spy: The Intertextual Power of International Intrigue." In *International/Intertextual Relations: Postmodern Readings of World Politics,* ed. by James Der Derian and Michael Shapiro. Lexington: Lexington Books, 1989.

———. "Boundaries of Knowledge and Power." In *International/Intertextual Relations: Postmodern Readings of World Politics,* ed. by James Der Derian and Michael Shapiro. Lexington: Lexington Books, 1989.

———. "The (S)pace of International Relations: Simulation, Surveillance, and Speed." *International Studies Quarterly* 34 (3) (1990): 295–310.

———. *Antidiplomacy: Spies, Terror, Speed and War.* Cambridge, Mass.: Blackwell, 1992.

Der Derian, James, and Michael Shapiro, eds. *International/Intertextual Relations: Postmodern Readings of World Politics.* Lexington: Lexington Books, 1989.

Derrida, Jacques. *Of Grammatology.* Trans. by G. Spivak. Baltimore: Johns Hopkins University Press, 1976.

———. *Writing and Difference.* London: Routledge and Kegan Paul, 1978.

Deutsch, Karl. *Nationalism and Social Communication.* Cambridge, Mass.: MIT Press, 1953.

———. *The Analysis of International Relations.* Englewood Cliffs, N.J.: Prentice Hall, 1968.

Deutsch, Karl, and J. D. Singer. "Multipolar Power Systems and International Stability." *World Politics* 16 (1964): 390–406.

Dews, Peter. *The Logic of Disintegration: Post-structuralist Thought and the Claims of Critical Theory.* London: Verso, 1987.

Dillon, Michael. *Defence, Discourse and Policy Making.* Institute on Global Conflict and Cooperation. Working Paper 4. San Diego: University of California, 1988.

———. "Modernity, Discourse and Deterrence." *Current Research on Peace and Violence* 12 (2) (1989): 90–94.

———. *The Falklands, Politics and War.* London: Macmillan, 1989.

———. "The Alliance of Security and Subjectivity." *Current Research on Peace and Violence* 13 (3) (1990): 101–125.

Donelan, Michael, ed. *The Reason of States.* London: George Allen and Unwin, 1978.

Dougherty, J. E., and R. L. Pfaltzgraff. *Contending Theories of International Relations: A Comprehensive Survey.* New York: Harper and Row, 1981.

Doyle, Michael. "Thucydidean Realism." *Review of International Studies* 16 (3) (1990): 223–237.

Dreyfus, H., and Paul Rabinow, eds. *Michel Foucault: Beyond Structuralism and Hermeneutics.* Brighton: Harvester Press, 1982.

Dubois, Marc. "The Governance of the Third World: A Foucauldian Perspective on Power Relations in Development." *Alternatives* 16 (1991): 1–30.

Dumm, Thomas. "The Politics of Post-Modern Aesthetics: Habermas Contra Foucault." *Political Theory* 16 (1988): 209–228.

Dunn, John. *Western Political Theory in the Face of the Future.* Cambridge: Cambridge University Press, 1979.

Dunnigan, James, and Albert Nofi. *Dirty Little Secrets: Military Information You're Not Supposed to Know.* New York: William Morrow, 1990.

Ehrenreich, Barbara. "Battlin' Bill's Initiation Rite." *The Nation* (May 24, 1993): 700–702.

Eisenstadt, S. *Modernization, Protest and Change.* Englewood Cliffs, N.J.: Prentice Hall, 1966.

Eisenstein, Zillah. *The Radical Future of Liberal Feminism.* Boston: Northeastern University Press, 1981.

Ellsberg, Daniel. *Papers on the War.* New York: Simon and Schuster, 1972.

Elshtain, J. B. "Reflections on War and Political Disourse: Realism, Just War and Feminism in a Nuclear Age." *Political Theory* 13 (1) (1986): 39–57.

Engels, Freidrich. *Anti Duhring.* London: Lawrence and Wishart, 1975.

Enloe, Cynthia. *Bananas, Beaches and Bases: Making Feminist Sense Out of International Politics.* Berkeley: University of California Press, 1989.

Escobar, A. "Discourse and Power in Development: Michel Foucault and the Relevance of His Work to the Third World." *Alternatives* 10 (1984): 377–400.

Evans, Graham. "Some Problems with a History of Thought in International Relations." *International Relations* 4 (1974): 720–732.

Factor, Regis, and Stephen Turner. *Max Weber and the Dispute over Reason and Value.* London: Routledge and Kegan Paul, 1984.

Ferguson, Yale, and Richard Mansbach. "Between Celebration and Despair: Constructive Suggestions for Future International Theory." *International Studies Quarterly* 35 (4) (1991): 363–387.

Feyerabend, Paul. "How to Be a Good Empiricist: A Plea for Tolerance in Matters Epistemological." In *The Philosophy of Science,* ed. by P. H. Nidditch. London: Oxford University Press, 1968.

Findlay, J. *Four Stages of Growth.* Stanford, Calif.: Stanford University Press, 1966.

Fitzpatrick, John. "The Anglo-American School of International Relations: The Tyranny of Ahistorical Culturalism." *Australian Outlook* 41 (1) (1987): 45–52.

Flax, Jane. "Why Epistemology Matters: A Reply to Kress." *Journal of Politics* 43 (1981): 1006–1024.

———. "Postmodernism and Gender Relations in Feminist Theory." *Signs: Journal of Women in Culture and Society* 12 (4) (1987): 621–643.

———. *Thinking Fragments: Psychoanalysis, Feminism, and Postmodernism in the Contemporary West.* Berkeley: University of California Press, 1990.

Foucault, Michel. *The Archaeology of Knowledge.* Trans. by A. M. Sheridan Smith. London: Tavistock, 1972.

———. *The Order of Things: An Archaeology of the Human Sciences.* Trans. by A. M. Sheridan Smith. New York: Vintage Books, 1973.

———. *The Birth of the Clinic: An Archaeology of Medical Perception.* Trans. by A. M. Sheridan Smith. New York: Vintage Books, 1975.

———. *Discipline and Punish: The Birth of the Prison.* Trans. by Alan Sheridan. New York: Vintage Books, 1979.

———. *Power/Knowledge: Selected Interviews and Other Writings.* Ed. and trans. by C. Gordon. New York: Pantheon Books, 1980.

———. *The History of Sexuality* (vol. 1). Trans. by R. Hurley. New York: Vintage Books, 1980.

———. "What Is Enlightenment?" In *The Foucault Reader,* ed. by Paul Rabinow. New York: Pantheon Books, 1984.

Frank, Andre Gunder. *Latin America: Underdevelopment or Revolution.* New York: Monthly Review Press, 1969.

Fraser, Nancy. "Michel Foucault: A 'Young Conservative'?" *Ethics* 96 (1985): 165–184.

Freedman, Lawrence. *The Evolution of Nuclear Strategy.* New York: St. Martin's Press, 1981.

Frisby, David. "The Popper-Adorno Controversy: The Methodological Dispute in German Sociology." *Philosophy and the Social Sciences* 2 (1972): 105–119.

Frost, Mervyn. *Towards a Normative Theory of International Relations.* Cambridge: Cambridge University Press, 1986.

Fukuyama, Francis. *The End of History and the Last Man.* New York: Free Press, 1992.

Gadamer, Hans-Georg. *Truth and Method.* Trans and ed. by G. Barden and J. Cumming. New York: Seabury Press, 1975.

Gaddis, John L. *Strategies of Containment: A Critical Appraisal of Postwar American National Security Policy.* New York: Oxford University Press, 1982.

———. "The Cold War, the Long Peace and the Future." In *The End of the Cold War: Its Meanings and Implications,* ed. by Michael Hogan. Cambridge: Cambridge University Press, 1992.

———. "International Relations and the End of the Cold War." *International Security* 17 (3) (1992/1993): 5–58.

Garst, Daniel. "Thucydides and Neorealism." *International Studies Quarterly* 33 (1) (1989): 3–27.

Gelb, Leslie, and Richard Betts. *The Irony of Vietnam: The System Worked.* Washington, D.C.: Brookings Institute, 1979.

Gellner, Ernst. *Legitimation of Belief.* Cambridge: Cambridge University Press, 1974.

Genovese, Eugene. "William Appleman Williams on Marx and America." *Studies on the Left* 6 (1966): 70–86.

George, Alexander, and Richard Smoke. *Deterrence in American Foreign Policy: Theory and Practice.* New York: Columbia University Press, 1974.

George, Jim. "International Relations and the Positivist/Empiricist Theory of Knowledge: Implications for the Discipline." In *New Directions in International Relations? Australian Perspectives,* ed. by R. Higgott. Canberra: Canberra Studies in World Affairs 23, 1988.

———. "International Relations and the Search for Thinking Space: Another View of the Third Debate." *International Studies Quarterly* 33 (3) (1989): 269–279.

———. "Some Thoughts on the Givenness of Everyday Life in Australian

International Relations: Theory and Practice." *Australian Journal of Political Science* 27 (1992): 31–54.

———. "Of Incarceration and Closure: Neo-Realism and New/Old World Orders." *Millennium: Journal of International Studies* 22 (2) (1993): 555–592.

George, Jim, and David Campbell. "Patterns of Dissent and the Celebration of Difference: Critical Social Theory and International Relations." *International Studies Quarterly* 34 (3) (1990): 269–294.

George, Stephen. "The Reconciliation of the Classical and Scientific Approaches to International Relations." *Millenium: Journal of International Studies* 3–5 (1975): 28–40.

Geutzkow, H. "Some Correspondences Between Simulations and Realities in International Processes." In *New Approaches to International Relations,* ed. by Morton Kaplan. New York: St. Martin's Press, 1968.

Geutzkow, H. et al. *Simulations in International Relations.* Englewood Cliffs, N.J.: Prentice Hall, 1963.

Giddens, Anthony. *Capitalism and Modern Social Theory: An Analysis of the Writings of Marx, Durkheim and Max Weber.* Cambridge: Cambridge University Press, 1971.

———. *Politics and Sociology in the Thought of Max Weber.* London: Macmillan, 1972.

———. *Positivism and Sociology.* London: Heinemann, 1974.

———. *Studies in Social and Political Theory.* London: Hutchinson, 1977.

———. *Profiles and Critiques in Social Theory.* London: Macmillan, 1982.

———. *The Nation-State and Violence. Vol. 2 of A Contemporary Critique of Historical Materialism.* Oxford: Polity Press, 1985.

Giddens, Anthony, and Jonathon Turner, eds. *Social Theory Today.* Cambridge: Polity Press, 1987.

Gill, Stephen. *American Hegemony and the Trilateral Commission.* Cambridge: Cambridge University Press, 1990.

———. "Two Concepts of International Political Economy." *Review of International Studies* 16 (1990): 369–381.

———. "Historical Materialism, Gramsci and International Political Economy." In *The New International Political Economy,* ed. by Craig Murphy and Roger Tooze. Boulder: Lynne Rienner, 1991.

Gill, Stephen, and David Law. *The Global Political Economy.* NewYork: Harvester, 1988.

Gilpin, Robert. *War and Change in World Politics.* Cambridge: Cambridge University Press, 1981.

———. "The Richness of the Tradition of Political Realism." *International Organization* 38 (1984): 286–303.

———. *The Political Economy of International Relations.* Princeton: Princeton University Press, 1987.

Gilson, E. "Concerning Christian Philosophy." In *Philosophy and History,* ed. by R. Klibansky and H. J. Paton. Oxford: Oxford University Press, 1976.

Goetz, Anne Marie. "Feminism and the Limits of the Claims to Know: Contradictions in the Feminist Approach to Women in Development." *Millennium: Journal of International Studies* 17 (3) (1988): 477–497.

Goodwin, Barbara. "Utopia Defended Against the Liberals." *Political Studies* 28 (2) (1980): 384–400.

Gouldner, Alvin. *The Coming Crisis of Western Sociology.* New York: Basic Books, 1970.

Grace, D. "Augustine and Hobbes." In *Comparing Political Thinkers,* ed. by R. Fitzgerald. Sydney: Pergamon Press, 1980.

Grant, Rebecca. "The Sources of Gender Bias in International Relations Theory." In *Gender and International Relations,* ed. by Grant and Kathleen Newlands. Bloomington, Ind.: Indiana University Press, 1991.

Grant, Rebecca, and Kathleen Lewland, ed. *Gender and International Relations.* Bloomington: Indiana University Press, 1991.

Green, Phillip. *Deadly Logic: The Theory of Nuclear Deterrence.* Columbus: Ohio State University Press, 1966.

Greico, Joseph. "Anarchy and the Limits of Cooperation: A Realist Critique of the Newest Liberal Institutionalism." *International Organization* 42 (Summer 1988): 485–507.

Gunnell, J. G. "Political Theory: The Evolution of a Subfield." In *Political Science: The State of the Discipline,* ed. by A. W. Finifter. Washington, D.C.: American Political Science Association, 1983.

Gutting, G., ed. *Paradigms and Revolutions.* South Bend, Ind.: University of Notre Dame Press, 1980.

Haas, Ernst. *Beyond the Nation State: Functionalism and International Organization.* Stanford, Calif.: Stanford University Press, 1964.

———. "Words Can't Hurt You: Or, Who Said What to Whom About Regimes." In *International Regimes,* ed. by Stephen Krasner. Ithaca: Cornell University Press, 1983.

Habermas, Jurgen. *Knowledge and Human Interests.* Trans. by J. Shapiro. Boston: Beacon Press, 1972.

———. *Theory and Practice.* Trans. by J. Viertel. London: Heinemann, 1974.

———. *Legitimation Crisis.* Trans. by T. McCarthy. London: Heinemann, 1975.

———. *Towards a Rational Society: Student Protest, Science and Politics.* Trans. by J. Shapiro. London: Heinemann, 1976.

———. *Communication and the Evolution of Society.* Trans. by T. McCarthy. London: Heinemann, 1979.

———. "Modernity Versus Post-Modernity." *New German Critique* 22 (1981): 3–22.

———. *Theory of Communicative Action* (vol. 1). Trans. by T. McCarthy. Boston: Beacon Press, 1984.

———. "Questions and Counter Questions." In *Habermas and Modernity,* ed. by R. Bernstein. Cambridge, Mass.: MIT Press, 1985.

———. *The Philosophical Discourse of Modernity.* Trans. by T. McCarthy. Cambridge: Polity Press, 1987.

———. *Theory of Communicative Action* (vol. 2). Trans. by T. McCarthy. Boston: Beacon Press, 1988.

Halberstam, David. *The Best and the Brightest.* New York: Random House, 1972.

Halfpenny, Peter. *Positivism and Sociology: Explaining Social Life.* London: George Allen and Unwin, 1982.

Halliday, Fred. *The Making of the Second Cold War.* London: Verso, 1983.

Halperin, Morton. "The Decision to Deploy the ABM." *World Politics* 25 (1972): 62–95.

Harding, Sandra, and Merrill Hintikka, eds. *Discovering Reality: Feminist Perspectives on Epistemology, Metaphysics, Methodology and the Philosophy of Science.* Dordrecht: D. Reidel, 1983.

Heisenberg, Werner. "Planck's Discovery and the Philosophical Problems of Atomic Physics." In *On Modern Physics,* Heisenberg et al. New York: Clarkson Potter, 1961.

Hekman, Susan. "Beyond Humanism: Gadamer, Althusser and the Methodology of the Social Sciences." *Western Political Quarterly* 36 (1983): 98–115.

———. *Weber, the Ideal Type and Contemporary Social Theory.* South Bend, Ind.: University of Notre Dame Press, 1983.

———. *Hermeneutics and the Sociology of Knowledge.* Cambridge: Polity Press, 1986.

Held, David. *Introduction to Critical Theory: From Horkheimer to Habermas.* London: Hutchinson, 1980.

Herbert, N. *Quantum Reality: Beyond the New Physics.* London: Rider, 1985.

Hermann, C. "International Crisis as a Situation Variable." In *International Politics and Foreign Policy,* ed. by James Rosenau. New York: Free Press, 1969.

Hermann, C., and M. G. Hermann. "An Attempt to Simulate the Outbreak of World War I." *American Political Science Review* 61 (1967): 400–416.

Herz, John. "Political Realism Revisited." *International Studies Quarterly* 25 (2) (1981): 182–197.

Hesse, Mary. *Revolutions and Reconstructions in the Philosophy of Science.* Brighton: Harvester Press, 1980.

Higgott, Richard. *Political Development Theory: The Contemporary Debate.* London: Croom Helm, 1983.

Hindess, Barry. *Philosophy and Methodology in the Social Sciences.* Brighton: Harvester Press, 1977.

Hinsley, F. H. *Power and the Pursuit of Peace: Theory and Practice in the History of Relations Between States.* Cambridge: Cambridge University Press, 1963.

———. *Sovereignty.* 2d ed. Cambridge: Cambridge University Press, 1986.

Hobbes, Thomas. *Leviathan.* Ed. by M. Oakeshott. Oxford: Basil Blackwell, 1960.

Hoffman, Mark. "Critical Theory and the Inter-Paradigm Debate." *Millennium: Journal of International Studies* 16 (1987): 231–249.

———. "Conversations on Critical International Relations Theory." *Millennium: Journal of International Studies* 17 (1988): 91–95.

Hoffmann, E. "Platonism in Augustine's Philosophy of History." In *Philosophy and History,* ed. by R. Klibansky and H. J. Paton. Oxford: Oxford University Press, 1976.

Hoffmann, Stanley. "An American Social Science: International Relations." *Daedalus* 106 (3) (1977): 41–60.

———. "Hedley Bull and His Contribution to International Relations." *International Affairs* 62 (2) (1986): 179–196.

———. "Delusions of World Order." *New York Review of Books* (April 9, 1992): 37–42.

Holsti, Kal J. *The Dividing Discipline: Hegemony and Diversity in International Theory.* Boston: Allen and Unwin, 1985.

Holsti, O., R. Brody, and R. North. "Measuring Affect and Action in International Reaction Models: Empirical Materials from the 1962 Cuban Crisis." *Peace Research Society Papers* 2 (1965): 170–190.

Hook, G. D. "The Nuclearization of Language: Nuclear Allergy as Political Metaphor." *Journal of Peace Research* 21 (1984): 259–275.

Hooker, C. A. "Philosophy and Meta-Philosophy of Science: Empiricism, Popperianism and Realism." *Synthese* 32 (1975): 177–231.

Horkheimer, M. *Critical Theory: Selected Essays.* New York: Herder and Herder, 1972.

Horkheimer, M., and T. Adorno. *Dialectic of Enlightenment.* New York: Herder and Herder, 1972.

Huntington, Samuel P. *Political Order and Changing Societies.* New Haven: Yale University Press, 1968.

International Institute for Strategic Studies. *The Military Balance.* London: Brassey's, 1983–1988.

Jacob, Margaret C. *The Cultural Meaning of the Scientific Revolution.* Philadelphia: Temple University Press, 1988.

Jay, Martin. *The Dialectical Imagination: A History of the Frankfurt School and the Institute of Social Research, 1923–1950.* Boston: Little, Brown and Company, 1973.

———. "Should Intellectual History Take a Linguistic Turn? Reflections on the Habermas-Gadamer Debate." In *European Intellectual History: Reappraisals and New Perspectives,* ed. by D. LaCapra and S. L. Kaplan. Ithaca: Cornell University Press, 1982.

———. *Marxism and Totality: The Adventures of a Concept from Lukacs to Habermas.* Berkeley: University of California Press, 1984.

Jervis, Robert. *Perception and Misperception in International Politics.* Princeton: Princeton University Press, 1976.

———. "Deterrence Theory Revisited." *World Politics* 31 (1979): 289–324.

Jervis, Robert, J. Lebow, and S. Rosen. *Psychology and Deterrence.* Baltimore: Johns Hopkins University Press, 1985.

Joenniemi, Pertti. "The Social Constitution of Gorbachev: From an Intruder to a Communal Figure." Paper presented at the Joint Annual Conference of BISA and ISA. London, March 28–April 1, 1989.

———. "The Post Cold War Warsaw Treaty Organisation: The Pact That Unravelled." *Current Research on Peace and Violence* 13 (3) (1990): 125–140.

Jones, R. "The English School of International Relations: A Case for Closure." *Review of International Studies* 7 (1) (1981): 57–68.

Kahn, H. *On Thermonuclear War.* Princeton, Princeton University Press, 1960.

———. *Thinking About the Unthinkable.* New York: Horizon, 1962.

Kalb, Marvin, and Elie Abel. *Roots of Involvement.* New York: W.W. Norton, 1971.

Kant, I. *Perpetual Peace.* Ed. by L. W. Beck. New York: Bobbs-Merrill, 1957.

Kaplan, Morton. *System and Process in International Politics.* New York: Wiley, 1957.

———. "The New Great Debate: Traditionalism vs. Science in International Relations." *World Politics* 19 (1966): 1–20.

Kaplan, M., A. Burns, and R. Quandt. "Theoretical Analysis of the 'Balance of Power.'" *Behavioral Science* 5 (1960): 240–252.

Kattenburg, Paul. *The Vietnam Trauma in American Foreign Policy, 1945–75.* New Brunswick, N.J.: Transaction, 1980.

Keat, Russel, and John Urry. *Social Theory as Science.* London: Routledge and Kegan Paul, 1975.

Keenes, Ernie. "Paradigm of International Relations: Bringing Politics Back In." *International Journal* 44 (Winter 1988–1989): 41–48.

Kennan, George. *American Diplomacy, 1900–1950.* London: Secker and Warburg, 1952.

———. "After the Cold War: American Foreign Policy in the 1970s." *Foreign Affairs* 51 (1972): 210–217.

Kennedy, Paul. *The Rise and Fall of the Great Powers: Economic Change and Military Conflict from 1500 to 2000.* New York: Random House, 1987.

———. *Preparing for the Twenty-First Century.* New York: Random House, 1992.

Keohane, Robert O. "The Theory of Hegemonic Stability and Changes in International Economic Regimes, 1967–1977." In *Change in the International System,* ed. by Ole R. Holsti, Randolph M. Siverson, and Alexander L. George. Boulder: Westview Press, 1980.

———. "The Demand for International Regimes." In *International Regimes,* ed. by Stephen Krasner. Ithaca: Cornell University Press, 1983.

———. *After Hegemony: Cooperation and Discord in the World Political Economy.* Princeton: Princeton University Press, 1984.

———. "Realism, Neorealism and the Study of World Politics." In *Neorealism and Its Critics,* ed. by Robert O. Keohane. New York: Columbia University Press, 1986.

———. "Theory of World Politics: Structural Realism and Beyond." In *Neorealism and Its Critics,* ed. by Robert O. Keohane. New York: Columbia University Press, 1986.

———, ed. *Neorealism and Its Critics.* New York: Columbia University Press, 1986.

———. "International Institutions: Two Approaches." *International Studies Quarterly* 32 (1988): 379–396.

Keohane, Robert O., and Joseph P. Nye, eds. *Transnational Relations and World Politics.* Cambridge, Mass.: Harvard University Press, 1971.

———. *Power and Interdependence: World Politics in Transition.* 1st ed. Boston: Little, Brown and Company, 1977.

———. *Power and Interdependence: World Politics in Transition.* 2d ed. Boston: Scott, Foresman and Company, 1989.

Kindleberger, Charles. *The World in Depression, 1929–1939.* Berkeley: University of California Press, 1973.

———. "Dominance and Leadership in the International Economy." *International Studies Quarterly* 25 (3) (1981): 242–254.

Kirpatrick, Evron. "The Impact of the Behavioral Approach on Traditional Political Science." In *Changing Perspectives in Contemporary Political Analysis,* ed. by Howard Bull and Thomas Lauth. Englewood Cliffs, N.J.: Prentice Hall, 1971.

Klein, Bradley S. *Strategic Discourse and Its Alternatives.* Center on Violence and Human Survival Occasional Paper 3. New York: John Jay College of Criminal Justice, 1987.

———. "After Strategy: Toward a Postmodern Politics of Peace." *Alternatives* 13 (1988): 293–318.

———. "Hegemony and Strategic Culture: American Power Projection and Alliance Defense Politics." *Review of International Studies* 14 (1988): 133–149.

———. "The Textual Strategies of Military Strategy: Or, Have You Read Any Good Defense Manuals Lately?" In *International/Intertextual Relations: Postmodern Readings of World Politics,* ed. by James Der Derian and Michael Shapiro. Lexington: Lexington Books, 1989.

———. "How the West Was One: Representational Politics of NATO." *International Studies Quarterly* 34 (3) (1990): 311–326.

———. "Beyond the Western Alliance: The Politics of Post-Atlanticism." In *Atlantic Relations in the Reagan Era and Beyond,* ed. by Stephen R. Gill. Brighton: Wheatsheaf Books, forthcoming.

Knorr, K., and J. Rosenau, eds. *Contending Approaches to International Relations.* Princeton: Princeton University Press, 1969.

Kolakowski, L. *Positivist Philosophy.* Middlesex: Penguin, 1972.

Kolb, David. *The Critique of Pure Modernity: Hegel, Heidegger and After.* Chicago: University of Chicago Press, 1986.

Kolko, Gabriel, and Joyce Kolko. *The Limits of Power.* New York: Harper and Row, 1972.

Kolkowicz, Roman, ed. *The Logic of Nuclear Terror.* Boston: Allen and Unwin, 1987.

Krasner, Stephen D. *Defending the National Interest: Raw Materials Investments and U.S. Foreign Policy.* Princeton: Princeton University Press, 1978.

———. "Structural Causes and Regime Consequences: Regimes as Intervening Variables." In *International Regimes,* ed. by Stephen D. Krasner. Ithaca: Cornell University Press, 1983.

———, ed. *International Regimes.* Ithaca: Cornell University Press, 1983.

———. *Structural Conflict: The Third World Against Global Liberalism.* Berkeley: University of California Press, 1985.

———. "Realism, Imperialism and Democracy: A Response to Gilbert." *Political Theory* 20 (February 1, 1992): 38–52.

Kratochwil, Friedrich. "Errors Have Their Advantages." *International Organization* 38 (1984): 304–319.

———. "Regimes, Interpretation and the 'Science' of Politics: A Reappraisal." *Millennium: Journal of International Studies* 17 (2) (1988): 263–284.

———. *Rules, Norms and Decisions.* Cambridge: Cambridge University Press, 1989.

Kratochwil, Friedrich, and John G. Ruggie. "International Organization: The State of the Art on the Art of the State." *International Organization* 40 (1986): 753–775.

Kripendorf, E. *International Relations as a Social Science.* Brighton: Harvester Press, 1982.

Kuhn, T. *The Structure of Scientific Revolutions.* 2d. ed. Chicago: University of Chicago Press, 1970.

Lakatos, Imre. "Falsification and the Methodology of Scientific Research Programmes." In *Criticism and the Growth of Knowledge,* ed. by Imre Lakatos and A. Musgrave. Cambridge: Cambridge University Press, 1970.

Lakatos, Imre, and A. Musgrave, eds. *Criticism and the Growth of Knowledge.* Cambridge: Cambridge University Press, 1970.

Lange, Lynda, and Lorrene Clark, eds. *The Sexism of Social and Political Theory.* Toronto: University of Toronto Press, 1979.

Lapham, Lewis. "Apes and Butterflies." *Harper's* (May 1992): 1–10.

Lapid, Yosef. "*Quo Vadis* International Relations? Further Reflections on the 'Next Stage' of International Theory." *Millenium: Journal of International Studies* 18 (1) (1989): 77–88.

———. "The Third Debate: On the Prospects of International Theory in a Post-Positivist Era." *International Studies Quarterly* 33 (3) (1989): 235–254.

Larson, Deborah. *Origins of Containment.* Princeton: Princeton University Press, 1985.

Lawrence, Philip. "Strategy, the State and the Weberian Legacy." *Review of International Studies* 13 (1987): 295–310.

Lebow, R. N., and J. G. Stein. "Rational Deterrence Theory: I Think Therefore I Deter." *World Politics* 41 (1989): 208–224.

Lijphart, Arend. "The Structure of the Theoretical Revolution in International Relations." *International Studies Quarterly* 18 (1974): 41–69.

Linklater, Andrew. "Realism, Marxism, and Critical International Theory." *Review of International Studies* 12 (1986): 301–312.

———. *Men and Citizens in the Theory of International Relations.* 2d ed. London: Macmillan, 1990.

———. *Beyond Realism and Marxism: Critical Theory and International Relations.* London: Macmillan, 1990.

Lloyd, Genevieve. *Man of Reason: Male and Female in Western Philosophy.* London: Methuen, 1984.

Locke, John. *Essay Concerning Human Understanding.* Ed. by A. Campbell-Fraser. New York: Dover, 1959.

Lukacs, Georg. *History and Class Consciousness.* London: Merlin Books, 1971.

Lyotard, J. F. *The Postmodern Condition: A Report on Knowledge.* Minneapolis: University of Minnesota Press, 1984.

Maclean, J. "Marxist Epistemology, Explanations of 'Change' and the Study of International Relations." In *Change and the Study of International Relations: The Evaded Dimension,* ed. by Barry Buzan and R. J. Barry Jones. London: Frances Pinter, 1981.

———. "Marxism and International Relations: A Strange Case of Mutual Neglect." *Millennium: Journal of International Studies* 17 (1988): 295–319.

Maghoori, Ray, and Bennet Ramberg, eds. *Globalism Versus Realism: International Relations' Third Debate.* Boulder: Westview Press, 1982.

Manzo, Katherine. *Domination, Resistance and Social Change in South Africa: The Local Effects of Global Power.* New York: Praeger, 1992.

Marcuse, Herbert. *One Dimensional Man.* London: Sphere Books, 1968.

Markwell, D. J. "Sir Alfred Zimmern Revisited: Fifty Years On." *Review of International Studies* 12 (1986): 279–292.

Masters, Roger. "Hobbes and Locke." In *Comparing Political Thinkers,* ed. by R. Fitzgerald. Sydney: Pergamon Press, 1980.

Maxwell, Nicholas. *From Knowledge to Wisdom: A Revolution in the Aims and Methods of Science.* Oxford: Basil Blackwell, 1987.

McCarthy, Thomas A. *The Critical Theory of Jurgen Habermas.* Cambridge: Polity Press, 1984.

McClelland, Charles. "The Beginning, Duration and Abatement of International Crisis." In *International Crises,* ed. by C. Hermann. New York: Free Press, 1972.

Megill, A. *Prophets of Extremity: Nietzsche, Heidegger, Foucault and Derrida.* Berkeley: University of California Press, 1985.

Mendelson, J. "The Habermas-Gadamer Debate." *New German Critique* 18 (1979): 40–55.

Millennium: Journal of International Studies, Special Issue on Feminism and International Theory, 1989.

Mills, Carl Wright. *The Sociological Imagination.* Middlesex: Penguin, 1970.

Mitrany, David. *A Working Peace System.* Chicago: Quadrangle Books, 1966.

Mohanty, Chandra. "Under Western Eyes: Feminist Scholarship and Colonial Discourses." *Feminist Review* 39 (1988): 60–80.

Moore, Barrington. *Social Origins of Dictatorship and Democracy: Lord and Peasant in the Making of the Modern World.* Berkeley: University of California Press, 1978.

Morgenthau, Hans J. *Politics Among Nations: The Struggle for Power and Peace.* 5th ed. New York: Alfred A. Knopf, 1978.

Morgenthau, Hans J., and Kenneth Thompson, eds. *Principles and Problems of International Politics: Selected Readings.* New York: Knopf, 1950.

Mueller-Vollmer, Kurt, ed. *The Hermeneutics Reader: Texts of the German Tradition from the Enlightenment to the Present.* New York: Continuum, 1985.

Murphy, Craig, and Roger Tooze. *The New International Political Economy.* Boulder: Lynne Rienner, 1991.

Nathanson, Charles. "The Social Construction of the Soviet Threat: A Study in the Politics of Representation." *Alternatives* 13 (1988): 443–483.

Neustadt, R. *Presidential Power.* New York: John Wiley, 1960.

Nicholson, M. "The Enigma of Martin Wight." *Review of International Studies* 7 (1) (1981): 15–22.

Niebuhr, Reinhold. *Christianity and Power Politics.* New York: Scribner's, 1948.

———. *Christian Realism and Political Problems.* New York: Scribner's, 1953.

Nisbet, Robert. *The Twilight of Authority.* New York: Oxford University Press, 1975.

Nye, Joseph S. "Nuclear Learning and the US-Soviet Security Regime." *International Organization* 41 (3) (1987): 371–402.

———. "Neorealism and Neoliberalism." *World Politics* 40 (1988): 235–251.

———. *Bound to Lead: The Changing Nature of American Power.* New York: Basic Books, 1990.

Oakeshott, Michael. *Rationalism in Politics.* London: Methuen, 1962.

O'Brien, C. C. *The Suspecting Glance.* London: Fairbain and Fairbain, 1972.

Olsen, William C., and Nicholas Onuf. "The Growth of a Discipline: Reviewed." In *International Relations: British and American Perspectives,* ed. by Steve Smith. Oxford: Basil Blackwell in association with the British International Studies Association, 1985.

O'Meara, Richard. "Regimes and Their Implications for International Theory." *Millennium: Journal of International Studies* 13 (1984): 245–264.

Organski, A., and K. Organski. *Population and World Power.* New York: Knopf, 1961.

Osgood, Robert E. *Limited Nuclear War.* Chicago: University of Chicago Press, 1957.

Outhwaite, W. *Understanding Social Life: The Method Called Verstehen.* London: George Allen and Unwin, 1975.

Packenham, Robert. *Political Development: Ideas in Foreign Aid and Social Science.* Princeton: Princeton University Press, 1973.

Pateman, Carol. *The Disorder of Women: Democracy, Feminism and Political Theory.* Cambridge: Polity Press, 1989.

Pears, D. *The False Prison: A Study of the Development of Wittgenstein's Philosophy.* New York: Oxford University Press, 1987.

Peterson, V. Spike, ed. *Gendered States: Feminist (Re)Visions of International Relations Theory.* Boulder: Lynne Rienner, 1992.

———. "Transgressing Boundaries: Theories of Knowledge, Gender and International Relations." *Millennium: Journal of International Studies* 21 (2) (1992): 183–206.

Pettman, Jan Jindy. *Living on the Margins: Racism, Sexism and Feminism in Australia.* Sydney: Allen and Unwin, 1992.

Phillips, D. L. *Wittgenstein and Scientific Knowledge: A Sociological Perspective.* London: Macmillan, 1977.

Plekhanov, Georgii Valentinovich. *Fundamental Problems of Marxism.* London: Lawrence and Wishart, 1969.

Popper, K. *Poverty of Historicism.* London: Routledge and Kegan Paul, 1961.

———. *The Open Society and Its Enemies.* 5th ed. London: Routledge and Kegan Paul, 1966.

———. *The Logic of Scientific Discovery.* London: Hutchinson, 1968.

———. *Conjectures and Refutations.* 3d ed. London: Routledge and Kegan Paul, 1969.

———. *Unended Quest.* London: Fontana, 1976.

Post, Tom. "How the West Lost Bosnia: Four Missed Opportunities on the Road to Chaos." *Bulletin/Newsweek* (November 3, 1992): 58–64.

Poster, Mark. *Foucault, Marxism and History.* Cambridge: Polity Press, 1984.

———. *Critical Theory and Poststructuralism: In Search of a Context.* Ithaca: Cornell University Press, 1989.

Puchala, Donald, and Raymond Hopkins. "International Regimes: Lessons for

Inductive Analysis." In *International Regimes,* ed. by Stephen D. Krasner. Ithaca: Cornell University Press, 1983.

Pye, Lucien. *Aspects of Political Development.* Boston: Little, Brown and Company, 1966.

Quine, W. V. "Two Dogmas of Empiricism." In *Can Theories Be Refuted: Essays on the Duhem-Quine Hypothesis,* ed. by Sandra Harding. Dordrecht: Reidel, 1976.

Rabinow, Paul, ed. *The Foucault Reader.* New York: Pantheon Books, 1984.

Rajchman, John. *Michel Foucault: The Freedom of Philosophy.* New York: Columbia University Press, 1985.

Rajchman, John, and Cornell West, eds. *Post-Analytic Philosophy.* New York: Columbia University Press, 1985.

Rapoport, A. *Fights, Games and Debates.* Ann Arbor, Mich.: University of Michigan Press, 1960.

———. *Strategy and Conscience.* New York: Schocken Books, 1964.

Ravetz, J. "Ideological Commitments in the Philosophy of Science." *Radical Philosophy* 37 (Summer 1984): 11–14.

Rengger, N. J. "Going Critical? A Response to Hoffman." *Millennium: Journal of International Studies* 17 (1988): 81–89.

Ricci, David M. "Reading Thomas Kuhn in the Post-Behavioral Era." *Western Political Quarterly* 77 (March 1963): 7–34.

———. *The Tragedy of Political Science: Politics, Scholarship and Democracy.* New Haven: Yale University Press, 1984.

Richardson, J. L. R. "Cold War Revisionism: A Critique." *World Politics* 24 (4) (1972): 579–602.

Richardson, Lewis. *Statistics of Deadly Quarrels.* Chicago: Quadrangle Books, 1960.

Ricoeur, Paul. *Hermeneutics and the Human Sciences: Essays in Language, Action and Interpretation.* Ed. and trans. by J. B. Thompson. Cambridge: Cambridge University Press, 1981.

Rifkin, Jeremy, with Ted Howard. *Entropy: A New World View.* New York: Viking Press, 1980.

Rorty, Richard. *Philosophy and the Mirror of Nature.* Oxford: Basil Blackwell, 1980.

———. "Habermas and Lyotard on Postmodernity." In *Habermas and Modernity,* ed. by Richard Bernstein. Cambridge, Mass.: MIT Press, 1985.

Rosecrance, R. "Bipolarity, Multipolarity and the Future." *Journal of Conflict Resolution* 10 (1966): 314–327.

Rosenau, James N. "Pre-theories and Theories of Foreign Policy." In *Approaches to Comparative and International Politics,* ed. by R. B. Farrell. Chicago: Northwestern University Press, 1966.

———. *The Scientific Study of Foreign Policy.* New York: Free Press, 1968.

———. "Before Cooperation: Hegemons, Regimes and Habit Driven Actors in World Politics." *International Organization* 40 (4) (1986): 849–894.

Rosenberg, Justin. "What's the Matter with Realism?" *Review of International Studies* 16 (4) (1990): 285–303.

———. "A Non-Realist Theory of Sovereignty?: Giddens' *Nation State and Violence.*" *Millennium: Journal of International Studies* 19(2) (1990): 349–259.

Rostow, W. W. *The Stages of Economic Growth: A Non-Communist Manifesto.* 2d ed. Cambridge: Cambridge University Press, 1977.

Rothchild, Donald, and Robert Curry, Jr. *Scarcity, Choice and Public Policy in Middle Africa.* Berkeley: University of California Press, 1978.

Rothstein, R. L. "On the Costs of Realism." *Political Science Quarterly* 87 (3) (1972): 348–362.

Ruggie, John G. "International Regimes, Transactions and Change: Embedded Liberalism in the Postwar Economic Order." *International Organization* 36 (1982): 379–415. Reprinted in *International Regimes,* ed. by Stephen D. Krasner. Ithaca: Cornell University Press, 1983.

———. "Continuity and Transformation in the World Polity: Toward a Neorealist Synthesis." *World Politics* 35 (1983): 261–285.

Russett, Bruce. "The Calculus of Deterrence." *Journal of Conflict Resolution* 7 (1963): 97–109.

———. "Pearl Harbor: Deterrence Theory and Decision Theory." *Journal of Peace Research* 2 (1967): 89–105.

———. "Components of an Operational Theory of International Alliance Formation." *Journal of Conflict Resolution* 12 (1968): 85–301.

Ryan, Michael. *Marxism and Deconstruction: A Critical Articulation.* Baltimore: Johns Hopkins University Press, 1982.

Said, Edward. *Orientalism.* New York: Vintage Books, 1979.

Sanders, Jerry W. *Peddlers of Crisis: The Committee on the Present Danger and the Politics of Containment.* Boston: South End Press, 1983.

Schact, R. *Classical Modern Philosophers: Descartes to Kant.* London: Routledge and Kegan Paul, 1984.

Scheer, Robert. *With Enough Shovels: Reagan, Bush and Nuclear War.* New York: Vintage Books, 1983.

Schelling, T. C. *The Strategy of Conflict.* New York: Oxford University Press, 1960.

———. *Arms and Influence.* New Haven: Yale University Press, 1966.

Scruton, Roger. *A Short History of Modern Philosophy: From Descartes to Wittgenstein.* London: Ark Paperbacks, 1984.

Shapiro, Michael J., ed. *Language and Politics.* Oxford: Basil Blackwell, 1984.

———. *The Politics of Representation: Writing Practices in Biography, Photography and Policy Analysis.* Madison: University of Wisconsin Press, 1987.

———. "The Constitution of the Central American Other: The Case of Guatemala." In *The Politics of Representation: Writing Practices in Biography, Photography and Policy Analysis.* Madison: University of Wisconsin Press, 1987.

———. "The Politics of Fear: Don DeLillo's Postmodern Burrow." *Strategies* 1 (1988): 120–141.

———. "Textualizing Global Politics." In *International/Intertextual Relations: Postmodern Readings of World Politics,* ed. by James Der Derian and Michael Shapiro. Lexington: Lexington Books, 1989.

Singer, J. D. "The Incompleat Theorist: Insight Without Evidence." In *Contending Approaches to International Relations,* ed. by K. Knorr and J. Rosenau. Princeton: Princeton University Press, 1969.

———. *The Correlates of War: II.* New York: Free Press, 1980.

Small, M., and J. D. Singer. "Formal Alliances, 1815–1965: An Extension of the Basic Data." *Journal of Peace Research* 6 (1969): 257–282.

Smith, Michael J. *Realist Thought from Weber to Kissinger.* Baton Rouge: Louisiana State University Press, 1986.

Smith, Steve, ed. *International Relations: British and American Perspectives.* Oxford: Basil Blackwell in association with the British International Studies Association, 1985.

———. The Development of International Relations as a Social Science." *Millennium: Journal of International Studies* 16 (2) (1987): 189–206.

Snell, B. *The Discovery of Mind: The Greek Origins of Modern Thought.* Trans. by T. Rosenmayer. New York: Harper and Row, 1960.

Snidal, Duncan. "The Limits of Hegemonic Stability Theory." *International Organization* 39 (1985): 579–614.

Snyder, Glenn H., and Paul Deising. *Conflict Among Nations: Bargaining, Decision-Making and System Structure in International Crises.* Princeton: Princeton University Press, 1977.

Spegele, Roger. "Richard Ashley's Discourse for International Relations." *Millennium: Journal of International Studies* 21 (2) (1992): 147–182.

Spero, Joan E. *The Politics of International Economic Relations.* New York: St. Martin's Press, 1977.

Spivak, Gayatri C. "Imperialism and Sexual Difference." *Oxford Literary Review* 8 (1986): 223–240.

———. "Can the Subaltern Speak?" In *Marxism and the Interpretation of Culture,* ed. by C. Nelson and L. Grossberg. Urbana University of Illinois Press, 1988.

Sprout, H., and M. Sprout. *Foundations of National Power.* New Jersey: D. Van Nostrand, 1951.

Spykman, Nicholas. *America's Strategy in World Politics: The United States and the Balance of Power.* New York: Harcourt, Brace, 1942.

Steadman-Jones, G. "History: The Poverty of Empiricism." In *Ideology in the Social Sciences,* ed. by R. Blackburn. London: Fontana, 1972.

Stein, Arthur. "Coordination and Collaboration: Regimes in an Anarchic World." In *International Regimes,* ed. by Stephen D. Krasner. Ithaca: Cornell University Press, 1983.

Stockman, Norman. *Antipositivst Theories of the Sciences: Critical Rationalism, Critical Theory and Scientific Realism.* Dordrecht: D. Reidel, 1983.

Strange, Susan. "Cave! Hic Dragons: A Critique of Regime Analysis." In *International Regimes,* ed. by Stephen D. Krasner. Ithaca: Cornell University Press, 1983.

Suganami, Hidemi. "Reflections on the Domestic Analogy: The Case of Bull, Beitz and Linklater." *Review of International Studies* 12 (2) (1986): 145–158.

Sullivan, Michael P. "Competing Frameworks and the Study of Contemporary International Politics." *Millennium: Journal of International Studies* 7 (1978): 93–110.

Suppe, Fred. *The Structure of Scientific Theories.* Chicago: University of Illinois Press, 1977.

Sylvester, Christine. *Feminist Theory and International Relations in a Postmodern Era.* Cambridge: Cambridge University Press, 1993.

———, ed. "Feminists Write International Relations," *Alternatives* Special Issue 18 (1) (Winter 1993).

Taylor, Charles. "Overcoming Epistemology." In *After Philosophy: End or Transformation?* ed. by K. Baynes, J. Bohman, and T. McCarthy. Cambridge, Mass.: MIT Press, 1987.

Thompson, John B. *Critical Hermeneutics: A Study in the Thought of Paul Ricoeur and Jurgen Habermas.* Cambridge: Cambridge University Press, 1981.

Thompson, John B., and D. Held, eds. *Habermas: Critical Debates.* Cambridge, Mass.: MIT Press, 1982.

Tickner, J. Anne. "Hans Morgenthau's Principles of Political Realism: A Feminist Reformulation." *Millennium: Journal of International Studies* 17 (3) 1989: 429–441.

———. "On the Fringes of the World Economy: A Feminist Perspective." In *The New International Political Economy,* ed. by Craig Murphy and Roger Tooze. Boulder: Lynne Rienner, 1991.

———. *Gender and International Relations: Feminist Perspectives on Achieving Global Security.* New York: Columbia University Press, 1992.

Todorov, T. *The Conquest of America.* Trans. by R. Howard. New York: Harper and Row, 1984.

Tooze, Roger. "The Unwritten Preface: International Political Economy and Epistemology." *Millennium: Journal of International Studies* 17 (2) (1988): 285–293.

Trevor-Roper, H. *Religion, the Reformation and Social Change.* London: Macmillan, 1967.

Tucker, Robert W. *The Inequality of Nations.* New York: Basic Books, 1977.

———. "Morality and Deterrence." *Ethics* (April 1985): 461–478.

Tyroler, Charles, ed. *Alerting America: The Papers of the Committee on the Present Danger.* Washington: Pergamon Brassey's, 1984.

U.S. Government. *The Report of the President's Bipartisan Commission on Central America.* New York: Macmillan, 1984.

Vasquez, John A. *The Power of Power Politics: A Critique.* London: Frances Pinter, 1983.

Walker, R. B. J. *Political Theory and the Transformation of World Politics.* World Order Studies Program, Occasional Paper 8. Princeton: Princeton University Center for International Studies, 1980.

———, ed. *Culture, Ideology and World Order.* Boulder: Westview Press, 1984.

———. "Culture, Discourse, Insecurity." *Alternatives* 11(4) (1986): 485–504.

———. "Realism, Change, and International Political Theory." *International Studies Quarterly* 31 (1987): 65–86.

———. *One World, Many Worlds: Struggles for a Just World Peace.* Boulder: Lynne Rienner, 1988.

———. "*The Prince* and 'The Pauper': Tradition, Modernity, and Practice in the Theory of *International Relations." In International/Intertextual Relations: Postmodern Readings of World Politics,* ed. by James Der Derian and Michael Shapiro. Lexington: Lexington Books, 1989.

———. *Inside/Outside: International Relations as Political Theory.* Cambridge: Cambridge University Press, 1993.

Walker, R. B. J., and Saul Mendlovitz, eds. *Contending Sovereignties: Redefining Political Community.* Boulder: Lynne Rienner, 1990.

Walt, Stephen. "The Renaissance of Security Studies." *International Studies Quarterly* 35 (1991): 211–239.

Waltz, Kenneth A. *Man, the State and War: A Theoretical Analysis.* New York: Columbia University Press, 1959.

———. "The Stability of the Bipolar World." *Daedalus* 93 (1964): 907–982 .

———. *Theory of International Politics.* Reading: Addison-Wesley, 1979.

———. "Realist Thought and Neorealist Theory." *Journal of International Affairs* 44 (1990): 22–33.

Wardell, M., and S. Turner, eds. *Sociological Theory in Transition.* Boston: Allen and Unwin, 1986.

Weber, Cynthia. "Representing Debt: Peruvian Presidents Belaunde's and Garcia's Reading/Writing of Peruvian Debt." *International Studies Quarterly* 34 (3) (1990): 353–366.

———. "Writing Sovereign Identities: The Wilson Administration's Intervention in the Mexican Revolution." *Alternatives* 17 (1) (1992): 313–337.

Wendt, Alexander E. "The Agent-Structure Problem in International Relations Theory." *International Organization* 41 (1987): 335–370.

Whitebook, Joel. "The Problem of Nature in Habermas." *Telos* 40 (Summer 1979): 50–62.

Wight, Martin. "Western Values in International Relations." In *Diplomatic Investigations,* ed. by Herbert Butterfield and Martin Wight. London: George Allen and Unwin, 1966.

———. "Why Is There No International Theory?" In *Diplomatic Investigations,* ed. by Herbert Butterfield and Martin Wight. London: George Allen and Unwin, 1966.

———. "The Balance of Power." In *Diplomatic Investigations,* ed. by Herbert Butterfield and Martin Wight. London: George Allen and Unwin, 1966.

———. *System of States.* Ed. by Hedley Bull. Leicester: Leicester University Press, 1977.

———. *Power Politics.* Ed. by Hedley Bull and Carsten Holbraad. Leicester: Leicester University Press, 1978.

Williams, William A. *The Tragedy of American Diplomacy.* Cleveland: World Publishers, 1959.

Winch, P. *The Idea of a Social Science and Its Relation to Philosophy.* New York: Routledge and Kegan Paul, 1958.

Wittgenstein, L. *Tractatus Logico-philosphicus.* Trans. by D. F. Pears and B. F. McGuiness. London: Routledge and Kegan Paul, 1961.

———. *The Philosophical Investigations.* Trans. by G. E. M. Anscombe. Oxford: Basil Blackwell, 1984.

Wolin, Sheldon. *Politics and Vision: Continuity and Innovation in Western Political Thought.* Boston: Little, Brown and Company, 1960.

———. "Political Theory as a Vocation." In *Politics and Experience,* ed. by P. King and B. Parekh. Cambridge: Cambridge University Press, 1968.

Wright, Quincey. *A Study of War.* Chicago: University of Chicago Press, 1942.

Yergin, Daniel. *Shattered Peace: The Origins of the Cold War and the National Security State.* Boston: Houghton Mifflin, 1977.

Young, Oran. *The Politics of Force.* Princeton: Princeton University Press, 1968.

Zimmern, Alfred. *The League of Nations and the Rule of Law, 1918–1935.* London: Macmillan, 1936.

Index

About the Book and the Author

An unusual combination of synthesis and original scholarship, this new text considers the contemporary agenda of international relations within a broad historical-philosophical context.

George first deals explicitly with precisely how, and with what effect, the dominant post–World War II approaches to international relations are located in this larger context. He then concentrates on the application of these approaches in the theory and practice of the IR community. Going beyond the conventional accounts of, for example, the "Americanization" of the discipline and its development via a "great debates" scenario, he suggests an alternative way of reading and understanding international relations.

The book offers at least three new dimensions to the available IR literature: George takes seriously the question of how we understand ourselves and our world, adding to the IR agenda a comprehensive discussion of the way we "know," and the way we apply that knowledge (e.g., via policy decisions). Though he brings a critical focus and tone to this discussion, he investigates the dominant disciplinary perspectives in their own terms. And not least, he explores some of the most significant of the critical perspectives that have been at the forefront of the challenge to traditional and disciplinary orthodoxies.

Jim George is lecturer in international relations in the Department of Political Science, Australian National University.

Other Books in the Series

The State in Transition
Joe Camilleri

Politics Without Principle: Sovereignty, Ethics, and the Narratives of the Gulf War
David Campbell

A Question of Values: Johan Galtung's Peace Research
Peter Lawler

The Global Economy as Political Space
Stephen J. Rosow, Naeem Inayatullah, and Mark Rupert, editors